Developments in European Politics

Developments in European Politics

2nd Edition

Edited By

Erik Jones
Paul M. Heywood
Martin Rhodes
Ulrich Sedelmeier

palgrave
macmillan

First published 2006

This edition published 2011 by
PALGRAVE MACMILLAN

Palgrave Macmillan in the UK is an imprint of Macmillan Publishers Limited, registered in England, company number 785998, of Houndmills, Basingstoke, Hampshire RG21 6XS.

Palgrave Macmillan in the US is a division of St Martin's Press LLC, 175 Fifth Avenue, New York, NY 10010.

Palgrave Macmillan is the global academic imprint of the above companies and has companies and representatives throughout the world.

Palgrave® and Macmillan® are registered trademarks in the United States, the United Kingdom, Europe and other countries

ISBN-13: 978–0–230–22187–1 hardback
ISBN-10: 0–230–22187–4   hardback
ISBN-13: 978–0–230–22188–8 paperback
ISBN-10: 0–230–22188–2   paperback

This book is printed on paper suitable for recycling and made from fully managed and sustained forest sources. Logging, pulping and manufacturing processes are expected to conform to the environmental regulations of the country of origin.

A catalogue record for this book is available from the British Library.

A catalog record for this book is available from the Library of Congress.

10   9   8   7   6   5   4   3   2   1
20   19   18   17   16   15   14   13   12   11

Printed and bound in Great Britain by
CPI Antony Rowe, Chippenham and Eastbourne

Contents

List of Figures and Tables

Figures

Tables

Notes on Contributors

Arno Behrens is Research Fellow and Head of Energy at the Centre for European Policy Studies (CEPS).

Christian Egenhofer is Senior Research Fellow and Head of the Energy, Climate and Environment Programme at the Centre for European Policy Studies (CEPS) and Senior Research Fellow and Jean-Monnet Lecturer at the Centre for Energy, Petroleum and Mineral Law and Policy at the University of Dundee (Scotland). He is Visiting Professor at the College of Europe (Bruges/Natolin), SciencesPo (Paris) and LUISS University (Rome).

Rainer Eising is Professor of Comparative Politics at the Ruhr-University Bochum.

Elisabetta Gualmini is Professor of Comparative Public Policy in the Department of Political Science at the University of Bologna.

Bob Hancké teaches European political economy at the London School of Economics and Political Science.

Paul Heywood is Sir Francis Hill Professor of European Politics at the University of Nottingham.

Jonathan Hopkin is Senior Lecturer in Comparative Politics in the Department of Government, London School of Economics and Political Science.

Erik Jones is Professor of European Studies at the SAIS Bologna Center of the Johns Hopkins University.

Christian Joppke is Professor of Sociology at the University of Bern.

John Madeley was (until his recent retirement) a Senior Lecturer in the Department of Government at the London School of Economics and Political Science.

Pippa Norris teaches at the John F. Kennedy School of Government, Harvard University and she will be a visiting professor at Sydney University during 2011.

Romain Pasquier is CNRS Senior Research Fellow at the research centre on political action in Europe of the Rennes I University.

Thomas Poguntke is Professor of Comparative Politics at the Heinrich-Heine-University Düsseldorf and co-director of the Düsseldorf Party Research Institute (PRuF).

Martin Rhodes is Professor of Comparative Political Economy at the Josef Korbel School of International Studies, Denver University, Denver, Colorado, USA.

Ulrich Sedelmeier is Senior Lecturer in International Relations at the London School of Economics and Political Science.

Alexander Spencer is Assistant Professor at the Geschwister-Scholl-Institute for Political Science, Ludwig-Maximilians-University Munich, Germany.

Emma J. Stewart was awarded her Ph.D. from Loughborough. She recently undertook postdoctoral work on the South Caucasus at the University of Bath.

Paul Webb is Professor of Politics at the University of Sussex.

Richard G. Whitman is Professor of Politics and International Relations at the University of Kent.

Chris Wood is a Ph.D. student at the University of Nottingham.

Acknowledgements

This project was much longer in gestation than originally foreseen. As editors we are extremely grateful to our contributors for their patience, diligence and dedication through what seems like an almost endless cycle of updating and revision. The same gratitude extends to our colleagues at Palgrave who made significant efforts to produce the book in a timely manner once the final manuscript was delivered. Finally, a particular note of thanks goes to Ms Barbara Wiza for her considerable efforts compiling and formatting the final manuscript. We could not have completed our work without her assistance.

List of Abbreviations

AKP	Justice and Development Party (Turkey)
AER	Assembly of European Regions
AU	African Union
BKA	Federal Criminal Policy Office (Germany)
BRICs	Brazil, Russia, India and China
BZO	Alliance for the Future of Austria
CCS	carbon capture and storage
CCTV	closed-circuit television
CDU	Christian Democratic Union (Germany)
CEE	Central and Eastern Europe
CEECs	Central and East European Countries
CEMR	Council of European Municipalities and Regions
CFSP	Common Foreign and Security Policy
CDM	clean development mechanisms
CID	Citizenship, Involvement, Democracy (Survey)
CIA	Central Intelligence Agency
CIG	*Cassa Integrazione Guadagni* (Italian Wage Guarantee Fund)
CME	Coordinated Market Economy
CoR	Committee of Regions
COSAC	Conference of European Affairs Committees
CPMR	Conference of Peripheral and Maritime Regions
CSCE	Conference on Security and Cooperation in Europe
DPP	Danish Peoples Party
DTP	Democratic Society Party (Turkey)
EAC	European Affairs Committees
ECB	European Central Bank
ECHR	European Court of Human Rights
ECJ	European Court of Justice
ECPHR	European Convention for the Protection of Human Rights
ECSC	European Coal and Steel Community
EEA	European Economic Area
EES	European Employment Strategy
EFTA	European Free Trade Association
EMS	European Monetary System
EMU	Economic and Monetary Union
ENEP	effective number of electoral parties

ENP	European neighbourhood policy
ENPP	effective number of parliamentary parties
EP	European Parliament
EPI	Energy Policy Index
ESDP	European Security and Defence Policy
ESS	European Social Survey
ETA	Basque Separatist Group (Spain)
ETS	Emission Trading System
EU	European Union
EU-15	European Union of 15 (West European) member states
EU-27	European Union of 27 member states
Euratom	European Atomic Energy Community
FATF	Financial Action Task Force
FDI	foreign direct investment
FDP	Liberal Party (Germany)
FLNC	Corsican Separatist Group (France)
FPA	Foreign Policy Analysis
FPO	Freedom Party (Austria)
FrP	Progress Party (Norway)
GCHQ	Government Communications Headquarters (UK)
GDP	gross domestic product
GHG	greenhouse gas
GIA	Algerian Islamist Group
ICT	Information and Communication Technology
ICTY	International Criminal Tribunal for the former Yugoslavia
IEA	International Energy Agency
IMF	International Monetary Fund
IRA	Independent Regulatory Agencies
ISAF	International Security Assistance Force
JI	joint implementation
LECs	local employment councils
LME	liberal market economy
LNG	liquefied natural gas
MENA	Middle East/North Africa
MME	mixed market economy
MP	Member of Parliament
Mt	metric tons
NAPs	national allocation plans
NATO	North Atlantic Treaty Organization
NGOs	non-governmental organizations
NRMs	new religious movements
OECD	Organization for Economic Cooperation and Development
OEF	Operation Enduring Freedom

OLS	ordinary least squares
OSCE	Organization for Security and Cooperation in Europe
PKK	Kurdish Separatist Movement (Turkey)
PD	Democratic Party (Italy)
PDL	People of Freedom (Italy)
PR	Proportional Representation
PSOE	Spanish Socialist Party
PVV	Freedom Party (Netherlands)
RegLeg	Network of Regions with Legislative Powers
REML	restricted maximum likelihood
SEA	Single European Act
SERPS	State Earnings-Related Pension Scheme
SIS	Slovak Intelligence Service
SPD	German Social Democratic Party
SRAS	Separation of Religion and State
TEC	Treaty on the European Community
TEU	Treaty on European Union
TFEU	Treaty on the Functioning of the European Union
TKB	Anti-Terrorist Coordination Committee (Hungary)
UK	United Kingdom
UMP	Union for a Popular Movement (France)
UN	United Nations
UNIFIL	UN Monitoring Team in Lebanon
U.S.	United States
USSR	Union of Soviet Socialist Republics
VoC	varieties of capitalism

Chapter 1

Introduction: Developments in European Politics 2

The Editors

The first edition of *Developments in European Politics* was published in 2006. Writing in the shadow of the 'old Europe–new Europe' debates that surrounded the Iraq War and the historic enlargement of the European Union to include ten new member states, we sought to show how the two parts of Europe could be treated analytically as a coherent whole. We urged our contributors to look for lessons that could travel from East to West as well as the other way around. We analysed common patterns, we examined common challenges, and we evaluated common projects. This was a big departure in scope from our previous efforts with *Developments in West European Politics* but it was not much of a change in form or method. The chapters were still pitched to an upper-level undergraduate or postgraduate audience eager to learn how to piece together the various isolated incidents they read about in the newspaper and form a deeper understanding or interpretation of Europe.

The timing of that volume was propitious. The French and Dutch referenda rejecting the European Constitutional Treaty occurred in the late spring of 2005, just as our contributors were revising their first drafts. The European Union began its 'year of reflection' and the European integration project experienced an existential crisis. Narratives as well as analysis that could tie together the whole of the continent were in demand, focusing not only on countries within the enlarged European Union but on those outside as well. The principal requirement was that any account of developments in Europe pay careful attention to domestic politics – meaning the institutions, parties, cultures and patterns of behaviour that draw flesh-and-blood Europeans into public life. East and West was no longer the central division, although on some issues (such as the weakness of civil society, or the volatility of party systems) it retained a high degree of relevance. Instead, what mattered was connecting the dots within countries over time and from one country to the next – while remaining sensitive to the fact that the countries are changing both through interactions among themselves and as a result of forces acting upon them from outside.

1

The situation has only become more complicated in the intervening half decade and the central significance of domestic politics has become more apparent. It is commonplace to describe Europe in terms of multi-level governance; but the fact remains that even as other levels of governance grow in significance, domestic politics trump external pressures on many issues. As domestic politics changes in Europe, the superstructure of multilevel governance must adapt. Much of this transformation is found in the culmination of long, slow developments as they affect demographic structure, environmental conditions, industrial models, confessional devotion, and social convention. To take but one example, political elites no longer command the respect they once took for granted and voters no longer show as much loyalty to traditional parties (nor in some countries much desire to participate) as they once did. Electoral volatility has continued to increase and new political movements have proliferated as a result. This shift in norms has been evolutionary rather than abrupt. That evolutionary character nevertheless gives rise periodically to clear political expression – the emergence of grand coalitions in Germany and the Netherlands; a fracturing of the left in Italy and Poland; an ongoing federal crisis in Belgium; and the first formal coalition government in the United Kingdom since 1945.

This mix of slow progression leading to abrupt change is hardly limited to politics. The impact of global warming is another example; the sudden onset of the economic crisis is a third. Indeed, we have learned through the exercise of reading and writing the contributions to this volume that the mix of long causality and sudden expression is the greatest common factor at work across European experience. Similar causal mechanisms may work faster in some countries and slower in others, the influence of different factors may vary from one place to the next, and yet no part of Europe is isolated and virtually every experience is shared to some extent.

The structure of this book reflects the general problematic. Each of the chapters addresses a set of issues that has been long in development and yet also immediate in terms of impact. We begin by looking at the broader context of globalization and interdependence. Erik Jones analyses the economic crisis that has dominated the headlines since 2007. The origins of the crisis lay deep in the structure of the post-Second World War economic system, the growth of cross-border capital flows, and the emergence of significant macroeconomic imbalances, most notably between creditor and debtor countries. The immediate expression took shape in the freezing of interbank lending markets, the collapse of successful models for financial intermediation, and the erosion of bank solvency and creditworthiness. As the interaction between slow-moving structural factors related to trade and interdependence and fast moving flows of credit, investment, and domestic demand, even the most isolated or economically unsophisticated countries were soon caught up in the crisis, and all countries felt its effects.

The impact of the crisis nevertheless differed from one country to the next. Moreover, this differentiated impact is not limited to the immediate effects of the economic shock. The underlying character of globalization and interdependence differs across countries as well. This is surprising in so far as Europe is probably the most globalized and interdependent region in the world. It is also a place where relations across countries and with the wider world are highly institutionalized – most obviously (although not exhaustively) by the supranational institutions of the European Union (EU). Those institutions in turn exercise their own influence, 'Europeanizing' not only those countries that participate within them but also those that desire to join. Nevertheless, as Uli Sedelmeier finds, the Europeanization of countries is differentiated as well – both within the EU and along its borders. Inside the EU, continued diversity results from national opt-outs from common policies (usually temporary), non-compliance with EU law, and the fact that much EU law sets minimum standards or makes reforms that can be adapted to national traditions. On the EU's borders, the interplay between domestic politics and EU incentives has some paradoxical results. Governments that pursue EU membership cannot simply choose to adapt to those influences that suit their broader purposes and resist those that do not. The broader political agenda of the EU in candidate countries and more intensive monitoring of compliance can reduce the room for manoeuvre available to politicians – perhaps more so than inside the EU itself. On the other hand, national politicians who view EU influences as a threat to their domestic political goals can sometimes choose to ignore or delay implementation of the EU's agenda. Differentiated Europeanization across Europe is the result.

The existence of this diversity focuses attention on domestic decision-making and specifically on the institutions that determine who governs and how they are held accountable for their actions. Hence Chapter 4 by Rainer Eising and Thomas Poguntke draws attention to the architecture of power. The emphasis is on regime types that are at the same time familiar and unfamiliar. They look at majoritarian and consensual democracies where decision-making authority may be united or divided, parliamentary or presidential. They also look beyond the countries that are located within Europe to examine the institutions of the EU itself. What they find is a continued strengthening of core executives and a progressive 'presidentialization' of politics, a theme returned to further on in Chapter 5 by Paul Webb. Institutional structures have become fragmented, but power has become concentrated within them. This is consistent with the view that politicians strive to maximize the scope for policy-making control. It fits with the notion of differentiated Europeanization as well. But it does not fit with conventional notions of accountability and representation. Hence the developments that Eising and Poguntke reveal can be used to explain moments of great decisiveness in politics as well periods of institutional conflict and stagnation.

In European democracies, political parties have traditionally performed an essential function in constraining and countervailing any excessive concentration of government executive power. If they are no longer fulfilling that role as well as they once did, and if their representative functions are also weakening, we need to ask what is happening to Europe's political parties. This is the set of issues examined by Paul Webb in his contribution. His analysis is – by his own admission – somewhat less than optimistic. What he finds is not only that some voters have drifted away from traditional parties but also that they have in some cases actively turned against them by expressing anti-party sentiments or by supporting non-partisan populists and occasionally putting them in power. Power presents such politicians with a dilemma, however, and creates pressures to move into the mainstream: they can try to retain their radical and usually simplistic approach to policy issues (and heavily restrict their electoral appeal), or they can adapt, and sometimes grow, by becoming more orthodox right- or left-of-centre parties – at the risk, of course, of losing credibility in the eyes of their original supporters. The most important findings of this chapter, and those with the greatest implications, are that parties have been hollowed out by the rise of charismatic leaders and powerful leadership groups, and that traditional linkages between party institutions and loyal constituencies are weakening over time. If political parties no longer represent voters as consistently or as completely as in the past, it becomes harder for them to legitimize their privileged access to the institutions of state. As parties resort to an increasingly personalized appeal, a gap emerges between what they say to the voters and what they may actually end up doing once in government. Political parties still make a great difference in terms of what governments do and who gets into power. But there is a growing disconnection between the process of governing and the process of voting as the representative capacity of parties declines. The quality of European democracy is diminished as a result.

A closer examination of the empirical data is necessary to appreciate the significance and implications of this dynamic. There are two dimensions to the analysis. One concerns the experience of national electoral systems, the other the underlying phenomenon of political activism and mobilization. Chapter 6 by Jonathan Hopkin focuses on the first dimension, elections. He looks at both the durability of specific electoral cleavages and the rise of electoral volatility more generally. What he finds is a pattern of destabilization that differs subtly between the mature democracies of Western Europe and the younger, post-communist democracies found in Central and Eastern Europe. Despite the differences, however, both parts of Europe seem to be converging on a common trajectory. They experience a greater, if still quite moderate, destabilization of traditional cleavages (the relationship between socio-economic groups and political parties) – even if class position, religious persuasion and territorial identity are still strong predictors of how people vote – and higher levels of electoral volatility, especially in the new democracies of Central and eastern Europe. Hopkin concludes by arguing that the key forces behind electoral change are a greater frequency of vote switching, the explosive growth of protest parties in some countries, and an overall weakening in loyal partisan electoral behaviour. These findings confirm Webb's conclusion that political representation is becoming more fluid and political parties subject to a greater organizational and electoral stress.

Chapter 7 on citizen participation and engagement by Pippa Norris takes the analysis to the individual level. She examines the extent to which patterns in the electoral behaviour of citizens reveal underlying tendencies within the general electorate to play a more active role in politics or to withdraw from participation altogether. What she finds is mixed. There are significant cases in Europe (and elsewhere) where levels of political engagement are either very high or very low. What is harder to identify is the causal direction or overarching significance. Voters may become more active when they are offered greater choice; democracies may not require high levels of voter activism to maintain representativeness or stability over the long term. Moreover, Norris cautions against rushing to conclusions about voter turnout and partisan identification, which often reveal trendless fluctuations over time, and against assumptions concerning any systematic linkages between mass political behaviour and the stability of democratic states. This nuanced conclusion moves the analysis from the manifestations of politics to the wider institutional or cultural context. If patterns of political behaviour are not self-evident in their implications, then it is necessary to consider the structures within which that behaviour occurs.

There is no obvious ordering for a survey of the different elements that constitute political life in Europe. Nor is there any reason to believe that such elements have remained constant over time. In fact, it is possible to see how each of the basic building blocks of European politics has changed over time. Consider the territorial basis of political organization, which is at least as old as the Westphalian state system itself. On the one hand it is tempting to believe that the forces of modernity are pushing us beyond (and above) the Westphalian nation-state with its strong emphasis on territorial control. On the other hand it is noteworthy that not only is all politics local (as Tip O'Neill would say) but that it may be increasingly so. This is the point made by Romain Pasquier in his analysis of cities and regions (Chapter 8). He finds that the territorialization of politics has increased rather than decreased over time, due, somewhat paradoxically, to the supposedly homogenizing and supranational forces of globalization and Europeanization. This rescaling of governance does not necessarily rescue or condemn the nation-state. Precisely because this transformation depends heavily on the development of governance capacity at the regional and local levels, there is considerable scope for *national* political elites to resist the centrifugal effects of decentralization. The progress of this territorialization will therefore differ markedly from one country to the next. Nevertheless, Pasquier's analysis makes it clear that the interplay of internal politics and external incentives identified by Sedelmeier operates at the subnational level as well.

Territory is of course not the only basis upon which to construct a polity, and associational behaviour can rest on different principles. Just as it is possible to accept Pasquier's assertion that the territorial basis for politics has strengthened over time, it is also possible to acknowledge that other forms of association have become less prominent. With their decline, citizens lose many of the virtuous side effects of their repeated and diffuse interaction, and national political stability as well as economic performance may weaken as a result. This is the central argument in the now famous debate about social capital, trust and corruption as analysed by Paul Heywood and Chris Wood in Chapter 9. They note at the outset that popular trust in political institutions has declined and they question whether this is the result of changing social capital or some other causal force. What they find is ambiguous. Social capital may have deteriorated in many European countries but the evidence for this is questionable and the causal links to political trust are not at all clear-cut, as the chapter by Pippa Norris also emphasizes. Instead, it is more plausible to argue that voters have turned their backs on politicians simply because politicians have failed to deliver on their promises. This analysis raises questions about what precisely the determinants of political effectiveness are. Having failed to resolve the representative dilemma raised by Webb, Hopkin and Norris, Heywood and Wood push the argument further to consider whether governments have become more incompetent.

The phrasing of the question exposes a gulf between the notions of governments and governance. Governments operate from within the institutions of state; governance involves a wide array of non-state actors as well. If governments are failing to deliver, it is necessary to consider whether the process of governance has broken down as well, or whether to some degree it provides some compensation – at least potentially for reasons outside any individual government's control. This explains the interest in 'varieties of capitalism', which is an argument that links the organization of finance, industry and labour to both the pattern of economic development and the possibilities for state intervention and control. Bob Hancké (Chapter 10) uses this 'varieties of capitalism' framework to look at how countries are organized economically across Europe, to assess how those patterns of organization have changed over time, and to explain what this means for both performance and control. His analysis centres on three major innovations: the completion of the single European market, the introduction of the euro, and the expansion of the EU to the East. What he reveals is that national distinctiveness has deep institutional foundations; that some models are more successful than others; and that considerable basis for optimism still exists. This is true with particular reference to the countries of Central and Eastern Europe where much of the turmoil that was witnessed at the end of the 1990s and beginning of the 2000s may be best understood as different models for organization settle down and consolidate. These countries are not all alike to any great extent; instead, they should be clustered into different specializations, which will likely prove more pronounced and more stable over time.

The 'varieties of capitalism' framework provides an analytic toolkit for understanding why national distinctiveness persists. But it does not answer all the questions raised by Heywood and Wood about why government performance is perceived by voters as worsening over time. A fuller answer to the question demands some understanding of the challenges to labour markets and the welfare state. Some of these challenges are obviously specific to particular formulas for taxation or redistribution, others derive from more general trends in demographic developments or industrial performance, while still others – such as the tendency of politicians to under-resource their welfare state institutions and then use borrowing to finance the resulting over-commitments – are ubiquitous. Elisabetta Gualmini and Martin Rhodes tackles this broad palette of issues in their contribution (Chapter 11) and reveal both the difficulty of engaging in necessary reforms – due to sometimes powerful vetoes and the fear of electoral unpopularity by political parties already vulnerable to the forces mentioned above – and the paucity of existing political commitment. Some governments have made great strides in balancing their resources and commitments; some countries have had to (or been able to) draw support from wider governance networks to recalibrate welfare state institutions. But many governments have delayed taking necessary action and many non-government actors have put up considerable resistance to change.

Gualmini and Rhodes' analysis of welfare states straddles the bound-aries between structures that might explain developments in European politics, the measures of that performance, and the challenges to be faced in holding ground or making improvements. As such, it creates a pivot in the book from a wider focus on contextual factors to a narrower focus on specific issues. The next five chapters rotate from that pivot to highlight major issues that have come into play: issues relating to religion, immi-gration, environment, foreign policy and counter-terrorism.

The issue of religion is examined by John Madeley (Chapter 12) in an expansion of his contribution to the previous edition of *Developments in European Politics*. Madeley looks at how different European countries manage the relationship between church and state. This has become important because of the growing presence, politicization and securitiza-tion of practitioners of the Islamic faith. As Madeley shows, Europeans have had difficulty accommodating to the increasing prominence of Islamic immigrants and citizens because they do not have a history of secularism as state and societal neutrality towards the presence of differ-ent faiths; instead, they are more likely to establish, privilege, cooperate with and accommodate those different faiths according to longstanding traditions and deeply embedded cultural norms. Islam does not fit easily within this framework, because it does not fit the traditional pattern and because it suggests a different normative framework as well. Hence while it may not be true that Europe is explicitly a Christian construct, it cannot be denied that European countries more easily accommodate Christian migrants. Somewhat ironically, however, the heavy emphasis on human rights and general principles within the process of European integration may work to tip the balance. As countries begin to converge on what are common European values (and common rules to protect those values), they are likely to lose their distinctive approach to church–state relations along the way.

A similar dynamic appears to be at work with regard to immigration. Christian Joppke (Chapter 13) returns to the analysis of European immi-gration policies that he posited in his 2002 contribution to *Developments in West European Politics 2*. Joppke finds that Europe is still at a cross-roads in trying to strike a balance between attracting those immigrants most likely to contribute economically and politically and rejecting those most likely to add to the burden on public institutions. Here the EU has played an increasingly prominent role, and he notes that almost one-third of all new European legislation concerns immigration. Nevertheless, the results are still mixed and the implications vary consid-erably from one country to the next. Moreover, the political salience of the issue continues to rise as right-wing populists agitate against the perceived threat posed both to employment and to law and order, and as more mainstream parties try to steal this populist thunder. The Italian case is a striking example, with both a centre-left Prodi government tightening the borders and a centre-right Berlusconi government putting soldiers on street corners as an alarmist response to an immigrant-related crime scare. As Denmark, Austria, the Netherlands and many other countries demonstrate, however, Italy is hardly alone in its concern.

Energy and environmental policy is another area of emergent concern and immediate passion. Christian Egenhofer and Arno Behrens (Chapter 14) examine the evolution of European energy policy from a long period of foot-dragging in the 1990s to a commitment to greater activity in the decade that followed. Their focus is primarily on the EU dimension because this has been the arena within which European efforts have increasingly concentrated; national governments are now less essential for legislation than for innovation and implementation. The challenge at all levels has been to connect two domains of policy – energy and the environment – and to use that connection to forge an integrated agenda to tackle the threat of global warming. The hope now is that the EU can succeed in coordinating responses across the multiple levels of European governance. And despite their optimistic conclusion, it is worth wondering whether the decentralization identified by Pasquier and the ineffectiveness of national governments underscored by Heywood and Wood will combine to undermine European efforts at coordination.

Concern for European coordination is hardly novel. In the area of foreign and security policy, for example, it has long been the norm. And despite the rhetoric of close European foreign and security policy cooperation, there is little evidence that the predominance of national foreign policies will soon diminish. This is the starting point for Chapter 15 by Richard Whitman and Emma Stewart, who then go on to consider whether the implications are so dire as the critics of European foreign policy might predict. What they find is that divisions within Europe continue to hamper its foreign policy. This was evident in the recognition of Kosovo, in Darfur, South Ossetia and Gaza. More generally, intra-European divisions represent a powerful constraint on European crisis management. To the extent that voters care about these issues, Whitman and Stewart's argument compounds the sense of governmental ineffectiveness. In doing so, it may further undermine popular trust in national political institutions along the way.

Nevertheless, it would be premature to suggest that European politicians would resort to extreme measures to bolster their reputations. Here the reaction to international terrorism offers an interesting contrast with the behaviour of the United States. As Alexander Spencer shows in his analysis of counter-terrorism efforts (Chapter 16), the countries of Europe have responded to the threat of terrorism in an incremental fashion with a mix of measures and relying on the lessons of their own experience. Cooperation across countries has not always been easy and some of the newer member states had to erect the institutions for cross-border coop-eration from scratch after the tragic attacks on New York and Washington on September 11, 2001. In doing so, many of these countries placed greater emphasis on relations with the United States than relations within Europe. This has created a division between countries – made famous by then Secretary of Defense Donald Rumsfeld when he pointed to the distinction between 'old' Europe and 'new' Europe. As Spencer concludes his analysis, however, it is unclear whether this division will be as persistent or meaningful as the underlying patterns of national distinc-tiveness witnessed elsewhere.

The list of challenges facing European politics is obviously much longer than those we analyse in this collection. The developments in European politics we analyse do not provide for an obvious conclusion, neither do they reveal that there is a consistent set of outcomes across countries. Instead they reveal patterns and raise questions. Doubtless there are other developments and issues which different editors would have highlighted, but we have chosen to focus on the ones which seem most salient to us. Our hope is that the students and scholars reading through these chapters will be sufficiently stimulated to engage in further reflection and continue the debate on the issues raised.

Chapter 2

Globalization and Interdependence

Erik Jones*

The global economic and financial crisis provides a stark backdrop for analysing developments in European politics. The crisis delivered a powerful shock to Europe, changing the fates of individual countries and challenging the function of common institutions. Some countries such as Great Britain, Hungary, Iceland, Ireland and Latvia were hit hard already towards the end of 2007. Others, such as France, Italy, Poland or the Czech Republic seemed better able to manage the initial blow. Over time, however, it became apparent that no country was immune to the effects of the crisis, which reverberated across the continent as a whole. Moreover, while the initial shock waves started outside Europe and then moved inward, the later effects took root in Europe before spreading to the outside world. The collapse in European demand for exports from emerging markets was one example; the sovereign debt crisis was another. When Greece began to have difficulties refinancing its government bonds in 2009, it was obvious that other governments were also in difficulty. The banks (and governments) that invested in those bonds were in trouble as well. Unfortunately, no country could rescue itself acting alone and neither was there any obvious formula for collective action. Both national politics and European unity stumbled as a result (Jones 2010).

There is always that chance that Europe's politicians will pull themselves together in order to turn the situation around. That is what happened – albeit with varying delays – during those crises of the past. The dollar gap of the late 1940s resulted in the European Payments Union, the breakdown of the Bretton Woods System in the early 1970s stimulated the creation of the European Monetary System, the dollar crisis of the late 1980s nurtured the formation of Europe's single currency, and so forth. Moreover, each of these 'European' innovations

* As author, I would like to thank Robert Dover for his many helpful comments and suggestions. The usual disclaimer applies.

only worked because of significant changes at the national level. Hence, if Europe's post-Second World War history is any guide, future readers will look back at this episode with less concern; more generous critics will place it in the 'crisis, what crisis?' file.

However the crisis plays out, the events of 2007 to 2010 point to something significant. If there was ever a strong presumption that Europe was heading towards unity (and, indeed, that external challenges can only hasten that integration), then the record of recent events offers a correction. Unity may be the end result, but that is hardly inevitable. If, instead, the presumption was that Europe had reached a stable balance between continental unity and national diversity, then that is under challenge as well. European countries have behaved very differently during the economic crisis. More important, these differences have run against rather than with the grain of integration. Neither European economic performance nor European integration has proved as stable as we might have imagined. Perhaps a better formulation would be, neither national economic performance nor European integration has proved as successful as we might have wished.

The problem is political at least as much as it is economic. Although European innovations have been matched by national adjustments in the past, those adjustments were at best only partial and the difference between what was required and what was achieved was often glossed over along the way. The Maastricht 'convergence' process necessary to qualify for adoption of the euro is one example; the stability and growth pact to keep medium-term fiscal positions close to balance or in surplus is a second; the Lisbon strategy to re-forge Europe into to the world's most competitive and dynamic knowledge based economy by 2010 is a third. The rhetoric of action exceeded the reality of achievement in each of these cases by a significant amount. The economic crisis has brought these shortcomings into sharp relief. Far from encouraging governments to redouble their efforts, however, the crisis seems to have had the opposite effect.

The longer this crisis wears on, the more it appears to be grinding up incumbents in its wake, particularly on the centre-left. The Italian Democratic Party, the German Social Democrats, the Dutch Party of Labour, the Hungarian Socialists and the British Labour Party have all left office since 2007. That does not mean, however, that the political right is reascendant. Silvio Berlusconi's centre-right coalition has been beset by infighting (De Giorgi 2010). Angela Merkel's Christian Democrats suffered setbacks, including the loss of their majority in the Bundesrat (or upper chamber of parliament) in the May 2010 regional (or *Land*) election in North-Rhine Westphalia. The Dutch and the Hungarians experienced an embarrassing growth in support for the extreme right. And the British elections resulted not in a victory for the Conservative Party but rather in a hung parliament. Those politicians who have managed to hold onto power across the crisis have fared little better. Both Nicolas Sarkozy, the centre-right French President, and José Luis Rodríguez Zapatero, the centre-left Spanish Prime Minister, saw their public approval ratings fall to all-time lows. Meanwhile, Robert Fico lost power in Slovakia despite the fact that his opposition was so divided.

The argument in this chapter is that the current crisis has revealed the underlying tensions between integration at the global level (or globalization) and interdependence within Europe. Globalization encourages European countries to be different from one another, often in unpredictable ways; interdependence ensures that the fates of these different countries are inextricably intertwined. Hence, when one European country suffers from its position in the global economy, all countries are likely to be affected. Moreover, this combination of influences is no coincidence. Europeans nurtured their interdependence at least partly so that they could maximize the benefits of interacting with the outside world. In doing so, they inadvertently pooled the costs as well. The future of Europe depends upon how well its leaders manage the distribution of unintended consequences. So far they have been doing a bad job. We can only hope that they will learn to do better.

This argument has five sections. The first looks at the relationship between globalization and national distinctiveness. The second highlights the 'European' role in helping countries get the best of their relationship with the outside world. The third examines the influence of big external shocks, and the current economic crisis in particular. The fourth describes how European politicians have begun to respond. The fifth concludes with implications for the future.

Divergence and convergence

When countries interact with the outside world, they become both less alike and more alike at the same time. They become less alike in so far as they play a specialized role in the global division of labour. They become more alike because they are all increasingly subject to the influences of the outside world on what happens at home. Both of these effects are well established in the literature. Where there is less agreement is on which set of forces predominates. Critics of globalization point to a process of convergence through which the forces that make countries more similar deprive the citizens of those countries of both identity and choice (Grieder 1998; Stiglitz 2002). Supporters of globalization paint a different picture. They show how national diversity is persistent. And while admitting that globalization changes participating countries, they argue that there is still plenty of scope for political choice (Bhagwati 2004; Rodrick 2007).

In unpacking this debate, it is useful to start with the sources of difference. The basic claim is that countries become less alike because they specialize. Some countries emphasize tourism, such as Greece, while others focus on manufacturing, such as Germany. The same is true for finance (Great Britain), transport (the Netherlands), agriculture (France and Poland), fishing (Iceland) and energy (Norway). This pattern of specialization is not always easy to anticipate before the fact. Some countries benefit from an absolute abundance of resources (such as coal deposits in Belgium and Germany or long Mediterranean coastlines in Greece, Italy and Spain) but others make best use out of whatever they have most abundant. Some specializations take root because they exploit a new niche to lasting advantage, such as banking in Britain or insurance in the Netherlands; others develop because they are ignored or unwanted elsewhere, such as the chemical sector in Germany or adult entertainment industry in Hungary. There are even specializations within specializations. Germany produces machine tools and heavy industry, Belgium and Slovakia emphasize productive intermediates (or goods that are used to make other goods), and France and Italy place more stress on designer brands and luxury goods. Hungary and Slovenia have processed foods, Romania and Bulgaria have fruits and vegetables, Poland has meats and grains.

Both institutions and policies have a role to play as well. It is now well recognized in the literature that the success or failure of certain kinds of enterprise is often a function of how trade unions and employers interact, how business is financed, and how taxes are levied by the state (Hall and Soskice 2001). Such institutions can influence the productivity of the workforce, patterns of investment and the diffusion of technology. By changing these institutions or altering their effects, politicians can influence the role played by national industries in the global economy.

Whatever the sources of specialization, the results are long-lasting. If we only look at trade, specialization is important for two reasons: it maximizes value added (or the return to productive inputs) and it makes it possible to acquire goods and services more readily and more cheaply that are produced in other parts of the world. The implication is not just that Greek shipping magnates or luxury beach resort owners can drive Mercedes made in Germany; it also means that German automotive makers can rely on parts carried by Greek ships and that German manufacturing workers can take their holidays in Greece.

Specialization is about more than just trade, however. It also implies the concentration of activity because it draws together both directly relevant and supportive expertise; it builds tightly knit networks between firms and their suppliers; and it sets in train a process where success builds upon success. In turn, this concentration of activity begins to create economies of scale that attract other forms of activity as well (Krugman 1991; Schwartz 2007). This other activity is important because not everyone in a country can become a global 'specialist' – even two or three steps removed via domestic supply chains. On the contrary, there are always likely to be more teachers, shopkeepers, restaurant workers, hoteliers, cleaners and hairdressers in any country, than workers in the traded sectors of agriculture, manufacturing, financial or business services. Northern Italy has a reputation for automotive and white-goods industries and southern Germany for its high-quality cars equipment. What is more important, however, is that both regions are relatively densely populated and also relatively prosperous. Hence these regions benefit from the specialization made possible through international trade. In that sense, being different means becoming better off.

The process of specialization creates similarities as well as differences. Some of these similarities are salutary, such as the diffusion of wealth and technology that helps to promote growth and innovation. These are the similarities most often celebrated by the proponents of globalization. Other similarities are more ambivalent (Keohane and Milner 1996). To begin with, once a country plugs into the world economy it begins to depend upon access to global supply for its imports and demand for its exports. This has two separate implications for how that country does business – one structural and the other cyclical or stochastic (meaning changing from time to time). The structural implication is that the relative rates of return to capital and labour begin to move towards global norms. In other words, where workers are relatively well paid, they will start to earn less; where they are relatively poorly paid, they will start to earn more. This 'factor price equalization' is not immediate, it is at least partly offset by the general rise in living standards, and it does not affect all parts of the economy to the same extent. Some contracts (or capital–labour relationships) are slow to adjust, some sectors are hardly affected, and some firms look to offset this equalization by changing investment patterns and therefore labour productivity levels. Nevertheless, it is not necessary to insist on a mathematical equivalence across countries; the point is simply that opening up to world markets alters the relative rates of return within the country from what they were before.

The cyclical or stochastic implication is that the relative rates of return to capital and labour become subject to the influence of economic conditions abroad, including both changes in the business cycle from boom to bust and back again and external shocks. Hence when foreign demand for domestic production falters or foreign supply of goods (oil, gas, metal, food) dries up, this can have a powerful impact on domestic incomes. Wrapped in the arid language of economics, these implications for the relative returns to productive factors may not seem all that important. Once this is translated into a redistribution from labour to capital or capital to labour, however, it is easier to see the connection to the political left and right. What countries have in common once they choose to open up to world markets is the fact that the distribution of income across labour and capital moves – at least partly – outside of political control (Frieden and Rogowski 1996).

Macroeconomic policy instruments are also affected by the flow of goods to and from other countries. Efforts to stimulate demand during a period of economic weakness will draw in imports alongside any strengthening of domestic consumption, dissipating the impact of the stimulus policy by spending money on goods produced elsewhere. The reverse is true when the government tries to slow down the economy. At a minimum, this means that government efforts must be enhanced to have the desired effect. Even enhancement may not be enough, however, depending upon what other governments are doing when the policy is enacted and how they react to the impact of any change in domestic policy once it begins to be felt abroad. If other countries are moving in the opposite direction or if they push against the international effects of the policy, the domestic government may find itself having little or no impact on economic performance at all.

This last point about the tension between macroeconomic policies at home and abroad raises a new consideration. If all countries that open to world markets are similar in facing the prospect that their domestic policy choices will be negated by choices made abroad, then each has an incentive to work towards international policy coordination. This is the essence of interdependence. The point is not that one country influences another and the reverse; rather, it is that no country can achieve its domestic objectives without taking the actions (and reactions) of other countries into account (Cooper 1968).

There is another, more important consideration. So far the discussion has focused on the integration of goods markets. This focus is built into how students learn international macroeconomics. The movement from closed economy macroeconomics to open economy macroeconomics involves the introduction of goods sold abroad and goods purchased from other countries. Hence it is only natural that economists first study open economy macroeconomics by asking questions about how changes in domestic policies or other external conditions will alter the direction of trade and the volume of goods involved. Meanwhile, capital flows accommodate the flow of goods.

This tendency to look first at the impact on flows of imports and exports is at odds with the way the world seems to work. Put simply, capital markets dwarf goods markets both in volume and – more worryingly – potential. If the sum total of global output in 2008 was $61 trillion, the total value of global financial assets was $221 trillion, and the notional value of derivatives contracts was $605 trillion. Moreover, these differences are more important within Europe than in most other places. The ratio of financial assets to gross domestic product for the world as a whole was just over 3.6 in 2008; the same ratio for the European Union was just under 5.1 (IMF 2010: 19, 20). Therefore, it may be necessary to consider the prospect that capital markets – rather than goods markets – lie at the core of global interdependence. This does not change the basic structure of the problem. Countries still need to coordinate if they are to achieve their domestic agendas. Nevertheless, it does change the speed and magnitude of the implications; a failure to coordinate could trigger a run on the currency, domestic banks or bond markets. As the British case demonstrated in 2007 and the Greek case demonstrated in 2010, the implications of such a run are system wide.

Hence countries get to specialize, share technology, and benefit from rising standards of living, but they face the same sword of Damocles in the form of capital market volatility. Moreover, the more they become dependent upon one sector of production, one key market for exports, or one major source of finance, the sharper and heavier that sword of Damocles becomes because of the danger that capital will respond adversely to news about the economy and suddenly decide to take flight. Countries benefit from globalization only by making themselves vulnerable to it. That is the principal lesson coming from Greece, Iceland, Ireland, Hungary and Latvia. What unites these countries is not that they are small, corrupt, incompetent or even unfortunate. Rather, it is that they experienced sooner what others may yet have in store.

Embedded liberalism

Globalization does not have to be so fatalistic. All it requires is appropriate institutions to coordinate national policy-making and to manage the threat of capital flight. This was the realization made by the architects of the post-Second World War international economic order. They believed that they only way to embrace free trade while preserving sufficient national political autonomy was by restricting the flow of capital from one country to the next. If countries wanted to use dollars to pay for imports, then they would have to earn those dollars by selling exports. With few exceptions, money could not be moved from one country to another unless there was some equal and underlying trade in goods and services involved. These architects of the post-Second World War economic system also nurtured institutions for policy coordination, industrial planning and the joint removal of barriers to trade. In a now classic essay published in *International Organization*, John Gerard Ruggie (1982: 393) referred to their strategy for combining these elements as 'the compromise of embedded liberalism'. The post-war architects compromised their ambitions for a liberal economic order by extending free market principles only to the goods trade and then they embedded it in the underlying social consensus of the participating countries by ensuring that these countries had enough room for manoeuvre to respond to their separate political wants and needs.

This compromise depended upon two conditions: one was that countries had access to sufficient liquidity to meet their international payments obligations; the other was that they could count on stable exchange rates. Liquidity in this context is any money that is accepted internationally as a form of payment. Given the prominence of the United States (US) economy immediately following the Second World War, the principal form of liquidity was the dollar. The relevant exchange rates are those between domestic currency and international currency. If a country lacks liquidity (international currency such as dollars), it cannot pay for its imports. And if it faces volatile exchange rates, then it has difficulty participating in international trade.

The challenge is to meet both conditions at once so that countries have both ample access to international currency and a stable exchange rate with which to acquire it. To a large extent, the series of attempts at different forms of monetary integration in Europe is the response. And it is a response that stretches all the way back to the post-Second World War reconstruction of Western Europe. For example, the European Payments Union of the 1950s helped countries to use their relatively scarce dollar holdings more efficiently as an international currency by allowing them to net out their payment obligations across the Union as a whole. Similarly, the Werner Plan and the European 'snake' mechanism sought to stabilize exchange rates between European currencies as the original post-Second World War economic order began to break down.

By the middle of the 1970s, it became clear that for countries to have access to sufficient liquidity to meet their international payments obligations, the original constraints on international capital mobility would have to go (Helleiner 1994). This way, countries with more imports than exports could effectively borrow the money to pay their import bills from those countries where the situation was the other way around. The word 'effectively' is important because it hides a lot of complicated economic machinery that is not vital to the story in broad brush. Another way to look at the same problem would be to ask what countries with more exports than imports are supposed to do with the money they earn abroad and yet do not want to spend. The answer is that they put the money into banks that in turn look for opportunities to make loans. Given that the net importing countries are looking for more to borrow to cover their import bills, it should be easy to anticipate how the story ends.

The problem with the growth of international capital markets is that it brought back the destabilizing effects of international capital flows; as international capital markets became more liquid, exchange rate stability became harder to maintain. Domestic policy autonomy became more difficult to protect as well, because policy differences across countries meant they began to work at cross purposes. Countries could choose to adopt whatever policy they wanted; what they could not choose was for the policy they adopted to have their desired effect. This problem became apparent even at a relatively low level of international capital mobility in the 1960s and early 1970s and it explains why neither the Werner Plan nor the 'snake' mechanism was much of a success. The European Monetary System (EMS) introduced at the end of the 1970s was designed to provide a more robust framework for exchange rate stabilization. Even that did not work properly, however, until it was underpinned by effective macroeconomic policy coordination after 1983 (McNamara 1998).

The decision to move from the EMS to a monetary union with a single currency was a logical extension of this historical trajectory. The completion of the European internal market created concerns that not all parts of the European Community would have sufficient access to liquidity and so fuelled interest in further capital market reform. As the EU countries planned for full capital market liberalization, however, they recognized that this would jeopardize exchange rate stability. Even relatively tight macroeconomic policy coordination might not be enough to ward off ever larger speculative financial flows. Hence they took the decision to move from a system of exchange rates that are fixed but adjustable (and so subject to speculation) to a system where exchange rates are irrevocably fixed – which is the definition of a monetary union. It was a short step from the irrevocable fixing of exchange rates to the introduction of a single currency, the euro.

Of course there were many motives for European monetary integration. The usefulness of this account is to highlight one line of reasoning and not to assign it an exclusive or even predominant role. Whatever its other advantages, the single currency was a source of economic empowerment as well as constraint – much as was the compromise of embedded liberalism that preceded it. Although participating countries face irrevocably fixed exchange rates and a common monetary policy, they have much greater access to liquidity and no obvious limitations financing their balance of payments; a government cannot suffer a flight from its currency if it does not have a currency for investors to flee. By the same token, the single currency emerged as a source of stability for the European Union as a whole. With the principal exception of the United Kingdom, most European countries manage their exchange rates with the euro – hoping to benefit from better access to liquidity and increased exchange rate stability as a result.

The combination of financial market integration and irrevocably fixed exchange rates changed the structure of European interdependence in two ways. To begin with, it freed countries to run ever larger current account surpluses and deficits because it guaranteed that surplus countries would find open capital markets to invest their excess savings and deficit countries would find the liquidity to pay for additional imports (Jones 2003). Hence, for example, Swedish banks could put their money in the Baltic states; Austrian banks into Central Europe; German banks in Mediterranean countries such as Greece, Italy, Portugal and Spain. Not all of these relationships lie within the euro. The Swedish example is outside, the Austrian example is both inside and out, and the German example is wholly internal to the eurozone. Moreover, while current account positions describe relative flows – the relative volume of imports and exports crossing borders during the course of a year – the net investment patterns give rise to stocks as well. This means that over time Swedish, Austrian and Germany bankers have built up a significant exposure to foreign debt.

The second change in interdependence took place through a lowering of the implicit requirements for macroeconomic policy coordination. During the 1980s and 1990s, countries had to coordinate their monetary and fiscal policies in order to maintain exchange rate stability (McNamara 1998). Once the single currency came into being, only countries outside the eurozone needed to worry about policy coordination because the countries inside the eurozone no longer had an exchange rate to manage. As a result, most non-eurozone countries apart from the United Kingdom target their monetary policy instruments to fix their national currency to the euro to a greater or lesser extent (Dyson 2006: 127–233 and 2008: 243–321). Of course it is true that countries inside the eurozone have a common monetary policy. The same is not true for fiscal policy, however, which is largely free from mechanistic constraint. There are rules to govern excessive deficits and norms for the stabilization of fiscal accounts over time, but the enforcement of these negotiated constraints has been patchy at best. Meanwhile, the market showed little interest in punishing governments that took advantage of newfound flexibility in their fiscal accounts. The cost of sovereign borrowing within the eurozone from the start of the single currency through the summer of 2007 varied no more than one half of one per cent between the most disciplined countries and their least disciplined counterparts; this was the case with Germany versus Greece (Jones 2009).

A powerful shock

European monetary integration evolved over time to maximize access to international liquidity while stabilizing exchange rates. This was not the sole purpose of the project but it was one of the more prominent effects. And, in doing so, the process of monetary integration made it easier for countries to participate in the global division of labour, primarily by facilitating the consolidation of Europe's internal market, but also by increasing the effective representation of European interests in the global economy as a whole. Moreover, the system was remarkably effective at stabilizing intra-European exchange rates in the face of external shocks. The start of economic and monetary union at the end of the 1990s coincided with the end of the Asian financial crisis and the onset of Russia's default. Such events would otherwise have been very likely to introduce volatility in intra-European exchange rates. Given the start of monetary union, however, it did not. Instead, intra-European exchange rates remained stable and long-term interest rates across Europe began to converge downward on more favourable German norms. Subsequent shocks had similarly little effect. Although the European Union struggled with the breakdown of fiscal coordination efforts and the shortcomings of welfare state reforms, intra-European exchange rates remained stable and the relative cost of liquidity remained low.

The crisis that started in 2007 posed a problem of a different sort. Instead of threatening exchange rate stability, it struck at the process of liquidity creation. The broad outlines of the story are well known. Complex investment securities backed by mortgages taken out in the United States began to lose value rapidly as the growth in US housing prices levelled off and unexpectedly high numbers of borrowers began to have trouble meeting their monthly payments. The problem snowballed as mortgage losses triggered derivatives contracts designed to compensate lenders in the event of default. Worse, many of the investors who owned the mortgage-backed securities had borrowed the money to make the investments and many of the institutions that sold the derivatives did not have the capital to cover default losses. This set off an increase in demand for liquidity as borrowers had to post ever higher amounts of collateral on the loans they had outstanding and as other institutions called in resources to honour their derivatives contracts. The problem was that no one who had liquidity was particularly eager to lend it out. Worse, banks were even reluctant to lend money to one another because they could not be sure of the scale of their respective losses or whether they would ever get that money back. In the scramble, banks began to horde their cash, inter-institutional lending dried up, and liquidity creation ground to a halt (Shiller 2008; Akerlof and Shiller 2009: 86–97).

The shutdown in liquidity creation spread almost instantly from the United States to Europe (Brender and Pisani 2009: 79–96). The first countries hit were those with the greatest relative exposure to financial services. The most obvious example is the run on the Northern Rock mortgage bank that took place in the United Kingdom in September 2007. The Northern Rock had a very successful business model for converting short-term lending in the interbank market into long-term loans to home owners. Once the interbank market dried up in August 2007, however, that model collapsed. By September, the Northern Rock had to appeal to the Bank of England for emergency financing which the Bank of England then had to announce to the public. Customers immediately queued up outside Northern Rock branches and the British government had to step in to guarantee their deposits (House of Commons 2008).

The Northern Rock, which was nationalized in February 2008, proved to be only the tip of the iceberg. As the financial crisis continued to deepen in the United States, losses continued to mount on the balance sheets of banks in Europe. Moreover, liquidity conditions eased only gradually in the early months of 2008 and then began to tighten again around the rescue of the US investment bank Bear Sterns in March. This tightening continued through the nationalization of US mortgage lending giants IndyMac, Fannie Mae and Freddie Mac to culminate with the collapse of Lehman Brothers in September. Almost immediately, banks in Iceland, Ireland, Belgium, the Netherlands and Luxembourg had to be nationalized or liquidated as a result (Gamble 2009: 19–35). German banks were also seriously damaged; because they are less connected to the outside world, however, French banks were not (Hardie and Howarth 2009).

The next countries affected were those outside the eurozone that still faced a balance of payments constraint. This included small, Central and East European countries such as Latvia and Lithuania, but also larger countries such as Hungary and Poland and wealthier countries such as Denmark and Sweden. During the crisis, the two Scandinavian countries had to choose between stabilizing their exchange rates with the euro or loosening monetary policy. Denmark chose to stay pegged to the euro and so raised its policy interest rates in October 2008 even as the

European Central Bank (ECB) moved in the opposite direction; Sweden opted instead to follow the ECB's decision to cut interest rates and so saw the relative value of its currency decline (Jones 2009: 51–2). Meanwhile, the Central and East European countries were battered by the markets. Lithuania undertook a major policy adjustment to cut government expenditures and shore up domestic banks; Latvia and Hungary had to appeal to the International Monetary Fund (IMF) for interim financial support; and Poland became the one of the first-ever recipients of an IMF contingency line of credit.

Trade and investment offered a third channel for contagion. Hence even countries without well-developed financial sectors experienced the contraction. In Central and Eastern Europe, this group includes Bulgaria, Romania and Slovakia. Romania had to appeal for IMF support in March 2009, making it the third country in Europe to do so – after Latvia and Hungary. Bulgaria, by contrast, was able to weather the storm with the aid of its currency board and pegged exchange rate to the euro. Indeed, it is likely that any credible suggestion that Bulgaria was seeking IMF support would have undermined market faith in the currency board's ability to support its exchange rate peg. Having adopted the euro in January 2009, Slovakia did not have to face such concerns. Moreover, the country's financial sector and central bank were both well insulated from the impact of tightened lending conditions. Nevertheless, Slovakia remained exposed to the crisis through the slowdown in its export markets and the country's unemployment rate increased while output growth slowed as a result.

The trade and investment channel also affected countries in Western Europe. Among these, the most prominent was Italy which was believed for a long time to have escaped the worst of the crisis. The Italian banking sector is notoriously provincial and so suffered less from the deterioration of credit conditions abroad. The principal exception was UniCredit, which maintained significant operations in Central and Eastern Europe. The Italian government under Silvio Berlusconi refused to bail out that banking group (some say because it is traditionally identified with the centre-left) and so UniCredit had to turn to Libyan investors for support (Alunni 2009). Despite the self-confidence of the Berlusconi government, the relentless pressure on Italy's traditional export markets soon took its toll on growth and employment and by the end of 2009 the Italian economy was among the hardest hit by the crisis.

The market for sovereign debt instruments offered a further channel through which the crisis could be felt. Bond yields began to diverge already in the early months of 2009, particularly for Greece and Ireland as compared to Germany. This was due both to the increasing risks attached to Greek and Irish debt and to the flight of investors towards the relative safety of German bonds. This pressure on bond markets lessened somewhat over the summer but returned with a vengeance when the incoming Greek Socialist government revealed that its centre-right predecessor had substantially under-reported the country's fiscal deficits. Concern over Greek solvency continued to strengthen in 2010 and spread to Spain and Portugal as well. Despite the fact that the three Mediterranean countries were actually in different financial conditions, market actors worried that each might be headed towards default (Jones 2010).

From unity to diversity

The ECB played a leading role in responding to the crisis. As the collapse in US mortgage markets began to have an impact across the European banking system, the ECB undertook exceptional measures to ensure adequate liquidity was available. This was made easier by the fact that the ECB could lend to banks under normal circumstances against a wide range of collateral. Hence, if the Northern Rock had been located within the eurozone rather than in the United Kingdom, it would never have had to ask for the exceptional financing that triggered the bank run. In addition to accepting a wide range of assets as collateral for lending, the ECB also announced a package of exceptional loans available to the banking sector. Moreover, it offered this liquidity for three months and not just overnight. These loans were first made available in September 2007 and the programme was extended the following November. Shortly thereafter, the ECB announced a new cooperative regime with the US Federal Reserve and other major central banks to make exceptional liquidity available in dollars as well. This made it possible for European banks to continue to fund their dollar positions, meeting both their collateral needs and payment obligations without forcing them to go into foreign exchange markets which were already showing signs of increasing turmoil.

Even as the ECB worked to stabilize the European banking system, however, the member states began pulling in opposite directions. As mentioned, the British found themselves having to underwrite (and in some cases even nationalize) important financial institutions. In the shadow of that experience, the UK government believed that the most important goal is to recapitalize and so underscore confidence in domestic banks. The German government was more circumspect and instead expressed concern about the moral hazard that bank recapitalization could create. A similar divide emerged around the question of deposit insurance. When the Irish government began to worry that it would experience bank runs of its own, the German government disagreed. In the end, both issues were resolved unilaterally following the collapse of Lehman Brothers. The Irish government insured the deposits of all Irish and then all Irish-domiciled banks, forcing other countries (including Germany) to offer similar guarantees across the eurozone. Meanwhile, the UK government pushed through a 'concerted action plan' to support the European banking system as a whole. The implementation of this plan was not well coordinated across countries and it left many gaps in coverage, nevertheless it did manage to stabilize the situation through the worst period at the start of 2009 (Quaglia 2009).

The crisis reached its nadir in March 2009 and then national economies began slowly to recover. Meanwhile the divisions between and within European countries got worse. The catalyst was a debate about the need for fiscal stimulus and the countervailing imperative to gain control over the growth public debt. This argument is best explained through a ratio: the stock of debt outstanding divided by the level of national income or gross domestic product (GDP). The basic insight is that if you have a high income, you can afford to pay down a large debt. The question is whether efforts to cut your debt will slow the growth of income even faster (which would drive the ratio higher because the bottom would decrease more quickly than the top), or whether it would not make more sense to accelerate the rate of income growth even at the cost of increasing the level of the debt (which means that the top of the ratio would increase but the bottom would increase even faster). The German government believes that the answer to both sides of the question is 'no'. By implication, debt reduction can run faster than it causes the economy to slow down (and it may even help the economy to grow) but government cannot stimulate growth more quickly than the debt caused by such efforts will mount. Most other countries in Europe were sceptical of this German point of view – and many voices in the UK were outright opposed.

The problem is that neither Germany nor the rest of Europe can afford to go it alone. If Germany pursues a deficit reduction strategy, any drawdown on German economic performance will have a negative impact on the European economy as a whole. Moreover, it will mean that German exports will soak up a growing share of any fiscal stimulus undertaken elsewhere: the rest of Europe will see its debt burden mount but the German economy will hold back their GDP growth. The Greek sovereign debt crisis brought this debate to a boil and at the same time illustrated how far the German government would go in asserting its preferences (Jones 2010). The other countries of Europe – and France in particular – responded by insisting that it is time to move towards more centralized European macroeconomic control.

No country in Europe is very eager to sacrifice its fiscal autonomy. Hence when Europe's heads of state and government finally agreed in May 2010 first to bail out Greece and then to create a fund to support other distressed European governments, the UK government opted to remain on the sidelines for all but a small share of balance-of-payments assistance. The German government showed similar reluctance to lend Greece support. Its unwillingness to extend aid to a wide range of countries was palpable. This left the ECB to pick up where national efforts left off – buying sovereign debt instruments outright to support their prices in secondary markets. The German government expressed scepticism with this approach as well. In a rare display of open disagreement, German Bundesbank President Axel Weber even went so far as to criticize the ECB's role in buying up distressed bonds.

The danger now is that the ECB will lose its struggle to maintain the liquidity of the European marketplace even as the German government succeeds in its efforts to push through a sharp fiscal contraction. The fear is that such a combination of factors would trigger an even deeper recession than the one we just experienced and might even cause the European single currency to unravel. This is not a likely possibility and most observers believe that European leaders will pull back having looked over the brink. Nevertheless, the prospect of a further deep depression has become a legitimate source of concern – made all the more so by the growing disparity in market competitiveness between the German powerhouse and the rest of Europe. Faced with a widening disadvantage in relative cost structures and having failed to ensure liquidity, the Europeans might give up on irrevocably fixed exchange rates as well. This would remove the last vestiges of Europe's re-wrought compromise of embedded liberalism. Without the structures for managing their interdependence, national governments would face the forces of globalization alone.

Implications for the future

It does not have to end that way. Globalization does not confront Europeans with a Hobson's choice. National governments are not forced to choose between convergence and divergence. The countries of Europe are different now and they are likely to remain distinctive well into the future. The question they face is whether and how they will retain effective economic control. Having opened up to world markets, these countries are now subject to world market influences. Historically they have insulated themselves from the forces of globalization through common institutions and coordinated policies. They have become more sensitive to each other as a result. This is unlikely to change either and European countries are likely to become more interdependent rather than less. Hence the challenge is to develop the political will to manage that interdependence. The experience of the recent economic and financial crisis suggests they may not be up to the task. That suggestion is unexpected. In the past, European countries have usually responded to economic crisis with a constitutive politics – building new institutions to help address the problems of the past. The politics this time around is more distributive than constitutive; it is more concerned with who pays and who benefits than with how the underlying causes of the crisis should be managed or addressed. Of course Europe's leaders may be roused to change this pattern and take command of their fate. Certainly they have always done so in the recent past. Let's hope that this time is no different.

Chapter 3

The Differential Impact of the European Union on European Politics

Ulrich Sedelmeier

There are many different definitions of the term 'Europeanization', but it broadly refers to the impact that the European Union (EU) has in the domestic realm of particular countries. In this sense, Europeanization is not a concept or a theory, but rather denotes a specific research area. Sometimes it is considered a second wave of research into the EU. After the main focus of the first wave was the study of European integration – the agreement on common rules and the delegation of tasks to intergovernmental and supranational institutions – researchers have turned their attention to studying the domestic impact that European integration and the EU has on its members. The main questions of the study of Europeanization of EU member states is the extent to which the EU has an impact, and how we can explain differences in its impact across countries. A related question is whether Europeanization induces convergence among EU member states.

What are the more recent developments with regard to the impact of the EU on European politics? Developments in the EU's impact are connected to changes in the adjustment pressures that the EU brings to bear on domestic politics. For EU member states, such changes are primarily caused by an expansion of EU rules. But despite the entry into force of the Treaty of Lisbon, there has been little development in this regard in recent years. This chapter therefore suggests that although the EU certainly continues to have an impact on its member states, the most striking recent developments with regard to Europeanization concern the EU's external impact on European states outside the EU.

In the context of the EU's Eastern enlargement, which cumulated in the accession of 12 predominantly Eastern European countries in 2004 (Czech Republic, Estonia, Hungary, Latvia, Lithuania, Poland, Slovakia, Slovenia, as well as Cyprus and Malta) and 2007 (Bulgaria and Romania), the EU has initiated a range of policies that allow it to exercise its influence outside its borders. The EU has directed such attempts at 'external governance' (Lavenex and Schimmelfennig 2009; Schimmelfennig and Sedelmeier 2004) primarily at two groups of European countries: (potential) candidate countries that aim to achieve EU membership and that the EU has formally recognized as (potential) candidates for accession, and neighbouring countries for which either the EU or the countries themselves do not envisage accession to the EU, at least not in the foreseeable future. This chapter suggest that the EU's impact on domestic politics varies between these two groups of countries, as well as within each group and across issue areas within the groups.

The chapter starts with a review of the key sources that account for differences in the EU's impact among its members, and then turns to the EU's external impact. The next section discusses the EU's pre-accession impact on the countries that joined in 2004 and 2007. The chapter then explores the sustainability of this impact after accession. The EU's impact on current candidate countries in South-East Europe, including Turkey, is then considered. The next section focuses on the successor states of the Soviet Union for which the EU does not currently consider the possibility of membership – Ukraine, Belarus, Moldova, as well as Georgia, Armenia and Azerbaijan. The chapter suggests that the EU's influence depends on target governments' calculations of whether the adjustment costs of compliance with the EU's conditions are outweighed by what they can expect in return from the EU. Two main factors then explain differences in the EU's external impact, both of which vary systematically across these groups of countries: first, the magnitude of the domestic adjustment costs, and second, the extent to which the incentive of eventual membership in the EU is credible.

The EU's differential impact within its membership

From early on, studies of 'Europeanization' have emphasized as a key finding that the EU's impact on its members is differential and that it does not lead to convergence but to continued national diversity (Héritier *et al.* 2001; Cowles *et al.* 2001). Yet it is useful to disentangle these two issues. 'Differential' impact means that both the *extent* to which the EU has an impact and its *outcomes* can vary across member states and policy areas. 'Convergence' only relates to the outcome of the EU's impact. Even if the EU's impact leads to similar outcomes in a specific policy area across countries, the depth of the EU's impact might vary if the starting positions of these countries different with regard to the extent of fit between EU requirements and pre-existing domestic rules. Both the depth and the outcome of the EU's impact varies across countries depending on mediating factors at the domestic level (Cowles *et al.* 2001). Rationalist institutionalism and constructivist institutionalism identify different sets of mediating factors, such as veto players, formal domestic institutions with a mandate to promote the goals of EU law, as well as domestic norm entrepreneurs, and the extent to which domestic political culture is conducive to overcoming formal veto players.

The claim that Europeanization has not led to convergence in Western Europe is correct in the sense that the EU has not produced uniform policies among its members. Otherwise, however, the EU has certainly induced more similar policies compared to the status quo ante. In environmental policy, for example, there is evidence of significant convergence in the policy instruments used (see e.g. Jordan and Liefferink 2006).

A number of factors limit the scope for convergence in the sense of uniformity. EU legislation often gives national legislators a wide margin of discretion rather than prescribing the adoption of identical rules across the EU. Still, even if EU law only specifies minimum standards, it limits the extent of persistent diversity and hence induces greater cross-country convergence. Member states' non-compliance with EU law (Börzel 2001) means that divergent national policies can persist, but such divergence is usually only temporary. If infringements of EU law are detected, member states generally correct them sooner, rather than later.

The most fundamental obstacles to convergence are explicit provisions for 'flexible integration' in the treaties, which grant specific member states permanent derogations from EU law (see e.g. Dimitrova and Steunenberg 2000). The possibility for individual EU member states to 'opt out' of cooperation in specific issue areas make the EU's impact uneven within its geographical borders. The area of 'flexible integration' has seen some more recent developments that militate against convergence inside the EU. From the outset, some member states chose not to join Economic and Monetary Union (EMU) – Denmark, Sweden and the UK – while among the EU's new member states, so far only Slovenia, Cyprus, Malta, Slovakia and Estonia have qualified since accession. Similarly, the UK and Ireland opted out of the Schengen Agreement's free travel area without border controls, while Romania and Bulgaria have not yet been accepted and its implementation in Cyprus has been delayed due to the Cyprus conflict. A more recent example of flexible integration is the European Security and Defence Policy (ESDP), for example with regard to the opt-out for Denmark, the 15 battle groups in which one to five different countries participate (except for Malta), or the contribution of member states to particular ESDP missions. Finally, the Lisbon Treaty codifies more opt-outs – such as from the Charter of Fundamental Rights (for the UK, Poland and the Czech Republic) and facilitates further moves towards 'flexible integration'.

At the same time as flexible integration reduces the scope for convergence within the EU, in some areas of flexible integration the EU induces policy convergence beyond its borders through the inclusion of non-member states. For example, Norway, Iceland and Switzerland are Schengen members. The euro has been introduced as the currency of Kosovo after Nato's intervention by the UNMIK administration, while Montenegro has adopted the euro unilaterally having used the German Mark as official currency already since 1996 during the State Union with Serbia. Concerning ESDP, Norway and Turkey contribute to battle groups, and various non-member states have contributed troops to specific ESDP missions, for example Ukraine with regard to the EU Police Missions in Bosnia-Herzegovina and in Macedonia. While flexible integration is thus one example of the EU's external impact, even outside these areas, it is precisely with regard to the EU's external impact that the most significant recent developments with regard to Europeanization are taking place.

EU impact beyond its borders

Although the study of Europeanization has focused traditionally on EU member states, the EU's impact has always extended beyond its borders. In the past, this impact manifested itself primarily in various forms of unilateral adjustment that outsiders undertook in order to alleviate the negative externalities of EU integration on outsiders – such as trade diversion, relocation of firms, or in the area of monetary policy or free travel. Such adjustments were therefore highly selective and did not result from deliberate attempts by the EU to induce an alignment with its rules.

A qualitative change in the EU's impact on outsiders occurred in the 1990s with regard to two groups of countries whose adjustment was much more comprehensive and much more directly influenced by the EU, making these Europeanization processes comparable to the EU's impact on member states. First, most members of the European Free Trade Association (EFTA) entered in 1992 into the European Economic Area (EEA) agreement, which provided for their unilateral adoption of the EU's rules and regulations – the *acquis communautaire* – as a precondition for their participation in the EU's internal market (except for agriculture). Second, in the late 1990s, the EU directly and explicitly influenced adjustment processes in the post-communist Central and Eastern European countries (CEECs) as part of their preparations for membership by providing yardsticks, schedules and regular monitoring of the progress achieved. Studies of the EU's impact on the CEEC candidate countries started to appropriate the term 'Europeanization' that the literature had hitherto reserved for studies of EU member states, to frame their analysis (see e.g. Schimmelfennig and Sedelmeier 2005a; Hughes *et al.* 2004; Grabbe 2006; Bauer *et al.* 2007). At the same time, Europeanization of candidate countries has distinctive characteristics from the Europeanization of EU member states.

First, and maybe counter-intuitively, the scope of the EU's adjustment pressures on the candidate countries has been much wider than on EU member states. Any international institution would expect new members to be able to comply with its rules. Yet the EU's membership conditions for the CEEC were not limited to their ability to apply the entire body of EU law – the *acquis communautaire*. In addition, the EU used the strength of the membership incentive to pursue broader political goals through its enlargement policy. Its membership conditions thus focused on a broad range of political and economic criteria, covering many rules for which EU institutions have no legal competences vis-à-vis full member states (such as democracy and minority rights). Second, EU institutions cannot rely on the treaty-based sanctions to illicit compliance. Instead, they have to use softer instruments, including conditional positive incentives (such as EU membership), or processes of socialization to persuade candidate countries that compliance with EU demands is normatively appropriate, rather than just a means to obtain the rewards offered by the EU. Third, in contrast to full members, the candidates' lack of voice in the making of the rules that they have to adopt deprives them of an opportunity to reduce their adjustment costs. While the CEECs considered many EU templates to suit their goal of a transition to the market despite high adjustment costs (Jacoby 2004), not all areas of the *acquis* provided the most cost-effective and functionally effective option.

In recent years, this external dimension of Europeanization has become more differential across distinctive groups of countries. The following section provides an overview of the findings of studies of the EU's impact on the (then) candidate countries that joined the EU in 2004 and 2007. While the EU's impact on the candidate countries that joined in 2004 and 2007 has been far from uniform, it has been generally pervasive. The EU's strong impact on these countries provides a certain yardstick of the extent to which the EU can have an external impact if the conditions for such an impact are favourable. It leads us to expect differences in the EU's impact across three groups of European countries where these conditions are – to different extents – generally less favourable. These groups are the new members after accession; the EU's current candidate countries in South-East Europe, including Turkey; and the European successor states of the former Soviet Union that are included in the EU's ENP and its more recent 'Eastern Partnership' initiative without the declared end-goal of membership.

EU impact on candidate countries in East Central Europe

The literature on the EU's Eastern enlargement and particularly of its accession conditionality towards the CEECs started to extend the study of 'Europeanization' beyond the member states (this section draws partly on Sedelmeier 2006). The main questions in this literature are to what extent and under what conditions the EU has a domestic impact in candidate countries. Similar to the study of Europeanization in member states, theoretically informed studies are largely set within the framework of institutionalist theory, and in particular the debate between rationalist institutionalism and constructivist institutionalism (see e.g. Goetz 2002; Kubicek 2003; Dimitrova and Steunenberg 2004; Jacoby 2004; Kelley 2004; Schimmelfennig and Sedelmeier 2005a; Grabbe 2006; Schimmelfennig *et al.* 2006; Epstein 2008). Rationalist and constructivist approaches identify distinctive mediating factors for the EU's influence at the domestic level in the target countries, just as in the study of member state Europeanization. Yet, in contrast to analyses of EU member states, the study of the external impact also focuses on differences in the strategies that the EU uses to achieve its impact.

The strategy that rationalist approaches focus on is the use of conditionality as an incentive-based strategy to achieve, or lock in, domestic changes in target countries. The EU's impact on target countries then depends on their governments' cost–benefit calculations, namely whether the rewards that the EU offers for complying with its demands outweigh the domestic adjustment costs of compliance. Factors both relating to the EU's use of the strategy and domestic conditions account for different outcomes of these cost–benefit calculations and hence account for variation of the EU's impact of across target countries. At the EU level, these factors include the credibility of the EU's conditionality, the size of the EU's rewards and whether they will be obtained in the short or long term, and how clear the EU's conditions are. The domestic factors that determine the adjustment costs include the strength of actual or de facto veto players on whom the EU's conditions impose costs.

By contrast, constructivist institutionalism also considers the possibility that the EU can generate an external impact through alternative strategies to the use of conditionality, namely such as persuasion and socialization. Target governments then comply with the EU's conditions if they are persuaded of the legitimacy of the rules in question. Within this framework, EU impact depends on the perceived legitimacy of its conditions (which increases e.g. if the more these rules are internationally codified, and consistently practiced by the EU members), on the target government's positive identification with the EU and a positive normative resonance of EU demands with existing domestic rules and political discourses.

Although the two approaches thus emphasize analytically distinctive factors, many studies do not consider these factors mutually exclusive (Jacoby 2004: 20–40; Kelley 2004; Schimmelfennig and Sedelmeier 2005b: 25) or focus precisely on their interaction (Epstein 2008; Johnson 2006). At the same time, most studies of candidate country Europeanization find that rationalist institutionalism best explains the broad patterns of compliance with EU demands by non-member states. Some studies suggest that the EU's influence cannot be explained fully without attention to processes of persuasion and socialization (Andonova 2005; Epstein 2008; Grabbe 2005; Johnson 2006) or the positive normative resonance of EU demands with pre-existing domestic political culture (Schwellnus 2005). However, the literature generally finds that cross-country and cross-issue variation in the EU's influence on non-members depends primarily on governments' cost–benefit calculations. More specifically, EU impact is mediated by the following two factors emphasized by rationalist institutionalism.

The key factor that explains differences in the EU's impact are the domestic adjustment costs for governments. The EU has made all of its rewards – from free trade to full membership – conditional on a target state meeting certain political criteria, in particular respect for the principles of democracy and human rights. For authoritarian and nationalist governments, the political adjustment costs of compliance can be prohibitively high, as it might undermine their hold on power. The EU's influence has crucially depended on the regime type and party political constellations in the non-member states according to which the costs of meeting the EU's political conditions vary (see e.g. Kelley 2004; Schimmelfennig *et al.* 2006; Vachudova 2005). When confronted with authoritarian regimes and anti-liberal party constellations, such as in the case of Belarus, or Slovakia under Vladimir Meciar and Croatia under Franjo Tudjman, the EU has to hope for domestically driven electoral turnover that brings liberal democratic parties into power for which the EU's political conditions do not impose prohibitive costs (see e.g. Schimmelfennig *et al.* 2006). At best, the EU can have an indirect influence on such electoral turnover between authoritarian/nationalist and liberal democratic parties in government. The EU can empower liberal reformers by informing electorates about the implication of their choices for the country's accession prospects and facilitating cooperation and moderation of a fragmented opposition (Vachudova 2005). In contrast to countries with anti-liberal governments, if a country's political competition is dominated by liberal democratic parties, the domestic costs of complying with the EU's political conditions have generally not been prohibitively high. In such cases, even high adjustment costs in specific policy areas have not necessarily inhibited the EU's influence on public policy (see e.g. Schimmelfennig and Sedelmeier 2005a).

However, in such cases, the EU's influence on public policy depended on two factors: first, if issue-specific adjustment costs were high, the EU had to offer its biggest possible reward for compliance – only the prospect of full membership was sufficiently big for governments to discount the adjustment cost in particular sectors against the overall benefits of membership. Second, the EU's conditionality – and its offer of membership – needed to be credible. Credibility in turn depends on a consistent and meritocratic application of conditionality (i.e. that the EU *always* rewards compliance – rather than only in some cases – and *only* rewards compliance – rather than offering membership to countries that do not comply fully), along with clear and consensual messages from the EU about what a target states needs to do (Grabbe 2006; Hughes *et al.* 2004; Schimmelfennig and Sedelmeier 2005b; Vachudova 2005). Variation in the credibility of conditionality – over time, across issue areas, or across countries – explains differences in the EU's impact on public policy. Issue-specific credibility problems are inconsistent messages from the Commission about the adjustment requirements in the area of regional policy (Hughes *et al.* 2004) or divergent messages from different EU actors with regard to the importance of adjustments in social policy for obtaining membership (Sissenich 2005). With regard to cross-country and temporal variation of credibility, a key act that made the prospect of membership credible was the opening of accession negotiations, which generally prompted the most far-reaching influence of the EU on public policies in the non-members (Schimmelfennig and Sedelmeier 2005a).

In sum, the study of the Europeanization of candidate countries in the second part of the 2000s has established that the EU's external impact depends, on the one hand, on the size and credibility of the incentives that the EU can offer. Generally, its most sizeable reward is membership; and this generally accounts for the strong influence of the EU if this incentive is credible. On the other hand, a precondition is that the EU's political conditions do not impose prohibitively high domestic adjustment costs on incumbent governments. Variation in the costs of compliance, the kinds of incentive on offer, and the credibility of conditionality explain the EU's differential impact across countries, issues and over time. At the same time, the conditions in the countries that joined the EU from 2004 to 2007 were arguably particularly conducive for the EU to have a generally strong impact on public policy. We could therefore expect the EU's impact to be also highly differential across three groups of countries: the new member states after accession, the current candidate countries and the successor states of the Soviet Union participating in the Eastern Partnership initiative without a clear prospect of EU accession.

EU impact on new members after accession

The finding that the conditional incentive of membership was the key factor that enabled the EU's external impact on candidate countries raises the question of how sustainable compliance with EU rules will be after the countries in question have joined the EU (Schimmelfennig and Sedelmeier 2004: 677–9; Epstein and Sedelmeier 2008; Sedelmeier 2008; Schimmelfennig and Trauner 2009). The importance of external incentives for pre-accession adjustment to the EU suggests that the changes in the incentive structure affect governments' decision whether to maintain these adjustments and whether to (continue to) apply and enforce EU rules. Of course after they have become EU members, the European Court of Justice can ultimately impose financial penalties on states that infringe EU law. But these sanctions are clearly not as powerful as the threat of withholding membership altogether. The reduced sanctioning power of EU institutions after accession is particularly salient in issue areas in which the EU has applied political conditionality beyond the reach of EU law and where the EU treaty hence gives EU institutions little leverage vis-à-vis full members.

However, studies of post-accession compliance of the new members with EU law generally do not find a deterioration of compliance after membership has been achieved (Sedelmeier 2009b; Trauner 2009b). Moreover, this finding also seems to hold with regard to issue areas beyond EU law, such as minority rights (Pridham 2008, 2009; Sasse 2008b; Schwellnus *et al.* 2009), party orientation (Vachudova 2008), or the respect for democratic principles more generally (Levitz and Pop-Eleches 2010). Developments with regard to judicial reform and the fight against corruption show a more mixed picture (Pridham 2009; Vachudova 2009), although this is a key area where the EU maintained monitoring and the possibility of sanctions with regard to Bulgaria and Romania after their accession in 2007.

Yet even if compliance with EU law in the new member states does not markedly deteriorate after accession compared to the pre-accession period, we might still expect it to be generally more problematic than in the older member states. Key explanatory factors emphasized in the study of compliance in the EU are generally unfavourable in the new members, namely high adjustment costs due to the post-communist transition and low administrative capacities. However, comparisons of the implementation of EU law in particular issue areas between old and new members do not find more significant problems in the latter (Blauberger 2009; Leiber 2007; Steunenberg and Toshkov 2009). More generally, a cross-country analysis of infringements of EU law recorded by the European Commission between 2004 and 2009 suggests that the great majority of new members that joined in 2004 even outperform virtually all of the older member states (Sedelmeier 2008, 2009a). Poland and the Czech Republic lag behind the other newcomers, but they still have better infringement records than the median old member state. Preliminary and anecdotal evidence suggests that this surprisingly good performance can be explained by two different legacies of the experience of pre-accession conditionality (Sedelmeier 2008: 820–2): the pre-accession institutional investment into administrative and legislative procedures that enable the fast transposition of new legislation (see also Dimitrova and Toshkov 2009), as well as a pre-accession socialization into a process of compliance that makes the new member states that aspire to be respectable member states more susceptible to regarding good compliance as appropriate behaviour.

At the same time, these factors might not only explain why the formal transposition of EU law into national law is generally better in the new members. They can also provide an explanation for the gap between good transposition and serious problems with regard to application and enforcement of law in practice that the first detailed studies of application of EU law in the new members observe (Falkner and Treib 2008). Pre-accession monitoring by the European Commission focused primarily on legislative changes, and the creation of administrative, or rather legislative, capacity emphasized the ability to transpose EU conform laws rapidly, rather than an investment in administrative capacities required for a proper enforcement and application of laws in practice.

In sum, the impact of the EU might be indeed differential between old member states and new members after accession. However, these differences do not manifest themselves as a general 'Eastern problem' of infringements of EU law, but with regard to a particular pattern of timely and correct transposition of EU law combined with a lack of proper enforcement and application (a pattern that however can be also observed in some old members in specific issue areas; see Falkner and Treib 2008).

EU impact on current candidate countries in South-East Europe

Compared to the candidate countries of Central and Eastern Europe that joined the EU in 2004 and 2007, the main condition for the EU's external impact – low domestic adjustment costs and a credible membership perspective – are less conducive in the current candidate countries. The EU's current candidate countries for EU membership include Turkey, the remaining successor states of the former Yugoslavia, Albania and most recently Iceland as a result of the financial crisis, which increased the attractiveness of membership in EMU via EU membership. Except for Bosnia-Herzegovina, all these countries have submitted applications for membership. Accession negotiations Croatia and with Turkey opened in October 2005, and Iceland in July 2010. However, with the exception of Croatia and possibly Iceland, which could finish its accession negotiations in 2011 and gain membership within the following years, the remaining candidate countries will move much more slowly towards membership.

Domestic adjustment costs

Among the successor states of Yugoslavia, only Serbia has sufficient administrative capacities to make rapid legal and institutional adjustments for membership. At the same time, in most of the current candidate countries, and in Serbia and Turkey in particular, the costs of meeting the EU's political accession conditions are generally much higher than in the CEECs (see Schimmelfennig 2008; Epstein and Sedelmeier 2008: 799). Standards of democracy and human rights are generally lower. The EU's political conditions are both more intensive and more far-reaching, and in some cases directly affect questions of statehood and national identity. This is particularly salient in the case of Serbia (with regard to the status of Kosovo or cooperation with the International Criminal Tribunal for the former Yugoslavia (ICTY)) and Turkey (with regard to perceived threats to the Kemalist state relating to the role of the military in politics, cultural rights of the Kurdish minority, or limitations on the freedom of expression).

Identity politics in relation to the EU are far more controversial than in the case of the CEECs, where they were generally a factor that facilitated adjustments to the EU's demands in order to obtain membership as part of a 'return to Europe'. While some in the Yugoslav successor states identify the EU with a positive political project that stands for overcoming the legacy of national tensions and ethnic conflict, for others the EU's attempts to influence domestic politics present a threat to key elements of national identity. For example, the arrest and extradition of former army generals indicted by the ICTY but considered war heroes by large parts of the population became the major stumbling block for Croatia to start accession negotiations in 2005 and for the implementation of an association agreement with Serbia. Since the start of negotiations in 2005, positive identification with the EU has also become increasingly problematic in Turkey, where previously across the political spectrum the EU had stood for the Western orientation on which the modern republic is based. The EU's political agenda became increasingly caught up in domestic debates about the role of religion in public life, especially in the face of attempts by the military and the judiciary to limit the powers of the government formed by the religious–conservative, pro-Western Justice and Development Party (AKP).

Not only are the EU's political conditions generally more costly to the current candidates, but the perception of the economic benefits of EU membership are a less compelling factor in domestic politics than in the CEECs (Grabbe and Sedelmeier 2009: 390–1). Through the conflicts surrounding the breakup of Yugoslavia and their aftermath, the Balkan countries missed the post-communist reform drive of the 1990s and the high levels of foreign direct investment (FDI) stimulated both by these reforms and high global liquidity. These countries therefore cannot build on the virtuous circle between economic reforms and regulatory convergence with the EU, FDI inflows, and accession prospects that worked well in the CEECs.

Credibility of the EU's membership incentive

At the same time as the domestic costs of adjustments to the EU are higher, attitudes in the EU towards enlargement have become much more negative, both among elites and particularly in public opinion. Montenegro and Albania submitted their membership applications despite explicit warnings from EU institutions that they were unlikely to lead to accession negotiations anytime soon. Despite starting accession negotiations, open opposition to Turkish membership has been voiced by the French and Austrian governments and the Christian Democratic Union in Germany. The conflict over the recognition of Cyprus has been the touchstone for such opposition to slow the pace of accession negotiations. Moreover, the reluctant member states are attempting to redefine the meaning of 'accession negotiations' with Turkey. Suggestions that the negotiations might not lead to accession but to an ill-defined 'privileged partnership' challenge the notion that the negotiations imply a mutual commitment to concluding them successfully. Another attempt to break the path dependency of accession negotiations are the changes to the French constitution

in 2005 and 2008 that will subject future enlargements to a referendum –
unless a high threshold for parliamentary approval is met.

Scope and limits of the EU's external impact

As a result of the domestic constellation in the current candidates and
attitudes in the EU, the conditions for the EU's impact are therefore
generally much less favourable than in the case of the CEECs. Domestic
cost–benefit calculation are much less straightforward, despite the very
high potential welfare benefits, since the EU's political conditionality
front-loads significant adjustment costs. In addition to the higher domestic adjustment costs, the EU's membership incentive is much less credible
– especially for Turkey – or at least much more distant. The weaker
membership incentive can create a vicious circle. The more the benefits of
membership are uncertain or are expected to materialize only in the long
term, the less conducive they are to overcoming short-term domestic
adjustment costs and reforms are more likely to stall. In turn, stalled
reforms make membership an even more distant prospect, further reducing its ability to stimulate adjustment efforts.

The generally less conducive conditions for the EU's impact on the
current candidates explain why the EU's impact has been generally
weaker in South-East Europe than in Central Eastern. Yet this does not
mean that the EU's impact has been insignificant. The incentive of EU
membership still has been a source of domestic change in South-East
Europe, but the EU's impact has been much more selective and partial
than in the CEECs. For example, Turkey has not only carried out far-
reaching political reforms in the run-up to the start of accession negotiations in 2005. Despite the diminished credibility of accession, the
government made further progress in certain areas, especially with
regard to the cultural rights of the Kurdish minority, such as the opening
of a public TV channel broadcasting nationwide in Kurdish. At the same
time, attempts at dialogue with the minority were undermined by the
Turkish Constitutional Court's decision in December 2009 to ban the
principal pro-Kurdish party, the Democratic Society Party (DTP),
accused of having links with the Kurdish separatist PKK. Likewise,
Macedonia achieved sufficient progress by 2009 with political reforms
demanded by the EU – concerning the conduct of elections, dialogue
between parties, effectiveness of parliament, the legal and institutional
framework for the protection of minorities, and tackling corruption in
the police, the judiciary and the public administration – for the European
Commission to recommend opening accession negotiations, although
these remain blocked by Greece due to the dispute with Greece over the
use of the country's name.

In view of these problems with using the prospect of membership as an incentive, the EU has focused more on making intermediate steps on the path to membership subject to specific conditions – such as recognising a country officially as a candidate for accession, or starting accession negotiations. But the EU has also used more issue-specific rewards, especially in areas where adjustments also serve its security interests in the region. A key area here is border security to combat illegal immigration and cross-border organized crime (Trauner 2009a). In addition to financial and technical assistance to upgrade border management, the EU's main incentives in this area are visa facilitation and ultimately the lifting of visa requirements, as it did for Macedonia, Montenegro and Serbia in December 2009. In December 2010, it abolished visa requirements for Albania and Bosnia after sufficient progress with meeting specific conditions, which include the conclusion of readmission agreements (in which the neighbouring countries from which refugees/asylum seekers have entered the EU commit to take them back), the introduction of biometric passports, improved border and police controls, and the fight against corruption and crime.

In sum, the less conducive conditions – higher adjustment costs particularly of the EU's political conditions and the less credible or more distant membership incentive – account for a generally weaker impact of the EU in South-East Europe compared to the CEECs in the late 1990s and early 2000s. Still, the presence of the prospect of membership – albeit less credible and more distant – has been a source of EU influence that introduced elements of convergence in public policies and democratic governance. Yet compared to the CEECs, the impact of EU conditionality has been much more selective and partial, slower, more incremental and more vulnerable to reversals, with variation according to country and issue-specific cost–benefit calculations by the target governments.

EU impact on Eastern European countries without membership prospect

The apparent success of accession conditionality in the CEECs led the EU to use similar policy instruments in order to influence domestic politics in the European successor states of the Soviet Union (Kelley 2006; Schimmelfennig 2009) when the prospect of Eastern enlargement led the EU to think about a framework for relations with the new Eastern neighbours. The result was the European Neighbourhood Policy (ENP), established in 2004 (Smith 2005; Weber *et al.* 2007). The ENP did not include Russia, which preferred bilateral relations with the EU, but at the same time the EU's southern member states successfully pushed to include the southern neighbours in the Mediterranean. The EU subsequently created a more specific framework for relations with the Eastern members of the ENP through the 'Eastern Partnership', endorsed by the European Council in December 2008. The Eastern Partnership partly responded to an initiative to strengthen the EU's relations with the southern neighbours through the 'Union of the Mediterranean', but also to the desire to strengthen democratic forces following the 2004 Orange Revolution in Ukraine and the Rose Revolution in Georgia, which became more salient after the conflict between Georgia and Russia in summer 2008.

Although the ENP uses similar instruments and pursues similar goals as the enlargement policy, it does not provide similarly strong incentives. It is organized around bilateral 'Action Plans' that identify priorities and timeframes for 'approximation and convergence towards the European Union', especially with regard to democracy, human rights and the market economy. Monitoring reports by the European Commission assess the progress made. However, the EU does not offer its most powerful incentive for adjustments: the ENP explicitly does not envisage membership for the East European neighbours. Instead, it offers a vague 'stake in the internal market' that echoes the concept of the EEA, although it is doubtful that the high administrative and economic adjustment costs of full alignment with the *acquis communautaire* make it an attractive option for ENP partners if it is not connected to the other benefits of full EU membership. Moreover, market access excludes precisely the sectors most attractive to ENP partners, especially agriculture.

The EU recognizes the weaker incentive structure in that it emphasizes participatory mechanisms that involve the ENP partners in the setting of priorities according to their own goals for economic developments, rather than (implicitly) expecting full and strict alignment to the *acquis* (Noutcheva and Emerson 2007; Sedelmeier 2007). The advantage of such a version of 'conditionality-lite' might be that it provides a 'loose framework for socialization' and an external reference point that can facilitate long-term, gradual adjustment even when faced with Eurosceptic actors within the ENP partners (Sasse 2008a). A more sceptical view is that the uneasy coexistence of conditionality and socialization might undermine each other's potential as instruments to promote the EU's external impact (Sedelmeier 2007: 200–1). The Eastern Partnership partly addresses the weakness of the incentive structure by offering association agreements that envisage the creation of bilateral free trade areas, and particularly the possibility of visa facilitation.

The incentive structure in the Eastern Partnership is thus still considerably weaker than for the current candidate countries. It offers otherwise very similar benefits and links with the EU, but not the crucial promise of eventual membership as a reward for adjustment. Some of the Eastern neighbours still perceive membership as a long-term possibility and hence might have a stronger motive for adjustment than non-European countries. Yet such motives are not suited to overcoming adjustment costs where they are high – as is generally the case with regard to principles of liberal democracy or more far-reaching regulatory alignment.

In the absence of the broader membership benefits, sector-specific benefits are unlikely to be sufficiently powerful to lead to convergence in sensitive areas of democratic principles and human rights. EU actors are either internally constrained from offering economic incentives where they are most powerful – such as with regard to agricultural free trade or free movement of labour – or attach their own, sector-specific conditions, such as the conclusion of readmission agreements for offering visa facilitation (Sedelmeier 2007).

Indeed, studies of the EU's impact on the East European neighbours find no evidence that the ENP or the Eastern Partnership have induced processes of convergence towards EU standards of democracy and human rights (Maier and Schimmelfennig 2007; Schimmelfennig and Scholtz 2008). However, there is some evidence of a strengthening of principles of democratic governance – such as transparency, participation and accountability – in sectoral policies, especially in areas where these principles are strongly legalized inside the EU and in international conventions (Freyburg *et al.* 2009). Similarly, although the EU might not have been able to induce convergence towards its own specific rules, its impact appears to have been stronger when promoting internationally codified rules as a basis for convergence (Barbe *et al.* 2009).

Otherwise, the EU's impact on its Eastern neighbours is strongest in individual policy areas where it can offer specific incentives for adjustments. Similar to the current candidate countries, the prospect of increased mobility for their citizens through visa facilitation is a strongly motivating factor for reforms in border management and controls, readmission of asylum seekers, and cooperation to prevent cross-border crime and illegal immigration. On the other hand, although the EU opened sector-specific governance networks to facilitate horizontal integration of ENP partners (Lavenex *et al.* 2009) such networks do not necessarily function as frameworks to transfer EU rules to non-member states.

In sum, although the ENP and the Eastern Partnership were specifically designed to extend the EU's external impact to its new Eastern neighbours, the EU's influence has been rather limited. Without an explicit prospect of membership, the incentive structure is too weak as it confronts generally high adjustment costs both in the political and regulatory realm. The EU's influence on domestic change is restricted to areas in which adjustment costs are not high due to financial support or outweighed by direct rewards.

Conclusions

Studies of the Europeanization on European politics have established that although the EU's impact is pervasive, it is also differential across member states and policy-areas. A key recent development with regard to the EU's impact on European politics is the extension of Europeanization effects beyond the EU's borders.

The EU made first targeted attempts to systematically influence political and regulatory adjustments in the context of its Eastern enlargement to the CEECs. Studies of the Europeanization of the CEECs generally agree that differences in the EU's impact across countries and issues depend on the extent of target government's adjustment costs with the EU's political conditions, as well as on the credibility of the EU's membership incentive.

Differences with regard to the incentive structure and adjustment costs also explain variation of the EU's impact across different groups of countries. The changing incentive structure after the CEECs achieved EU membership in 2004 and 2007 did not lead to a general deterioration of their compliance with EU law. Compliance – at least at the formal level of legislative adjustment – even appears generally better in these new member states than in the old member states. In contrast to the EU's generally strong impact on regulatory alignment and to some extent on political reforms in the candidate countries of the 2004 and 2007 enlargements, Europeanization effects are generally weaker in current candidate countries and the European successor states of the Soviet Union.

In the current candidate countries, the membership incentive is much less credible or much more distant. Adjustment costs with the EU's political conditions are particularly high in Turkey and most successor states of Yugoslavia where they touch on sensitive questions of statehood and national identity. In the Eastern neighbours that are the target of the EU's 'Eastern Partnership', the incentives for adjustment are even weaker, as the EU has explicitly ruled out the prospect of membership for the foreseeable future. Differences in the incentive structure explain why the EU's impact is still considerably stronger in South-East European candidate countries than in the Eastern neighbours, but in both groups, adjustments to the EU are much more selective and partial than in the case of the CEECs.

Chapter 4

Government and Governance in Europe

Rainer Eising and Thomas Poguntke

Europe comprise both a fairly uniform and very diverse group of countries. This inherently contradictory statement flows from the fact that we are dealing with a group of countries defined by geographic location which are all democracies. As such, they are uniform and differ from many other countries in the world. However, once we start inspecting the nature of their democracies somewhat closer, we quickly discover substantial differences. In the first instance, we are dealing essentially with two groups of countries, some of which achieved democracy only at the beginning of the 1990s, and are characterized by their post-communist heritage, while democracy dates back further in the remaining countries. The latter again divide into three groups: those where democracy survived the challenges of Fascism (though many of them were occupied by Germany during the Second World War), those where democracy was finally established after the Second World War, and those where authoritarianism lingered on until the 1970s.

These very different historical pathways to democracy suggest that we should be able to find their traces in the political structures of these countries. We have deliberately chosen the term 'institutional structures' as this includes not only institutional architecture but also less formalized governance structures. This distinction is important because historical traces and legacies are likely to be as visible in less formalized political process and routines as in the highly formalized institutional architecture to which we now turn.

Who governs?

The question 'who governs' refers to the core of political analysis, namely the locus of power and mechanisms to ensure its democratic control and accountability. This includes the formal structures of government, including parliament and the core executive, which make binding decisions for the nation. However, modern political science has moved beyond this narrow concept of government and now includes a wider range of formalized arenas of decision-making, including private or semi-private and supranational structures which are captured by the concept of governance.

Governance is a buzzword in the social sciences. In our understanding governance means all forms and mechanisms of coordination among more or less autonomous actors whose actions are interdependent, that is, they might support or impede each other (see Benz *et al.* 2007: 9). Thus we do not consider governance to be the opposite of government as is often the case. Rather, governance should be understood as an extension of government towards less formalized mechanisms to reach binding decisions, including the variety of social structures that coordinate political behaviour, ranging from hierarchies, markets and networks to communities as well as the concomitant forms of interaction such as negotiations, governing by decree or political competition.

Presidents and prime ministers

When looking at the formal structures of power, one obvious distinction between different political systems meets the eye immediately. Executive power is either in the hands of a president or a prime minister – or, and now things get complicated, power is shared between them. Let us begin with the pure systems. They represent very different attempts to solve one of the core problems of democratic government, namely to find the right balance between the needs of executive power if it is to be capable of governing effectively, and the need to limit this executive power through constraints imposed by parliament, through legislation and budgetary control.

Presidential systems have solved this problem by creating an executive which is legitimated through popular (not necessarily direct) election and cannot be removed from office by parliament. The president *is* the executive and the head of state; all other executive offices derive their legitimacy in the first instance from appointment by the president. This feature has been called the 'uni-personal' executive and clearly differs from the collective executive responsibility that characterizes parliamentary systems where the prime minister is the chief executive. A clear institutional separation of power is the defining criterion of presidentialism. President and legislature are elected separately and they live separate lives in that the survival of the executive is independent of a majority in the legislature.

This institutional configuration aims at achieving the dual goals of strong executive leadership and meaningful democratic control through guaranteeing the survival of the executive (presidents are elected for fixed terms) while limiting its steering capacity through the need to obtain the consent of the legislature. A president can neither spend money nor implement significant policy changes without its approval, even though the survival of his or her government remains unchallenged.

Parliamentary government follows a substantially different institutional strategy. The head of state can either be an elected president or a hereditary monarch and has a largely ceremonial role. There is no separation of legislative and executive power. On the contrary, parliamentary systems are characterized by a fusion of these powers. Governments need the consent (that includes toleration) of parliament in order to remain in office, and they also need parliamentary consent to govern effectively. Among the parliamentary parties, it is up to the opposition to control government and hold it in check. At first sight, prime ministers would appear substantially weaker than presidents in that they seem to depend entirely on the majority of parliament when it comes to their survival and scope for action. Yet, they have a powerful weapon because they can usually initiate early elections and this is an effective tool for disciplining dissenting MPs who often do not want to risk their jobs.

The British political system comes closest to the ideal type of a parliamentary government where parliamentary majority and government form a unified political camp, usually led by a strong prime minister who is capable of dominating and controlling his or her parliamentary party to a considerable degree. The power of the chief executive may be more limited under conditions of coalition government or in federal systems where a prime minister needs to deal with a larger number of veto players (see below).

An alternative way of analysing the regime types is to focus on the way the chain of delegation runs from mass publics to the public administration. While parliamentary systems are characterized by one single chain of delegation, presidential systems have parallel chains running from voters via the legislatures and via the president to the machinery of government (Strøm 2000: 269). It is typical of semi-presidential systems that they combine these parallel chains of delegation with the core feature of parliamentary government, namely the parliamentary accountability of a prime minister. In other words, semi-presidential regimes amalgamate parliamentary government with a directly elected president who has – *de jure* or *de facto* – substantial executive powers. This hybrid constellation has given rise to considerable debate in the literature over the inherent logic of semi-presidential systems. Some go as far as denying that semi-presidentialism represents a regime type in its own right (Strøm 2000: 266), while others have alluded to the fact that the actual working mode of such systems depends substantially on the political configuration (divided or unified government), and on unwritten codes of behaviour (Döring and Hönnige 2008; Sartori 1994; Duverger 1980).

Two Western European states exemplify the difficulties of classifying regime types. Even though the Austrian president has very considerable powers including the right to dismiss the prime minister, the Austrian political systems functions largely like any other parliamentary system. The French constitution, on the other hand, gives no such right to the president yet he has always been able to enforce the resignation of the prime minister as long as the head of government belonged to his own party political majority. In times of a hostile majority in parliament, that is, under conditions of 'cohabitation', things change substantially and the president is reduced to his role in foreign and security policy while the system functions largely like any other parliamentary regime (Elgie 1999: 73). In the past decade, constitutional reforms have aimed at preventing this constellation by reducing the president's term of office from seven to five years (once renewable) bringing it in line with that of the Members of the Assemblée Nationale.

Yet, in formal terms, both countries are correctly categorized as semi-presidential (see Table 4.1), because the considerable powers of the Austrian presidency cannot be ignored even though they have thus far been used very cautiously. Other Western nations have moved towards a purely parliamentary system over past decades. A series of constitutional reforms has reduced the powers of the Finnish president to an extent that suggests a classification as parliamentary even though the president is still directly elected. However, the same applies to Ireland which is also normally regarded as parliamentary, while Portugal has now become a weak form of semi-presidentialism (Costa Lobo 2007; Paloheimo 2007).

This drift towards parliamentarism in Western Europe is also indicative of the trajectory of post-communist countries. During the early transition from authoritarian to democratic rule that began in 1989, most of the formerly communist countries opted for constitutions that gave considerable powers to a president. In part, these choices reflected power struggles between newly formed (opposition) parties and the former ruling (post-)communist parties. Even in those countries where a president was not directly elected (as in Hungary and the Czech Republic), the low degree of party system institutionalization and a lack of familiarity with parliamentary politics allowed presidents to assume a strong position, sometimes over and above their constitutionally circumscribed role. Over the past decades, however, post-communist countries began to curtail the role of the presidency (Goetz 2006: 77; Elgie 2009: 253ff.) and operate according to the logic of parliamentary democracies, even though several of them still fall under the semi-presidential rubric

Table 4.1 Structures of government in Europe

Country	Head of state	Method of selection	Type of representative democracy	Head of government	Appointment of cabinet	Parliament
Austria	President	Popular election; six-year term	Semi-presidential	Federal Chancellor appointed by President	Chosen by President on the advice of Federal Chancellor	Bicameral
Belgium	Monarch	Hereditary	Parliamentary	Prime Minister appointed by Monarch, then approved by parliament	Formally appointed by Monarch	Bicameral
Bulgaria	President	Popular election; five-year term	Semi-presidential	Chairman of the Council of Ministers nominated by President and elected by parliament	Nominated by Prime Minister and elected by parliament	Unicameral
Croatia	President	Popular election; five-year term	Parliamentary	Prime Minister appointed by President with the approval of parliament	Appointed by Prime Minister with approval of parliament	Unicameral
Cyprus	President	Popular election; five-year term	Presidential	President	Appointed by President	Unicameral
Czech Republic	President	Elected by parliament; five-year term	Parliamentary	Prime Minister appointed by President	Appointed by President on nomination of Prime Minister	Bicameral
Denmark	Monarch	Hereditary	Parliamentary	Prime Minister appointed by Monarch	Appointed by Prime Minister and approved by parliament	Uricameral
Estonia	President	Elected by parliament or Electoral Assembly; five-year term	Parliamentary	Prime Minister, nominated by President, approved by parliament	Appointed by Prime Minister and approved by parliament	Unicameral
Finland	President	Popular election; six-year term	Parliamentary	Prime Minister, appointed by President, approved by parliament	Appointed by President and responsible to parliament	Unicameral

continued overleaf

Table 4.1 *continued*

Country	Head of state	Method of selection	Type of representative democracy	Head of government	Appointment of cabinet	Parliament
France	President	Popular election; five-year term	Semi-presidential	Prime Minister, nominated by lower house, appointed by President	Appointed by President on the suggestion of Prime Minister	Bicameral
Germany	President	Elected by Federal Convention, five-year term	Parliamentary	Federal Chancellor elected by lower house	Appointed by President on the nomination of the Federal Chancellor	Bicameral
Greece	President	Elected by parliament; five-year term	Parliamentary	Prime Minister appointed by President	Appointed by President on the nomination of the Prime Minister	Unicameral
Hungary	President	Elected by parliament; five-year term	Parliamentary	Prime Minister appointed by parliament on recommendation of President	Elected by parliament on the nomination of the President	Unicameral
Ireland	President	Popular election; seven-year term	Parliamentary	Prime Minister appointed by President on nomination by lower house	Appointed by President with previous nomination by Prime Minister and approval of lower house	Bicameral
Italy	President	Elected by Electoral College, seven-year term	Parliamentary	Prime Minister appointed by President and confirmed by parliament	Nominated by Prime Minister and appointed by President	Bicameral
Latvia	President	Elected by parliament; four-year term	Parliamentary	Prime Minister appointed by President and confirmed by parliament	Nominated by Prime Minister and elected by parliament	Unicameral
Lithuania	President	Popular election; five-year term	Semi-presidential	Prime Minister appointed by President with the approval of parliament	Appointed by President on the nomination of the Prime Minister	Unicameral

Luxembourg	Monarch	Hereditary	Parliamentary	Prime Minister appointed by Monarch	Nominated by Prime Minister and appointed by Monarch	Unicameral
Malta	President	Elected by parliament; five-year term	Parliamentary	Prime Minister appointed by President	Appointed by President on the advice of Prime Minister	Unicameral
Moldova	President	Elected by parliament; four-year term	Parliamentary	Prime Minister nominated by President upon consultation with parliament; must seek a vote of confidence	Nominated by the President, subject to approval by parliament	Unicameral
Montenegro	President	Popular election; five-year term	Semi-presidential	Prime Minister appointed by President, accepted by parliament	Parliament shall simultaneously vote on the government's programme and election of the Prime Minister and members of the government	Unicameral
Netherlands	Monarch	Hereditary	Parliamentary	Prime Minister appointed by Monarch	Appointed by Monarch	Bicameral
Norway	Monarch	Hereditary	Parliamentary	Prime Minister appointed by Monarch with the approval of parliament	Appointed by Monarch with the approval of parliament	Unicameral
Poland	President	Popular election; five-year term	Semi-presidential	Prime Minister appointed by President and confirmed by lower house	Prime Minister proposes, President appoints and lower house approves	Bicameral
Portugal	President	Popular election; five-year term	Semi-presidential	Prime Minister appointed by President	Appointed by President on the recommendation of Prime Minister	Unicameral
Romania	President	Popular election; five-year term	Semi-presidential	Prime Minister appointed by President	Appointed by Prime Minister	Bicameral

continued overleaf

Table 4.1 *continued*

Country	Head of state	Method of selection	Type of representative democracy	Head of government	Appointment of cabinet	Parliament
Serbia	President	Popular election; five-year term	Semi-presidential	Prime Minister elected by parliament	Parliament shall simultaneously vote on the government's programme and election of the Prime Minister and members of the government	Unicameral
Slovakia	President	Popular election; five-year term	Semi-presidential	Prime Minister appointed by President	Appointed by President on the recommendation of Prime Minister	Unicameral
Slovenia	President	Popular election; five-year term	Parliamentary	Prime Minister nominated by President, elected by lower house	Nominated by Prime Minister and elected by lower house	Unicameral
Spain	Monarch	Hereditary	Parliamentary	Prime Minister elected by parliament on proposal of Monarch	Designated by Prime Minister	Bicameral
Sweden	Monarch	Hereditary	Parliamentary	Prime Minister elected by parliament	Appointed by Prime Minister	Unicameral
Switzerland	President	Elected by parliament, one-year term	Collegial government elected by parliament for a fixed term	Elected by parliament	Elected by parliament	Bicameral
Ukraine[1]	President	Popular election; five-year term	Presidential	Prime Minister appointed by the President	Appointed by the President	Unicameral
United Kingdom	Monarch	Hereditary	Parliamentary	Prime Minister appointed by Monarch	Appointed by Prime Minister	Bicameral

[1] Until October 2010 the Prime Minister and the Cabinet needed the consent of parliament. This was abolished by a ruling of the Constitutional Court which effectively means a return of Ukraine to a presidential system. *Sources:* Goetz (2006); Döring and Hönnige (2008); own research.

(Table 4.1). The protracted struggles between Prime Minister Yulia Tymoshenko and President Viktor Yushchenko in Ukraine were a conspicuous example of the still not fully settled institutional balance in some post-communist countries. Similarly, the Czech president Václav Klaus has attempted to assume a role that arguably goes beyond that of a president who does not enjoy popular legitimacy but who is elected by parliament.

Two countries stand out in the universe of parliamentary or semi-presidential regimes in Europe. Cyprus is the only European nation with a presidential system, and Switzerland is notoriously difficult to classify because its collegial executive is elected by parliament but cannot be removed by it. Furthermore, Switzerland is unique in not having a separate head of state. Instead, government members take turns in taking over the representative functions of a head of state for one year each without assuming a formally more senior position during this period of time.

Another feature of Western European democracies is politically largely unimportant and can be explained by diverse historical developments. Hereditary monarchies have survived in several parliamentary democracies which experienced a usually gradual transition to democracy during which the monarch was reduced to a largely ceremonial role. The notable exception is Spain where the monarchy was reinstated at the end of the Franco dictatorship and played a crucial and supportive role in the country's transition towards democracy.

Majoritarian and consensus democracies

We have started the discussion of regime types by pointing out that different institutional configurations represent alternative solutions of striking a balance between facilitating strong executive leadership and ensuring democratic control and accountability. From this perspective, our threefold classification remains insufficient in that it ignores a large number of systemic factors which also influence the distribution of power between executive and legislature. Arend Lijphart has suggested that a more complete picture can be obtained by including a larger number of institutional variables ranging, among others, from the electoral system, the type of party system, the power of the constitutional court to the degree of federalism and the power (and existence) of a second legislative chamber. These factors make democratic decision-making either more majoritarian or more consensual and allow us to place political systems on a continuum ranging from strongly majoritarian to strongly consensual (Lijphart 1999). Single-party government, the absence of strong judicial review, subnational units of government and a weak second chamber serve to concentrate the power in the hands of the prime minister. The paradigmatic example of this configuration is the United Kingdom before the Blair government initiated a process of devolution and made the central bank politically independent. The Scandinavian multiparty systems and the strong German federalism are examples of political systems where the central government needs to negotiate with a considerable number of veto players in order to achieve desired policies.

Other analyses have drawn attention to additional factors that were not included in Lijphart's analysis. The structure of the core executive is one of them. The core executive denotes '*all those organizations and procedures which coordinate central government policies, and act as final arbiters of conflict between different parts of the government machine*' (Rhodes 1995: 12, emphasis in original). It includes the 'prime minister, cabinet, cabinet committees and their official counterparts' as well as the surrounding set of formal and informal institutions and practices (*ibid.*: 12). The German chancellorship is an example of a constitutionally strong chief executive whereas other countries ascribe a *primus inter pares* role to the prime minister. This is often reflected in a relatively modest number of senior civil servants who are under the direct control of the prime minister. While a German chancellor has a powerful chancellor's office at his or her disposal, which is capable of screening the activities of cabinet members, other European prime ministers are largely dependent on the input of government departments which are under the control of their cabinet members when it comes to designing policies. It is indicative of the growing role of prime ministers, however, that the prime ministers' offices have been strengthened over the past decades almost everywhere in Western Europe (Webb and Poguntke 2007).

The resources available to the core executive point to another important feature of parliamentary democracies: the overwhelming share of legislation originates from within the machinery of government, and the resources of the prime minister are an important indicator of the extent to which he or she is capable of controlling and steering this legislative initiative. This is, however, only part of the picture. A more detailed analysis of executive agenda control over parliamentary procedures adds further differentiation. A full assessment of the balance of power between executive and parliament needs to take into account how the powers of parliament are regulated when it comes to the process of legislation. This includes the rights of members of parliament (MPs), as individuals or in groups, to initiate or amend legislation and to influence the parliamentary agenda (Döring 1995). After all, the fact that prime ministers may be able to dominate their cabinet does not automatically mean that they are equally capable of achieving their legislative goals. It has been suggested that the Italian bicameral system, where the Chamber of Deputies and the Senate have equal powers, is a conspicuous example of an institutional design that makes it notoriously difficult for the government to achieve parliamentary approval for legislative initiatives. Again, the British political system is situated at the other end of such a continuum, because parliamentary rules allow the government largely to control the legislative process. The parliamentary agenda also used to be determined by the government in France. Here, the latest constitutional reforms have significantly strengthened the rights of parliament to set its own agenda.

Overall, consensual elements are prevalent in Europe. Proportional representation dominates which furthers multiparty systems and coalition governments. There has been a trend towards strengthening subnational units of government in several countries. Spain, the UK and Italy, for example, have shifted substantial governmental competencies to subnational units, and Belgium is now almost fully separated along linguistic lines. The Central and East European countries (CEECs), on the other hand, tend to prefer a more centralized institutional setup (Keating 2008). Another tendency is the delegation of decision-making powers to non-majoritarian institutions which has been said to 'hollow out' the core executive. The growing importance of supranational regulation has added further constraints to the control of national institutions over national policy. Last but not least, the large majority of European nations are EU members, which means that a considerable portion of decisions which mould national politics are made on the European level. These are limitations on executive and legislative power which will be analysed in the following sections.

Governance in Europe – or: who decides?

As we have indicated above, the analysis of the institutional architecture of European democracies yields only an incomplete picture of the location of powers to make binding decisions for the nation. For many European countries, the institutions of the European Union have now become a powerful rival to domestic decision-making structures. They reshape the policy-making capacities of executives as well as the domestic legislative–executive relations that have been at the core of the national regime typologies. At the same time, all European countries have undergone, to a greater or lesser extent, processes of delegation of powers to regulatory bodies which are at best indirectly controlled by political actors. While both developments surely enhance the complexity of governance in European democracies, they do not necessarily stand in the way of a strengthening of national core executives and the 'presidentialization' of domestic politics, which is characterized, among other aspects, by a shift towards a stronger role of chief executives in parliamentary, semi-presidential and presidential systems alike (Poguntke and Webb 2007).

The EU institutional setting

The typologies of national political regimes rest on the assumption that national political systems form independent units that can be sorted according to some commonalities and differences regarding their organization and distribution of power. Given that they transfer ever more policy competencies to international organizations such as the United Nations, the World Trade Organization, and the North Atlantic Treaty Organization, the independence of nation-states can hardly be taken for granted any more. Their political organization becomes ever more integrated into international multilevel governance structures. It is likely that the internal dynamics and structures of states change as they become integrated into these larger systems of cooperative effort (see Olsen 2007: 24). Ironically, these developments are most pronounced in Europe which is the birthplace of the modern nation-state. The scope of policy delegation to the supranational European Union (EU) institutions exceeds by far the amount of delegation to other international organizations.

The EU has acquired substantial competencies in a variety of policy areas since the early 1950s. While regulatory policies, foreign and security policy, citizenship policies, expenditure policies and agricultural price support were exclusively steered by national governments in 1950, the EU member states have since lost their exclusive say in these matters. Having allocated a wealth of policy competencies to the EU they must increasingly share decision-making powers among each other and with the supranational institutions (for a detailed overview, see Hix 2011). One should note, however, that the core competencies of the EU are still its regulatory powers to create, police and correct the common market as well as in adjacent policy areas. Here, European integration clearly circumscribes the policy options that are available to national government and parliament. Moreover, for the most part, the EU needs to rely on the member state administrations to implement common policies.

Now, owing to its genesis as a supranational organization for the regulation of the coal and steel industries in a limited number of Western European countries, the institutional setup of the EU differs significantly from national representative democracies. The union is not marked by an institutional separation of powers as are presidential democracies. Nor does it showcase the fusion of parliamentary majorities and the executives that is typical of parliamentary democracies.

The EU differs from presidential democracies in that the President of the European Commission is not elected by popular vote. Being nominated by the European Council he (all have been male to date) is subject to a vote of approval by the European Parliament. Even though the President's powers vis-à-vis the college of Commissioners have increased in recent treaty revisions, the Commission operates clearly more in terms of a collegial executive than in terms of presidential government. However, in several other respects, the institutional setup corresponds to the characteristics of presidential democracies: the European Commission cannot be removed by the European Parliament for political reasons. Moreover, although Members of the European Parliament or of the EU Council are not legally prohibited from serving in the Commission, empirically, membership in both the executive and legislative EU institutions has so far been incompatible (with a notable exception in the area of EU foreign policy) as is the case in presidential democracies. Finally, the parties in the European Parliament are fairly independent of the President of the European Commission. Note, however, that the parliament's vote of approval ensures that the person holding the office of President of the Commission must be acceptable to a majority of the members of the European Parliament.

As a corollary, the setup of the EU institutions differs from that of parliamentary democracies in nearly all respects: membership in the parliament and in the European Commission has so far been incompatible, the executive exists independently of the political will of the legislature, it cannot dissolve parliament, and party discipline in the European Parliament is below that of longstanding parliamentary democracies. Finally, as in federal systems, the EU legislature consists of two chambers. However, unlike in federations, the chamber that represents the territorial interests, the EU Council, still has the upper hand. The legislative powers of the chamber representing citizen interests, the European Parliament, still vary in different policy areas even though the Lisbon treaty which came into legal force on 1 December 2009 includes another substantial increase in its legislative powers.

The EU impact in the member states: empowering executives and 'victimizing' parliaments?

Given that the institutional configuration at EU level has given rise to the heated debate on the democratic deficit of the EU (see also below), we do not suppose that the member states are going to adopt this institutional model in their domestic contexts. That is, the member states will stick to their domestic regime types, be they parliamentary, presidential or semi-presidential. Moreover, the EU institutions do not have the competencies to intervene directly in the administrative or parliamentary structures of the member states. Unsurprisingly, studies on the adaptation of domestic executive institutions indicate incremental change and modifications rather than a fully-fledged transformation of executive structures and practices. Cross-country comparisons illustrate that domestic contexts and traditions mediate EU pressures and suggest that they have the capacity 'to modify, accommodate, internalise and, perhaps, even neutralise European pressures' (Goetz 2000: 216).

Nonetheless, we expect that the delegation of policy competencies to the EU and the involvement of the member states in the EU institutions have a profound impact on national executives, parliaments and legislative–executive relations. In particular, Andrew Moravcsik (1994) has suggested that the involvement of national executives in EU politics strengthens the role of the executive in domestic politics. He claims that four mechanisms strengthen domestic executives vis-à-vis domestic parliaments and societal actors: (a) the control over domestic agendas shifts to the executives because they are more involved in EU negotiations; (b) decision-making procedures change in order to accommodate the need of executives to enter into credible commitments at the EU level; (c) domestic executives enjoy better access to information about supranational developments than other actors because they are represented in the EU Council machinery; and (d) their involvement in European politics also enhances their ability to justify domestic politics ideologically. Robert Putnam's notion of two-level games delivers additional insights: according to this theorem, domestic executives use their involvement in EU negotiations strategically in order to pursue EU policies that are closer to their own preferences than to those of other domestic actors. Wolfgang Wessels and his collaborators concur that European integration has brought about 'a shift in the internal national balance of powers towards governments and administrations' in the old EU member states (EU-15) (Wessels *et al.* 2003: xvi). However, it is controversial whether core executives or their administrative staffs benefit from this process: according to Larsson and Trondal (2005), involvement with the European Commission strengthens the lower echelons of the national bureaucracies in the Nordic countries whereas their presence in the Council apparatus strengthens the core executives. Arguably, the EU policy-making process puts a premium on technical knowledge privileging civil servants over elected politicians.

More generally, Europeanization is often equated with de-parliamentarization. In a study on the national coordination of EU policy, Hussein Kassim and his collaborators found that parliaments have 'very little ability to scrutinize Union proposals, still less to influence their content, and are able only in very exceptional cases to direct the actions of their respective governments' (Kassim *et al.* 2000: 258). In conjunction with the strengthening of party leaders vis-à-vis their parties (Poguntke *et al.* 2007), the increasing fragmentation of political institutions in Europe might actually nourish tendencies towards the strengthening of the core executive in domestic political systems.

The Eastern enlargement of the EU lends some empirical support to these arguments. It has, at least temporarily, strengthened the position of 'the core executive' in these countries. In Central and Eastern Europe, the EU impact evolved in parallel to the build-up of the institutions of government. The enlargement process has provided the core executives in the CEECs with a central role (Grabbe 2001: 1016). The executive branch has been 'privileged over the legislature and judiciary in terms of political attention and commitment of resources' (*ibid.*), because of the need to implement the *acquis communautaire* and the Copenhagen criteria. In several CEECs, prime ministerial offices or foreign ministries orchestrated the accession process. Implementing the 31 chapters of the *acquis communautaire* also required stronger inter-sectoral coordination. However, it is important to note that the scope and depth of the EU's impact was limited (see also Chapter 3, in this book). The EU did not aim at broad horizontal changes in national government machineries. Rather, it sought effective sectoral cooperation partners that were able to administer EU funds and ensure the implementation of the *acquis communautaire*. Moreover, administrative centralization in CEECs was by no means a response that was unique to the enlargement process. Rather, the centralization of power was often deemed to be a suitable response to the pervasive governance problems of these transition countries (Dimitrov *et al.* 2006: 255). In some cases the supranational authorities even had to overcome the substantial capacities of resistance to change of administrative and political institutions. Finally, it was not uncommon that CEECs such as Hungary, Poland, Bulgaria or the Czech Republic created flexible and reversible institutions in order to avoid institutional lock-in effects in uncertain circumstances. Accordingly, the EU's impact provided additional impetus to centralizing tendencies in CEECs.

De-parliamentarization has been noted as a general side effect of European integration. National parliaments have often been portrayed as the ' "victims" of integration' (O'Brennan and Raunio 2006a), thus contributing to a further presidentialization of domestic polities. However, since the late 1980s, national parliaments have reformed their organizational structures and procedures and reshaped the terms of their interaction with domestic governments and EU institutions. They have gained some ground in holding their governments accountable in EU affairs. Thus, all parliaments have set up European Affairs Committees (EACs) to coordinate parliamentary scrutiny and also involve specialized committees more closely in processing EU affairs. Interaction within COSAC, the Conference of the European Affairs Committees, has contributed to the spread of best-scrutiny practices across the Union. Thus, in CEECs, parliamentarians were well aware of the advantages and deficits of existing scrutiny practices. For instance, the Slovene parliament essentially copied the Finnish institutional model (O'Brennan and Raunio 2006b: 274).

Despite such efforts to strengthen the role of parliaments, a landmark decision by the German Federal Constitutional Court on the Lisbon treaty (Federal Constitutional Court 2009) has re-emphasized that the EU might undermine parliamentary democracy in the member states. The Court generally held that the Treaty of Lisbon is compatible with the German Basic Law. But it also ruled that the concomitant Act regulating the rights of the Bundestag and the Bundesrat (the two German legislative chambers) to participate in EU affairs after the enactment of the Treaty, infringes the Basic Law. Measuring the EU rule system against the yardstick of parliamentary democracy, the Court finds a structural democratic deficit at EU level. In the Court's view, the EU still forms an 'association of sovereign national states' to which these countries delegate powers (*ibid.*: 3). Asserting that the EU institutions lack the necessary social and institutional prerequisites for achieving democratic legitimacy themselves, the member states' peoples are regarded as the decisive holders of public authority in Europe. Accordingly, the national legislatures that represent these peoples must have a meaningful say in treaty amendments as well as in areas that are of particular importance for democracy, including criminal law, the monopoly on the use of force, fundamental fiscal decisions as well as social and important cultural policy decisions.

However, strengthening national parliaments does not necessarily cure the democratic deficiencies of the EU. When considering the self-interest of party-political actors in re-election, a rather low level of scrutiny over European integration policy need not even indicate parliamentary weakness but may well be the outcome of quite rational strategies (see Saalfeld 2005). Several political parties such as the British Conservative Party are less cohesive on the European integration dimension than in traditional left–right issues. Accordingly, they seek to avoid party-political disputes over European policies that might cost them votes. Furthermore, majority parties have far less incentives to scrutinize government than do opposition parties. But even opposition parties might refrain from such activities because the majority parties could blame them for contributing to outcomes of EU negotiations 'that are inferior to compromises that might have been obtained if the government had enough room for manoeuvre' (Auel and Benz 2005: 373). Finally, politicizing EU issues may be far less important to the re-election of parliamentarians than domestic or regional issues.

Now, the Lisbon Treaty provides national parliaments with the opportunity to scrutinize the subsidiarity and proportionality of Commission proposals. They have the right to demand a review of Commission proposals and can even forestall them if they think that these proposals violate the subsidiarity principle. One-third of national parliaments need to object to a proposal in order for the Commission to review it. And if a majority of the national parliaments opposes a Commission proposal under the co-decision procedure, and either the European Parliament or the Council agrees, the proposal will not proceed any further. However, while empowering national parliaments, the resulting change in domestic relations between the legislature and the executive is bound to be limited. The fusion of the executive and legislatures in parliamentary democracies makes it unlikely that majority parties will take a different stance than government. Moreover, the attention that national parliaments pay to the subsidiarity of Commission proposals will vary significantly across countries and issues (Raunio 2009: 11–12).

'Agencification' of the state apparatus?

European governance is not just marked by an increase in the vertical dimension of policy-making and implementation. Since the 1980s, administrative reforms have transformed the horizontal structure of the state apparatus throughout Europe. As Rhodes (2003: 69) has put it: 'The state has been hollowed out from above (e.g., by international interdependence), from below (by marketization and networks), and sideways (by agencies).' Independent regulatory agencies (IRAs) have proliferated throughout Europe and in international arenas. To an increasing extent, elected politicians hand over social and economic regulation to specialized agencies, thus lengthening the chain of accountability that stretches from citizens to parliaments and governments in representative democracies by yet another element. Some agencies have arisen from delegation to public bodies, 'others are private bodies that have acquired regulatory power' (Coen and Thatcher 2005: 342). The introduction of these changes reflects new strategies of national governments to cope with the perceived failure of Keynesian demand management, public ownership and increasing international competition. On the one hand, in social policy areas such as labour, environmental and health policy, 'protective norms and standards have taken on greater importance' (Eberlein and Grande 2005: 90). On the other hand, the privatization of public firms and the liberalization of markets triggered a need to control economic power and behaviour in newly formed and rather imperfect markets. Political delegation to independent regulatory authorities supposedly allows credible long-term policy commitments. It is a way to avoid the vagaries of party competition and the policy fluctuations that are frequently attributed to party politics. Comparative analyses of regulatory agencies in Northern Europe and in the four largest European countries – Britain, France, Germany and Italy – demonstrate indeed that these agencies enjoy substantial independence from elected politicians in their daily work (Martens 2008; Thatcher 2005). According to Mark Thatcher, 'elected politicians rarely used their formal controls to appoint party political IRA members, to overturn IRA decisions, or to punish IRAs with budget changes' (2005: 363). In that sense, IRAs form a group of actors that is separate from elected party politicians.

Some authors have associated these developments with a move towards a European regulatory state in that many regulatory institutions would be located at the supranational level (Majone 1996). But comparative studies indicate that we are not witnessing the emergence of a European regulatory state (Eberlein and Grande 2005; Thatcher 2005). Those agencies that have been set up at the European level tend to have informative and consultative tasks in order to prepare EU legislation or implementation rather than regulatory powers. They are also mostly focused on social regulation, whereas the institutional sites for the economic regulation of markets are located within national confines. The discussion on responsible political authorities has therefore focused on national ministries or cabinet offices. Recent studies within five different fields – telecoms, food safety, environment and statistics – confirm that national agencies are, for the most part, elements of national government machinery. However, they are also involved in European regulatory networks 'in which the Commission or an EU-level agency makes up the hub' (Egeberg 2008: 247). Especially when EU legislation is put into practice, the national agencies tend to work closely with the Commission bureaucracy or ' "sister agencies" in other member states' (*ibid.*: 248). Accordingly, national chains of political delegation and accountability gain in complexity through the horizontal delegation of agencies and the added vertical dimension of the EU multilevel system. Trends towards national and transnational self-regulation within the context of the regulatory state reinforce such developments.

Conclusion

Our analysis identified two apparently countervailing trends in Western European representative democracies. The first is the increasing vertical and horizontal fragmentation of the state apparatus and the concomitant development of power-sharing mechanisms and long chains of political delegation and accountability. These structural changes in governance structures are by now heavily institutionalized and will remain important conditions of democratic governance in Europe.

The other is what we called the strengthening of the core executive and the 'presidentialization' of democratic politics. While this seems paradoxical at first sight, a closer view reveals that both developments can easily coincide. In fact, the growing importance of complex governance structures and the weakening of the traditional mode of national government is one of numerous structural factors that increase the opportunities for governmental leaders to assume a stronger political role in the governance process, resembling that of a chief executive in a presidential system (Poguntke and Webb 2007). It needs to be emphasized that such shifts towards a presidentialized mode of governance do not necessarily amount to more power for the chief executive vis-à-vis the legislature. Rather, it is characterized by a tendency that individual leaders assume a more central role in the policy process while collective actors (such as cabinets or parliamentary parties) lose influence. Yet, to the extent that they assume nodal positions and 'boundary roles' (Grande 2000: 18) in international or European multilevel systems their strategic repertoire to obtain outcomes closer to their own preferences *can* actually broaden. Hence, institutional fragmentation is not equal to the fragmentation of political power. Other factors furthering presidentialization include the growth of the state, a weakening of cleavage politics, and the increasing role of the media in national political processes. All represent a structural change in the political conditions of modern democracies and provide chief executives with more opportunities than in the past to assume a stronger role in the governance process. They are accompanied by similar strengthening of party leaders vis-à-vis their parties (Poguntke and Webb 2007). Such potential shifts in the functioning of modern democracy do not normally involve changes in the formal configuration of national political institutions. All regime types described above can move, within their specific institutional borders, towards a more presidentialized mode of governance.

It needs to be emphasized, however, that such power gains are also contingent on the political situation, and that parliaments remain powerful veto players that can block political initiatives by chief executives or, under conditions of parliamentary accountability, even remove them from office. The resignations of Margaret Thatcher and Tony Blair from the office of prime minister in the United Kingdom are important reminders. Hence, to some extent, such changes are reversible as has been the case in many CEECs and they are also contingent upon a range of factors, including the personality of individual leaders. As the anchorage of political parties in clearly defined segments of the population has eroded, the appeal of leaders has become more decisive in election campaigns. To be sure, it is difficult to ascertain the exact leadership effect on voting choice; but what matters is the perception of politicians and parties that leaders count more than in the past. As a result, electoral campaigns and party strategies have become more dominated by leaders, and they can use the consequent power gains to assume a more independent role from their parties once they are in government. However, not all leaders are equally gifted in making use of such opportunities. Also, the overall political context may strengthen the power of parties. Under such conditions, a political system may reverse once more towards a more party-based mode of governance.

There are two trajectories of presidentialization. Under a more majoritarian system, an incoming chief executive needs to defend his or her power and autonomy, while in a more consensual setting they can use their increasingly prominent role as negotiator in chief to widen their autonomy and power. In both cases, the tendencies towards the fragmentation of decision-making described above, the weakening of the organizational power of political parties and the drastically increased exposure of leaders in the media provide a powerful set of opportunities for strong leaders to act as those who 'bring together' the fragments of governance.

To be sure, much may remain on the level of symbolic politics. 'Summitry' may convey the message that fundamental decisions are reached even though there may be little real substance. Furthermore, the increased ability of political leaders to govern 'past their parties' may not achieve the intended outcomes because powerful interests and veto players may still be able to obstruct. Finally, while the opportunities for strong leadership have grown, so have the structural constraints that flow from power sharing in multilevel governance structures. In other words, those who present themselves to the public, their national parliaments and their parties as powerful leaders who have reached decisions without much interference by their domestic agents often want us to forget that they have themselves been involved in a painstaking search for compromise.

Chapter 5*

Political Parties, Representation and Politics in Contemporary Europe

Paul Webb

Political parties across the democratic world come in for much criticism these days. The challenges to party are multiple and frequently rehearsed, both in the academic literature and in broader political debate. Across Europe, both East and West, there is widespread evidence of popular mistrust and disillusionment with party politics; electoral turnout is often disappointingly low and has declined since 1990 in many cases; party membership and activism have collapsed; 'dissatisfied democrats' deride parties for stifling public engagement with politics and call for more radical forms of participatory democracy, while 'stealth democrats' have little innate interest in politics, deride party conflict, and are susceptible to the appeals of populist demagoguery and fringe movements; interest groups and social movements are widely seen as more popular vehicles for political engagement and representation than parties; the collective identities and action that parties once embodied are increasingly undermined by the erosion of distinctive social or programmatic profiles and the emergence of a form of politics obsessed with individual personalities; and critics often lament the failure of parties to 'make a difference' to policy outputs.

If this litany of failure, decline and under-performance carries any real weight, then it does indeed make for a dismal outlook for the party government model of representative democracy. But how accurate is this portrayal of parties in Europe today? In this chapter I shall review some of the criticisms, evidence and arguments, before suggesting that, while the reality of party performance is not always unremittingly negative, it seems that popular perceptions of weakness and failure are increasingly widespread in the face of mounting challenges to political parties.

---

* Note that parts of this draw heavily on the findings reported in Webb (2002) and Webb and White (2005).

Challenges to party in Europe: the evidence

The popular standing of political parties

There is widespread evidence of the low standing of parties in electorates across Europe, which suggests that party penetration of society has eroded (or in the cases of the new democracies of Eastern and Central Europe, never much developed) in a multifaceted fashion. *Electoral turnout* may vary over time for contingent reasons related to short-term developments in the pattern of party competition, and a drop does not necessarily reflect a general loss of party legitimacy. However, in the established democracies of Western Europe the near universality of significant turnout decline since 1990 raises general concern that 'there is less of a market for the parties' product' (Wattenberg 2000: 76). By the same logic, in the new democracies of Eastern Europe, stable and high turnout could be regarded as demonstrating a growing 'market for party politics', which is to say, an indicator of the institutionalization of parties. However, there is little evidence that any such thing has happened, for turnout has generally emulated the established democracies by declining in recent years. Only in Hungary has it more or less held up, and then only until 2006. Comparison of average turnout levels shows that the newer democracies remain behind the longer established democracies, moreover: Eastern Europe's average of 61.8 per cent is some way behind the established democracies' average of 75.9 per cent. All calculations include Belgium, where voting is legally compulsory. If Belgium is excluded the average falls to 73.2 per cent.

Electoral volatility (the Pedersen Index) is a well-known indicator of the stability of voter choices from one election to the next, and as such can be taken as an indicator of the stabilization, institutionalization and consolidation of patterns of party politics. Although, once again, this is an indicator that can fluctuate in the short-run for quite contingent reasons, it is clear that there has been a general increase in levels of electoral volatility since 1970 in Western Europe as a whole. Even so, it remains considerably higher in Eastern Europe. Using data reported by Mainwaring and Torcal (2006: 208) we can calculate an average level of electoral volatility since democratization of 44.0 across 11 East European countries, compared to 12.5 in Western Europe since the 1970s. This again suggests that party institutionalization is not as well established yet in the newer democracies, even though it has risen in the latter case.

On the face of it, *party identification* is perhaps the most direct measure of party attachment. Once again, however, there is little evidence of party institutionalization in Eastern Europe. If anything, rates of partisan identification have been more likely to go down – or stabilize at low levels – than to increase across the populations of these new democracies, although there is modest cause for optimism in that two countries have experienced slight increases from low baseline levels (Ukraine and Hungary). Overall, the average rate of partisan identification in the East European cases is 39 per cent; while it remains higher in the established democracies, at 49 per cent (Enyedi and Tóka 2007: Table 6.4; Webb *et al.* 2002), it is nonetheless well attested that the proportion of voters claiming strong partisan affinities has dropped in almost all established democracies since the 1960s (Dalton and Wattenberg 2002). In most West European cases, moreover, we find a combination of weakening partisan identification and increased volatility, which is not surprising since we would expect voting behaviour to become less stable as people's partisan loyalties wane. In similar vein, it is no surprise to find that the proportion of citizens willing to become *party members* has fallen dramatically across Western Europe. Nevertheless, party membership remains higher there than in the newer democracies: on average 5.5 per cent of registered electors in Western Europe still join political parties as individual members, compared to just 2.3 per cent of voters in the new democracies of Eastern Europe (Mair and van Biezen 2001; Webb and White 2005). Apart from some communist-successor organizations, few parties have achieved substantial levels of membership in these countries. Only Hungary has experienced anything approaching impressive growth in recent years; Slovakia also did throughout the 1990s, but this has begun to reverse since then, while Ukraine has enjoyed more modest growth. The other East European cases have either remained stagnant at low levels or – as in the case of the Czech Republic – have declined from an initially promising level in the immediate aftermath of transition.

The final indicator of the standing of parties in the electorate is the popular expression of *anti-party sentiment*. It is necessary to be cautious here, since one can virtually guarantee finding evidence that some people are disaffected with parties in any country. It is therefore necessary to consider how widespread expressions of anti-party sentiment are, and their nature. This too is difficult, however, given the very wide variety of survey instruments that researchers draw on to gauge the phenomenon; such inconsistency makes direct comparison virtually impossible. We are inevitably left with rather impressionistic comparisons, therefore. In conceptual terms, it is useful to think of a distinction between 'hard' and 'soft' anti-party sentiment; the latter is disparaging of parties in various ways, but nevertheless accepts that they remain central and necessary elements of any system of open, plural and democratic politics.

By contrast, hard anti-party sentiment consists of genuine antipathy, based on the notion that parties are pathological to the body politic in some way. One can further conceive of at least two variants of this: the first might be consistent with a broad preference for competitive democratic politics, but would favour a highly personalistic system of presidential rule; central to this conception of democracy is a preference for charismatic leaders who are capable of being 'above politics' and expressing the will of the nation. Parties are regarded as embodiments of partial group interests, and sources of national disunity and weakness. General de Gaulle's approach to politics when he was President of the French Republic in the 1960s provides a classic example of such a phenomenon (Graham 1993). The second variant of hard anti-party sentiment goes further still, in as much as it represents an element of a fundamental hostility towards democracy per se.

In these terms, we can see that soft anti-party sentiment is evident virtually everywhere in Europe. The most recent wave of World Values Survey data (gathered since 1999 across more than 70 countries) reveals that on average some 18.8 per cent of East European respondents have 'quite a lot' or 'a great deal' of confidence in political parties, compared to 21.9 per cent of those from the established democracies. It is equally apparent that overall confidence in parties is low across the continent. Confidence is particularly low in Russia, Ukraine and Poland, while a preference for personalist presidential politics is widespread, so it is reasonable to infer that the citizens of these countries are especially likely to harbour more profound antipathy towards political parties. Moreover, the former two are among the countries characterized by the lowest levels of confidence in democracy per se, which suggests that anti-party sentiment is often of the 'hard' variety here. For example, in Russia only 47 per cent see democracy as the best form of government (compared to the East European average of 74 per cent), while the corresponding figure for Ukraine is 64 per cent. Conversely, countries such as the Czech Republic and Hungary are less prone to such pathological forms of anti-party sentiment. Poland occupies a position in between: while parties are deeply distrusted, democracy is widely preferred (with 77 per cent of Poles regarding it as the best form of government).

To sum up, the picture regarding the popular standing of political parties, then, we can say the following. The post-communist new democracies of Eastern Europe have more volatile electorates than their longer established West European counterparts, while electoral turnout, partisan identification and party membership rates are also lower. However, each of these indicators has registered a significant drop across Western Europe since 1970, as well. Anti-party sentiment is universal in democratic society, though this is often about 'soft' lack of trust in parties rather than a deep-rooted hostility. In most countries, there is widespread recognition that parties remain important to democracy. Where antipathy towards parties is harder, it is not always associated with a preference for authoritarianism, but rather, for a personalistic form of democratic leadership. The popular belief that democracy is the best form of government predominates within all types of existing democratic regime, though hostility towards democracy per se, and therefore towards competitive forms of party politics, is more prevalent among some of the recently transitional cases.

Anti-party sentiment in the wider context of democratic theory

Anti-party sentiment should be understood as part of a wider political malaise. It is not just parties that so many citizens seem to be disaffected with, but a broader array of institutions – indeed, the political system as a whole. Thus, it is not difficult to uncover evidence of citizens' low regard for a variety of actors and institutions that constitute key elements of the democratic system – parliaments, governments, politicians, and so on (see, e.g., Pharr and Putnam 2000; Dalton 2004; Stoker 2006; Hay 2007). A reading of the comparative literature on this theme suggests that there might actually be two quite distinct groups of disaffected citizens. The first largely comprises middle-class educated individuals, who are unusually interested and active in politics and who are committed to a democratic vision of highly engaged citizens. These people are cognitively mobilized in that they have access to a considerable amount of political information and have the educational background and intellectual skills to feel confident about acting politically. While these are the very groups that have most directly benefited from the spread of affluence, they are also the people whose expectations have increased the most, as has their tendency to criticize political elites, institutions and processes. Yet they do not represent a threat to democracy per se; on the contrary, these 'dissatisfied democrats' are driven by a passion for the democratic creed that fosters disillusionment with the way current political processes operate. For them, the system of representative politics and its key institutions – among which political parties are central – is flawed in various ways, above all because it does not offer sufficient opportunity for political participation by citizens.

However, there is a quite different group as well, whom I shall refer to as 'stealth democrats', taking a cue from research conducted in the USA by John Hibbing and Elizabeth Theiss-Morse. On the basis of their findings, they conclude that:

the last thing people want is to be more involved in political decision-making: They do not want to make political decisions themselves; they do not want to provide much input to those who are assigned to make these decisions; and they would rather not know the details of the decision-making process ... This does not mean that people think no mechanism for government accountability is necessary; they just do not want the mechanism to come into play except in unusual circumstances. (2002: 1–2).

They discovered a widespread belief that people generally shared similar basic goals, but were betrayed by elites in hock to the 'special interests'. This was seen to create a cacophonous power struggle based on the pursuit of self-interest, whereas it was felt that an impartial technocratic elite should be able to make policies based on the public interest. There is perhaps more than a hint of populism in all this, and in the consequent belief 'that the common good is not debatable but, rather, will be apparent if selfishness can be stripped away' (*ibid.*: 9). Hibbing and Theiss-Morse summarize the orientations of American citizens as a preference for some kind of 'stealth' arrangement, whereby citizens know that democracy exists, but expect it to be barely visible on a routine basis – an attitude that they describe as naive and unfeasible.

While it remains a matter for empirical research to verify whether such attitudes are equally prevalent among Europeans, it is certainly a very plausible hypothesis. It is also likely that such 'stealth democrats' are generally of lower socio-economic status and are less well educated than the cognitively mobilized 'dissatisfied democrats', have little interest in politics, and are largely absorbed by private concerns. Thus, they are very different critics of parties; whereas dissatisfied democrats are primarily disappointed with the failure of parties to provide adequate *participatory* linkage between state and society, stealth democrats are disappointed with the failure of parties to provide effective *representative* linkage. They do not want much participation in politics, but do expect intermediary actors such as parties to represent them effectively and to be accountable. They have traditionally depended on parties (among others) to act as key interlocutors and tribunes of their social group interests, but their parties (typically social democratic or labour in orientation) have often lost this role through strategic adaptation. Without representative parties that express their social identities and to serve as communities of political learning, as was once the case in the era of the mass party, these citizens retreat into a disaffected and alienated take on contemporary politics (Bengtsson and Mattila 2009; Webb *et al.* 2010).

Challenges to party as a channel of representative linkage

Central to political representation are the twin functions of the *articulation and aggregation of interests*, and it has frequently been suggested that parties face considerable challenges as articulators and aggregators of interests. In particular, there is little doubt that citizens' political participation in Western Europe through interest groups and non-governmental organizations (NGOs) has grown enormously since the 1960s, at precisely the time that their involvement in parties has declined. It seems undeniable that in an era when fewer citizens are linked to parties by virtue of their social group identities, they are more likely to engage with politics through concerns over particular issues. This has led commentators such as Jeremy Richardson (1995) to claim that parties are being squeezed out of the 'market' for political activism in Western Europe. Historically, interest group activity has not been a challenge to party so much as a complement to it, as in those instances when parties have jointly articulated group demands with trade unions (for instance, in Britain and Scandinavia), or churches (as per the Christian democratic parties of Italy, Germany, Netherlands, Belgium), or environmentalist NGOs since the 1970s (most obviously in the case of the German Greens). Even so, the erosion of links between the social democrats/unions and Christian democrats/churches has been notable where catch-all strategies have been adopted since the 1960s, thus de-emphasizing party roles as an expression of class or denominational identities (Kirchheimer 1966).

The *aggregation* function is particularly interesting. Do parties succeed in bundling together the demands of their various support constituencies in a coherent and stable fashion? The answer is broadly 'yes, but the job has become harder'. In parliamentary democracies, parties are still central to this function, and indeed, it is not difficult to see why: the aggregation of group demands into more or less coherent programmes for governmental action cannot be done by interest groups, social movements or the media – it is a task that simply has to be undertaken by parties competing for elective office, or at least, by their elites. Yet the aggregation function has become a more challenging and complicated task for parties. In some cases, this is precisely because parties have adopted catch-all strategies, thus embracing a broader array of social group interests than hitherto. Beyond this, however, the task of aggregation has become intrinsically more complex because of social changes which have generated incompatible demands from different components of the support base, and/or because of the emergence of new issue cleavages (Dalton 2004). This is most obvious in cases where cleavages that threaten national unity have emerged (as in Belgium), but it is not an insignificant problem in a number of other advanced industrial societies that have become more socially heterogeneous since the 1960s. In particular, the emergence of new issue agendas relating to gender, ethnicity, regionalism, environmentalism and European integration has undoubtedly complicated the vital task of aggregation for the major parties.

In general, political parties in Eastern Europe face even greater challenges in struggling to articulate and aggregate group interests. This is particularly true of countries like Russia and Ukraine, where large numbers of legislators are not party members – or are so only notionally, because of their propensity to 'hop' from one parliamentary group to another; under such circumstances it is virtually impossible for a party to act as the main conduit of representational linkage. Individual politicians may fulfil the articulation function to some extent, often on a clientelistic basis, or it may be provided by loose and impermanent cross-party groupings of legislators. However, the legacy from the communist era of a relatively under-developed autonomous civil society somewhat reduces the nature of the challenge from pressure groups and social movements, but it does not necessarily mean that it will be left to parties to articulate and aggregate demands: individual candidate-centred politics is an alternative, a point to which we will return in due course.

Popular choice and control through party government

Representative linkage between state and society is not simply about the articulation and aggregation of interests. It is also about the key democratic objective of popular choice and control over government (Ware 1987). Parties should be central to this, as E. E. Schattschneider (1942) argued, so long as they ensure a connection between the competing programmes put before the electorate and the policies a government implements. This is the idea of party government. How far do parties actually fulfil this objective in contemporary Europe?

It is a common refrain of critics across Europe that parties fail to offer voters a meaningful choice, as they converge around a limited range of ideological or programmatic options. An interesting example of this critique has recently been developed by Colin Hay (2007) who argues that the current political malaise among citizens owes much to the narrowing of political space in Europe around a neo-liberal consensus. This has impacted on the scope and ambition of the state by generating a 'depoliticization' of public life, incorporating 'privatization, the contracting out of public services, the marketization of public goods, the displacement of policy-making autonomy from the formal political realm to independent authorities, the rationalization and insulation from critique of neo-liberalism as an economic paradigm, and the denial of policy choice' (*ibid.*: 159). These trends have been exacerbated by the narrowing of electoral competition which has been driven by the adoption of political marketing techniques by parties. The net effect of this has been to restrict the domain within which politicians may act, or articulate a convincing case for political action. This in turn simply serves to undermine the point of politics in the eyes of many citizens.

Note that in order to meet Schattschneider's criterion, parties must not only offer a choice of *programmes*, but they must also enact these programmes in such a way that they make a meaningful difference to policy *outputs*. This issue bears directly upon the issue of accountability, for if parties are fundamentally unable to shape public policy, who does (if anyone), and who should be held to account (if anyone)? It is an issue of obvious importance for democratic performance, then. It is of course well recognized that a variety of macro-social developments can seriously constrain the scope for autonomous action by party governments, including technological changes, demographic trends, social changes and economic cycles. The whole question of global economic constraints on national governmental autonomy has of course become one of the most insistent political themes of the contemporary era, and a highly vexed issue for politicians and intellectuals alike. The power of these implacable and impersonal forces can seem daunting, and they make it unsurprising that commentators should question the ability of parties to make any real difference. But what is the evidence?

First, do parties actually offer the electorate reasonably distinct *programmatic* alternatives, or are they so convergent as to render the idea of 'choice' meaningless (Hay's point)? Long-term manifesto analyses of shifting party ideologies demonstrate that ideological convergence between major parties has been particularly evident in matters of macro-economic management since the 1960s (Klingemann *et al.* 1994; Caul and Gray 2000: 213–15). This should not lead us to the simplistic conclusion that there are no important differences between the major parties, but it does suggest that those who struggle to discern the differences have picked up on something tangible. The second issue is whether or not the growing indistinctiveness of ideological emphases, at least in certain areas, renders insignificant party impacts on policy *outputs*. There is a large literature on which to draw, but unfortunately, it does not provide a clear consensus. Results vary considerably according to the precise cases, methods, data and variables selected for analysis. A 'meta-analysis' by Imbeau *et al.* (2001) – that is, a review of nearly 700 statistical tests reported in published analyses of party effects – reveals that only a minority of them confirm the party effects thesis. However, they concede that the party effects model is much more successful in predicting some dependent variables – such as the overall size of the state – than others (such as level of state welfare expenditure). They note too that qualitative studies are generally more likely to confirm that parties make a difference than quantitative studies are. It should also be borne in mind that this study does not take into account the impact of centre parties, even though research has shown that such parties can influence policy in a distinctive and coherent way; Christian democratic parties in particular have proposed their own brand of solutions with respect to social welfare (van Kersbergen 1995) and foreign aid (Thérien and Noël 2000).

Overall, this suggests that, even if it is an exaggeration to claim that there is 'a remarkably high congruence between the themes stressed in party election programs and the subsequent policies enacted by the parties that get into government' (Klingemann *et al.* 1994: 268), political parties continue to make a significant difference to policy outputs across Europe. A degree of convergence might have occurred, and yet parties still offer meaningful choices in many European countries. This does not, however, prevent confusion and incomprehension in the minds of many voters about the differences between parties. Such perceptions may emanate from parties' own self-limiting behaviour, as critics like Hay claim, or from the impact of the media which, as Gerry Stoker has pointed out, is often guilty of 'dumbing down' politics by focusing on the 'immediate, the scandalous and the negative', of fusing reporting and opinion in a provocative way, and even of spreading a 'culture of contempt' about politics and its main protagonists (2006: 128–9). Dumbing-down, trivialization and generalized contempt all tend to feed the sense that party politics cannot really achieve positive outcomes, and that consequently it matters little which of the major alternatives is in power.

The populist alternative

Where citizens, justifiably or otherwise, are unconvinced that political parties can 'make a difference', the case for them as mechanisms of representative linkage is critically undermined. Put differently, it is no longer clear that they facilitate democratic choice and control over political decision-making. This, among other things, feeds a variety of pathological reactions that we have already noted – declining partisan attachment, electoral abstention, anti-party sentiment, and so on. There is one other response, however, not yet touched on. This is the temptation to turn from mainstream to fringe parties, many of which are broadly populist in orientation.

Since the 1980s populist parties in established European democracies such as France, Italy, the Netherlands, Denmark, Belgium and Austria have achieved excellent results at the ballot box and, in several cases, have entered government. Typically, the list of parties referred to as populist in Western Europe includes List Pim Fortuyn and more recently Geert Wilders' Freedom Party (PVV) in the Netherlands, the Progress Parties of Scandinavia, the Danish People's Party, the Sweden Democrats, the Austrian Freedom Party, the Flemish Vlaams Blok, Front National in France, and Lega Nord in Italy. In Eastern Europe, the candidates for the populist label include the Czech Civic Democratic Party, Fidesz in Hungary, the League of Polish Families, Self-Defence, Law and Justice (all in Poland), and the Liberal Democratic Party of Russia. Many of these parties are of the radical authoritarian (though not fascist) right (Kitschelt 1997), though not all are. Some, such as the Dutch Fortuyn List and the Lega Dei Ticinesi in Switzerland, only adopt authoritarian positions towards ethnic and religious minorities that are regarded as a threat to the indigenous community and its values. In fact, contemporary populist movements may well be staunch defenders of liberal values, as in the case of List Fortuyn. What these populist organizations share in common, however, is their notion of a virtuous and homogeneous national or regional community – the 'people' – who may be contrasted with a corrupt or ineffectual elite and certain 'others' who are perceived as a threat to their identity, values and culture. They regard themselves as 'true democrats' who articulate the interests and common sense aspirations of the people. As often as not, these parties have charismatic leaders at the helm who boast 'an apparent ability to see through the machinations of the professional political class combined with the superior vision which allows them to identify simple solutions to complex problems' (Albertazzi and McDonnell 2007: ch.1).

The surge in support for populist parties flows from a number of things, including the perceived failure of mainstream parties to 'make a difference' in the face of complex issue challenges, and the impact of economic and cultural globalization, the speed of European integration, corruption scandals, the decline of traditional cleavages which once tied social groups to major parties, the impact of immigration, and the perceived threat to identity and security posed by Islam. In the former Soviet bloc countries, one might add the challenge of adapting to market order and a post-Cold War international system, with the attendant turmoil and insecurity which this has brought to many.

However, while populist parties and politicians might benefit electorally from the tribulations of their mainstream counterparts, they rarely flourish upon actually attaining (a share of) power. Office confronts them with a dilemma: either they can seek to retain their radical and often simplistic approach to public policy questions, or they can adapt to the realities of office by mutating into more orthodox right or left-of-centre parties – thereby losing credibility in the eyes of their supporters (Minkenberg 2001; Heinsich 2003). The latter scenario – sometimes called the 'filtration effect' model – is particularly likely when populists find themselves in coalitions with mainstream (normally conservative) parties, as in Austria (i.e., Haider's Freedom Party), the Netherlands (List Fortuyn) and Italy (Lega Nord), or by supporting bourgeois minority cabinets (Danish People's Party). Thus, the populist temptation is unlikely to offer a panacea for disaffected voters in the long run.

The challenge of personalized politics

It is not only populist organizations that are characterized by dominant and even charismatic leadership. It seems increasingly likely that many mainstream parties can also be described in such terms, which opens up a further line of criticism of parties – that is, not parties per se, but rather individual politicians who now perform the key representative functions we have discussed above. This suggests, in effect, that the collective identity and presence of political parties in Europe are being hollowed out by the phenomenon of personalized politics, in which the primary focus is the individual politician.

In the new democracies, this phenomenon occurs in a context where strong executive leadership was the norm prior to democratization, and where it has inevitably taken time for party politics to institutionalize and stabilize around a defined set of organizational options and mobilized socio-economic cleavages. As we have already noted, citizens in some countries find it difficult to identify parties and what they stand for – but it is far easier to identify individual politicians and decide what is or is not appealing about them. In the older democracies of Western Europe the context is generally quite different. In most of these countries, democracy is more established, cleavages longer mobilized, and party organizations more developed. The major parties there are more likely – even today – to have significant memberships (the former communists of Eastern Europe being their only counterparts in this respect), and are clearly more institutionalized. Even so, there is plenty to suggest that individual leaders are achieving an unprecedented degree of prominence and independence from their parties.

The theme of the concentration of power around leaders in democratic political systems is by no means new. Nearly 40 years ago Brian Farrell (1971) observed that 'in almost all political systems, executive dominance and the personification of this domination in a single leader is a central fact of political life'. Yet it is hard to avoid the impression that perceptions of the personalization of politics in the putatively party governments of Western Europe have become more widespread in recent years. Poguntke and Webb (2007) have gone so far as to refer to the 'presidentialization' of politics in these countries. This does not imply a shift in the formal constitution from parliamentarism to presidentialism, but rather to informal changes in the working of these political systems, such that they increasingly come to operate according to a logic resembling that of presidentialism. Others, such as Karvonen (2010), prefer the term 'personalization', but either way there is broad agreement that there are three broad aspects of this process, encompassing change in three distinct political arenas: the electoral process, the party and the executive of the state.

With respect to the electoral process examination of available evidence confirms that leader-centred election campaigning and media coverage are nowadays much in evidence across Western Europe. Moreover, although parties still preponderate in voter assessments when it comes to parliamentary elections, leader effects on voters do appear to be significant and/or increasing in most cases (Webb and Poguntke 2005: Table 15.1). While it is methodologically extremely difficult for researchers to untangle the direction of causality in the relationship between party images and leadership images, it is hard to deny that in an age of increasingly competitive elections, electorally appealing leaders can make all the difference. Undoubtedly, a large (and growing) number of voters in modern societies are less constrained by stable party loyalties, and are thus likely to be freer to base their voting decisions on the personal and political qualities of the leading candidates; this perception encourages party strategists to respond by focusing their campaigns increasingly on leaders. Indeed, this perception of the importance of leaders can matter as much as the reality: even if leaders actually only have a modest direct effect on voting behaviour, the fact that the strategists tend to be convinced of their importance nevertheless results in campaigns which are increasingly centred on party leaders. This, in turn, furnishes leaders with additional legitimacy (and hence power), as they are increasingly able to claim a personalized mandate to lead their party. Thus, party leadership rests less on a dominant coalition within the party and more on the claim that it delivers electoral success.

Within the party and (in the case of governing parties) the state executive, enhanced leadership power and autonomy are evident in developments such as: the growth of resources or strategic coordinating capacity available to the leader; reduced opportunities for collective decision-making within the executive (for instance, diminished frequency or length of Cabinet meetings); the growth of bilateral decision-making processes involving the leader and individual (shadow) ministers to the exclusion of the (shadow) Cabinet collectively; and a tendency to promote non-party technocrats or politicians lacking distinctive party power bases. Such developments have been widespread throughout Western Europe. This is not to deny that parties and parliaments remain important actors, especially in parliamentary systems with strong traditions of party government, such as Sweden. But even in multiparty systems where coalitional and consensus models of politics are the norm, it is fascinating to observe that premiers have apparently often become more 'presidential'. In the Low Countries, for example, Fiers and Krouwel (2007: 128) report that 'within the last two decades, party leaders and Prime Ministers alike, both in Belgium and the Netherlands, acquired more prominent and powerful positions, transforming these consensus democracies into a kind of "presidentialized" parliamentary systems'. In majoritarian systems, such as the UK, the growth of the prime minister's underlying structural power within the executive has been even more notable (Foley 2000; Heffernan and Webb 2007). None of this overlooks the fact that the party colleagues of a political leader usually retain the means by which to constrain him or her in the last resort; but there does appear to have been a discernible shift over time in favour of leaders, which affords them considerable scope to governing past their own parties.

What factors lie behind the personalization of politics? It is tempting to explain the dominance of leaders such as Thatcher, Blair, Berlusconi or Schroeder by short-term contingent factors, such as the size and cohesion of the parliamentary support on which they can draw, their current standing with the electorate, their personalities, and the sheer and inevitably unpredictable impact of 'events'. Indeed, these factors can certainly be significant, but it is also possible to identify a number of underlying long-term factors. In Eastern Europe, it has more to do with the enduring influence of recent traditions of strong leadership under dictatorship and the failure of new parties to institutionalize. In Western Europe, the phenomenon and its causes are rather different. Four things seem to have been of particular importance here, the first of which is the *internationalization of political decision-making*. It is widely recognized that many of the most challenging political problems facing governments can only be dealt with via international cooperation. Examples abound in policy contexts as diverse as the policing of ethnic conflict (as in the former Yugoslavia), the fight against international terrorism, the battle against environmental pollution, the establishment of effective and just asylum and immigration policies, and the control of global financial markets and patterns of transnational investment. Where such issues are dealt with via intergovernmental negotiation, this shifts power to the heads of governments and some of their key advisers or governmental colleagues. Increasingly, parliaments and even cabinets can only ratify the decisions which have been taken elsewhere. In particular, it would seem likely that the process of European integration means that a substantial part of domestic politics is now decided like international politics, which is a traditional domain of leaders and senior members of governments (as opposed to cabinets, parliaments and parties).

The second factor behind personalization of politics is the *growth and complexity of the state*. This has been a long-term process which has generated greater bureaucratic complexity and organizational specialization (Peters *et al.* 2000: 8), and has generated a variety of responses. Some of the latter would seem to be relevant to the phenomenon of personalization, including the centralization of power as the core executive seeks enhanced 'steering capacity' in order to coordinate the 'institutional fragments' of the state. The third development driving personalized politics is *the changing structure of mass communications*. The growing role of electronic media since the early 1960s (van Deth 1995: 59) has fundamentally altered the nature of mass communication in modern democracies. By its very nature, television tends to focus on personality rather than programme in order to reduce the complexity of political issues, and politicians frequently respond by concentrating on symbolism rather than substance and detail in order to cater for the media's inherent needs (Bowler and Farrell 1992; Farrell and Webb 2000). To be sure, it works both ways: to a degree the media require and force politicians to adapt to their logic and their format. Much of this so-called mediatization of modern politics, however, may be the result of a conscious choice by politicians to *exploit* the visual media's potential for simplification and symbolism for their own ends. Thus, governmental leaders may use the potential of modern media communications techniques to bypass other executive actors in setting political agendas.

Finally, *the erosion of traditional social cleavage politics* since the 1960s has entailed the weakening of traditional links between mass parties and their bases of social group support (Franklin *et al.* 1992). As a consequence, where social group identities no longer dictate voter loyalties and sharp ideological conflicts fail to provide unambiguous cues, the personal qualities of actual or prospective heads of governments (*inter alia*) may become more important for the conduct of election campaigns and voting decision cues.

Conclusion

Overall, then, mainstream parties across Europe face a number of significant challenges, evidenced among other things by anti-party sentiment, the erosion of partisan attachments and memberships among voters, the emergence of populist alternatives, a rise in electoral volatility and a fall in turnout. The hollowing-out of political parties that these developments signify, in conjunction with the emphasis on personalized leadership, stem from a number of factors, including the weakening of traditional electoral cleavages, the changing nature of political communication, the desire for maximum strategic autonomy and directive capacity on the part of leaders, and the internationalization of political decision-making. In terms of democratic theory, these developments amount to perceived or real shortcomings in representative and participatory linkages, which serve to undermine party government.

Does this complex catalogue of problems imply that parties are, as has so often been suggested over the years, in crisis? This is perhaps one of those glass half-empty–half-full issues. Over the years, I personally have tended to lean towards the 'half-full' perspective in view of the various ways in which parties have continued to contribute significantly to processes of mobilization, representation and governance. In view of the challenges before Europe's parties today, I would concede that it is becoming harder to remain sanguine. This is not necessarily to say that parties are generally moribund or redundant; indeed, in some ways the need for parties as communities of political learning and recruitment, and as mechanisms of aggregation and accountable governance, may be as great as ever. Indeed, in many countries they do continue to offer meaningful political choices, even if those choices are constrained by broader historical and institutional contexts, and may not be susceptible to easy detection through quantitative analysis. But the significance of political parties in such terms certainly appears to be ever less tangible in the eyes of European publics.

Chapter 6

Elections and Electoral Systems*

Jonathan Hopkin

The competition between political parties for votes in periodic elections remains the cornerstone of democracy in Europe, and in many respects little seems to have changed over the last few decades. Seymour Martin Lipset and Stein Rokkan famously stated in the 1960s that 'the party alternatives, and in remarkably many cases the party organizations, are older than the majorities of the national electorates' (1967: 50) in Europe. Although this is obviously not the case for the newer democracies of Central and Eastern Europe, it is still not so far off the mark in many of the older democracies of Western Europe. A quick glance at some of the parties in government in large European democracies at the end of the 2000s suggests a high degree of continuity. Centre-left parties in government are almost always older than any of their voters: the Labour party (in government until 2010) in the UK was founded in 1900, the Socialist party in Spain (PSOE) in 1879, the Social Democratic Party (SPD) in Germany in 1863. The Conservatives and Liberal Democrats in Britain date back (in one form or another) to the eighteenth century. Even among the newer governing parties, the Christian Democratic Union (CDU) in Germany was founded in 1945, and Nicolas Sarkozy's Union for a Popular Majority (UMP), although founded in 2002, is in large part the same party that has represented the 'Gaullist' tradition under various names ever since the 1950s. Dramatic changes have occurred in some countries, most notably Italy and Belgium. But on the surface, the broad picture for Western Europe is one of stability, with the principal political parties becoming part of the national political heritage, passed down through the generations.

How can we square this substantial continuity with the important changes in politics, culture, the economy and society that have taken place in the lifetime of these parties? The survival of most European party systems over such long periods of time appears, on the face of it,

* The author thanks Brenda van Coppenolle and Jan-Emmanuel de Neve for research assistance.

surprising. In many cases, the period since democratic elections were first held has seen the transformation of predominantly agrarian societies into first industrial and then post-industrial ones, the decline of organized religion, the transformation of gender roles, mass migratory flows and a revolution in patterns of social communication. How could all this happen without profound changes in the political parties represented in the institutions of the state?

In fact, there is a great deal of evidence of fundamental changes in electoral politics, and the apparent stability of party systems often masks dramatic underlying changes. This chapter will present an account of continuity and change in electoral politics in European democracies, looking particularly at social structural factors and political cleavages, electoral systems, voters' relationship with political parties, and the growth of new political forces such as the extreme right. Although most of the academic research on European electoral politics has focused on developments in the older democracies of Western Europe, the chapter will draw parallels and contrasts with the party systems emerging in the new democracies of Central and Eastern Europe.

Frozen politics? Party systems and voter volatility in the new Europe

The survival into the twenty-first century of political parties founded in the nineteenth century poses a puzzle. If democratic elections are the chief mechanism for the representation of social interests and popular opinion in the institutions of the state, how could so many political parties have survived the radical changes that have affected all European societies over the past century? Some of the pioneering works in the study of European politics set out to explain precisely this. Stein Rokkan's 'cleavage structures' approach to understanding party systems focused on long-term social structural variables and emphasized the continuities in Western European party politics (Lipset and Rokkan 1967; Rokkan 1970). The 'Rokkanian' approach explained the shape of European party systems in terms of the ways in which particular historical conflicts – landed versus urban interests, workers versus capitalists, centre versus periphery, the religious versus the secular – had played out in each country. In the UK, for example, most of these conflicts had declined in importance by the time of democratization, leaving only the 'class conflict' between workers and capital to drive political competition. In Italy, by contrast, conflicts between Catholic and secular interests, between North and South, between industry and agriculture were added to the class conflict to produce a complex combination of cross-cutting conflicts.

These varying cleavage structures went some way towards explaining why the UK had a simple two-party system, while Italy had a highly fragmented multiparty system.

As well as explaining the shape of electoral competition, the cleavage-centred approach predicted substantial electoral stability: Lipset and Rokkan famously argued that Western European party systems had become 'frozen' during the consolidation of democracy, so even after several decades of free elections patterns of party competition faithfully reflected the dividing lines of the initial democratization phase: as they put it, 'the party systems of the 1960s reflect, with few but significant exceptions, the cleavage structures of the 1920s' (1967: 50). This was a paradoxical finding, since the nature of social cleavages had in almost all cases changed dramatically in the intervening period. Lipset and Rokkan's explanation for the persistence of electoral divisions based on anachronistic social conflicts was that political parties were capable of adapting their appeal to their electorates in such a way as to maintain their support when the original circumstances for mobilization had changed. One striking example of this is the persistence of the Irish party system structured around Fianna Fáil and Fine Gael, two parties which emerged out of opposed positions in the Irish Civil War, yet have continued to structure the party system ever since (Mair 1987), although the results of the 2011 election have challenged this established pattern.

However the period since the early 1970s has seen the emergence of an increasingly volatile electoral politics in the advanced democracies, with dramatic electoral shifts in previously 'frozen' party systems (i.e., systems undergoing apparently little real change over time), and the rapid growth of 'new' parties which do not reflect traditional cleavages (Inglehart 1997; Bartolini and Mair 1990; Franklin *et al.* 1992). Table 6.1 and Figure 6.1 document the steady increase in electoral instability in Western Europe since the 1960s, measured in terms of electoral volatility (the total percentage net vote shifts between successive elections, a proxy for the overall instability of voter preferences; see Pedersen 1979). After a little turbulence in the immediate post-war period, average volatility was stable and low in the 1950s and 1960s, began to increase in the 1970s and 1980s, and has been consistently higher in the 1990s and 2000s. These data suggest beyond reasonable doubt that electorates in the oldest European democracies have become less predictable in their behaviour in recent years.

Voters' increased willingness to shift their allegiances is not the only sign of change. Mair (2002) reported that as well as increased volatility, West European countries had seen the emergence of a series of new political parties which were playing increasingly important roles in the party system, often becoming decisive in government formation. The average percentage vote share of 'new' parties (defined as those which did not

Table 6.1   *Electoral and party system indicators (Europe, 2000s)*

Country	DM	LSQ	ENEP	ENPP	Volatility	New parties
Western Europe						
Netherlands	150.0	0.99	5.61	5.36	16.0	8.86
Germany	37.69	3.39	4.28	3.72	4.9	7.46
Italy	24.23	6.52	5.28	4.48	23.4	14.58
Austria	20.33	2.35	3.84	3.5	18.8	7.29
Sweden	15.86	2.27	4.59	4.19	13.6	5.9
Finland	13.3	3.18	5.77	5.03	5.4	8.46
Portugal	11.3	5.2	3.08	2.53	3.0	0.0
Denmark	9.72	1.35	5.1	4.9	11.7	9.22
Norway	8.68	2.95	5.65	4.96	14.5	13.41
Switzerland	7.7	2.52	5.53	4.99	6.4	9.96
Belgium	7.5	4.27	8.94	7.47	9.9	11.22
Spain	6.73	4.95	2.97	2.46	8.7	0.0
Greece	5.14	7.05	2.77	2.34	4.5	0.39
Ireland	3.93	6.24	3.95	3.21	6.5	1.97
France	1.0	17.77	4.77	2.38	16.3	17.84
UK	1.0	17.25	3.46	2.32	2.9	0.26
av. W. Europe	20.26	5.18	4.55	3.87	10.41	7.57
Central and Eastern Europe						
Slovakia	150.0	6.25	7.49	5.47	34.3	0.67
Latvia	20.0	6.03	7.14	5.51	32.0	0.0
Czech Rep.	14.29	5.73	4.37	4.37	13.6	1.4
Poland	11.21	5.99	4.56	3.56	27.9	6.42
Slovenia	11.0	3.4	5.37	4.66	23.5	0.87
Estonia	9.18	3.47	5.22	4.52	22.5	3.32
Rumania	7.79	6.15	4.58	3.46	19.2	9.7
Bulgaria	7.74	5.9	4.86	3.86	40.9	0.0
Hungary	1.96	6.67	2.87	2.31	8.9	2.32
Lithuania	1.96	7.73	6.5	4.84	46.5	3.25
av. CE Europe	24.9	5.73	5.3	4.26	26.93	3.11
av. all Europe	4.94	4.09	5.6	21.93	16.76	5.79

Legend:
DM – district magnitude;
ENEP – effective number of electoral parties;
ENPP – effective number of parliamentary parties;
LSQ – least squares measure of disproportionality.
Averages for the 2000s, except new parties (1990–2006)

Source: Comparative Study of Electoral Systems database, University of Michigan.

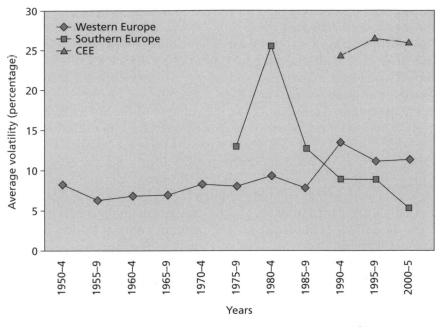

Figure 6.1 *Electoral volatility in Europe (1950–2005)*

Sources: Pedersen 1979; Lane and Ersson 1999; Koole and Katz 2000; Sikk 2005; Budge et al. 2006

contest elections before 1960) grew from 9.7 per cent in the 1970s to 23.7 per cent in the 1990s (Mair 2002: 134). Of course, parties formed in the 1960s are no longer so 'new', but their strength undermines the 'freezing' hypothesis advanced by Lipset and Rokkan, both because they were not present at the origin of democratic elections, and because for the most part these parties represent the kinds of 'new' political cleavages characteristic of the 'post-modernization' of democratic politics since the 1960s (Inglehart 1997). The emergence of 'post-materialist' concerns in the form of Green parties, and the even stronger reaction to rapid social change on the extreme (usually anti-immigrant) right, show the ability of electorates and political elites to move beyond the original cleavage structures which gave life to the democratic system. Added to the decline in support for many established parties and the increasingly unstable behaviour of voters, the strength of parties such as the Northern League and People of Freedom (PDL) in Italy, the Front National in France, and the Progress Party in Norway, suggests that the 'freezing' thesis needs to be revised. Table 6.1, which defines 'new' parties as those that mobilize around ethno-regionalist, post-materialist, extreme right or extreme left themes, finds that an average of around 8 per cent of voters vote for such parties, with figures as high as 18 per cent in France, 15 per cent in Italy and 13 per cent in Norway.

A further reason for thinking anew about how to understand European party politics is the emergence of new democracies lacking the decades of voter experience and party institutionalization of most Western European states. The 1970s added Greece, Portugal and Spain to the democratic family, and then the collapse of the Soviet bloc effectively completed the democratization of the continent up to the border of the former Soviet Union. The bottom part of Table 6.1 presents volatility scores for these newer democracies, while Figure 6.1 contrasts these scores with those of the older Western European democracies. What these data show is that volatility is much higher in the new democracies, a situation familiar to students of democratization. In the initial phase of democratization, political parties and aspirant political leaders have to connect with an electorate unaccustomed to free and open political competition, and lacking the stable associational ties typical of civil society in the democratic world. In these circumstances, instability is the norm, but as time passes voters get the chance to develop stable partisan identities (Gunther *et al.* 1995). In Southern Europe, this process can be observed in Figure 6.1: volatility is quite high in the early years of democracy, peaking in the early 1980s (the data point is skewed by the spectacular collapse and disappearance of the Union of Democratic Centre in Spain in 1982), and then declining as the party system consolidates.

In Central and Eastern Europe, this initial volatility has been even higher than in Southern Europe, with only one case of volatility falling below 10 per cent (Hungary in 2000 to 2004). Although we have data for only three five-year periods, this suggests a strikingly weak relationship between voters and political parties, even by the standards of new democracies. To give some idea of the magnitude of this instability, the *average* volatility for Central and Eastern Europe since 1990 – 26 per cent – is higher than *all but two* country scores for Western Europe between 1950 to 2005 (the sole exceptions being Italy in 1990 to 1994, and Spain in 1980 to 1984).

This means that legislatures elected in Central and Eastern Europe usually bear little resemblance to their predecessors, and that party 'systems' as such – stable, patterned interactions between parties – have yet to develop. In some cases, volatility is the result of major reconfigurations of the party system resulting from politicians changing their alliance-building strategies, but in others, parties standing under the same name have received vastly different vote shares in successive elections. This suggests at the very least a failure of the political parties to bed down and develop stable relationships with their electoral clienteles.

Subsequent elections will tells us whether Central Eastern European party systems will stabilize or whether voting behaviour will remain unstructured and unpredictable.

After the Ice Age: what kind of voters in Western Europe?

The evidence against the 'freezing' hypothesis is by now substantial, but there is still a good deal of uncertainty about how to characterize electoral politics in the new Europe. In particular, the growth of instability in Western Europe generated a debate over how to interpret high levels of volatility: was it a sign of *realignment* – one-off shifts in voting patterns ('critical' elections), where some voters swap stable allegiance to one party for equally stable allegiance to another – or of *dealignment* – in which voters were becoming detached from political parties and partisan identities altogether, shifting their allegiances on a regular basis? The general trend towards higher volatility in Western Europe, and the consistently high levels in Central and Eastern Europe, point very much in the direction of the second interpretation, since realignment would imply short-term increases in volatility followed by declines to the original level as voters found new stable allegiances. Although the average increase in volatility is more linear than the trend in most individual countries, the data show increasing instability across almost all West European countries since 1990, rather than stability punctuated by 'critical elections'.

Most studies therefore conclude that some degree of dealignment has taken place, and that European voters are less attached to partisan identities than in the past (e.g., Franklin *et al.* 1992; Nieuwbeerta 1996; Dalton 2000; Thomassen 2005; Knutsen 2006; see the review in Enyedi 2008). However, it is less clear what kind of alignments, if any, influence voting behaviour in the more unstable electoral environment of early twenty-first-century Europe. There are two broad positions adopted by scholars in this debate. The first draws on the Rokkanian 'sociological' approach and defends the continued relevance of social structural factors such as class, religion and territory on voting behaviour. Most of the research in this tradition recognizes that there has been some weakening of the classic social cleavages as a predictor of the vote, but that these cleavages remain important: as Elff (2007: 289) puts it, 'reports of the death of social cleavages are exaggerated'. A second line of scholarship instead sees dealignment as a consequence of a process of 'modernization' which has led to the 'cognitive mobilization' of the population (more discerning political behaviour resulting from higher levels of

education) and the 'individualization' of political behaviour, with collective identities such as class and religion less and less important in determining voting choices. Various alternative interpretations of the vote are
proposed by this school. One line of argument stresses the role of 'values'
held by citizens (such as their position on social–cultural issues or the
environment) which drive their voting behaviour independently of their
position on the old lines of cleavage (Inglehart 1978). Another sees voters
'beginning to choose' (Rose and McAllister 1986) on the grounds of their
proximity to parties on major policy issues, or in terms of broad 'valence'
concerns such as the state of the economy and the perceived relative
competence of politicians (Clarke *et al.* 2004).

Neither of these approaches is entirely inconsistent with the observation that electoral behaviour has become more unstable. High levels of
volatility provide some indirect support for 'individualistic' models of
voter behaviour, which emphasize voter choice. If voters are free to
choose, it is more likely they will choose differently from one election to
the next. For proponents of the sociological approach, instability could
be the consequence of the changing nature of the social structure in
contemporary Europe, with major shifts in the political economy leading
to the shrinking of some occupational groups (e.g., industrial manual
workers) and the growth of others (both high and low-end service workers). Low-skilled workers may become less likely to support labour or
social democratic parties if they are in non-unionized workplaces where
there is little social pressure to maintain left partisanship. Higher living
standards and social mobility for most citizens may affect partisan loyalties (Thomassen 2005). Declining religiosity, reflected in lower church
attendance, is likely to reduce the influence of religion on voting behaviour, opening up the prospect of more unstable behaviour. However,
notwithstanding these changes, certain social characteristics remain
powerful predictors of voting behaviour in Western Europe (Evans 2001;
Elff 2007). As Enyedi concludes: 'the cleavage model of politics is less
relevant, but far from irrelevant' (2008: 299).

Which cleavages are relevant to voting behaviour in twenty-first-
century Europe? Socio-economic position – usually characterized as
'class' – remains an important predictor of the vote in Western Europe,
although to varying degrees in different countries. According to early
studies in the post-war period, class voting was more prominent in
Northern Europe than in Catholic and Mediterranean Europe, with
Britain and the Scandinavian countries presenting the strongest relationship between occupation and party allegiance (Lijphart 1971; Korpi
1983). Subsequent research confirmed this comparative picture, while
documenting the overall decline in the class–vote relationship, particularly in those countries where it had been strongest (Nieuwbeerta 1996).

Despite the waning of the class cleavage, data for seven West European countries from the late 1990s show significant differences (mostly over 20 per cent) in support for social democratic and labour parties between manual workers and the middle-class ('salariat' and self-employed) (Elff 2007: 280). Class still makes a difference to the way people vote in Western Europe, which helps account for the much lower rates of volatility in 'old' Europe compared to the newer Central and Eastern European democracies.

Another important stabilizing force in Western Europe is the religious cleavage. Like class, religion has historically been a strong predictor of the vote in the established democracies, particularly in Catholic Europe where the battle between the church hierarchy and the secular state has been just as conflictual as the class struggle (Lipset and Rokkan 1967). However, social change has weakened the intensity of the religious cleavage, with church attendance and compliance with church norms on social behaviour in steep decline. Surprisingly however, the declining social influence of organized religion in Western Europe has not brought a parallel decline in its relationship to voting behaviour. Differences in support for conservative and Christian parties between churchgoers and non-churchgoers remain very high in countries with a tradition of religious cleavage (over 60 per cent in the Netherlands, over 50 per cent in Belgium and nearly 50 per cent in Italy; Elff 2007), and the decline in the religious cleavage is less sharp than is the case for social class. The clear secularization of social behaviour across Western Europe has left the political impact of religious belief largely intact.

A third major cleavage identified by Rokkan – the territorial tensions between centre and periphery – has also proved resistant to the forces of modernization. In the early phase of democratization through the post-war period, a tendency towards an increasing 'nationalization' of politics can be observed (Caramani 2004), with the decline of localistic concerns and the growing strength of political parties representing positions on 'functional' cleavages (such as class and religion) across the territory of the democratic state. The nationalization thesis implies the disappearance of the territorial cleavage, with voters behaving in similar ways in all parts of a national territory. This prediction has only partially been fulfilled, and in some cases has been reversed (Swenden and Maddens 2009): in Britain and Italy new 'ethno-regionalist' parties have emerged, or old ones have re-emerged, obtaining substantial vote shares in their territories. In Spain, the consolidation of democracy has not weakened the territorial cleavage, and ethno-regionalist parties have become entrenched in their territories at the expense of the main state-wide parties. In the most extreme case, Belgium, state-wide parties representing functional cleavages have divided on ethno-regionalist lines, with the territorial–linguistic cleavage cutting clearly through the other political divisions. Most of these cases involve territorial differences underpinned by linguistic differences and separate national identities, but there is also evidence of territory reinforcing the electoral effect of socio-economic cleavages, by further separating the social experiences of wealthy and poor groups in large democracies (for example Johnston and Pattie 2006).

So cleavages are not dead in Western Europe, despite growing electoral instability. But what about new democracies, where volatility is on average twice as high? The extraordinary levels of vote switching in East-Central Europe are hard to square with a role for cleavages such as social class in structuring the vote. Some early studies of elections in East and Central Europe argued that the long period of Communist rule had not only undermined the development of civil society, but had also dismantled the social stratification characteristic of Western democracies, leaving an atomized society: a sociological *tabula rasa* (see the review in Evans 2006). The failure of party systems to bed down after almost two decades offers some support to this interpretation. However, research using data comparable to that gathered on Western European electorates suggests otherwise: although less clear than in Western Europe, social structural models of voting behaviour do have some explanatory power in new East-Central European democracies (Gjisberts and Nieuwbeerta 2000; Evans and Whitefield 2000), and there is some evidence that social structure has grown in importance as democracy has consolidated (Evans 2006).

Other research suggests that the higher volatility of the new democracies may be permanent: in a cross-national analysis of 47 democracies in Europe, America and Asia, Mainwaring and Zoco (2007) find that democracies established after 1978 have systematically and stably higher levels of volatility than those established before that date. This may be an indication of parties' declining ability to mobilize around social cleavages, rather than an indication of the decline of such cleavages. This suggests another, often neglected, explanation for the growing unpredictability of electoral politics in Europe: the instability of political parties themselves.

The causes of instability: volatile voters or volatile parties?

The Central-East European experience so far suggests that political parties themselves have been a source of instability, with frequent changes of alliances, names and leaderships (Sikk 2005). Since modern media systems provide political elites with little incentive to invest in building grassroots organizations, political parties in Central and Eastern Europe may have locked themselves into permanently high levels of electoral instability, with volatile voters and equally volatile parties. However, political parties have become weaker organizations in Western Europe too. New technologies have made it possible to fight elections with lightweight and top-heavy organizational structures and few grass-roots members (Hopkin and Paolucci 1999). Voters therefore have a more detached relationship to political parties than was the case in the post-war Europe analysed by Lipset and Rokkan (Katz and Mair 1995), and this is in itself a plausible source of change in electoral behaviour.

Figure 6.2 displays some key indicators of party weakness in Europe after the end of the Cold War. Average levels of party membership in the 'old' (pre-1975) democracies of Western Europe (data from Mair and van Biezen 2001) has been on a downward trajectory since 1980, and declined at an accelerating rate through the 1990s, leaving the Western European average at little above one party member for every 20 voters. Levels of party identification – the extent to which voters feel close to a particular party, usually a good predictor of reliable electoral support for that party – are also in decline (Figure 6.2 shows the percentage of voters

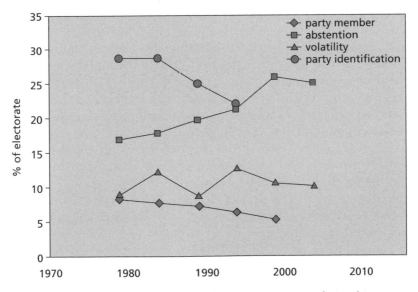

Figure 6.2 *Indicators of weakening party–voter relationship (Western Europe 1975–2005)*

Sources: Party membership (Mair and van Biezen 2001); party identification (Eurobarometer); volatility (Lane and Ersson 1999; *European Journal of Political Research*; Political Data Yearbooks 2000–5); turnout (International IDEA Voter Turnout Database 2009).

who 'feel very or quite close to a party', averaged across European democracies). Although there are numerous measurement problems, the scholarly consensus is that party identification has fallen consistently in the 'old' European democracies since the 1970s, and remains low in the new democracies (Dalton and Wattenberg 2002; Thomassen 2005). So citizens are less and less likely to join political parties, or to identify closely with them. Added to this, there is evidence of a steady, although unspectacular, decline in electoral turnout, with voters increasingly likely not to use their vote (although the vast majority in Western Europe still do) (Franklin 2004). These indicators match the steady rise in volatility discussed earlier.

How are we to interpret these changes, and what do they tell us about the nature of electoral politics in Europe? Here establishing causality is difficult, since there are a considerable number of factors which could potentially have undermined political parties' ability to connect with citizens and reliably win their support. The previous section outlined the kinds of social changes which could have made voters more independent and less reliant on parties for their political orientations, such as shifting social structure, higher levels of education and mobility, individualization, and declining religiosity. However parties themselves have changed as organizations in ways which have undermined their connection with their electoral bases. The fall in party membership, for instance, is consistent with the theory of cognitive mobilization, which portrays voters as increasingly independent-minded citizens who choose candidates and policies rather than slavishly supporting 'their' party. But it is also consistent with theories of party organizational change which emphasize the growing centralization of power around party leaders and the declining role of grassroots mobilization in an age of rapid technological advances in social communication (Panebianco 1988; Katz and Mair 1995; Hopkin and Paolucci 1999). From this perspective, it could be argued that party members and identifiers have been abandoned by political parties, rather than the other way around.

Indeed one important source of electoral volatility in recent years has been changes to party organizations and labels prior to elections, meaning that voters have simply not have the option to confirm their support for a political party or coalition. This has been particularly frequent in the new Central and East European democracies, but there have also been high profile cases in Western Europe. Between 1992 and 1994, all the major governing parties in Italy were hit by a wave of corruption scandals, with at one stage up to two-thirds of parliamentarians officially under investigation. As a result, the Christian Democrat and Socialist parties, the linchpin of government coalitions for decades, effectively ceased to exist. By the subsequent elections in 1994, the party system was unrecognizable, with Silvio Berlusconi's newly created Forza Italia dominating a right-wing coalition of new or renamed parties, and substantial changes on the left too. In 2008, Forza Italia merged with its right-wing partner National Alliance to form the People of Freedom party (PDL) while the main parties on the centre-left merged in the Democratic Party (PD) (despite the many name changes, most of the main party leaders remain the same as in the early 1990s). Although this is the most dramatic case, party splits and the creation of new formations, often by political leaders defecting from the established parties, have featured in party system realignments in a number of other cases. In the Central and East European case, high levels of volatility are in part the result of elite manoeuvrings rather than any marked shift in electoral behaviour.

In Western Europe, parties have mostly responded to their increasing weakness on the ground by strengthening the party organization at the central level and in public office, and have compensated for the fall in membership by awarding themselves ever more substantial public subsidies and other forms of state support (Katz and Mair 1995; Detterbeck 2005). However, in responding to the threats of electoral instability and grassroots weakness, parties may well have been storing up even more serious problems for themselves, since their penetration of the state machinery is likely to exacerbate the distance between parties and citizens which has caused parties' organizational and electoral decline (Mair *et al.* 2004). In fact there is also some evidence that European citizens are more distrustful of their elected politicians, with high profile corruption scandals overturning governments and even, in the exceptional case of Italy in 1992 to 1994, an entire party system. Often these scandals have revolved around cases of corrupt or unethical financing of party activities, particularly in the cases of Italy, Spain and Belgium, and to a lesser extent France, Germany and the United Kingdom. After revelations of systematic abuses of expenses allowance by British parliamentarians, fringe parties won record shares of the vote in the 2009 European elections, and the 2010 elections saw an unprecedented turnover of MPs, as targets of public ire over the expenses issue opted to leave politics rather than face humiliation at the polls. As in the case of volatility though, public trust seems to be weaker in the new democracies than in the established democracies. The European Values Survey finds that 'confidence in parliament' – a reasonable proxy for trust in parties, given that parliament is almost exclusively the territory of party politicians – is consistently lower in Central and East European democracies than in Western Europe (Webb and White 2007). This lack of trust in the political elite is yet another piece of evidence supporting the notion of a failure of political parties to connect adequately with voters in the newer European democracies.

Electoral systems and electoral behaviour

Electoral systems play an important role in structuring democratic politics through the incentives they give voters and parties to behave in particular ways. Electoral rules are particularly important because they perform the function of transforming votes into representation, allocating parliamentary seats to different parties according to their vote shares. There is a potentially infinite variety of electoral systems, because there are a number of features of the electoral rules that can be modified. Broadly, however, the main dimension along which electoral systems vary is proportionality – the degree to which parties receive a share of representation which is proportional to their share of the popular vote. The degree of proportionality of an electoral system is affected by a variety of mechanisms, including the mathematical formula used to allocate seats, the adoption of thresholds below which a party is excluded, mechanisms to reallocate surplus votes once seats have been allocated, and the size of the electoral districts (district magnitude). The latter measure is a reasonable proxy for the overall level of proportionality.

Tables 6.1 and 6.2 present some indicators of the relationship between electoral systems and party systems (countries in each table are ordered by district magnitude, with the most 'proportional' systems at the top). Some effects of electoral systems can be gauged quite clearly. First, smaller district sizes have a mechanical effect of under-representing smaller parties and over-representing larger ones, leading to a higher disproportionality between vote shares and shares of parliamentary representation (reflected in the scores on the 'least squares index' – Gallagher 1991). Second, greater district magnitude is related to a higher 'effective number of parties' (a measure of party system fragmentation which considers both the absolute number of parties and their relative sizes – Laasko and Taagepera 1979). Higher district magnitude is associated with greater fragmentation not only in the allocation of parliamentary seats (as measured by the 'effective number of parliamentary parties' (ENPP)), but also a greater fragmentation in the vote shares won by the parties standing for election ('effective number of electoral parties' (ENEP)). This shows that electoral systems not only affect the number of parties represented in parliament, but also affect the number of parties receiving significant vote shares, as voters tend to recognize the higher likelihood of minor parties receiving seats in more proportional systems. However, electoral systems are not the sole determinant of party systems, and there are numerous exceptions. Belgium, for example, has the most fragmented party system in Western Europe, despite not having exceptionally proportional electoral rules: here the powerful effect of cleavage – in this case the territorial/linguistic cleavage dividing

Flanders and francophone Belgium which has effectively created two separate party systems – is the main cause of the large number of parties. The UK, as one would expect given its single-member district majoritarian electoral system, has a low degree of fragmentation, but France, which has a two-round single member district system, has a higher than average effective number of parties. Among the new democracies, Slovakia has the highest district magnitude, yet a less fragmented party system than Lithuania, which has the lowest district magnitude. This reminds us that party systems have a 'life of their own' (Mair 1996), and are not simply an artefact of the electoral system.

The data presented in Table 6.1 also suggest that electoral systems are relevant to explaining the growing instability of party politics in Europe. Although the relationship is not linear and there are notable exceptions, most of the cases of high volatility in the older democracies in the recent period occur in countries with more proportional electoral systems. For the Central and East European cases, the relationship is less clear, in part because volatility levels are very high across all of these countries. Two implications can be drawn from this. First, electoral systems do not structure party systems on their own: the new democracies in Central and Eastern Europe have lower average district magnitudes than in the West, but far higher volatility, suggesting that the ability of parties to articulate social interests acts on stability independently of the electoral system. A second implication is that, where party systems have enjoyed periods of substantial stability – the old democracies of Western Europe – higher district magnitude is associated with higher volatility. The reasons for this are related to the greater ability of new parties to penetrate the electoral arena in countries with more proportional electoral systems, since these systems offer parliamentary representation even to very small parties, allowing new formations to get a foothold in the institutions.

The rightmost column in Table 6.1 reports the vote shares won by extreme right, protest and green parties in the 2000s. These are the main types of new parties that have made an impact on West European party systems over the past quarter-century. Again we see a relationship – albeit not a particularly clear one – between high vote shares for these types of parties and higher district magnitudes. In Spain, Greece, Ireland and the UK, new parties are conspicuous by their absence, and all share relatively low district magnitude. The effects of the electoral system on the prospects of these parties can be estimated by observing the relatively strong performance of green parties and anti-Europe parties in the UK in European Parliament elections, held under a form of proportional representation, and their generally weaker performance in Westminster parliamentary elections. New parties on the ecological left and extreme right are less present in the Central and Eastern European democracies, suggesting a relationship between the success of these parties and the degree of past institutionalization of the party system.

The rise of new parties, particularly extremist parties on the right of the political spectrum, is an important development in West European electoral politics. For a long time West European electorates voted for parties which had been established decades earlier. But voters have not only begun to switch party more often, but also are increasingly likely to support new, recently created political parties. Moreover, these parties often represent political positions which directly challenge the range of policy options considered acceptable by the established parties, as well as questioning the legitimacy of the established party elites themselves. In some cases, the challenge to the mainstream has been taken up by parties representing, and at times reviving, the territorial cleavage, such as nationalist parties in Scotland, Wales, Catalonia, the Basque Country or Northern Italy.

Figure 6.3 illustrates the changing levels of support of these 'challenger' parties; not all of these parties are new, but for the most part, extreme-right parties, green parties and ethnic/regionalist parties tend to constitute a challenge to the existing order, and define themselves as being outside the established party system. In much of the post-war period, the main challenge to the mainstream parties came from communism. Figure

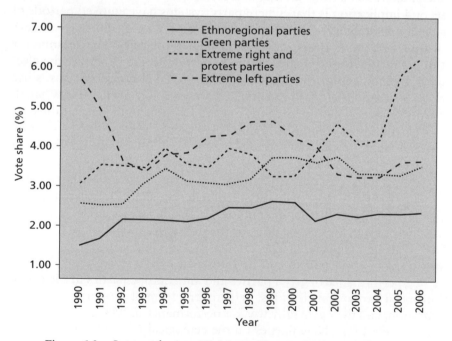

Figure 6.3   *Support for 'new' parties in Western Europe (1990–2006)*

6.3 shows that the main shift over the past two decades is the decline of the extreme left (usually represented by communist parties, which suffered a rapid decline in support after the collapse of the Soviet Union), and the broad growth in support (from less than 5 per cent on average in 1990 to almost 9 per cent in 2006) for all other kinds of challenger parties, many of which are relatively new parties, some even created during this period.

Few Western European countries remain unaffected by this phenomenon. Curiously, protest parties of the radical right have been particularly popular in stable, wealthy established democracies such as Austria, Norway, Denmark and the Netherlands, possibly in part because of the openness of their electoral systems. In these small democracies challenger parties – mobilizing particularly around the issue of immigration – have won sufficient support to condition government coalition formation. In Austria, the Freedom Party (FPO) – traditionally a liberal party, but under the leadership of Jorg Haider transformed into a radical right, anti-immigrant formation – peaked at 27 per cent of the vote in 1999, and although the party's support subsequently fell back after an unsuccessful period in national government, the total far right vote (FPO and the splinter Alliance for the Future of Austria (BZO)) again reached over 27 per cent in the 2008 legislative elections. In Norway, the anti-tax and anti-immigrant Progress Party (FrP) has grown to winning 23 per cent of the vote in the 2009 elections, making it the second largest party in the parliament (although excluded from government coalition formation). In Denmark, the Danish People's Party (DPP, a successor to the Danish Progress Party) occupies a similar position in the party system, and has won more than 10 per cent of the vote since 2001, offering parliamentary support to a centre-right coalition government. In the Netherlands the Pim Fortuyn List – a curious mix of social liberalism and anti-immigrant rhetoric – won 17 per cent in the 2002 election after its leader's assassination, but disappeared shortly afterwards. Geert Wilders, another outspoken critic of immigration, and particularly Muslim immigration, formed the Party of Freedom (PVV) in 2004, winning 6 per cent of the vote in the 2006 elections, and 16 per cent in the 2010 elections, making it decisive in the formation of the new government.

Extremist challenger parties have also been successful in some of the large Western European democracies. This is particularly the case in Italy, where the wholesale transformation of the party system in the early 1990s left a power vacuum which has been exploited by previously marginal challenger parties to establish themselves as the mainstream. The right-wing coalitions led by Silvio Berlusconi have allied his own party with the National Alliance, formerly a neo-fascist party, and the Northern League, which despite its origins as a regionalist and anti-tax party has recently adopted a strident anti-immigration discourse. In France, the extreme-right National Front has won between 10 to 20 per cent of the vote since the mid-1980s, and in the late 2000s the Anti-Capitalist Party, bringing together hard left factions around 2007 presidential candidate Olivier Besancenot, challenged the traditional parties of the centre-left. In Germany, the Social Democratic Party SPD is increasingly under pressure from the new Links party formed by former SPD leader Oskar Lafontaine, but right-wing extremists have been largely excluded from elective institutions.

In the UK and Spain, in contrast, challenger parties have found it hard to gain access to state-wide elective institutions, although in the former case the UK Independence Party and the British National Party have won European Parliament seats and local council representation, and together polled an unprecedented 5 per cent of the total vote in the 2010 elections, although the workings of the first-past-the-post electoral system denied them any parliamentary seats. In both Britain and Spain, ethno-regionalist parties demanding self-government for their territories have been relatively strong: the Welsh and Scottish nationalists have been a presence since the 1970s and have successfully campaigned for devolution, while the decentralization issue has been placed at the centre of the political agenda in Spain since the transition to democracy after Franco. Support for ethno-regionalist parties has tended to be more stable than that for protest parties of the right and left, but their relative success in second-order elections at the subnational level suggests an element of protest underpinning their electoral support.

Conclusion

This short account of recent developments in European party politics has sought to do two things. First, to take stock of the accumulation of empirical evidence on the nature and evolution of electoral politics in European democracies over the post-war period. Second, to look at what recent developments tell us about the validity of the various theoretical tools and interpretations that have emerged out of the study of elections and electoral behaviour in Europe.

The strongest conclusion that can be drawn is that electoral democracy in the 'old' democracies of the West is becoming increasingly unstable and unpredictable, although it still does not match the volatility of voting behaviour in the new democracies of Central and Eastern Europe. In general, therefore, theories of electoral stability based on social structure and the development of political cleavages appear less and less relevant to our understanding of contemporary European politics. Although the majority of voters in the more established democracies have stable patterns of voting behaviour, the dominant picture emerging out of the past decade is of vote switching, the explosive growth of protest parties in some countries, and an overall weakening in loyal partisan electoral behaviour.

Explaining and interpreting these recent developments remains in part speculative, since we are dealing with events that 'haven't finishing happening yet'. But it is worth concluding that some of these are consistent with the 'cartel party' thesis advanced by Richard Katz and Peter Mair (1995; also Blyth and Katz 2005). They argued that parties were becoming more distant from their supporters and voters, but colluded to distribute public subsidies and shares of state patronage among themselves, while using electoral rules to obstruct new parties from gaining access to the system. Although in the short run such strategies can be successful, at the same time collaboration and collusion between the established parties plays into the hands of 'challenger' parties, who seek to represent themselves as the voice of the 'outsiders'. The pressures facing West European party systems, where parties are more deeply institutionalized, come in large part from protest parties building on popular resentment against entrenched partisan elites. In Central and Eastern Europe, where parties are weakly institutionalized and protest parties correspondingly less prominent, instability is even greater. It is too soon to dismiss theories of electoral stability based on cleavage structures and institutionalized political parties, but in early twenty-first-century Europe the challenge is to explain electoral change rather than stability.

Chapter 7

Political Activism

Pippa Norris

Many believe that in recent decades European democracies face a hazardous and difficult pathway steering between the twin dangers of political activism where the public is neither too lukewarm nor over-heated, the Scylla and Charybdis of contemporary politics.

One potential danger is that European citizens are becoming increasingly disengaged from civic affairs, as indicated by falling electoral turnout since the early-1990s and eroding grassroots party membership. In the June 2008 elections to the European Parliament, for example, more than half of the electorate (57 per cent) stayed home. Voter turnout in these elections fell to a new low of 43 per cent in 2008, down from 62 per cent in 1979. Post-war turnout in parliamentary national elections, illustrated in Figure 7.1, show a pattern of trendless fluctuations until the 1990s, when there was a significant decline in Western Europe, as well as sharper falls in Central and Eastern Europe. Turnout was about 76 per cent on average in 52 Western European parliamentary elections in 2000 to 2009, down about 10 percentage points from its peak during the 1960s. Similarly average turnout in Central and Eastern European parliamentary elections fell from 71 per cent in the 1990s to 60 per cent during the following decade. Such indicators are widely regarded as signalling public disaffection and the growth of more critical citizens, especially if coupled with low or declining levels of trust in core state institutions, including parliaments, parties and elected politicians (Norris 1999b, 2011; Dalton 2004; Hay 2007).

The alternative risk is that citizens are indeed intensely involved but in ways which may potentially destabilize the state and undermine democratically elected authorities. This threat is illustrated most vividly by the sudden outbreak of violent street riots, including firebombs outside of parliament and anarchist shop looting in Greece. But there are many other recent events which show similar outbursts, from cases of fuel strikes in London to violent riots among immigrants living in Paris suburbs, protests over the Muhammad cartoons in Copenhagen, and farmer's dumping food on the streets of Brussels. Such actions are exemplified by the wave of widespread demonstrations in European capitals

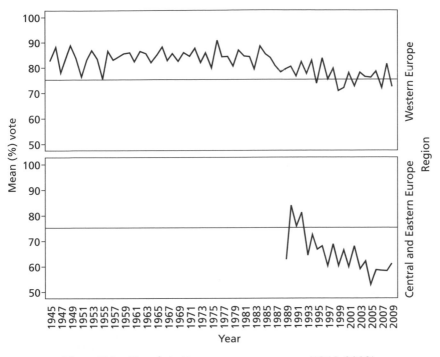

Figure 7.1   *Trends in European voter turnout (1945–2009)*

Note: Votes cast as a proportion of the eligible electorate in national parliamentary elections, 1945 to 2009.

Source: International IDEA Voter Turnout database.

protesting proposed austerity cuts in public services, triggering a general strike in Spain and tens of thousands of protesters on the streets of Brussels. In the United States, voter anger is widely assumed to have fuelled noisy shouting matches at town hall meetings over health-care support and Tea Party rallies, as well as growth in militia movements. These diverse cases may or may not have similar underlying roots. But interpretations commonly perceive contentious politics as threatening to political stability.

The democratic state is often assumed to flourish best with moderate participation, especially acts channelled through the conventional mechanisms of elections and parties in liberal democracies. This argument is far from novel – indeed its roots can be traced back more than half a century (Eckstein 1961). But it is heard today with increasing urgency. The risks to order and stability are most real in fragile states, exemplified by outbreaks of 'people power' overthrowing Ramos in the Philippines, populist uprisings supporting Chavez in Venezuela, and political crisis leading to a military coup in Thailand. No one believes that this phenomenon poses a major risk today to the ultimate stability, cohesion and unity of most contemporary European states. But if long-established democratic societies lack the capacity to contain sporadic outbreaks of contentious politics, and if they are simultaneously unable to bring citizens to the ballot box, this becomes a matter of serious concern.

To examine these issues, the first part of this chapter considers the standard paradigm which evolved in social psychology to explain individual-level citizen engagement in public affairs. The next section then identifies the major contemporary normative and empirical challenges to the classic model and the revised contextual model of political activism which informs current research. This is followed by a review of some of the evidence about the patterns of voting participation available from the European Social Survey. Lastly, the conclusion summarizes the main results and reflects upon their implications for democracy.

The standard social psychological paradigm of political participation

Research on political activism compares the ways that citizens participate in the public sphere, the processes that lead them to do so, and the consequences of these acts. The standard social psychological model of political participation quickly became adopted as the orthodox paradigm following Gabriel Almond and Sidney Verba's path-breaking *The Civic Culture* (1963, 1980). The intellectual roots of this study, and the sociological and psychological explanation for political behaviour, originated during the inter-war era with the Chicago school, notably Charles Merriam's study on *The Making of Citizens* (1931), as well as Harold Lasswell's *Psychopathology and Politics* (1930). Harry Eckstein's (1961) work *A Theory of Stable Democracy* was also highly influential. Building upon this foundation, *The Civic Culture* theorized that stable democracies ideally required equilibrium with the mass public finely balanced between the dangers of either an excessively apathetic and disengaged citizenry, on the one hand, or an overly agitated and destabilizing engagement, on the other.

The idea that societies differed in their political culture was hardly novel; indeed it had been the subject of philosophical speculation and normative debate for centuries, in classic works from Aristotle and Montesquieu to de Tocqueville. But one of the more radical aspects of the civic culture study was the way that empirical support for the theory was derived from a path-breaking cross-national opinion survey, demonstrating that citizen's orientations could be examined empirically among the mass publics in Mexico, Italy, Britain, France and Germany. The civic culture study and the use of cross-national survey methods established a quantum leap in the methods and concerns common in comparative political science. It was followed in 1963 by the eight-nation *Political Participation* study sponsored by the International Social Science Council, with Asher, Richardson and Weisberg *et al.* as the principal investigators. A few years later, Sidney Verba expanded upon his earlier work in the US (Verba and Nie 1972) and developed the *Political Participation and Equality* survey in seven nations in 1966 (Verba, Nie and Kim 1978). The eight-nation 1973 and 1981 *Political Action Surveys* by Samuel Barnes, Klaus Allerbeck, Max Kaase, Hans-Dieter Klingemann, Alan Marsh and Ronald Inglehart expanded upon this foundation to understand 'unconventional' forms of protests and mass demonstrations which were widespread among the trilateral democracies during this decade (Marsh 1977; Barnes and Kaase 1979; Jennings and van Deth 1989).

The paradigmatic approach derived from *The Civic Culture* used mass surveys to document levels of activism within and across nations, distinguishing several distinct 'modes' or dimensions of political action. The literature established a series of well-known findings about the distribution and the causes of mass activism, illustrated schematically in Figure 7.2, which continue to inform conventional wisdom today.

1   Political participation is a multidimensional phenomenon, with acts differing in the demands they placed upon citizens and their modes of engagement.
2   Voting turnout was the only mode of political participation involving a majority of citizens, and it was distinctive since it required only minimal investment of time, skills, and money.
3   Beyond this, only a minority of the population were engaged in the more demanding forms of 'conventional' participation, including campaigning and party work, contacting officials and community organizing.
4   Protest politics, exemplified by involvement in demonstrations, petitions and political strikes, and regarded as another distinct form of activism, was similarly confined to small elites.
5   In explaining who became active, the 'baseline model', developed by Almond and Verba (1963) and Verba and Nie (1972), suggested that social structural resources played a significant role, notably the distribution of educational qualifications, income, and occupational status, along with the related demographic factors of sex, age and ethnicity/race.
6   Cultural attitudes and social psychological predispositions, closely related to socioeconomic status and education, were also important

Figure 7.2   *The standard social psychological theory of individual political activism*

for motivating engagement; participation was greatest among those who felt informed, interested and efficacious, who cared strongly about the outcome, who had a sense of party identification, and who felt a sense of duty to participate in civic affairs.

The prime focus of social psychological analysis was therefore something about the individual citizen, not something about the context within which they acted. Throughout this body of literature, the roles of specific formal and informal institutions, as well as the broader political system, were acknowledged as theoretically important for mass activism. For example, Verba *et al.* (1978) noted that national levels of voter turnout were influenced by registration procedures and by group affiliations with mobilizing agencies and organizations, such as labour unions, religious organizations and political parties. They also drew attention to the broader political institutions and historical legacy which differentiated each of the countries under comparison. In the empirical analysis, however, these macro-level contextual factors were essentially designated as bit players, relegated to the side of the stage. The ways that the political environment established the hurdles and incentives for citizen engagement in public life was given far less emphasis than the social psychological predispositions of individual citizens.

In part, this approach arose from the bias towards methodological individualism in the sub-field; the predominance of individual-level behavioural survey analysis, based on samples representative of the general adult population within each nation, meant that the empirical analysis of macro-level contextual effects remained underdeveloped. Comparisons within each country are typically made between groups (for example, turnout among African-Americans versus Hispanics), over time (for example, trends in electoral turnout since 1960), and occasionally across regions or states (such as the effects of registration requirements). Single nation surveys, such as the standard series of national election studies, are usually not well designed to study institutional effects unless there are significant variations across sub-units (such as the registration or balloting procedures used in different US states) or major systemic changes functioning as natural experiments over time (such as electoral reforms occurring in New Zealand or Italy). Most cross-national surveys during the 1970s and 1980s were commonly based on convenience samples of a small number of established democracies and post-industrial societies, implicitly based on the 'most similar' comparative design. This tries to compare like with like, such as selecting post-industrial societies with relatively similar levels of democratization or development to analyse variations in behaviour. As a result, individual-level variance among groups of citizens *within* each society was usually greater than systematic national-level institutional variance *across* types of societies, for example by levels of economic development, global cultural region or types of regimes. The importance of individual-level structural resources and cultural attitudes was replicated and confirmed in numerous survey-based studies of specific nations and types of participation. The core theoretical claims of the social psychological model became the standard textbook view of political participation from the 1960s until at least the late-1980s, particularly in the American literature (see, for example, Milbrath and Goel 1977; Bennett 1986; Conway 2000). Normal science research continues to replicate, applying the old classic theoretical paradigm to expand the geographic basis of our generalizations. The paradigm continued to fit diverse countries. For example, an edited volume by Krishna (2008) examined whether social inequality helps to explain patterns of political participation in Sub-Saharan Africa, South Asia and Latin America. The study concluded that lack of education – but not wealth – continued to be one of the most important barriers to participation in these countries, reflecting one of the key findings originally observed by Verba *et al.* (1978) three decades earlier.

The revised model of political activism

The *normative* underpinnings of the standard paradigm of political participation have come under sustained critique, however, especially from theorists emphasizing the virtues of deliberative democracy. *The Civic Culture* evaluated the consequences of civic engagement, such as voting and working for parties, mainly by how far this established the legitimacy of the democratic state and the accountability of elected officials. By contrast, ideas of deliberative democracy have been heavily influenced by the philosopher and social theorist Jürgen Habermas, who argued that citizen involvement should be valued for the quality of informed public opinion and for rational deliberation within the public sphere (1991). This provides a richer and more comprehensive vision of the quality of democratic participation and its educational potential for citizen awareness, as much as for state legitimacy (Gutmann and Thomson 2004). Ideas of deliberative democracy are not merely theoretical and confined to academic debate; instead they have been embodied in innovative forms of citizen decision-making which embody the deliberative ideal. Diverse new channels have expanded in the last decade, exemplified by the use of participatory budgeting in Brazil, social audits in India, deliberative opinion polls, national issue forums, online consultation processes, citizen juries, experiments in community decision-making processes, and the growing use of referenda and plebiscites in many states (Gastil and Levine 2005). It remains difficult to monitor the extent of mass public engagement in each of these diverse channels and forums, which lend themselves best to quasi-experimental 'before' and 'after' research designs among participants, but these are clearly very different to the standard notions of political activism which informed the behavioural tradition.

Moreover the *empirical* basis for the standard account of political participation has also been challenged. One reason has been the growth of electoral democracies worldwide, and the export of social scientific surveys which accompanied this process. This allowed the study of public opinion to expand around the globe, as exemplified by the Global-barometers, the European Social Survey, and the World Values Survey (Norris 2009). This has strengthened the capacity of analysts to compare political activism within a wide range of contexts.

These developments have encouraged sustained attacks on the standard social psychological model (Books and Prysby 1988; Norris 2007). It is increasingly recognized that 'context matters', with individual citizens embedded within specific mezzo-level informal institutions of organizations, communities, neighbourhoods and social networks, as well as being nested within the even broader environment set by the formal state institutions and the social context within each nation (see the schematic model illustrated in Figure 7.3).

One popular perspective is offered by theories emphasizing the role of *formal state institutions*, which rational choice accounts explain through the role of institutions in shaping the incentives for citizens to participate. Of course this is far from a novel claim; rational choice theorists had long emphasized the conscious calculation of 'costs' and 'benefits' involved in any political act, as argued by Downs' *An Economic Theory of Voting* (1957) and by Olson's *The Logic of Collective Action* (1965). Nevertheless the strong assumptions underpinning rational choice

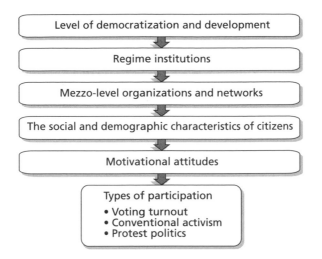

Figure 7.3 *The contextual model of political activism*

accounts of participation, and the empirical evidence supporting these claims, has always proved highly controversial (Blais 2000).

The role of formal institutions has most often been applied to compare electoral turnout across countries or subnational units. In particular, voter turnout studies now commonly include the effect of formal electoral rules, such as those governing the registration and balloting processes used within American states (Wolfinger and Rosenstone 1980; Teixeira 1992) and voting facilities such as the use of weekend polls, and postal or absentee ballots (Pintor and Maria Gratschew 2004; Massicotte *et al.* 2004); the franchise qualifications including the legal minimal voting age for suffrage (Franklin 2004); the eligibility criteria disqualifying felons, immigrants and related minorities (McDonald and Popkin 2001; Miles 2004); the frequency of subnational, national and supranational contests (Franklin 2004); the closeness of party competition (Powell 1980, 1982, 1986); the use of compulsory voting (Norris 2002, 2004); and the impact of the type of electoral system (Jackman and Miller 1995; Blais and Dobrzynska 1998; Blais 2000; Norris 2004).

Moreover the role of institutional rules is also recognized theoretically as an important aspect of other types of participation, although reliable cross-national data coding these rules is usually less easily available. For example, campaign funding laws and regulations which either provide public finance or else cap donations to parties and candidates are likely to affect patterns of grassroots party membership and local campaigning, such as how far parties depend upon raising resources from members or whether they rely upon public funding, and whether they campaign using a network of local volunteers or else employ paid workers (Austin and

Tjernström 2003). The legal requirements governing the taxation status of the non-profit sector, as well as the safety net provided by state-funded welfare services, are also likely to affect levels of volunteer activism within philanthropic organizations and interest groups. The even broader context of levels of democratization, including respect for basic human rights and fundamental freedoms of association, assembly and expression, also set the context for engagement in public life. Major limits on human rights persist in states such as Belarus, Russia, Uzbekistan and Kazakhstan, influencing how far citizens are free to express criticism of those in authority through public demonstrations, protests, and the mass media. Turnout in newer democracies is also affected by the historical legacies of authoritarian regimes, the modes of transition, and the initial 'founding' election (Kostadinova and Powers 2007). Interest has also expanded to consider the plebicitory role of electoral participation within electoral autocracies; states like Belarus which allow multiparty competition although manipulating or rigging campaign coverage and the outcome in favour of the predominant party or leader (Schedler 2006).

By contrast to the macro-approach, the *campaign mobilization* approach has focused attention upon informal mezzo-level institutions drawing citizens into activism. This includes a diverse range of organizations, notably the traditional role of informal political discussion within local communities (Huckfield and Sprague 1995), the activities of political parties in grassroots campaign organizations (Rosenstone and Hansen 1993; Whiteley and Seyd 2002), and the impact of the mainstream media (Norris 2000; van Kempen 2007; de Vreese 2005). The newer development of viral communications and social networking on the Internet also fall into this category, such as through blogging, text messages, Facebook and videos on YouTube, engaging people in transnational social movements and virtual communities (Kluver *et al.* 2007).

The closely related *social capital* approach, associated most closely with Putnam (2000, 2001), has reinvigorated interest in the role of horizontal social networks in civil life (see Chapter 9 in this book). An expanding range of comparative studies has examined participation in voluntary associations and organizations, and the consequences for social trust, tolerance and the ties of sociability which root us to local communities (van Deth 1997; Hooghe and Stolle 2003; Howard and Gilbert 2008; Castiglione *et al.* 2009).

Lastly, another strand of the literature has theorized about the *opportunity structure* for contentious politics, emphasizing the importance of tolerance of dissent by regimes, the strength of group alliances, and the impact of specific catalytic political events in triggering outbursts of mass protests and demonstrations via new social movements (Tarrow 1994; Tilly 1978; Adrian and Apter 1995; McAdam *et al.* 1996).

Re-examining the European evidence

These studies focus on the broader environment conditioning the role of both individual-level resources and social psychological attitudes. To re-examine some of the empirical evidence, comparing individual and institutional contexts, this study uses multilevel regression analysis to analyse patterns of political activism across two dozen European nations. The danger of using ordinary least squares (OLS) regression for analysis is that the standard errors of the regression coefficients can be inaccurate for contextual and cross-level variables, by overestimating the degrees of freedom, and therefore tests of significance can prove misleading. The models in this chapter use restricted maximum likelihood techniques (REML) to estimate direct effects for hierarchical data. Individual respondents are grouped into nation-states. Each nation-state has a different set of parameters for the random factors, allowing intercepts and slopes to vary by nation. In hierarchical linear models, as is customary, all independent variables were centred, by subtracting the grand mean (which becomes zero). The standardized independent variables all have a standard deviation of 1.0. This process also helps to guard against problems of collinearity. The independent variables were treated as fixed components, reflecting the weighted average for the slope across all groups, while nation was treated as a random component, capturing the country variability in the slope. The strength of the beta coefficients (slopes) can be interpreted intuitively as how much change in the dependent variable is generated by a 1per cent change in each independent variable.

For individual-level data, the study draws upon the cumulative file for the European Social Survey (ESS) (see www.europeansocialsurvey.org). This is a rich resource which monitors multiple dimensions of political activism as well as containing a variety of social psychological, structural and demographic characteristics of respondents. The pooled ESS dataset covers three waves in 2002, 2004 and 2006, which contain in total almost 125,000 respondents, a sufficiently large number to compare subsamples, such as non-citizens. Moreover the survey covers respondents living in two dozen European countries, including Nordic, Northern and Mediterranean and post-communist Central European societies. To measure pattern of political activism, the ESS included a number of standard items, listed in Table 7.1, including those which factor analysis revealed fell into three dimensions. (Principal components factor analysis

Table 7.1 *Distribution of political activism in Europe*

European region	Country	Voted	Conventional activism				Contentious politics			
		Voted in last national election	Contacted official	Worked in party or action group	Member of political party	Worked in another organization	Signed petition	Demonstrated lawfully	Boycotted certain products	Worn campaign badge/sticker
Nordic	Denmark	87	19	4	6	22	31	7	25	7
	Finland	73	22	4	7	32	27	2	28	15
	Norway	79	23	8	9	27	38	9	23	23
	Sweden	82	15	4	7	25	44	6	33	13
Northern	Austria	74	20	10	14	23	24	7	20	8
	Belgium	81	17	5	7	21	29	8	11	7
	France	66	16	4	2	16	33	15	27	12
	Germany	74	12	4	4	20	30	9	24	5
	Ireland	74	22	4	5	13	25	6	12	8
	Luxembourg	56	20	4	8	20	25	18	15	5
	Netherlands	79	14	4	5	22	22	3	9	4
	Switzerland	53	15	7	8	15	38	8	28	8
	United Kingdom	65	17	3	3	9	39	4	23	9
Mediterranean	Spain	73	12	6	3	16	24	23	11	10
	Greece	84	14	5	6	5	4	5	7	3
	Italy	82	13	4	4	8	15	11	7	8
	Portugal	68	8	2	4	4	5	4	2	4
Central	Czech Republic	55	19	4	4	10	14	4	8	5
	Estonia	51	10	3	3	4	5	2	4	3
	Hungary	76	12	2	1	2	5	3	5	2
	Poland	61	8	2	1	5	7	1	4	3
	Slovenia	70	13	3	5	2	10	3	4	2
	Slovakia	67	8	3	2	8	21	3	11	4
	Ukraine	83	9	4	4	2	7	14	1	9
	Total	72	15	4	5	15	23	7	15	8

Note: Mean distributions for each nation by each type of activism.

Source: European Social Survey Cumulative file (2002–6). Number of respondents: 124,659; countries: 24.

with varimax rotation revealed that the nine items clustered into three dimensions, as described in the text.)

Reported *voting participation* in national elections engaged on average almost three-quarters (72 per cent) of the European public, although the proportion ranged from just over half the electorate in Estonia, Switzerland, Luxembourg and the Czech Republic up to over 80 per cent in Italy, Belgium, Greece and Demark. The patterns of reported voting closely related to official records of voter turnout, measured as a proportion of the registered electorate, in national elections to the lower house of parliament (see Table 7.3). Although the most widespread type of political activity, as many have observed, voting turnout is also atypical of other forms of engagement.

Forms of *conventional* activism undertaken during the preceding 12 months were monitored by three items which were closely related, including contacting an official (elected or bureaucratic) (15 per cent), belonging to a political party (5 per cent) and working for a political party or action group (4 per cent). Each of these can be regarded as conventional ways to become involved in representative democracy, making higher demands upon cognitive skills and knowledge, time and energy than voting. What these traditional repertoires share is that they are focused primarily upon how citizens can influence representative democracy indirectly (through parties and public officials).

Lastly, activism in *contentious* or *protest* politics during the preceding twelve months was measured by five items which clustered together, including working for another organization (15 per cent), signing a petition (23 per cent), boycotting certain products (15 per cent), demonstrating lawfully (7 per cent), and wearing a campaign badge or sticker (8 per cent). Although contentious politics was once regarded as confined to a small group of students and workers, the distribution shows that all these activities are now more common today than party work. Petitioning and consumer boycotts are particularly popular activities in the Nordic region as well as in many North European societies, while contentious politics was less widespread in the post-communist societies of Central Europe as well as in most of the Mediterranean nations.

How reliable are these survey estimates? Often sample surveys are the only evidence which is available to gauge how many people have experience of certain acts, such as demonstrations and consumer boycotts. But for comparison some independent evidence can be derived from other official sources. Table 7.2 provides national estimates of the number of party members expressed as a proportion of the electorate, derived from official party records, as collated by Mair and van Biezen (2001). The comparison with the estimates provided by the ESS shows a remarkably strong correlation ($R=0.898***$), given the different time periods, the

Table 7.2   *Comparison of party membership estimated in the ESS and in official party records*

Country	Party membership, 2002–6, ESS	Party membership as a % of the electorate, late1990s	Difference
Austria	14	17.7	–3.7
Norway	9	7.3	1.7
Switzerland	8	6.4	1.6
Finland	7	9.6	–2.6
Sweden	7	5.5	1.5
Belgium	7	6.5	0.5
Denmark	6	5.2	0.8
Greece	6	6.8	–0.8
Netherlands	5	2.5	2.5
Ireland	5	3.1	1.9
Italy	4	4.0	0
Czech Rep.	4	3.9	0.1
Germany	4	2.9	1.1
Portugal	4	3.9	0.1
Spain	3	3.4	–0.4
France	2	1.6	0.4
Slovakia	2	4.1	–2.1
Hungary	1	2.1	–1.1
All above	**5**	**5.2**	**–0.2**

Note: Party membership in the late 1990s is measured as a proportion of the electorate.

Sources: Mair and van Biezen (2001).

potential measurement errors for both sources and the different methods of data collection. Comparisons can also be drawn in Table 7.3 from official estimates of electoral turnout, measured as the proportion of the eligible age population who cast a valid ballot in national elections held during the 1990s. Again there is usually quite a high correlation (R=0.611**) between the ESS estimates and official data on electoral turnout, given the difference in time periods, with some notable exceptions where reported voter participation in the ESS survey was either substantially higher than the official average electoral turnout (Hungary, Switzerland and Ukraine) or else substantially lower (Slovakia, Czech Republic).

What factors are more plausibly linked to each of these dimensions of political activism? Without testing all potential components or types of activism identified in Figure 7.3, in this chapter we can examine a

Table 7.3   Voter turnout in Europe

Country	Reported voting, ESS 2002–6	National elections for the lower house of parliament				EU contests
		Official voter turnout in the latest election	Year of latest contest	Electoral system	Compulsory voting	Official voter turnout in EU elections June 2004
Luxembourg	59	91.7	2004	PR	Strict	90.0
Belgium	81	91.1	2007	PR	Strict	90.8
Cyprus	87	89.0	2006	PR		71.2
Denmark	82	86.6	2007	PR		47.9
Sweden	82	82.0	2006	PR		37.8
Austria	75	81.7	2008	PR	Partial (a)	42.4
Italy	83	80.5	2008	Mixed	Weak	73.1
Netherlands	80	80.4	2006	PR		39.3
Norway	79	77.4	2005	PR		n/a
Spain	73	75.3	2008	PR		45.1
Greece	84	74.1	2007	PR	Weak	63.4
Ireland	76	67.0	2007	STV		59.7
Finland	73	65.0	2007	PR		39.4
Czech Republic	55	64.5	2006	PR		28.3
Hungary	76	64.4	2006	Mixed		38.5
Portugal	69	64.3	2005	PR		38.6
Slovenia	70	63.1	2008	PR		28.3
Ukraine	82	62.0	2007	Mixed		N/a
Estonia	51	61.9	2007	PR		26.8
United Kingdom	67	61.4	2005	PR		38.9
Latvia		61.0	2006	PR		41.3
France	67	60.0	2007	Majoritarian		42.7
Slovakia	67	54.7	2006	PR		16.9
Poland	61	53.9	2007	PR		20.9
Germany	74	53.4	2008	Mixed		43.0
Lithuania		32.4	2008	Mixed		48.4
Switzerland	55	48.3	2007	PR	Partial (b)	n/a
Total	72	72.0				47.6

Note: Official voter turnout is measured as the number of valid votes cast expressed as a proportion of the total registered electorate (Vote/Reg) in the latest national parliamentary and European elections. Compulsory voting either strictly or weakly enforced: (a) only in the regions of Tyrol and Vorarlberg; (b) only in one canton. Otherwise none is used. N/a: not a member state of the EU.

Sources: European Social Survey Cumulative file (2002–6); International IDEA Voter Turnout database www.IDEA.int; European Parliament (www.europarl.europa.eu).

simpler two-level model of voting turnout where a representative sample of individual respondents (level 1) is nested within national-level contexts (level 2).

The theory offered in this chapter predicts that *individual structural and social psychological characteristics* will have a significant direct effect on voting turnout. In particular, we expect that those who are more educated and more affluent will also prove more active, as numerous studies have documented over the years since *The Civic Culture*. Education provides cognitive skills, strengthens a sense of internal efficacy (a feeling of competence to engage), and increases knowledge and awareness about public affairs, which facilitate taking part in all types of activism. Educational qualifications are also closely associated with subsequent levels of household income and social status, which function in similar ways. Traditionally, men have usually been slightly more engaged than women in activism within unions and parties, although the voting gap has closed and even reversed in some contemporary societies, and the social capital gender gap depends heavily upon the type of association under comparison (Burns *et al.* 2001; Inglehart and Norris 2004). The age effects are expected to prove curvilinear for voting (peaking in late middle age) with the older generation slightly more engaged than average in conventional forms of activism, while the younger generation is slightly more involved than average in types of protest politics (Norris 2002). Patterns of citizenship also have a direct link to voting turnout, and the proportion of non-citizens who are entitled to vote in each country varies across Europe depending upon legal citizenship and suffrage qualifications, as well as patterns of immigration and the openness of labour markets to migrant workers across national borders.

In addition to all these familiar patterns, the account predicts that *the national context* will also prove important. To simplify the factors under comparison, we can test for the macro-level effects of contemporary levels of economic development (measured by per capita GDP in 2006 in US$) and the historical legacy of democratization in each state (measured by the sum of Freedom House annual index of political rights and civil liberties during the third wave era from 1972 to 2006). The comparison includes some of the most affluent societies in the world, including Luxembourg, Switzerland and Norway, as well as those which have experienced rapid economic development during recent decades (such as Portugal and Spain) and other emerging economies which have moderate or low-income levels today (Hungary and Ukraine). The level of development is expected to increase participation; in part because more affluent societies have populations with higher levels of education and the cognitive skills derived from schooling, as well as more access to a range of independent news media and new information and communication technologies

(ICTs). During the third-wave period, Europe also contains states with very different historical legacies and political traditions, including long-standing stable democracies, interrupted democracies (such as Greece), and consolidating democracies emerging from dictatorships in Spain and Portugal, and from communist party rule in Central Europe. Longer experience of living in democratic states is expected to reinforce habitual forms of political activism, such as voting turnout.

Moreover we can also compare the impact of certain institutions on voter turnout, including whether the state uses a proportional, mixed or majoritarian electoral system for national parliamentary contests, and whether there are any compulsory voting laws, as classified and discussed in detail elsewhere (Norris 2005). We would predict that proportional electoral systems and compulsory voting laws will both exert a positive impact upon voter turnout in national elections, the former indirectly by expanding party choice and the latter directly, where enforced with any penalties, by increasing the cost of non-compliance.

Table 7.4 presents the results of the analysis. As expected, all the individual-level factors proved significant and in the expected direction; voting turnout was indeed higher among the middle-aged and older generation, among those with greater educational qualifications, and among those with national citizenship. At the same time, the traditional gender gap has now been reversed in Europe, with women voting today at slightly higher rates than men (as well as predominating in numbers among the older electorate, due to patterns of longevity). As numerous other studies have documented, political interest and internal efficacy (where someone felt competent about civic affairs) were also significant predictors of whether people cast a ballot. Verba *et al.* (1995) argue that education is a strong predictor of these civic attitudes, by strengthening civic skills and competencies, awareness and information which helps to make sense of electoral choices and issues in public life.

Turning to the contextual variables, the strongest factor proved the use of compulsory voting laws. This may not appear that surprising but it should be emphasized that the type of penalties and, in particular, whether these regulations are actually enforced in practice, does vary from one place to another (Norris 2002). The most stringent enforcement occurs in Luxembourg and Belgium, both countries which we have already seen had the highest turnout of any of the countries under comparison. By contrast, enforcement was far weaker in Italy and Greece. If the convention threshold for evaluating statistical significance is slightly loosened (P> .067), then the democratic history and traditions of a country can also be regarded as important; in general the longer that a country has enjoyed civil liberties and political rights (as measured by the total cumulative Freedom House score on these indices during the

Table 7.4   *Multilevel regression models explaining European voting activism*

	Estimate (beta)	Std Error	Sig (P)
Individual level			
Demographic and social characteristics			
Age (years)	.137	(.001)	.000
Gender (male=1)	−.009	(.001)	.000
Non-national citizenship	−.121	(.001)	.000
Education 9-pt scale	.071	(.001)	.000
Cultural attitudes			
Political Interest	.065	(.001)	.000
Political efficacy	.018	(.001)	.000
National level			
Societal and political context			
Democratic history	.025	(.013)	.067
Level of economic development	−.027	(.021)	.210
State Institutions			
Majoritarian electoral system	−.027	(.014)	.063
Compulsory voting law	.047	(.013)	.001
Constant (intercept)	.732		
Schwartz BIC	105,776		
No. respondents	116,120		
No. nations	19		

Note: All independent variables were standardized using mean centring (z-scores). Models present the results of the REML multilevel regression models. The dependent variable is whether the respondent reported voting in the last national election. Models report the estimated beta coefficient slopes (b), standard errors (in parenthesis), and their significance. Significant coefficients (probability less than the 0.10 level) are highlighted in **bold**.

Source: European Social Survey cumulative file (2002–6).

third-wave era), the greater the level of voter participation. This suggests that the more free and fair elections which a country has held, the more that citizens acquire the habits and party loyalties that encourage voting.

Yet, by contrast, contemporary levels of economic development (measured by per capita GDP in 2006), which might be expected to prove important, proved insignificant in the model. One possible reason is that, although there are some important variations in levels of economic development across the European countries under comparison, such as contrasts between Ukraine and Luxembourg, compared with the rest of the world, even the middle-income post-communist societies in Central Europe have almost universal literacy and relatively high tertiary education. The impact of macro-level education on voting partic-ipation worldwide seems to have the greatest impact in the early stages of societal development, where growing literacy in some of the poorest democracies around the globe, such as Mali and Ghana, provide access to mass media and related information sources (Norris 2003). Once primary and tertiary schooling is widely available to the general public, then educational levels within the general population no longer help to predict societal-level variations in turnout.

This is most clearly illustrated by the particular case of Switzerland, one of the most affluent and well-educated nations in the globe, but with one of the lowest patterns of voting turnout for national elections of any established democracy, in part due to the constitutional power-sharing arrangements used in this state. The type of electoral system was also significant at the lower level (P> .10) but as Table 7.3 showed, most countries under comparison used proportional representation (PR) party list electoral system for national parliamentary elections. There were only four cases of mixed (combined) systems (Italy, Hungary, Ukraine and Germany) and only two cases of majoritarian/plurality electoral systems (Britain and France) under comparison. A broader and more systematic comparison of major and minor types of electoral systems used worldwide showed far stronger effects on average levels of voting participation for the lower house of parliament during the 1990s, with proportional representation (PR) elections usually having about 10 per cent higher turnout than majoritarian systems (Norris 2004: 162). The most plausible reasons are that the broader range of parties typically standing for office and elected to parliament under PR systems expands party competition and voter choice at the ballot box, and the lower vote threshold of PR systems minimizes the 'wasted vote' syndrome, where supports of minor parties, which are destined to lose under plurality rules, decide to abstain.

Conclusions and implications

We can conclude that participation is indeed something about citizens (notably, as the standard model has emphasized, their age, education and motivational attitudes) and also something about elections (such as the institutional and political context) (Franklin 2004). What does this observation imply – especially for the broader issues of the consequences of participation for democratic health and stability? Political activism has always been central to the study of political behaviour, where wide-spread participation is commonly regarded as indicative of a healthy level of public support for the political system. Indeed disquiet about falling turnout during the last decade, coupled with eroding membership within mass-branch parties, has been widely interpreted as an indicator of public disaffection with democratic governance in Europe and elsewhere. Many commentators couple this phenomenon with other indicators – such as low or eroding trust in parliament and politicians – to diagnose signs of civic malaise (Hay 2007). At the same time, outbreaks of radical mass activism and contentious politics, such as violent street riots or occasional outbreaks of people power, are also usually viewed with alarm, as another danger symbolizing a breakdown of the state's capacity to safeguard law and order, or even a phenomenon capable of destabilizing or undermining fragile democratic states.

In practice, however, a glance at some of the persistent outliers quickly reveals that there is no optimal level of participation which ensures stable and effective democratic states. Interpreting the implications for democracy following from the behavioural evidence is far more complex than is often assumed. Political interest and efficacy are important attitudinal predictors of activism but, by contrast, although popular commentators commonly link declining participation to an erosion of trust and confidence in political institutions, in fact the empirical evidence for such a link is often thin or non-existent (Norris 1999b, 2002). Critical citizens who are mistrustful of institutions may become more motivated to become active, in order to reform the state, not less. The evidence for a long-term erosion of voter turnout in established democracies is not consistent, and even trends in basic indicators such as national levels of party membership, trade union membership and partisan identification often display patterns of trendless fluctuations over time, rather than an inevitable secular decline during the era since the Second World War (Schmitt and Holmberg 1995; Pintor and Gratschew 2004; Norris 2002). Much attention has focused upon the supposedly apathetic younger generation of Americans, but newer studies suggest that in fact young people are engaged and active, but in a diverse array of organizations, causes and movements, rather than through the traditional channels of civic activism (Dalton 2008).

Moreover countries such as Switzerland and the United States have persisted over the centuries as some of the most stable democracies around the world, despite the fact that they have experienced consistently low levels of voter turnout over a long series of national elections. There are multiple drivers of the democratization process, including the critical role of power-sharing institutions, and political culture is only one aspect among many (Norris 2008). Moreover the underlying normative judgements about what level of citizen participation is intrinsically valuable, which often colour evaluations of the empirical evidence, remain open to debate. It is commonly assumed that the democratic state which flourishes best is one which encourages moderate participation, as Eckstein asserted over half a century ago, but the systematic linkages between mass political behaviour and the stability of democratic states involves a long and complex chain, and a more cautious interpretation of the broader implications would be wise.

Chapter 8

Cities, Regions and the New Territorial Politics

Romain Pasquier

European states have been confronted for some years by the triple pressure of economic globalization, European integration and the growing desire for autonomy on the part of subnational political communities. As a result of decentralization reforms, the evolution of EU policies and, more generally, the increasing globalization of the overall economic context, the central administrative organs of Western states have lost their monopoly on political initiative (Keating 1998, 2008; Keating and Loughlin 1996; Jeffery 1997; Le Galès and Lequesne 1998; Négrier and Jouve 1998). The growing power of cities and regions in the public policy process is one of the most striking consequences of decentralization processes in most European states, all the more so as 'regionalization' has long been regarded with considerable suspicion by central governments, anxious to avoid any concession to political fragmentation. This desire notwithstanding, the new economic, social and cultural logics to which national governments are increasingly exposed, are contributing to the erosion of the nation-state mythology. Indirectly, but significantly, these developments serve to reinforce both the capacity and the growing legitimacy of the actions taken by cities and regions in Europe.

On the economic front, the growing internationalization of the economy calls into question voluntarist policies of territorial planning, while the promise of a post-Fordist model of production based on the flexible specialization of local units of production suggests the necessity of reinforcing intermediate levels of government (Amin 1994, 2004). On the political level, 'globalization' has tended to accelerate European integration and, with it, the emergence of multilevel governance (Hooghe and Marks 2001; Marks 1996). Central authorities in Western countries have been forced to face the emergence of a rival supranational 'centre', the European Commission, which has sought to establish relations of exchange and cooperation with subnational authorities either through the Community's regional policies or through the institutional representation of these authorities (local as well as regional) in the EU's Committee of Regions (Jeffery 2000; Loughlin 2005).

120

Some analysts have seen in this changing political opportunity structure the framework for a new type of territorial governance, based on the capacity of some cities and regions to create coalitions coordinating an array of public and private actors around a strategy for development (Keating 1998; Le Galès 2002; Pasquier 2003, 2004). The formation of such coalitions, however, requires a particular set of conditions. Institutional, political and economic resources clearly play a role in creating these, but they are not sufficient in and of themselves. Required in addition is a certain understanding of identity, and in particular of shared identity, among the actors in question. We can think of this as an additional resource, on the cognitive dimension, which plays a determining role along with institutional, political and economic resources.

One of the central claims of this chapter is that a new political opportunity structure has emerged for cities and regions in Europe. The building of a polycentric field of action characterized by the erosion of boundaries between public and private on the one hand, and among local, national and supranational authorities on the other – what we might call 'a new age of governance' – can, under certain conditions, provide resources for the definition of common interest and strategies of action for cities and regions in Europe. When they are activated, these resources contribute to the shaping of a new age of territorial governance. Regional and urban identities, where and when they exist, can contribute to the generation of models of collective action leading to the emergence of latent groups and interests, transforming these into active players in a policy community whose members are convinced that they have key interests in common.

We must be careful, however, to note not only the importance but also the limits of this phenomenon. Depending on the way in which collective identities are constructed and on the strategies chosen by state elites, cities and regions do not have similar political capacities across Europe. National policy styles and political territorial cultures can be a constraint or a facilitator of proactive strategies. The object of this chapter is precisely to understand how and why some cities and regions are able to increase their capacity for political action in this new age of territorial governance in Europe. This, we believe, is a critical question at a time when the distribution of power at all levels is being called once more into question.

A new opportunity structure for cities and regions

In this first section, we set out three parameters which change context for action of cities and regions: (a) globalization and the building of a new economic geography; (b) the impact of European integration on territorial actors; and (c) the development of political decentralization reforms in Europe.

Globalization and the building of a new economic geography

Recent decades have brought about a growing interest in the economic performance of regions and cities and, as a consequence, in the forms of subnational governance which are associated with different levels of economic dynamism. Economic dynamism in general has had a strong territorial component over the last two decades (Amin 2004; Brenner 2004; Crouch *et al.* 2003; Rodríguez-Pose 2003). Between the late 1970s and the 1990s economic development has shifted away from the regions of old industrialization and mass production (steel, shipbuilding, the car industry, and so on). The regions with higher growth rates were characterized by low initial levels of employment and value added in manufacturing (in the 1970s), and by an ensuing increase in both indicators. Contrary to what one could expect, it was not services but manufacturing that was the most important component in economic growth. Local and regional systems based on small firms have played a crucial role in this dynamism, both in large urban areas and in more peripheral regions. Through the processes of globalization, economic activities performed in a variety of regions and countries are becoming increasingly integrated into cross-national systems of production.

In industries such as automobiles, electronics and garments, the chain of value-adding activities leading to a final product is organized in global networks creating new interdependencies between firms, industries and labour markets. Although these networks are transnational in scope, they comprise specialized clusters of activities that remain strongly embedded in local industries and communities. Local embeddedness is particularly pronounced with regards to labour resources, which are much less mobile than capital, products and information within the global economy. The interactions between the global dynamics of production networks and the local operation of labour markets and labour market institutions generate new growth opportunities, as local firms can access new markets and resources by connecting to global networks. Global linkages also provide a means to acquire new skills and capabilities, enhancing the value content of local activities and their potential for sustainable growth. Both the quantity and quality of local jobs can potentially be increased in that process. At the same time, global connections might provide an unstable basis for growth and development. Locational advantage and the competitiveness of local firms have to be constantly realigned to the restructuring of global production networks. Moreover, becoming integrated into global networks can divide and fragment local industries and societies, marginalizing those economic actors that fail to develop strong global linkages.

The reasons behind this growing focus on meso- and micro-levels of economic performance and governance and on local production systems are manifold and come from different fields. First are the changes that certain researchers have identified in the evolution of the capitalist system. Aglietta (1977), Boyer (1989) or Scott and Storper (1986) have highlighted the profound transformation undergone by the traditional system of accumulation, based on mass-production and Taylorist principles, which is giving way to a post-industrial system in which flexibility seems to be the key word. Parallel to these structural changes, the dominant economic system of the post-war decades has been challenged from another angle. Advances in technology, information, goods and services transform traditional forms of governance. Economic globalization and the rise of the information society created a space of flows which has altered the traditional conception of space (Brenner 2004). Previously, space was usually conceptualized as distance – from raw materials and markets – and as a matter of cost, which could be compensated by subsidies for producers in disadvantages areas. Different approaches to the study of varieties of capitalism (see Chapter 10, in this book) showed how local societies can provide the conditions for successful development (Bagnasco and Trigilia 1993; Crouch and *al.* 2003; Scott 1998, Storper 1997). The old top-down regional policies, based on central government policies on industry, subsidies, tax incentives and infrastructure, have given way to a decentralized model in which the emphasis is on what regions, cities and localities can do for themselves.

The economic dynamism of a series of regions (Baden-Württemberg, Catalonia, the Third Italy) – whose basic common denominator is the presence of dense networks of small and medium-sized enterprises – caught the eye of researchers. In political science, the 'new regionalism' approach revealed for the first time this new economic trend and the transformation of the state and government (Balme 1996; Keating 1998, 2008). Local economies matter as such but most importantly in relation to the erosion of national models of economic governance or regulation. Localities and regions are becoming more important in Europe as units of the organization of social, political and economic life. If nation-states and national regulations carry less weight, it is not surprising to see in the European context the re-emergence of intra-national territories (Bagnasco and Le Galès 2002; Keating and Loughlin 1996). Economic globalization became a new parameter of the European territorial puzzle in the 1990s. This combination of socio-economic restructuring and economic globalization is posing serious challenges while also offering new opportunities for the development of regions, cities and localities (Le Galès and Voelzkow 2003; Rodríguez-Pose, 2001, 2003). Advances in technology, free flows of capital and goods, and the almost unified access to codified know-how, together with the need to respond rapidly to global competition, have put territories all over the world under considerable strain, facing the alternatives of adapting to the new environment or suffering economic decline. Large metropolitan areas, because of their ability to attract and generate pools of capital, technology and information have been expected to perform better (Le Galès 2002; Sassen 1991).

Thus, one can distinguish two ways in which the global–local question can be approached in European cities and regions. The first is to see globalization as a threat which tends to eliminate autonomy in local affairs and with it the local or regional actors who could offer resistance to the globalization process. From this perspective, local development becomes impossible or marginal as long as international conditions remain unchanged. This way of thinking sees globalization as a threat. The second way of approaching the global–local relationship is somewhat more complex. It attempts to set up a way of connecting the local to the global with the idea that globalization is an opportunity and a challenge to be met and exploited so as to promote local development. Good examples here are cities (Barcelona, Helsinki, Lyon, London, Milano, Paris) and regions (Bavaria, Basque Country, Catalonia, Rhônes-Alpes, Scotland) that have more or less successfully inserted into the new global logic, sometimes in a way that is passive or functional to the global situation, and sometimes exploiting characteristic and individual aspects of societies and districts and their productive networks with a distinctive strategy for competitiveness.

European integration and territorial actors

Since the mid-1980s, European regional policy has been identified as another key variable in the reorganization of public action at the territorial level within the European Union (EU). More generally, the process of 'Europeanization', i.e. the 'processes of a) construction, b) diffusion and c) institutionalization of norms, beliefs, formal and informal rules, procedures, policy paradigms, styles, 'ways of doing things' that are first defined and consolidated in the EU policy process and then incorporated in the logic of domestic (national and sub-national) discourse, political structures, and public policies' (Radaelli 2003), has also been analysed as a new political opportunity structure, providing political and economic resources for regional actors to strengthen their positions vis-à-vis central administrations (Börzel 2002; Elias 2008; Hooghe and Marks 1996, 2001; Pasquier 2004).

Thus, Europeanization can cause a significant redistribution of power among domestic actors and result in institutional change. However, this sort of 'resource dependency model' presents contradictory expectations about outcomes (Börzel 2002; Bourne 2003; Carter and Pasquier 2010b). Some claim that Europeanization, institutionalizing new political arenas and policy networks, creates direct opportunities for regional mobilization and strengthens the regions at the EU level (Hooghe and Marks 1996; Keating and Loughlin 1996). Others argue exactly the opposite: the centralist tendencies of the European integration process reinforcing the centralization of power at the centre, including a centralist institutional decision-making structure to which regional actors have limited access (Weatherill 2005). We shows that within this debate two competing research agendas have emerged which, read together, suggest that European integration has set in motion a dynamic of 'multi-level governance' which appears at one and the same time to both empower and disempower regions (Bourne 2003). These approaches are presented in the form of two strong (and competing) narratives on the impact of European integration on regional governance – the 'de-centralisation of power' narrative and the 'centralisation of power' narrative (Carter and Pasquier 2010b).

The 'decentralization' of power narrative takes as its source the acceleration of integration in the second half of the 1980s and finds its expression in the metaphor of 'Europe of the Regions' or 'Europe of the Cities' (Marks 1996; Hooghe and Marks 2001). This narrative analyses European integration as a new opportunity structure, providing political and economic resources for regions and cities to strengthen their positions vis-à-vis central administrations. In the 1990s, the nature of change brought about by this process was theorized by scholars who studied European integration as having both 'supranational' and 'subnational' effects, the mobilization of which was putting in motion a system of 'multilevel' governance (Hooghe and Marks 2001). In short, this narrative views the multilevel game played jointly by the European Commission with regional actors as a *normative* one. The Commission and regional actors are understood to be engaged in a governance process which seeks to institutionalize relations in ways which will enable both sets of actors to 'bypass' or 'evade' the centre *qua* central government, with a view to strengthening the supranational and regional 'tiers' of the system. This approach has to date driven research in specific ways and has led in particular to the study of four empirical phenomena – the strategy of the European Commission in regional policy design, the implementation of the EU Structural Funds policy, the institutionalization of regional representation at EU level and the transnational activity of the regions.

The second narrative – the 'centralization of power' – is well rehearsed in the literature (Bomberg and Peterson 1998; Jeffery 2005; Weatherill 2005). According to this approach, the deepening of European integration over the years has brought about a gradual and increasing transfer of policy competencies from the member states to the European 'level' with the result that today's EU exercises considerable legislative power over a wide range of public policies. Many of the EU's policy competencies are competencies over which regional governments have legislative or administrative authority at home, as set out in their domestic constitutions (Jeffery 2005: 34) and which have now been transferred 'upwards'. The centralizing effect brought about by this transfer of competencies to the European 'level' creates different types of 'regional deficit' which are the object of extensive study. For example, regions with legislative powers which now share competencies with EU institutions over a number of policy areas – e.g. environment, agriculture, transport – find themselves increasingly 'transformed' within their own territorial jurisdictions from political legislative regional actors (exercising primary powers within their respective territories) into administrative regional agents – implementing EU law and policy legislated upon within EU institutions. Another example is EU cohesion policy through which central governments use structural funds to better control regional authorities' development policies, in particular in central and Eastern Europe (Schimmelfennig and Sedelmeier 2005).

Political decentralization reforms in Europe

The two parameters of change discussed above directly question the European state and its potential reconfiguration. One essential dimension of this restructuring is the decentralization of state functions to subnational levels of government. Based on the persistence of centre–periphery cleavages, the nation-state building has produced resistances and conflicts since the nineteenth century in Europe (Rokkan and Urwin 1982, 1983). Cultural movements and ethno-regionalist parties claim for political autonomy in order to defend the specific cultural and linguistic rights of 'nations without states' (Keating 2008). During the last three decades of the twentieth century, European integration and globalization gave more resources to these regionalist mobilizations relative to the central state elites. This has clearly contributed to the acceleration of decentralization processes in many European countries (Belgium, Bulgaria, France, Italy, Romania, Spain and the UK). On this aspect, decentralization empowers subnational actors so they can more efficiently take part in competing for resources and developing their own assets (Carter and Pasquier 2010a).

After the Second World War, the old welfare state encouraged uniformity and standardization across the national territory in order to ensure there would be no deviation in the standards of services available to citizens of the nation. The aim of an earlier phase of administrative decentralization was to ease the excessive burdens of highly centralized political systems but gave little by way of political decision-making powers to lower levels of government (Sharpe 1988, 1993). By contrast, the political decentralization of the 1980s and 1990s has been much more about devolving political power and giving regional and local authorities greater decision-making discretion. Examples during this period were the establishment of the Autonomous State (El Estado de las Autonomias) in Spain on the basis of its 1978 constitution and the decentralization Act in France launched in 1982. During the 2000s this general shift has continued to increase asymmetrical diversity which can be political, administrative and/or fiscal.

In Spain, the first wave of decentralization involved the transfer of competencies from Madrid to the Autonomous Communities and, in the 2000s there has been a 'second wave' of decentralization from the Autonomous Communities to the provinces and municipalities (Aja 2003). However, relations between the central government and the Autonomous Communities – in particular with Catalonia and Euskadi – remain quite strong, increasing the fiscal decentralization of Spain in recent years. In France, decentralization reforms were running out of steam in the 1990s and this led governments of both left and right to launch a second phase of decentralization in 2003 to 2004 in an attempt to complete and/or correct some effects of the first phase. The Belgian reforms saw the country transform itself from being a classical Jacobin unitary state, dominated by the French-speaking population, to one where the federal state has an almost residual position. In Italy, if the reforms seeking to create a federal state finally failed in 2006, the emancipation of the local and regional authorities resulted from wider processes of reforms in the 1990s. There was a series of referendums which changed the electoral systems at both national and subnational levels, and permitted the adoption of direct elections of regional presidents and mayors. The UK was the last of the large European states to launch a programme of political decentralization (which it called 'devolution') after many years of centralization. Having been a state with a high degree of administrative diversity, devolution has also increased its political asymmetry by setting up devolved elected assemblies with differentiated powers, Scotland and Northern Ireland obtaining primary legislative powers and the Welsh assembly obtaining secondary ones

(Cole 2006). France changed its constitution in 2003 to redefine itself as a 'République décentralisée' and to incorporate the right to experimentation by local and regional authorities, even if the specific statute of Corsica and other overseas territories had already broken with the Jacobin myth. The Scandinavian countries, previously marked by a high degree of homogeneity and uniformity despite the vast area they cover have also been willing to accept some degree of diversity since the 1990s. Even Central and Eastern Europe has been affected by the political decentralization trend (Keating and Hughes 2003; Maurel; 2004, Pasquier and Perron 2008). In line with the EU membership process, several Eastern and Central European countries such as Poland or the Czech Republic, implemented decentralization reforms despite the centralist heritage of communism. However, these reforms vary according to nation-state traditions and political opportunities, ranging from functional regionalization in Bulgaria and Romania to political decentralization in Poland (Keating and Hughes 2003; Maurel 2004).

Towards a new age of territorial governance?

In this second section, we analyse the institutionalization of a new territorial governance characterized by three main elements: (a) the re-emergence of local economies; (b) the rescaling of governance; and (c) the development of territorial capacities.

The re-emergence of local economies

Globalization processes are not leading towards the end of differences, to a space of flows, a global economic order dismantling everything in Europe. Although it is often maintained that one of the trends in globalization is homogeneity (the same products, the same preferences, the same culture all over the world), the reality is that there is great heterogeneity between different places when it comes to opportunities and risks. While globalization opens up opportunities for different European cities and regions it also poses new threats. We can identify four ways in which these new threats are manifested. First, there is the threat of marginalization or exclusion for places or districts which are not, or which have ceased to be attractive and important for the world economy. Now that state protection has been removed, many places have to face the real possibility that they will stagnate, slip backwards or be abandoned. Second, some cities and regions may play a role of subordinate integration in that they will depend on external global actors who do not have roots in the region and who have no responsibility for local society there. Their links with local society are extremely fragile, so they can withdraw their investments when they see more advantageous conditions elsewhere. Third, there is the possibility of economic and social fragmentation, dismemberment and disintegration in certain territorial units, regions or cities. This depends on how those units are inserted into the global system. In some cities this fragmentation can result in a split between the 'globalized' population and that which is not globalized. Lastly, there is an environmental threat caused by the imposition of a development model that is not sustainable. Globalization can also be seen as an opportunity for regions to develop, and this can follow two main lines. First, for some cities and regions it can lead to better access to global resources in terms of technology, capital and markets, which can lead to a rise in the value of endogenous resources. When this happens, globalization is a window of opportunity for places which have strategic capacities that are in demand.

The changing scales point to what one might call the 'paradoxes of territories' (Le Galès and Voelzkow 2003). Economic globalization means an increased mobility of capital and the ability for capitalists to overcome spatial constraints to a certain extent. Hence the domination of local economies by large firms. Paradoxically, this goes hand in hand with an increased sensitivity to territory, especially in the form of cities as possible sites for investment and living. In Europe, regions, cities and localities are not passive spaces where localization takes place; they are more than just passive receptors. Cities and regions (or at least some of them) are structures of differentiated relations which tend to orient the behaviour of different groups of social and economic actors (Storper 1995). The extent to which local industrial communities can take advantage of global connections by engaging in a process of learning and upgrading largely depends on the social and institutional context of local economic activities. As emphasized by a number of approaches to local industrial development, the success of a local production system is based on interrelationships between the social, political and economic spheres, and the functioning of one is shaped by the functioning and organization of the others. The highly publicized case of the Third Italy shows that regional industries that succeed in the global economy have developed a culture of learning and innovation supported by local institutions such as governments, community-based associations and trade associations (Trigilia 1986; Putnam 1993). These institutions have developed formal and informal relations with local firms and workers that sustain a dynamic of continuous improvement and reinforce social ties within the local community. However, Rodríguez-Pose (2001) points out that only a limited number of localities seem to be taking advantage of the new opportunities thrown up by the globalization process in this way.

Above all, the development of global production networks is placing new demands on local elites and policy-makers, who need to redefine their role in relation to changes in the forms and logic of competition (Veltz 2008). At the local level (cities and regions), policies aimed at supporting industries and generating employment are increasingly geared to influencing a broad range of horizontal, location-specific factors that play an important role in economic growth and the international competitiveness of firms. There is growing awareness that restructuring and adjustment are part of a continuous process, and that policy interventions must be systemic, flexible and adjustable. Emphasis is being placed on strengthening collective intangible assets such as R&D, human resources, awareness of industry standards and relations of trust among local firms. Labour market institutions in particular are seen as capable of playing an important role in developing workers' skills, raising standards and contributing to building up intangible assets. Because skills and capabilities are essential sources of competitive advantage, industrial and labour policies appear as increasingly interlinked, reinforcing the need for a territorial approach to policy. Local institutions in cities and regions can help firms – small and medium-sized enterprises in particular – to integrate successfully into global networks, by identifying opportunities and threats in the global environment and supporting the establishment of connections to foreign markets and competencies (Veltz 2008). By such means, they may provide a necessary bridge between the global and the local.

The rescaling of governance

Rescaling is the second dimension of this new age of territorial governance in Europe. Policy regulation contributes to a polycentric context of action. Regional development policies illustrate this evolution well. The institutionalization of new vertical and horizontal policy networks contribute to reinforcing the roles of cities and regions.

The reform of the EU Structural Funds in 1988 is viewed as a turning point in the engagement of cities and regions in the public sphere of EU governance (Hooghe and Marks 2001). Specifically, the operationalization of the principle of 'partnership' at the regional level is seen as bringing together regional actors (public and private) with officials from national administrations and the European Commission. The effects of 'partnership' are complex; on the one hand, and through horizontal relations between public and private actors at the regional level, regional governance is apparently intensifying. New non-hierarchical relations between actors are established independently of pre-existing political relationships (Smith 1996). On the other hand, the partnership principle and the integrated involvement of the Commission in the administering and evaluating of the Structural Funds at the regional level encourages a strengthening of direct relations between local and regional actors and the EU level. This has produced an acceleration of inter-regional cooperation and the diversity and intensification of transnational regional activity (Jeffery 2000; Mazey and Richardson 1993). Cities and regions are increasingly viewing themselves as transnational actors whose economic and political interests are predominantly mediated at the EU rather than the national level. The deepening of integration has resulted in an increase in the number of policy areas over which cities and regions now share authority with the EU – environment, transport, culture and public services. This process has resulted in the establishment of direct links with the EU, as evidenced by the setting up of a number of regional offices in Brussels and the creation of regional associations and networks (Fleurke and Willemse 2006). In order to better follow EU-level decisional processes and negotiations, it is argued, regions require regional offices in Brussels. (The first of these were set up in 1984 and 1985 by the city of Birmingham and the regions of Hamburg and Sarre. There were 54 regional offices by 1993, 140 by the end of 1995, and more than 240 by the end of 2007.) The more that regions are able to mobilize institutional and financial resources, the greater the capacity for representation: for example, the average size of the offices of the Spanish autonomous regions is 11 staff; by contrast, French regional offices are normally no larger than two or three).

As far as inter-regional cooperation is concerned, here too we can find evidence of growth since the 1980s. Two types of association can be identified: those which primarily serve a representative function and those which are 'issue-based'. Representative associations represent sub-state authorities at the EU level and engage in a dialogue with other local authorities, regional governments, national officials and the EU. There are many such networks, such as the Assembly of European Regions (AER) and the Council of European Municipalities and Regions (CEMR), and the (new) network of regions with legislative powers (RegLeg). As was illustrated by the negotiations surrounding the European Convention, these associations at times defend particular ideological and territorial visions of the development of the EU. 'Issue-based' associations of regions normally tend to organize around a specific and shared set of economic and/or geographical interests – but can equally develop global visions around issues. For example, the Conference of Peripheral Maritime Regions (CPMR) initiated a collective campaign undertaken by both regional and local associations during the course of the European Convention to recognize the regional and local tiers of government in the application of the principle of subsidiarity in EU policy-making. We also observe an institutionalization of local and regional activities in European governance. In this regard, the Committee of the Regions (CoR), established by the Treaty on European Union 1993 (TEU) is viewed as the (logical) locus for the institutionalization and consolidation of direct links between the regions and the EU. Acknowledging that internal divisions within the CoR have at times undermined both its effectiveness and its political visibility, research has laid emphasis on the growing importance of the CoR highlighting *inter alia*: the *modus vivendi* established within the committee between local and regional representatives, and in particular between members of its two main networks – the AER and the CEMR; the number of opinions given by the CoR since 1994 which has increased, and continues to do so; the intensification of relations between the CoR and other EU institutions, namely the European Commission and the European Parliament; the increase in networking between cities and regional networks, and local and regional associations; and, finally, the further empowerment of the CoR under the provisions of the proposed Constitution which provides the CoR with new rights in the implementation of the principle of subsidiarity, and specifically, the right of judicial review to protect its own prerogatives.

We can also observe this rescaling through the multilevel transfer of EU governance models and norms. Territorial actors, and particularly urban and regional ones, participate in learning processes through a multilevel transfer of EU norms (Pasquier 2005). Further, this migration of norms, based as it is on the dissemination of new values and practices of territorial governance, is in turn building a new territorial policy 'model' and producing structural changes in the territorial governance of European states. Rather than being passive receptors of stimuli from Europe, local and regional actors and institutions use European policy norms as cognitive resources in order to elaborate and implement their own territorial policies. What we observe is an interactive policy transfer process – which we term 'cognitive Europeanization' – in which 'knowledge about policies, administrative arrangements, institutions etc. in one time and/or place is used in the development of policies, administrative arrangements and institutions in another time and/or place' (Dolowitz and Marsh 2000: 344). Significantly, this process of 'cognitive Europeanization' is an interactive process whereby territorial actors and institutions, socialized in to the principles of action of a European model of governance, are Europeanizing their policies without EU legislation. Regional actors and institutions reappropriate EU norms and use them according to their own strategies and policies. We are clearly in a process whereby 'the Commission serves as a "bourse" of ideas, "inseminating" solutions into national political systems' (Radaelli 2000: 25–9). For instance, we have analysed how the implementation of EU urban and rural development policies have given French, Italian and Spanish cities and regions new cognitive resources – such as vertical partnerships between levels of administrations and horizontal partnerships between the public sector and the civil society – to implement their own policies (Pasquier 2005; Pasquier and Pinson 2004).

The development of territorial capacities

Most analysts today agree that the manner in which public authority is wielded in Europe has evolved considerably. The state acts at the local and regional levels as much as at the national level. This said, however, the relative intensity and importance of these various levels of action remains the subject of considerable debate. Accordingly, any analysis of policy at the territorial level must avoid two pitfalls. In the first place, it is important to avoid overestimating the autonomy of territorial political actors and institutions. Considerable structural constraints continue to handicap their potential for action. At the same time, however, we should not underestimate the political capacity of territorial institutions and actors. The structural handicaps of cities and regions are well known. Cities and regions are intermediate levels that are dependent on other levels of government, and particularly on central government regarding the policies that regulate the implementation of different public policies. Depending on the European state in question, they must compete with the better-established power of other levels (intermediate levels such as the *départements* in France for instance, and/or capital cities). They must also contend with the expertise and administrative capacity of the national administration in the elaboration and management of policies for regional and urban development. Although the structural handicaps under which they labour are real and apply to all, cities and regions are far from homogeneous in their ability to overcome them.

The successful elaboration and implementation of public policy depends on more than just legal authority. Political capacity is, at least in part, a process of mediation in which elites and social groups produce a vision of the world that allows them at once to structure relations among themselves and to define the very 'interests' that they are pursuing collectively (Pasquier 2004). Once achieved, they can mobilize material and cognitive resources in elaborate strategies designed to attain desired objectives. It is this capacity of territorial elites to organize informal relations among relevant policy actors according to a coherent shared vision of desired outcomes that varies significantly among cities and regions. Along with it, the capacity of territorial policy-makers varies to adapt to social and economic change (Hudson 2007).

A city or a region, as such, will have significant influence in the public policy process only to the extent that a coalition of actors takes on itself the definition and defence of the 'territorial interest'. We can define such a territorial coalition as a set of actors coming from both public and private organizations who share a set of common beliefs and engage to a significant degree in coordinated activity in a given time and territorial space. Such a coalition stabilizes political exchange among public and private actors within the region and orients it towards certain objectives. As noted above, however, these regional coalitions are found to vary considerably in terms of their influence, homogeneity, and stability over time. In order to analyse these inter-territorial variations in Europe, we need a concept to grasp the constitution of territorial actors who are proactive in this fashion. For at least a decade now, several authors working on cities and regions have developed the concept of political capacity (Cole 2006; Stone 1989; Keating *et al.* 2003; Pasquier 2004). For us 'regional political capacity' refers to 'a complex process of interest definition, organization and coordination of collective action which enables institutions, public and private groups to regulate a wide range of public problems' (Pasquier 2004: 28). This concept, coming from urban sociology (see particularly the study of Clarence Stone (1993), who defines urban regimes as 'a capacity to govern', i.e. the capacity of actors' coalitions (private and public) to produce collective regulation over long-term periods) moves analysis from formal institutions and resources towards the social construction of logics of action. Capacity building most obviously comprises territorial political institutions, but also involves developing horizontal and vertical relationships based on trust (Cole 2006; Stone 1989). With this concept, we hypothesize that one must understand the political capacity of territorial actors as a socio-political process rooted in an ongoing social construction of territories and centre–periphery relationships. It is rooted too in identities understood as a set of social practices, beliefs and visions of the world, socially constructed, which shape and guide the strategies of territorial actors. Therefore, the capacity of territorial actors results from a complex interaction between inherited practices and beliefs and new dynamics of political change and encompasses both formal and informal institutional processes.

The political capacity of cities and regions can be conceptualized as comprising two closely related but distinct components: territorial models of collective action and intrastate territorial politics. Faced with evolving challenges and opportunities cities and regions do not dispose of identical resources. Over time, the strategies of regional and local elites have resulted in a distinct model of collective action in each city and region. The analysis starts with the examination of production of social identities and collective representations, which facilitate the definition of interests and strategies of actions. Research has shown that in this process new types of institutional actor become prominent and deploy constructions of territory in the development of strategies for regional transformation (Le Galès 2002). Territorial actors frequently use resources and norms as part of this process. Research shows that specific territorial identities can be found across a variety of groups and organizations such as political parties, administrations, trade unions, interest groups and/or firms (Trigilia 1986). At issue is the establishment of a 'positive' linkage between globalization and/or European integration on the one hand, and the different features of the regional territory on the other. For example, European integration can provide a new opportunity structure for social movements and political organizations who defend specific territorial identities and who want to 'modernize' the territorial structuring of their region. The existence – or non-existence – of territorialized ideologies within cities and regions, and their effect on political capacity, is a key element.

For example, faced with evolving challenges and opportunities French regions do not dispose of identical cognitive resources. Comparative analysis of Brittany and Languedoc-Roussillon sheds light on two such models, one largely consensual and the other more conflictual (Pasquier 2003; Smyrl 1997). In Brittany, the stabilization of relations among political, economic and cultural elites within an enduring regional coalition has made possible the elaboration of a regional development project and has forced the state to support it. The Breton regional council in its present form is not at the origin of this model. Rather, today's leaders have inherited the model from the preceding generation. In their hands it has been adapted to contemporary conditions and has allowed regional elites to meet successfully the challenge of socioeconomic change. In contrast, the elites of Languedoc-Roussillon have yet to succeed in overcoming the traditional system of local political mediation. The region remains highly fragmented, with most policy choices strongly politicized. Rather than coming together to pool their resources, each unit of political or administrative power has sought to expand its own political clientele. Competition remains the modal behaviour for elites in Languedoc-Roussillon.

The last component of territorial capacity includes analysis of the institutionalization of different 'styles' of intrastate territorial politics, i.e. the set of rules and policy procedures which shape interactions between cities, regions and central governments. In this respect, territorial capacity depends on the mobilization of networks. This is because political capacity is, at least in part, a process of mediation in which institutional elites and social groups produce a vision of the world that allows them simultaneously to structure relations amongst themselves and to define the very 'interests' that they are pursuing collectively. We can define such a territorial coalition as a set of actors coming from both public and private organizations who share a set of common beliefs and engage to a significant degree in coordinated activity in a given time and territorial space. As noted above, however, these territorial coalitions are found to vary considerably in terms of their influence, homogeneity and stability over time. French regions may lack the constitutional status of German *Länder*, Spanish autonomous communities or even Italian regions, but they have the potential nevertheless to constitute distinct spaces for economic regulation, social mobilization and political relations with the central state. To the extent that regional coalitions are structured around preferences and goals, this can only be the result of a combination of contemporary conditions and shared historical experience. In France, a number of factors contribute to the presence or absence of coalition cohesion at the regional level. Among the most important are: the territorial identity and socio-political cleavages that construct and define regional political space; the framework of exchange among political, economic and cultural elites; and the relations of cooperation or competition of regional-level political institutions with both national and local institutions and with interest groups.

Conclusion

In sum, changes over the last two decades in Europe have led to the creation of an economic, social and institutional panorama characterized by greater complexity, with local levels of governance embedded in regional levels, and these linked in turn to national and supranational levels. All are interdependent and interrelated. The combined effect of globalization, decentralization and of the Europeanization process has been a territorialization of governance and regulation. In the process, the central administrative organs of the European state have lost their monopoly on political initiative. Central states are pursuing their own reorganization by 'deconcentrating' power to its own agents in the field and adapting itself to European integration. Cities and regions, for their part, are also seeking to position themselves in the most advantageous way. The territorialization of this interdependent and interrelated game has clearly produced policy and cognitive changes for cities and regions. Most notably they have developed a set of new local policies (local development) and strategies (para-diplomacy) using economic and normative resources coming from the EU. The impact of change varies among countries, cities and regions in Europe, in particular between Western and

Eastern Europe. Western cities and regions benefit from more decentralized state structures. However, the successful elaboration and implementation of development strategies in this polycentric context of action depends on more than just legal authority. In European cities and regions, political capacity is, at least in part, a process of mediation in which elites and social groups produce a vision of the world that allows them at once to structure relations among themselves and to define the very 'interests' that they are pursuing collectively.

Chapter 9

Culture versus Institutions: Social Capital, Trust and Corruption

Paul M. Heywood and Chris Wood

Concern about public confidence in the political class and civic engagement with the political process is hardly a novel phenomenon. However, both in the established European democracies and in the post-communist countries of East-Central Europe, there are few signs of any arrest to the apparent disillusionment with politics and the political process. As Pippa Norris notes (Chapter 7, in this book), the 2009 European elections saw electoral turnout fall for the seventh time in a row to reach a new low of just 43 per cent across the 27 member states of the European Union (EU-27). In some of the newer member states, turnout was exceptionally low: 19.6 per cent in Slovakia, 21 per cent in Lithuania and 24.5 per cent in Poland. This contrasts sharply with the 1979 elections, when only in Denmark (47.8 per cent), the Netherlands (58 per cent) and the UK (32.4 per cent) did turnout fall below 61 per cent.

To be sure, there may be very specific reasons why turnout should have fallen so precipitously in elections to the European Parliament (EP), which may not reflect any wider sense of disengagement from politics – including the view that such elections are of limited importance given the EP's perceived lack of capacity to exercise significant influence. Moreover, some might argue that falling turnout in elections could signal satisfaction with the working of democracy, and others that some level of healthy scepticism on the part of the public helps keep pressure on politicians to be responsive (see Grönlund and Setälä 2007: 400). None the less, there is widespread acceptance that the so-called trilateral democracies (North America, the EU and Japan) are 'troubled' (Pharr and Putnam 2000) and their citizens disillusioned, based on the evidence of a steady decline over several decades in voter turnout at elections in established European democracies as well as in other forms of conventional political participation (Niemi and Weisburg 2001; Putnam 2001).

A number of arguments have been put forward to explain this decline, ranging from barriers to voting and lack of free time to a growth in competing calls on citizens' interest and engagement. However, by far the most attention has been paid in recent years to an alleged decline in a sense of civic community and trust, encapsulated most notably in concerns about an erosion in 'social capital'. Indeed, it seems easy to point to factors which have contributed to such an erosion, not least the growing sense that political corruption is a serious and increasing problem at both national and European levels and one which has contributed in a significant way to poor governance. A Eurobarometer (European Commission 2009) study of the attitudes of Europeans to corruption, conducted in September and October 2009, found that a strikingly high proportion of EU citizens (78 per cent average) saw corruption as a 'major problem' in their country, up three per cent from a similar survey conducted in 2007 (see Figure 9.1). In just three countries (Denmark, Luxembourg and Sweden) did fewer than half the respondents agree. Those seen as most likely to be corrupt were politicians at national level, followed by officials awarding public tenders and those issuing building permits, then politicians at regional level – although personal experience of corruption remained very low, with just 9 per cent of respondents having been asked to pay any form of bribe for access to services over the preceding twelve months.

Question QB1.1   For each of the following statements, could you please tell me whether you totally agree, tend to agree, tend to disagree, or totally disagree with it.

Option: corruption is a major problem in (OUR COUNTRY).

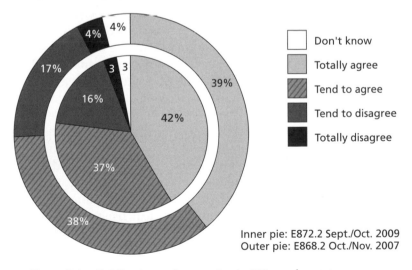

Inner pie: E872.2 Sept./Oct. 2009
Outer pie: E868.2 Oct./Nov. 2007

Figure 9.1   *Public views of corruption in EU member states*

Source: 'Attitudes of Europeans towards Corruption', *Eurobarometer* 72(2) (November 2009).

The gap between personal experience and perception may be explained to some extent by the regularity with which high-profile scandals involving national politicians seem to emerge. In the United Kingdom, for instance, there was significant public disquiet during 2009 over the perceived misuse of expenses claims by Members of Parliament (MPs), many of whom found themselves obliged to pay back large sums of money. In Italy, the alleged involvement with call girls of the Prime Minister, Silvio Berlusconi, further tarnished a personal reputation which was already subject to much speculation about corruption. Elsewhere in 2009 there were major corruption scandals involving national-level politicians in Bulgaria (money laundering and fraud), the Czech Republic (bribery), Poland (gambling bill), Portugal (attempted influence on judiciary), Russia (obstruction of justice) and Spain (party funding), to mention just some.

The seemingly endless stories of corruption involving senior political figures naturally feeds into the sense of a democratic process which is not functioning properly, and in which elected representatives are more concerned with extracting private rents than with serving the public which voted them into office. The response of many involved in the political process has been to focus on the need to repair the key institutions of government (notably, national parliaments, which are widely seen as lacking credibility). Many political scientists, meanwhile, have been prompted by a somewhat different approach, based on the theory that the 'social capital' which has been identified as key to the healthy functioning of democratic societies, is in decline or under threat. Among the key questions raised by these arguments are whether political disillusionment is a symptom of the atomization inherent in modern societies or are Europeans just becoming more critical of their governments? Do corruption scandals encourage citizens to distrust each other as well as politicians? Can trust be rebuilt by improving democracy, or has apathy become embedded in European political culture?

In this chapter, we look first at issues of political trust and explanations for its apparent decline across Europe. We then explore the continued influence of the concept of 'social capital', associated most directly with the work of Robert Putnam, and discuss issues of conceptualization and measurement. In the third section, we explore more closely the relationship between governance and political trust, and emphasize the importance of institutions acting as exogenous variables. The final section concludes, arguing that improvements to government effectiveness, not attempts to influence political culture, are more likely to be effective in tackling citizen disengagement from the democratic political process.

Political trust and participation

Theorists of democracy have long taken it as axiomatic that responsive, fair and effective government goes hand in hand with a population that is willing to become involved in the political process. Political participation is generally defined as actions by ordinary citizens directed towards influencing political outcomes. There are of course many different forms of participation, and levels vary across Europe, with East Europeans and Russians generally participating least and Scandinavians most (Teorell *et al.* 2006: 336, 340). It has been suggested that traditional forms of participation are in decline, being replaced by newer forms such as political consumerism (buying or boycotting goods) and the use of the Internet to contact officials and influence policy (Stolle *et al.* 2005). However, some research suggests this may not be the case. Both old and new types of participation seem to go together and are closely associated with the interest people have in politics (Teorell *et al.* 2006: 354; van Deth 2008).

So what does lie behind political participation? It has long been assumed that levels of trust are important. Where people have trust in politicians and the political process, they tend to see politics as important and relevant for them, and are more likely to get involved. Political trust is usually separated conceptually into trust in people and confidence in institutions. The latter measure avoids the short-term cycles of governments and elections, and is assumed to represent a more stable set of attitudes. Hence it is often used as the best indicator of political trust. Scholars vary in regard to which institutions are seen as most relevant, from simply confidence in parliament to confidence in multiple institutions. The 'Citizenship, Involvement, Democracy' (CID) survey asks respondents about a diverse range of institutions: politicians, cabinet, parties, parliament, the courts/legal system, the civil service, the police, municipal boards, the European Union and the United Nations. People are asked how much confidence they have in each of these, and the evidence suggests that individuals are either generally trusting of most of such institutions, or they are not. This is also true for individual countries: where citizens of a country have confidence in any one national institution, it is likely to be repeated for all others (Zmerli *et al.* 2006: 41).

How much Europeans trust their political institutions varies greatly from country to country. Surveys have consistently found the highest levels in Scandinavia and the Netherlands, where average levels of trust are double those of the post-communist democracies of Eastern Europe, which report the lowest levels (see Figure 9.2). The Iberian countries tend to be a little more trusting, but not by very much (Zmerli *et al.* 2006: 43; Norris 1999: 229). While the countries with the highest levels of political

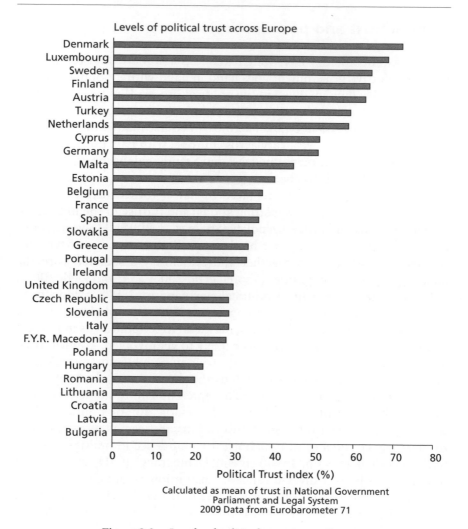

Levels of political trust across Europe

Political Trust index (%)

Calculated as mean of trust in National Government
Parliament and Legal System
2009 Data from Eurobarometer 71

Figure 9.2   *Levels of political trust across Europe*

trust *tend* to be established Western democracies and those with the lowest levels *tend* to be the former communist ones, there are some outliers: both Italy and the UK score quite low, in the former case probably on account of the *Tangentopoli* scandals and continued suspicions about the probity of Silvio Berlusconi; in the latter case, almost certainly on account of a series of issues, such as the so-called 'dodgy dossier' that was used to claim Iraq had weapons of mass destruction, 'cash for honours' and parliamentary expenses. Turkey also scores better than might be expected, particularly when compared to other 'Southern' democracies.

On the whole, however, it appears that Europeans distrust their politicians, have slightly more confidence in their parliaments, and a fair amount of trust in their legal systems (Gabriel and Walter-Rogg 2008: 222–3). Political trust across Europe has shown signs of decline since it first started to be tracked in the 1980s, even before the collapse of communism (McAllister 1999: 192; Norris 1999: 229). Although the decline has been found to be fairly small in most West European states, it holds true virtually across the board (Dalton 1999). Despite recent research showing that the decline may have stabilized (Marien 2008: 13), evidence of the long-term trend at least partly confirms anecdotal evidence that European citizens are becoming less trusting of elites and their political institutions (see Figures 9.3 and 9.4). It is notable and striking that since the democratization of the post-communist states, confidence in the political institutions of some of those countries has fallen precipitously (Klingemann 1999), which may have grave implications for their future political stability.

A particular reason for concern is the belief that low confidence in institutions will lead to low levels of political engagement, which in turn

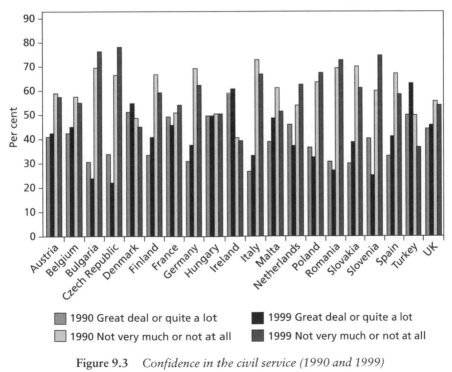

Figure 9.3 *Confidence in the civil service (1990 and 1999)*

Source: authors' calculation from World Values Survey data.

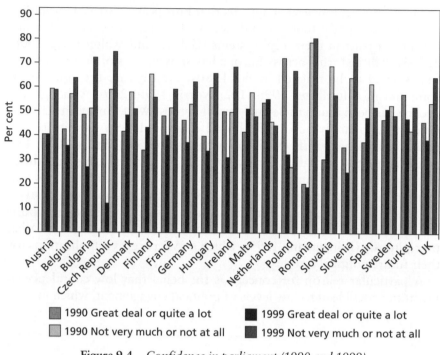

Figure 9.4   *Confidence in parliament (1990 and 1999)*

Source: authors' calculation from World Values Survey data.

will weaken the very foundations of democratic politics. The most important measure of participation, voter turnout, does seem to follow a similar pattern to political trust across Europe – with most of the Scandinavian countries having high levels of both, apart from Finland's curiously low turnout coupled with high levels of political trust. Poland suffers from both the most distrust and lowest turnouts, and some of its post-communist neighbours do not fare particularly well either. The correlation is not perfect, but it does seem to hold for most of Europe (Grönlund and Setälä 2007: 411, 418).

The pioneers of the study of political culture, Gabriel Almond and Sidney Verba (1963), originally argued that trusting, rational and informed people would be much more likely to participate, and that this would foster good governance. Robert Dahl (1971) also assumed for the same reason that a democratic society was unlikely to emerge without political trust. More recent studies have found that confidence in political institutions is strongly associated with democratic satisfaction (Zmerli *et al.* 2006). Such correlations do not demonstrate causality (nor the direction of the relationship, which some see as going in the other

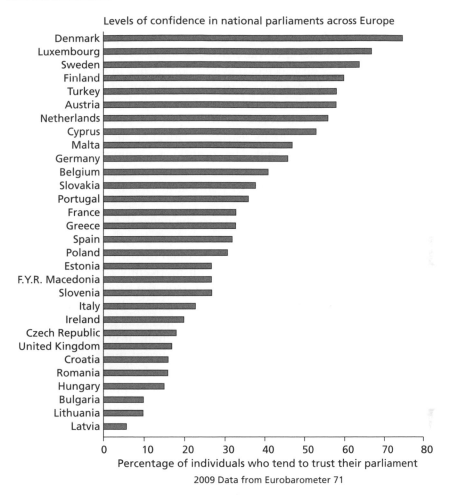

Figure 9.5 *Levels of confidence in national parliaments (2009)*

direction). However, throughout most of Europe, political trust, engagement and effective democratic systems do seem to go hand in hand. Therefore, if citizens across Europe are becoming less confident in their political institutions, as indicated in Figure 9.5, this does not augur well for the prospects of democratic governance.

Why is trust declining?

For a long time, the most widely accepted explanation for the decline of political trust was that it reflected citizens' rational interpretations of institutional performance. Expectations had been raised by politicians' promises of improvements, but these were not delivered: the decisions, outcomes and conduct of politics were deemed to be poor by ever more critical citizens (Gabriel and Walter-Rogg 2008: 219–20). As individuals became increasingly disaffected, they lost confidence in either politicians or the institutions of government to deliver the outcomes they wanted. Such an argument implies the reverse of the causal chain identified by Dahl and by Almond and Verba: by this logic, it was the low quality of institutions (coupled with an increasingly critical public) which was feeding distrust and disillusionment. The solution, according to the new institutionalists, was therefore to improve institutional design and enhance the capacity and accountability of political actors. Better performance would lead to increased confidence.

This response is relevant not only to the general decline in political trust but also to more immediate issues, such as the effects of corruption scandals. Following the 2009 expenses scandal involving UK MPs it was feared that a 'wave of anti-political populism' (Kenny 2009: 508) would lead to disengagement since it would destroy the moral authority not only of politicians themselves, but also of the political system as a whole. Many (especially those who stood to gain) called for a general election to address distrust of existing MPs by replacing them. It was widely argued that in order to rebuild confidence in the political institutions, certain parliamentary procedures and unwritten rules of conduct needed to be tackled to increase transparency. It also became popular to respond to popular clamour by calling for more radical electoral and parliamentary reforms (*ibid.*: 510).

However, it was also recognized by some that greater interaction with politicians, more political education, and greater participation in both politics and civil society might help to increase political trust (Kelso 2009). This argument reflects an alternative approach to that outlined above, which has also been applied to the general decline in political trust. In a large-scale study of Italian regional democracy, Robert Putnam (1993) argued that instead of being based on direct personal experience of institutions and individuals, the root of trust in politics lay in general trends of cooperation and shared norms which developed over a long period. It made sense that cultural values had a role to play since, as we have seen, citizens do not need directly to experience bad governance to feel negatively about officials. In effect, Putnam's thesis revived the 30-year-old theory of political culture, but took it further. Almond and Verba (1963: 178) had argued in the early 1960s that democratic political systems required civic political cultures, that is, beliefs, norms and attitudes that supported participation. Compared with other political cultures, citizens in a civic culture were better equipped to respond rationally to their political system. Almond and Verba distinguished the values and outlooks of citizens in various countries, and explored how these influence behaviour and what kind of political system, in aggregate, they create. Inglehart further developed these ideas in the late 1980s, arguing that political trust was part of a group of attitudes which allowed citizens to believe in and get involved in political processes, thereby creating an environment where effective and stable democracy was more likely to take hold:

> viable democracy does *not* depend on economic factors alone. Specific cultural factors are crucial, and they in turn are related to economic and macropolitical developments ... Stable democracy reflects the interaction of economic, political, *and* cultural factors. (Inglehart 1988: 1220 emphasis in original)

The renaissance of an interest in culture in the study of politics went alongside a broader critique of liberal conceptions of citizenship, including an emphasis on strengthening participatory attitudes and common values. The most notable exemplar of the trend was Putnam's thesis on the decline of civic life in America, outlined in his 2000 publication, *Bowling Alone*.

Social capital

Putnam argued that sports clubs, trade unions, religious groups, professional societies and all other forms of association were the key to civic life and ultimately civility in America. Membership of such associations, which had been very high in the nineteenth century (de Tocqueville 2000) and even up to the 1960s, was now in drastic decline. This reflected a drop in levels of 'social capital' across America, which would, he argued, make people more atomized, less involved in their societies, and less willing and able to participate in political life (Putnam 2000). The 'decline thesis' was widely taken on board in America and across the Western world, even where there was little evidence for a similar decline – as in Germany and the UK (Offe and Fuchs 2002; Hall 2002). Putnam's theory of what lay behind this trend was seen by many also to provide the basis of a potential solution.

His original argument was that social networks, common values and levels of trust between strangers in each region of Italy best explained how well governments worked. Thus, it is 'trust, norms and networks that can improve the efficiency of society by facilitating coordinated actions' (Putnam 1993: 167). Rather than the design of the institutions themselves, or socio-economic factors such as economic equality, modernization, ethnic diversity or individual wellbeing, it was social capital that led to people cooperating with each other and participating in the political process, thereby making democracy work. Where these factors were lacking, people distrusted each other and their politicians, institutions failed to govern efficiently or democratically, and corruption was likely to set in. There was a clear model here, with levels of social capital directly influencing the trust people had in public officials and institutions, which in turn conditioned politicians either to work efficiently towards common goals or to work for factional or selfish interests.

Putnam based much of his work on the membership and proliferation of voluntary organizations – part of the 'structural' rather than 'attitudinal' side of social capital – because relevant data were easy to find (Putnam 2001). In areas with high social capital, he argued, people are much more likely to join or form associations, in which they could learn to work together, building more social capital and forming networks which would allow them to participate in social and political life. Where there is no history of voluntary associations, democracy tends not to work. However, these claims are contestable. Voluntary membership in most types of organizations appears only weakly related to other measures of social capital (as discussed above). Moreover, there is at best only weak evidence for a relationship between membership of networks and either political involvement or confidence in institutions (see Uslaner 1999; Hooghe 2003; Zmerli *et al.* 2006; Delhey and Newton 2005).

Social and political trust

Research into trust and its socio-political impact was established long before social capital theory. Indeed, in measuring trust between strangers, most surveys still rely on the question originally used in 1948 to study post-war Germany: 'Generally speaking, would you say that most people can be trusted or that you can't be too careful in dealing with people'. This question was used to measure the 'generalised' social trust between strangers, as opposed to particularized trust which exists between insiders of specific groups (Delhey and Newton 2005: 311). It has been claimed that citizens who are generally trusting will also trust their politicians. Inglehart (1988), for instance, argued that along with a host of other factors such as economic development and education, trust between strangers and other cultural assets contributed to improvements in the political system. His view was that a 'culture of trust', consisting of both types of trust, was very important to democracy (see also Inglehart 1999). Ken Newton (1999) has also argued that social trust leads to good governance, and that the relationship is reciprocal, so governments can help to create trusting populations. He further argues, like Inglehart, that social and political trust are 'two sides of the same coin' (Delhey and Newton 2005), making it difficult to identify causality.

However, although social and political trust often seem to go together, research results have been inconclusive, with some finding at best only a weak association between the two (Kaase 1999: 1–21; Norris 2002: 160; Delhey and Newton 2003: 93–137). Newton himself has collected data showing little evidence of a link, and has highlighted an important exception which goes against the general trend. In Finland, as in most of Europe, political trust has been in decline, but social trust and associational life seem to remain very high (Newton 2001: 210). This has led some to abandon social capital theory because of 'poor empirical support' (Zmerli and Newton 2008: 707; see also Rothstein 2004), and some to argue that Putnam was wrong about the relationship between governance and social capital.

Few scholars still subscribe fully to Putnam's causal model, though many still argue that trust does play some part in contributing to effective democratic governance. Those who have found evidence for a relationship tend to think that it is political, rather than social, trust that is more important (Gabriel and Walter-Rogg 2008: 238; Delhey and Newton 2005). While the two types of trust may appear to be linked, albeit often weakly, they may simply have common antecedents (such as certain norms or attitudes) which feed into both clusters (van Deth 2008). For example, Zmerli *et al.* (2006: 60) argue that the key common factor is overall life satisfaction, which feeds into political confidence and supports social trust and satisfaction with democracy, whereas community attachment primarily promotes social trust, and municipal attachment supports satisfaction with democracy.

In the case of the post-communist countries, the onset of democratization saw a dip in recorded levels of social trust, although there is evidence that such trust has started to rise again in more recent years where democratic institutions have become more stable. It is certainly plausible that the establishment of more formal democratic mechanisms could lead to lower levels of social trust, since the need for people to trust and rely on each other to create collectively beneficial outcomes declines as responsive and accountable systems are created to do this instead (Letki and Evans 2005: 525; Warren 1999). A similar argument has been made in regard to state intervention: if people trust in and rely upon the government to provide solutions to their problems, they may allow the social ties that would otherwise be necessary to wither (Coleman 1990: 302–4; van Deth 2008). However, this does not fit well with the evidence from elsewhere, given that it is the Scandinavian countries with the largest welfare states that generally manifest high levels of social trust.

Given the time and effort devoted to studying the issue, it is perhaps surprising then that there is no accepted general theory of trust. A yes/no answer to the original question is often used and accepted as a good measure of generalized social trust (see Uslaner 2002; Delhey and Newton 2005), but recent surveys have produced more consistent and valuable data by using more questions and a scale rather than a binary answer. The European Social Survey (ESS) and the Citizenship, Involvement, Democracy (CID) survey both now measure social trust by using three questions and an 11-point scale (Neller 2008; Zmerli and Newton 2008). Overall, these data suggest that in contemporary Europe, social trust is highest in Scandinavia and the Netherlands and lowest in Eastern Europe, mirroring variations in political trust (Zmerli *et al.* 2006: 40). Although only a weak positive link has been found between social trust and satisfaction with democracy, the former has been shown to be fairly well associated with confidence in political institutions throughout Europe (*ibid.*). A 'tight three-cornered syndrome' linking the two types of trust and democracy has therefore been proposed (Zmerli and Newton 2008: 719), although it has been claimed, especially in studies of European cases, that this finding may be biased by those countries which score highly on all three. Removing these cases – sometimes referred to under the banner of 'Nordic exceptionalism' – reduces the level of correlation, but links do still seem to be present (Delhey and Newton 2005; Uslaner and Badescu 2004).

Governance, political trust and corruption

Despite the popularity of the social capital model, it has always had its critics, and the debate over the relationship between social trust, political trust and democracy has not been settled. Even Almond and Verba (1963: 224–5) were never convinced that the causal direction always ran from social trust to participation to democracy, arguing instead that this only happened in certain countries.

In fact, there is a growing body of evidence which supports the idea that if there is a relationship, it works in broadly the opposite direction, so that political factors impact on levels of social trust. If levels of social capital are maintained over generations, it seems likely they are based on something more than just individual characteristics. Inglehart (1999: 88), for instance, argues that country-level factors are important because social trust is a 'relatively enduring characteristic of given societies'. Others presume that contextual factors must matter because they direct the way people interact, and that therefore such interactions are the basis of social capital (Books and Prysby 1994; Schmitt-Beck 2008: 167).

Political cultures must at least partially be created by the processes of government, politicians themselves are often told they must act as role models, and political systems should involve checks on the abuse of power. Where individuals or institutions are perceived as failing, such as during corruption scandals, it is damaging to both politics and society – alienating and isolating people.

A recent study by Neller (2008) indicates that measures of good governance at the country level are, along with social equality, the most important factors influencing individual levels of social trust. Neller used the World Bank's data on governance, including measures of participation, stability, effectiveness, accountability, rule of law and 'control of corruption' and argued that, in countries with good results, citizens had more positive experiences of political institutions and actors, leading them to become more trusting.

It makes intuitive sense that lived experience influences how much we trust each other (Uslaner 1998: 331–68). Similarly, other studies have concluded that democratic governance must be able to create social trust. After all, the democratization of both Spain and Portugal took place despite low levels of social trust in both countries (Muller and Seligson 1994: 635–52). It has also been suggested that not only does democracy make people more trusting of politicians and so creates social capital, but also that the social capital that is created is less likely to be of the 'bad' type: anti-democratic phenomena such as corruption are hence doubly unlikely to occur (Warren 2001; della Porta 2000). A two-way relationship seems most plausible: social capital helps bolster democratic governments, but good institutions can foster a more sociable culture. It is likely that the top-down effects occur because such institutions prove they can be trusted, and this trustworthiness then has positive effects for social trust. If this is the case, we need to understand how the quality of democratic governance can create or destroy political trust.

However, if an effective political system is a root of both forms of trust, then changes in government institutions must be shown to influence political trust. The two are certainly correlated: studies have shown a strong link between satisfaction with democracy and confidence in political institutions (Zmerli *et al.* 2006; Zmerli and Newton 2008). The most logical explanation for this seems to be the original explanation given for a decline in political trust: citizens gain or lose confidence in institutions on the basis of how those institutions perform in practice. This can happen either gradually over time or quickly as a result of specific events. Political problems in the 1990s, including corruption, were behind the collapse in Finnish political trust, even while social trust remained very high (Newton 2001: 210). The most important factors influencing political trust are the belief that the government is responsive to people's needs, as well as satisfaction with both the sitting government and the overall system of democracy (Gabriel and Walter-Rogg 2008: 238). These factors are even more important than the type, or longevity, of political system, or a host of other socio-economic or cultural factors.

Pippa Norris (2002: 160, 164) found evidence of links between social capital, democratization and good governance, but no links between social capital and political trust. As in the Finnish example, other countries in Western Europe have experienced a general decline in political trust while social trust in some areas has remained high. This suggests that the quality of public services and governance is more important to levels of satisfaction. Specific bad experiences of democracy – such as of corruption – lead to political distrust:

> support for the political system among citizens seems to reflect, quite accurately, independent judgements of the actual performance of regimes in terms of the level of democratization ... where governments do not deserve trust, then it is indeed often absent. (Norris 1999: 231)

Where people experience corruption, it seems obvious that they should not have confidence in officeholders, but high-level corruption usually only directly affects small numbers of people, who are often interconnected. In these cases, the media has an important role to play, particularly given its tendency to sensationalize scandals. Certainly, perceptions of corrupt governance seem to have a significant effect on political trust. A reciprocal relationship between the two may spiral into a vicious circle of declining confidence and an increasingly corrupt system (della Porta 2000; Heywood and Krastev 2006). A classic example is Italy, where numerous scandals in the 1990s led to a crisis of confidence in government. However, such dramatic decline may be the case only where perceived levels of corruption start from a low base. Where corruption has become deep-rooted and endemic, the public seems simply to shrug it off as normal (Uslaner and Badescu 2004). As Italians became used to the idea that their politicians would act corruptly, levels of dissatisfaction dropped (della Porta 2000: 209–10), and there was little apparent long-term impact on standard measures of political participation such as turnout at general elections. Nonetheless, it does seem that in general, when governing institutions do not live up to expectations, political trust falls – certainly in the short term.

As well as arguing that direct experiences of democracy lead to changes in levels of political trust, Norris (2002) also claims that these can affect social trust. Bo Rothstein (2004) agrees that experiences of interaction with public officials and institutions are important and that, alongside general perceptions of the quality of governance, these explain levels of social trust. In particular, corruption scandals will lead both to distrust in politicians and a decrease in social trust more generally, as people assume that if even public authorities cannot be trusted, then no one else can either. It is therefore very important that institutions should be perceived to be effective and fair. Claus Offe (1999) offers a similar focus, arguing that submitting to the rules of democratic institutions leads to shared aims and values, and hence generates social trust. Honesty in the actions of our politicians may contribute to how individuals interact in our society, partly because they can act as role models.

Conclusion

Whatever their effects on the other values people hold, research indicates that political factors hold the key to political trust. How the performance of institutions is judged by the public, which in turn appears inherently linked to institutional design, certainly seems to be one of the paramount elements in determining levels of political trust:

> Results strongly support the superiority of institutional explanations of the origins of political trust, especially micro-level explanations, while providing little support for either micro-cultural or macro-cultural explanations. (Mishler and Rose 2001: 33)

For sure, citizens can get used to a certain level of corrupt governance and may not always respond to political changes in the way we expect them to – as has arguably happened in Italy and may be occurring in some of the former communist countries. On balance, however, it seems that the quality and effectiveness of democracy is a good predictor of support for democracy, better than for example the extent of bonds between citizens. If this is the case, then logic suggests that the recent decline in political trust across most West European countries may be reversed by ensuring that institutions are perceived to be more effective, fair and accountable, and by involving the public more in processes of government.

To return to the issues raised at the start of this chapter, declining turnout at elections and falling levels of interest in politics as a whole may reflect a rational assessment on the part of citizens that they actually lack the capacity to exercise genuine influence. In regard to the EU, it has often been observed that the lack of a 'demos' has generated a so-called 'democratic deficit'. However, it seems that even at the national level, citizens feel that their governments and the political class in general are unresponsive to their demands and generally unable to deliver on the promises they make. Such trends are visible across the whole of Europe.

None the less, there remains a clear divide in Europe between the newer and older democracies. As well as lower levels of all types of political participation, the newer democracies tend to have less social involvement, with people less civically minded and showing lower levels of social trust (Montero *et al.* 2006: 437). This does not mean that the relationship works the other way around, however: in specific studies of these countries, even less support has been found for social capital theory (Letki 2004: 665–79; Letki and Evans 2005: 515–29; Mishler and Rose 2001: 30–62). A more plausible explanation is the lack of genuinely effective, accountable and fair democratic institutions, procedures and politicians in some of these countries, which has caused difficulties, along with the fact that civic political cultures take time to become established. There are indeed some signs from post-communist countries that the decline in trust and participation that first followed democratization is being reversed, and consolidation of democracy may be leading to a gradual re-emergence of social trust (Catterberg and Moreno 2006).

In the account outlined here, the performance of democratic institutions is more a cause than a product of effective engaged citizenship. The movement towards democracy is sometimes found to be significantly related to political involvement and trust, but it is likely that only stable long term democracy will really make a difference. It is clear that in the short term, whatever the context, it is the general effectiveness of institutions that makes them trustworthy. Rather than trying to reform the cultures of European societies from the bottom-up, rejuvenating democracy and good governance may be a more effective strategy to follow. Otherwise widespread disillusionment with the political process may assume an unstoppable dynamic.

Chapter 10

Varieties of European Capitalism and their Transformation*

Bob Hancké

European capitalism, according to the conventional wisdom, is very different from the wilder forms of capitalism found across the Atlantic. It incorporates a strong sense of social justice with a larger role for the state and for regulation in the economy, without necessarily leading to a less efficient outcome in terms of growth and productivity. The key ingredient is the institutionalized balance of power between capital and labour, which follows from their mutual dependence: capitalists need the skills of workers and workers need investment in new sophisticated machinery by capitalists in order to bring about economic growth. That mutual dependence has led to institutions which make sure that economic decision-making, from the firm to the macro-economy, incorporates both capital and labour.

While this broad picture is not without merit, things are, in fact, considerably more complicated. Instead of one type of European capitalism, we have, over the last three decades, discovered two or even more (Hall and Soskice 2001; Amable 2003; Whitley 1999; Crouch 2005), and realized along the way that such diversity in socio-economic arrangements has probably always been a defining characteristic of the political economy of Europe (see, e.g. Shonfield 1965; Piore and Sabel 1984; Zysman 1983; Berger and Piore 1981). German capitalism always was different from French, Italian or British capitalism – and may well have become even more so. And the many small economies, predominantly located in North-West Europe, developed their own neo-corporatist model over the last century (Katzenstein 1985), while the Scandinavian economies combined that with political dominance by social democrats,

* The material in this chapter is in part based on the introduction to Hancké, Rhodes and Thatcher (eds), *Beyond Varieties of Capitalism: Conflict, Contradictions and Complementarities in the European Economy* (Oxford University Press, 2007), and on joint research with Alison Johnston and with Lucia Kurekova. The usual caveats apply.

broad encompassing trade unions, and a universal welfare state. Even though all of these economies are now closely linked to each other through trade, monetary union and single market regulation, and many governments in Europe have been looking at each other for institutional solutions to the problems of economic governance they face, the different countries still retain a distinct character that reflects the different organization of business, and the relations between capital, labour and the state in the economy.

This chapter has three goals: the first is to make sense of this surprising finding; the second to understand how European (monetary) integration and eastward enlargement have changed the basic parameters of European capitalisms; and the third to assess the future of this capitalist diversity within Europe. The chapter is organized around those three questions. I start by developing the basic analytics underlying capitalist variety, building primarily on the 'varieties of capitalism' (VoC) view developed by Hall and Soskice (2001) and how that could play out in Europe. The sections that follow, in turn, examine three exogenous shocks to the different political–economic systems in Europe – the Single European Market, Economic and Monetary Union (EMU) and enlargement – and assess their impact on pre-existing diversity. The emphasis here is on analytics rather than description: the key texts referred to in the chapter, as well as newspapers such as the *Financial Times* and *The Economist* offer a wide array of empirical material that can be explored.

'Varieties of capitalism' – the basics

The VoC approach identifies capitalist production regimes, relatively coherent institutional arrangements within which firms pursue their goals of making profit. It starts therefore axiomatically with the firm in the centre of the analysis, treating it as a relational network: the firm, operating in its markets and other aspects of the relevant environment, is institutionally embedded. These institutional frameworks, in turn, are mutually attuned in systemic ways, leading to institutional complementarities, and confer comparative and competitive advantages to countries, which are reinforced through specialization in rapidly integrating international markets. What emerges, in ideal–typical form, are two (or more, but at least two) institutional equilibria, one where coordination takes the form of contractual relations (liberal market economies (LMEs)) and another relying on strategic forms of coordination (coordinated market economies (CMEs)).

Two actors are therefore crucial in this analysis: business and (organized) labour. The first lays out the basic matrix of a capitalist system: in capitalism, capital rules, but it is not necessarily always the same everywhere, and often it has to play within a framework of rules set by organized labour through trade unions and their political allies in social and Christian-democratic parties. There is a vast difference, for example, between German associational business governance through collective organizations, and atomized business governance in the UK, where firms compete directly without significant collective representation beyond government lobbying. In the first, firms may recognize the benefits of collective labour organization in strong industrial trade unions in terms of social peace, predictability of wages and skills formation, while in the second trade unions and employers find themselves in a zero-sum arrangement: what one gains is at the expense of the other.

By placing the firm at the centre of the analysis, VoC explores capitalism from the vantage point of what it considers as its central actor – business. Where other perspectives have focused on descriptive macro-level attributes, and to a large extent have read the shape of markets and the nature of market participants as a function of those macro-structures, VoC instead starts with the analytics underlying the coordination problems that firms face in their strategic environment. A capitalist economy, according to VoC, is riddled with information and hold-up problems: how do owners know that managers maximize profits, managers that workers perform to the level of their abilities, and workers that managers will not fire them after they have put in their effort?

The solution to these potentially debilitating information asymmetries is offered by the historically given institutional frameworks within which management finds itself. Firms are permanently exposed to changing markets – product markets which structure relations between firms and their customers; labour markets where workers and management meet; and capital markets which provide firms with capital – and the governance of these markets takes very different shapes in different capitalist economies. Labour markets in Germany, Sweden and other countries in North-Western Europe, for example, are highly structured arrangements, where strong employers' associations meet strong trade unions and collectively negotiate wages. Capital provision has, up until very recently, been organized through banks in those countries, and even if international investors have made a dramatic and massive appearance on these capital markets over the last decade, the relations between firms and banks remain highly coordinated. Compare this with the dispersed shareholder systems associated with the City of London and Wall Street, or with the loose hire-and-fire labour market regulations in most Anglo-Saxon (but very few continental European) economies, and the differences are clear. Firms in these two types of systems do not operate in the same labour and capital markets.

This is not a coincidence: it makes little sense to link long-term capital provision along the lines of what banks usually provide to short-term, deregulated labour markets or vice-versa. Long-term investors are usually very willing to invest in the provision of specific skills for workers and accept that regulated labour markets are a useful way of doing so. Nervous institutional investors such as mutual funds, on the other hand, are loath to sink capital into a long-term training project with uncertain (and often even longer-term) payoffs and that ties their capital to the effort and skills of workers. The crucial issue is that once labour and product markets are linked in such systemic ways, the options for a company in terms of product markets are considerably narrower as well. Building machine tools in a competitive way, for example, requires that both employer and employee invest in skills that further a deep knowledge of the technology deployed and of the type of customers that would want to buy such complex capital goods. Specific skills and long-term capital are combined, in other words, in ways that produce important competitive advantages in relatively narrow market niches, where long-term, relationship-specific links between producers and consumers emerge.

VoC systematizes this insight into a key argument: the presence of several 'correctly calibrated' institutions that govern different markets determines the efficiency of the overall institutional framework. This argument for the existence of 'institutional complementarities' implies that for a framework to have the desired strong effect, the constituent institutions in the different markets – between labour relations and corporate governance, labour relations and the national training system, and corporate governance and inter-firm relations – reinforce each other. The tightness of the links between these institutional complementarities linking institutional subsystems determines the degree to which a political economy is, or is not, 'coordinated'. Coordinated market economies (CMEs) are characterized by the prevalence of non-market relations, collaboration and credible commitments among firms.

The essence of its 'liberal market economy' (LME) counterpart is one of arm's-length, competitive relations, formal contracting and supply-and-demand price signalling (Hall and Soskice 2001; Hall and Gingerich 2004). VoC argues that these institutional complementarities lead to different kinds of firm behaviour and investment patterns. In LMEs, fluid labour markets fit well with easy access to stock market capital, producing 'radical-innovator' firms in sectors ranging from biotechnology, semi-conductors, software and advertising to corporate finance. In CMEs, long-term employment strategies, rule-bound behaviour and the durable ties between firms and banks that underpin patient capital provision predispose firms to 'incremental innovation' in capital goods industries, machine tools and equipment of all kinds. While the logic of LME dynamics is centred on mobile assets whose value can be realized when diverted to multiple purposes, CME logic derives from specific or co-specific assets whose value depends on the active cooperation of others (Hall and Soskice 2001; Hall and Gingerich 2004).

The persistence of capitalist diversity is largely attributed to the 'positive feedbacks' referred to above: the different logics of LMEs and CMEs create different incentives for economic actors, which, in turn, generate different politics of economic adjustment.

> [I]n the face of an exogenous shock threatening returns to existing activities, holders of mobile assets will be tempted to 'exit' those activities to seek higher returns elsewhere, while holders of specific assets have higher incentives to exercise 'voice' in defence of existing activities. (Hall and Gingerich 2004: 32)

In LMEs, holders of mobile assets (workers with general skills, investors in fluid capital markets) will seek to make markets still more fluid and accept further deregulatory policies. In CMEs, holders of specific assets (workers with industry-specific skills and investors in co-specific assets) will more often oppose greater market competition and form status-quo supporting cross-class coalitions (*ibid.*: 28–9). Globalization thus reinforces this logic of divergent adjustment (Hall and Soskice 2001; Gourevitch and Hawes 2002). Since foreign direct investment (FDI) will flow to locations rich in either specific or co-specific assets, depending on the sector or firm-specific requirements that investors are searching for, globalization will often reinforce comparative institutional advantage. CMEs and LMEs are therefore likely to be located at different points in international production chains: high value-added, high skill-dependent, high-productivity activities will tend to remain in the core CMEs, while lower value-added, lower-skill, price-oriented production will relocate to lower-cost jurisdictions.

The final step in the argument therefore links the development of these coherent institutional frameworks to the processes of economic integration associated with globalization and European integration. It builds on two key insights in classical political economy. Ricardo's theory of comparative advantage suggests that if two trading nations specialize in what they do relatively better, the overall outcome will be beneficial. VoC suggests that in today's world the intricate institutional frameworks in different capitalist economies also confer such comparative advantages. Adam Smith's idea that the division of labour is determined by the extent of the market – the larger the market, the more market participants specialize – is the second. Therefore: since economic integration increases the size of the market, nations will specialize according to their comparative institutional advantages.

Varieties of capitalism in Europe

There is more going on in Europe, of course, than this simple CME–LME dichotomy suggests: countries such as France, Italy, Spain and Greece have or used to have large state-controlled industrial and credit sectors. Yet in the framework above, the state, does not really play an important part. That begs the question to what extent a framework that is built on the juxtaposition of strategic–associational and atomistic market governance can make sense of economies that rely heavily on ownership and regulation by the state? In addition, how do the new market economies in Central Europe fit in this picture? Even if we accept that economic actors adjust their behaviour according to the institutional framework they are embedded in, these frameworks were built through trial and error, conflict and institutional imposition over periods that ranged from several decades to several centuries; two decades (since the fall of the Berlin Wall) may simply not be long enough for such processes to play themselves out. In addition, the Copenhagen accession criteria made sure that a large part of the political–economic choices in Central Europe were conditioned by the views of the EU and its existing member states in 1994. Since the new member states in Central Europe are the subject of a section on their own below, I refer to that section and especially the conclusion of this chapter which will follow the presentation of all the relevant material.

The Mediterranean economies, on the other hand, pose a direct problem for VoC, precisely because they have on the whole been democratic–capitalist economies since at least the Second World War – in other words, as long as Germany, Sweden or Ireland. One of the ways to make sense of the differences between the Mediterranean Mixed Market Economies (MMEs) and CMEs or LMEs is to start from the different role of the state in those economies. As Molina and Rhodes (2007) point out, MMEs can perhaps best be understood in a two-tiered framework, in which firms attempt to coordinate the production of collective goods among themselves, but are forced to rely on the state to compensate for gaps in the institutional framework which preclude them to deliver those autonomously. In MMEs, in other words, the state is an integral part of the variety of capitalism, because it oils the machine at moments when institutional deficiencies would make it become stuck. Building on this insight which follows from an analysis of Italy and Spain, Hancké *et al.* (2007) reinterpret the VoC typology by bringing in both state and labour in addition to the organization of capital. This slightly wider perspective is useful, since it makes clear that the CME–LME distinction led to the assumption that the state was not a crucial actor in the original framework: in both types of capitalism, relations between the state and the rest of the economy are more arm's length today, often involving broad framework arrangements instead of ownership or micro-management through detailed regulation. France, Italy and Spain each have, in different ways, a state that has played and often still plays a central role in the economy, despite decades of liberalization and privatization.

These different capitalist models – coordinated, liberal and mixed-market economies – have faced a series of important shocks over the last two decades. The completion of the Single Market Programme, EMU, and Eastern enlargement all introduced new pressures on what once looked like relatively stable political–economic arrangements. How are we to understand these changes, both in terms of their causes and their effects? And when, where and how would such shifts in the political economy of Europe influence the viability of existing capitalist models? Perhaps the most interesting conceptual point of entry into these questions is offered by the notion of institutional complementarities. Since different elements in an institutional framework are tightly linked to one another, changes in one – say, in the sphere of firm ownership, corporate governance and finance – are likely to have important consequences for the organization of other spheres in the economy, for example the labour market. The reason is that at the level of firms, the incentive structure of the average manager would shift, for example from a longer-term to a short-term profit orientation, which might entail a change in wage-setting and training strategies. Aggregated over an entire economy, this would lead to a parallel but more gradual shift as firms adjust to new ownership arrangements. However, the actual mechanism through which such a translation of pressures from one sphere to another would happen is unclear and probably underdetermined: does the tight linkage imply that shifts are directly and rapidly transmitted or, on the contrary, that the pressures for change are neutralized since all institutional elements would have to change at the same time? In addition, how do we think about the effects of such pressures?

The Single European Market

The Single European Market is an excellent place to start such an inquiry. If product, labour and capital markets in different countries have been following different logics as a result of their national embeddedness, then the increased freedom of movement of capital, people, goods and services across the EU offers an opportunity to test the causes and effects of economic integration. The first observation is that increased trade and more broadly increased flows of capital and people have, on the whole, not affected the organization of individual European economies much: Germany, Italy, France and the UK have been exposed to trade since the mid-1970s, and developed very different but complementary export profiles, while small economies always knew how to use domestic institutions as instruments for manoeuvring through hard economic times (Katzenstein 1985).

However, entirely new pressures emerged from financial market integration via ownership on corporate governance, and in turn on labour market institutions along the logic outlined earlier. These direct effects have also been limited, however, especially in the large multinational firms. Even large German firms, which have come under pressure from new shareholders, have avoided massive labour market deregulation (Wood 2001) and instead have stuck to the existing wage-setting and training systems while negotiating adjustments in the margins (Hassel 2007). In other words, the articulation of ownership arrangements with labour market institutions, in which shifts in finance trigger adjustments in the labour market, is considerably looser than many had thought. Sometimes the relationship between finance and labour markets moves in unpredictable ways: explaining why hedge funds and mutual funds flock disproportionately to France and not Germany, Goyer (2007) notes that such funds demand unilateral management action without significant accountability to labour – something they can easily find in France, but not in Germany.

If the single market seems to have had few significant direct effects through trade or foreign investment, possibly the emergence of a pan-European regulatory framework in such network industries as transport, telecommunications and energy, often explicitly drafted to counteract 'protectionist' national regulations, would? Since market-making through regulation is what characterizes the EU more than anything else, effects of integration would be found here. A detailed analysis of regulation in different network utility industries in the UK, France and Germany (Thatcher 2007) suggests the situation is highly complex: EU regulation in these industries has forced change in the national systems, but much of the change has followed implementation patterns that suggest a profound procedural continuity with the old national models. The process of liberalizing and sometimes privatizing these public and semi-public utilities reflects the general state–economy links which had been in existence. EU-wide market-oriented liberalization often ratified existing practices in the UK, and their net effect was therefore negligible. In France the government relied on EU regulation to 'internationalize' the national champions, large firms such as Electricité de France and France Télécom, by supporting them in their strategy of expansion into other markets while slowing down transposition of EU rules into domestic law. And in Germany, the prevailing close links between different companies in these industries offered the institutional matrix for adjustment, which was largely governed through the industry associations (*ibid.* 167–9).

Drawing a picture of Western European capitalism that emphasizes persistent stability would be incomplete and wrong, however. It sidesteps many complex domestic changes, especially in the areas of welfare states and labour markets, where significant reorganizations often followed fiscal problems, persistent unemployment, and more generally a post-Keynesian view of the welfare state that favours employability over employment stability and income maintenance. Broadly speaking, welfare arrangements everywhere have become more 'incentive compatible', reflecting the shift from a passive support of weak income groups to an active shaping of employment chances. Sometimes, as in the case of employment policies and pension funding, many of the European nation-states have looked across the border, helped through the information exchanges taking place under the aegis of the Open Method of Coordination. Pension arrangements across Europe, for example, look more alike today than they ever did in the past, and some form of active labour market policy, which combines income support with retraining, is now standard in many European countries. But the previous existing institutional makeup shines through, even in these more activist welfare policies: where labour unions and employers were important in organizing the labour market and setting wages, they still play a central role; and where they were absent, as in the UK, or have played a marginal role, as in France, that still remains the case. Sectoral pension funds, for example, are run by the social partners in countries such as Germany, Belgium and Sweden, but are primarily private affairs, without labour union involvement, in the UK. Convergence in these areas of the labour market and the welfare state, while important, can therefore also be understood along the lines of the logics that preceded these new initiatives.

The fact that almost 20 years after the completion of the Single Market programme, institutional convergence across the European economies remains limited, should not really come as a surprise. Since the Single Market's aim was to increase trade, it effectively raised the scale of the relevant market for each of the different production regimes underlying capitalist diversity in Europe. French, German, Italian and British companies therefore developed their comparative advantages, which were largely built on the very different institutional frameworks in these countries. If specialization is a function of the size of the market, then a larger and growing market is bound to produce more not less differentiation. At the same time, the causes and especially the consequences of shifts in the European political economies are not always easy to examine. Europe is going through a phase of rapid change – and this was true even before the financial and economic crisis of 2008 – and key VoC insights, such as complementarities, comparative institutional advantage and the institutional embeddedness of production regimes, help us understand what has been going on in Western Europe since the mid-1980s. How then do these same ideas help us make sense of the main changes in the 2000s – EMU and enlargement?

Varieties of European capitalism in EMU

Institutional complementarities played an important role in the way EU member states have handled the dramatic shift in the European macro-economic policy-making following the introduction of the euro in 1999. EMU created a remarkable situation in the political economy of Europe, and especially of those member states that joined EMU, by centralizing monetary policy yet leaving national-level wage-bargaining systems (and fiscal policy) intact. What follows will discuss how complementarities between macro- and micro-level elements of the institutional frameworks operated.

These arguments are inspired by a debate on the links between labour market institutions and economic performance that emerged in the 1980s. One position in that debate, which is of crucial importance for understanding the effects of EMU, is related to the model developed by Calmfors and Driffill (1988). The basic intuition of that model is that semi-centralized systems of collective bargaining will perform less well than either highly decentralized or highly centralized wage-setting frameworks, since in the semi-centralized ones, each individual union is strong enough to be able to bargain above-productivity wage increases, but small enough not to have to bear the full cost of that decision in terms of inflation or unemployment. In contrast, actors in both highly centralized and decentralized wage-setting systems – strong trade unions in the first, individual employees or company-level bargainers in the second – are forced to take into account these consequences, and thus set wages at a sustainable level in terms of inflation and unemployment. The introduction of an independent conservative central bank into this model reinforces this logic without altering it (Soskice and Iversen 2000; Hall and Franzese 1998). In effect EMU moved, in terms of these models, wage-setting systems from highly coordinated national systems to an EMU-wide medium-coordination arrangement: in every country the unions are strong enough to extract high wage increases but small enough to have only a limited effect on the EMU-wide inflation rate and therefore on the European Central Bank's reaction function. Even Germany, easily the largest economy in Europe, only accounts for one-third of the overall inflation rate.

What do these developments imply in terms of capitalist diversity in Europe? Let us start with the Maastricht Treaty. Qualifying for EMU meant that prospective member states met several economic criteria which had to do with the monetary stability of their economy. Exchange, interest and inflation rates were supposed to converge to a stable level, while public debt had to fall to a sustainable level. In principle these criteria were relatively easy to meet: central banks have the power to impose currency stability unilaterally and governments can do the same with austerity plans. But such drastic strategies are likely to have dramatic social consequences, and thus negative electoral effects for the austerity-minded governments. Governments in the EU therefore adopted a strategy of bringing social partners around the table and negotiate social pacts with them that allowed them to meet the Maastricht criteria (Hassel 2006).

However, social pacts were not concluded everywhere (Hancké and Rhodes 2005). It turns out that two conditions have to be met for social pacts to emerge. The first is, quite simply, that the country must actually have a problem meeting the Maastricht criteria – inflation and public debt has to be sufficiently above the target rate for governments and others to recognize this as an issue that might create problems for EMU accession. Second, social partners have to be able to credibly commit to social pacts – and often this means that companies and labour relations have to be organized in such a way that they support, from the bottom up as it were, the macro-strategy associated with social pacts. And this is where EMU and VoC meet. Most CMEs in Europe did not face problems meeting the Maastricht criteria, largely because they had become members of the Deutschmark bloc – a sort of proto-EMU – in the 1980s, and had reorganized their domestic institutions to guarantee exchange rate stability through low inflation.

In the other economies, where problems were visible and important, credible commitments were considerably more likely to emerge in economies which were organized around stable micro-foundations, or, perhaps better, where a set of prior conditions supported the construction of inter-firm coordination in such areas as training and wage-setting (Hancké and Rhodes 2005). Social pacts are therefore, somewhat counter-intuitively, not found in most CMEs, but in those prospective EMU member states that were able to rearrange their institutional makeup to support 'macro-pacting'. Culpepper (2002) argues that the prior networks encouraged information flows and deliberation, which allowed the views of the relevant parties to converge. The various forms of capitalism found in Europe thus played a role in how countries experienced and handled the pressures associated with the Maastricht Treaty and EMU.

Capitalist variety continued to be important after the introduction of the euro as well. Many observers (e.g. Hall and Franzese 1998; Soskice and Iversen 1998, 2000), building on the Calmfors–Driffill model referred to earlier, predicted a surge in inflation, led by reinvigorated labour unions that were no longer subject to the hard constraints imposed by their national central bank. During the first ten years of EMU, however, wage inflation has been relatively subdued in the euro-zone: the aggregate year-on-year inflation rate jumped slightly from a very low 1.1 per cent at the start of EMU, but with very few exceptions, has oscillated between 1.5 per cent and 3 per cent since 2000. But this relative price stability hides quite dramatic variation across the different member states (Johnston and Hancké 2009). In 1999, at the start of EMU, inflation rates (indirectly imposed by the Maastricht Treaty) ranged from slightly less than 1 per cent in Germany and France to a little below 2.5 per cent in Portugal and Spain. In 2001, inflation rates varied between almost 5 per cent in Ireland, more than 4 per cent in Portugal and the Netherlands, and less than 2 per cent in Germany and France. By 2004, the range was below 0.5 per cent (Finland) and 4 per cent (Ireland).

The explanation for this variation appears to be related to the type of wage-bargaining system prevailing in each of these economies. Broadly speaking, those countries that have a tightly coordinated wage-bargaining system, in which strong unions in the tradable goods (export) sector lead wage-setting and other trade unions follow, have lower inflation rates in EMU than countries with weaker forms of wage coordination or where it is altogether absent. Since high domestic inflation translates into uncompetitive export prices, labour unions which are exposed to competition have to take domestic price movements into account. They therefore keep their own wages in check, and transmit those moderate wages to the other labour unions and thus onto the economy as a whole through coordinated wage bargaining. In economies which lack such a mechanism, labour unions in the sheltered sectors (especially though not solely the public sector) can claim higher wage increases without having to take the inflationary effects into account. Put differently, CMEs are, on the whole, low-inflation economies in EMU, while the continental economies that are organized along different, more hybrid, combinations of market, state and associational lines have, on average, higher inflation rates (Johnston and Hancké 2009).

The second important point in that debate deals with the effects of this shift on the supply side of the economy (Streeck 1992; Soskice 1999). It deals with the microeconomic effects of macroeconomic regimes, particularly those that are filtered through institutional frameworks. The key idea is that, under a fixed exchange rate regime – which is de facto what the Maastricht Treaty introduced for those countries that intended to join EMU from the start – a shift in wage setting towards more wage coordination across sectors forces companies to become more competitive, not by lowering wages but by relocating themselves in higher value-added product market niches. Wage setting acts, in other words, under such restrictive macroeconomic regimes, as a productivity whip by forcing underperforming firms 'up' or 'out'. During the 1990s, when the Maastricht regime imposed a set of hard macroeconomic constraints, firms indeed adapted and upgraded their product line to reflect strong wage pressures in countries where wages were set in a centrally coordinated system, while decentrally organized economies adjusted by adopting a more cost-sensitive product market strategy. Between 1992 and 2001, the simple correlation between wage bargaining system and product market strategy jumped dramatically from –0.4 to +0.3 (Hancké and Herrmann 2007: 130). Most of these adjustments reflected, in the case of upgrading, shifts in company organization that we usually associate with how workplaces are organized in CMEs (*ibid*: 131–6).

The different organizational logics of capitalism in Western Europe prior to 1990 are therefore very useful tools to understand the adjustment of national economies to the macroeconomic regime that EMU heralded. On the whole, CMEs were better prepared to enter EMU, and have lower inflation rates in EMU. Furthermore, EMU seems to have invited many countries to increase central coordination in wage setting as a way of bringing inflation under control, which forced companies to move into higher value-added market segments. And the outcome has been, at least until the 2008–10 financial and economic crisis, that different capitalist varieties persisted and flourished in Europe.

That crisis has put a very different complexion on the diversity of capitalisms in Europe. It started, both within and outside Europe, in the Anglo-Saxon LMEs, and branched out to include all the others, ultimately freezing the meanwhile highly integrated credit system. After that flattening process in 2007 to 2008, the fiscal problems that followed the bank bailouts in 2008 were, somewhat surprisingly, aligned along different capitalist systems: Greece, Spain and Ireland – but not Germany, Sweden or Austria – faced massive losses of competitiveness, draconian austerity plans, and often a loss of confidence of international investors in sovereign debt. North-West European countries appeared shielded from these shocks, with some observers even suggesting a return to the 'narrow' hard currency Deutschmark-bloc type exchange rate and mone-tary arrangement that was at the basis of the original EMU designs. In addition, the competitiveness of the North-West European economies improved primarily because of the importance of collective bargaining in wage setting, which allowed these countries to keep wage growth below productivity growth. However, in an almost closed monetary union the necessary implication is that other countries lose competitiveness – and thereby the tools to adjust. The crisis of EMU in 2010 was, therefore, to a large extent the product of different logics of capitalism that existed and implicitly competed.

Eastward enlargement

The third political–economic shift in Europe over the last two decades has, of course, been the fall of the Berlin Wall and the subsequent transi-tion to a capitalist democracy in large parts of Central and Eastern Europe (CEE). By 2004, eight of the countries that went through a peace-ful revolution in 1989 (and in 1991 in the case of the Baltic states) joined the EU, and by 2009, several of them were full members of EMU. How can a perspective inspired by VoC enlighten our understanding of these processes? Answering that question is easier when we split the period into one which covers late communism and the immediate transition and a second which takes a bird's-eye look back at the different patterns of economic organization in CEE.

The central problem that countries in CEE faced in 1990, relatively simple in principle but complicated in practice, was how to turn a state-led command economy into a privately owned market economy. One group of authors proposed a *shock therapy*: the rapid and simultaneous introduction of the central institutions of capitalism is a necessary condi-tion for a successful transition from a planned to a market economy. The information and incentives underlying a planned economy are so differ-ent from a market economy that hybrid systems are unlikely to function well, and may actually lead to perverse outcomes since the discipline of a market economy is dulled by non-market elements – 'you cannot jump over a chasm in two steps', thus the key legitimizing idea. Freely moving prices will quickly tell producers where to concentrate their activities, will guide the allocation of resources in the economy, and will allow consumers to balance free choice with a hard budget constraint. Relying on the price mechanism, however, is only possible if prices are stable, and a transition therefore entails a macroeconomic stabilization programme as well, led by tough central banks and finance ministries who can contain spending and thus stabilize inflation as well as exchange rates.

By the end of the 1990s, this orthodox interpretation was coming under fire. Stiglitz's (1999) analysis of transition, which criticized the wholesale destruction of existing pre-transition institutions and the problematic timing of different stages in the transition, was among the first systematic counter-arguments to emerge. Trust, so the argument goes, is a necessary ingredient of a market economy; however, since this trust is embedded in non-economic networks, the destruction of these networks ultimately undermines the capacity to choose different paths for the economy. Left to its own devices, the economy thus adopted a purely market-based form of coordination – but this was not an evolution that necessarily imposed itself. In a comparison of Estonia and Slovenia, Feldman (2007) took this critique one analytical step further: the difference between the CME Slovenia and the LME Estonia is related to the *network-promoting* versus the *network-disrupting* government policies adopted during the transition in the two countries. Combining these points and translating them into the language of VoC, these critiques of the orthodox political–economic positions suggest that by resolutely turning towards a minimal institutional and social embeddedness of the newly emerging market economy, the transitions in fact precluded alternative, institutionally 'thicker' forms of capitalism from emerging. If Central Europe is 'liberal', it is so by design rather than by default: business coordinating capacity, a necessary ingredient of the types of capitalism associated with the northern half of the continent (and Scandinavia), was simply unable to emerge.

The actual evolution of CEE may, however, be less dramatic than this suggests. After the initial transition, the region has become a major destination of FDI. It is not hard to guess why multinational companies located production sites in Central Europe: the region offered a relatively skilled workforce that worked for a fraction of the normal wage in the rich North-West European countries. Unsurprisingly, given the large relative wage differentials and geographic proximity, much of the FDI into the region was German in origin. But after a few years, a slightly more differentiated picture emerged. A careful comparison of investment in and export profiles of different CEE member states, based on the asset-specificity typology that Greskovits (2005) has constructed, suggests quite convincingly that broadly speaking two very different production profiles have emerged there over the last 10 to15 years. This typology is based on the degree to which industries are labour or capital intensive.

The first group has very few skilled inputs. One set of industries is intensive only in physical capital: a 'heavy-basic' profile, which can be found in such sectors as food, live animals, beverages and tobacco, fuels, vegetable oils, iron and steel, pulp and paper, non-ferrous metals. Another set is based on neither physical nor human capital, but unskilled labour ('light-basic'): typical sectors here are cork and wood, textile, rubber, furniture manufacturing, clothing and accessories and footwear. The second set of profiles, in contrast to these two, has important contributions from both physical and human capital ('heavy-complex'), found in industries such as chemicals, machinery and equipment, road vehicles and transport equipment. And the fourth relies almost entirely only on human capital ('light complex'), in such sectors as pharmaceuticals, office and data-processing machines, electrical machinery, scientific equipment, optical goods and clocks. Input factors such as skills and suppliers will differ across these different types: a country dominated by light or heavy complex industries will require a workforce with more sophisticated training and suppliers that are more technologically advanced than a country which specializes in light-basic industries.

Using this typology as a lens to look at reindustrialization and investment in Central Europe shows a remarkable differentiation across the region. Slovenia and the Visegrád 4 (V4: Czech Republic, Hungary, Poland and Slovakia) have increasingly specialized in heavy-complex and light-complex export industries, while in the others (the Baltics and South-Eastern Europe) heavy-basic and light-basic profiles dominate. In the V4 and Slovenia at least 40 per cent of exports – and usually considerably more, up to 70 per cent – over the last ten years consisted of complex goods; this figure of 40 per cent appears to be the ceiling for the other CEE countries. In addition, the trajectories of the V4 and Slovenia contrast sharply with the Baltics and South-Eastern Europe (SEE). In the first group, the share of complex products in exports rises almost immediately after the transition recession of the early 1990s, while that share first fell in the other group and began to rise only towards the end of the decade, and then only slowly. While it may be too early to treat these different outcomes as stable, there are reasons to believe that it is very difficult for the Baltics and SEE to catch up with the V4 in terms of the importance of complex manufacturing. The initial wave of investment in CEE seems to have produced network externalities which imply that complex manufacturing in future is likely to invest where other companies with a similar profile are located.

Again, rather than a single capitalist logic, different types seem to be emerging, each with their own coherent internal organization, leading to different specializations and economic performance. Yet, comparative advantage, reflected in the leading sectors, tends to be self-reinforcing over time. Tellingly, for example, the region between Prague, Katowice, Budapest and Vienna, has become the main hub of car assembly in the world, producing models in practically any segment, from relatively low value-added car models to sophisticated sport utility vehicles, while the Baltics are known worldwide for sophisticated software development and Internet applications. This pattern of specialization in different sectors is slowly working its way into the system: as more specific skills are required in the V4, for example, companies discover the need for inter-firm coordination as a way of overcoming collective action problems that block the development of training systems (Hancké and Kurekova 2008). And that, in turn, requires governance forms beyond firms, in which such quasi-voluntary institutions as chambers of commerce seem to play a central role. But such a coordinated system, if it is developed, is likely to be a 'Balkanized' version of coordination, which produces exclusive ('members-only') club goods. If that is the case – and it is, on current form, a likely outcome – the broader social effect will be a sharp segregation between those inside and those outside the networks, in a different labour market segment in the same region, or excluded from this beneficial regional development model altogether.

Conclusion

Thinking about European capitalism not as one, but as a collection of different types, turns out to be a very useful perspective on change and adjustment in European economies over the last three decades. It helps us make sense of many of the adjustment paths following the oil shocks of the 1970s, the fall of the Berlin Wall in 1989, the completion of the Single Market Programme in the early 1990s, and EMU and Eastern enlargement in the late 1990s and early 2000s. Such a perspective alerts us to several developments that other approaches might miss (see also Hall 2007). Adjustment often follows an institutional logic of change: similar shocks can be translated into very different outcomes; comparative advantage in an integrating single market reinforces that logic of adjustment; and institutional complementarities impose sometimes narrow paths of adjustment. Put differently, after two decades of almost permanent adjustment and change, it is still quite simple to recognize countries such as Germany, France and the small corporatist economies in North-West Europe as both very similar to their older versions and very different from the UK. And even in Central Europe, where alternatives appeared limited, different models of capitalist organization emerged, often on the back of foreign investment. Capitalist diversity is, it seems, here to stay, despite all the pressures for convergence that emanate from European economic integration, financial and economic globalization, and eastward enlargement.

But such a perspective is not a panacea. It does not capture all moments of change that Europe is or might be going through. Welfare states everywhere are facing problems, both of funding and of organization, and the reforms that have taken place in many continental European countries as often as not reflect similar pressures and intergovernmental learning and policy transfers. Some of the changes might simply be too small to notice today but can have large consequences a few decades down the road, and, of course, the financial crisis which started in 2007 and which engulfed the entire world by the time this book is published may have shifted the basic parameters of economic policy-making to such an extent that advanced capitalist economies over the entire world are forced to reinvent themselves. Some might even argue that the crisis, against the background of the pressures for adjustment in the welfare state and in global competition, will succeed where the assault of orthodox economics on the coordinated market economies failed over the last two decades – albeit, somewhat ironically, in the opposite direction of a more regulated, less 'turbo' capitalism. They might be right; but if the past is any guide, that is an unlikely outcome. Ten years from now, the various models of capitalism in Europe are likely to be recognizably different, and the way we started to think about those differences in the early 2000s is likely to be a very good guide to understanding why that is the case.

Chapter 11

Welfare States in Trouble: Policy Reform in a Period of Crisis

Elisabetta Gualmini and Martin Rhodes

The 'crisis' of welfare state has often been announced. There was a crisis in the 1970s, when European economies were hit by the twin oil shocks, putting a dramatic end to the *trente glorieuses*. Crisis returned in the 1990s when many national budgets were constrained by the need to comply with EMU debt and deficit criteria. In the 2000s, the emergence of 'new social risks' (increasing poverty and social inequalities) called for a recalibration of social protection systems; and in 2008 to 2010 the international financial crisis has pushed up government debt and threatened welfare spending.

But much like the boy who cried wolf, the word 'crisis' has been massively overused (Castles 2004). Welfare states have continued to grow, and the biggest issue facing governments is making welfare budgets sustainable. 'External shocks' have contributed to the complex set of forces, including domestic factors and ideational changes that have gradually impacted the scale and orientation of social spending. But radical reforms – even in the present crisis – are limited by popular support for welfare and the reluctance of politicians to antagonize public opinion (Pierson 2001; Vis et al. 2010). Welfare reform tends to be slow and incremental; but even gradual change can produce a substantial transformation over time.

This chapter examines social policy change in European countries over the last decade. Notwithstanding the structural distinctiveness of welfare systems, common adjustment features can be identified, especially in labour market policies and pension systems, the main focus of our analysis. In employment policy, the 'activation' paradigm – linking benefits to job search incentives and sanctions and in the best of cases training – has been strongly promoted by the European Commission and adopted widely in Europe. In pensions, which account for the largest part of European social spending (Figure 11.1), governments have promoted private funds and placed stricter rules on retirement age and contributions.

The second section of the chapter presents the major social and economic challenges confronting European welfare states; the third analyses recent changes in employment and pensions policies; the last section concludes by considering the consequences for efficiency and equity of a decade of welfare reform.

The challenges of the 2000s: new risks, new constraints and a paradigm shift

Welfare states are dealing with 'old' and 'new' social risks in a more difficult climate. To the traditional risks of sickness, unemployment and vulnerability in old age have been added the consequences of family breakdown for single parents and children, high rates of unemployment or precarious jobs among young people, increasing inequality and higher rates of poverty and social exclusion (Taylor-Gooby 2004; Armingeon and Bonoli 2006). Governments and their electorates have difficult choices to make given upward pressures on welfare budgets from different directions.

First, population ageing, due to longer life spans and lower fertility rates, has important implications for pension systems and welfare state

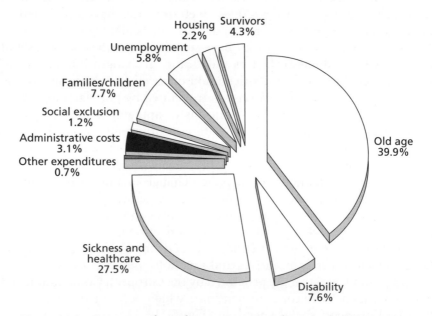

Figure 11.1   *Structure of social protection expenditure in the EU-27 (2005)*

Source: 'Statistics in Focus', Eurostat, 46 (2008), 3.

sustainability (Véron *et al.* 2007). In the EU-27, the number of over-65s increased by 9 per cent, or 6 million people, in 2001 to 2006 alone, while those under age 14 fell by 4.4 per cent. The elderly dependency ratio is forecast to rise by 50 per cent by 2020, implying an increase in social expenditure of 5 to 7 per cent of GDP (Eurostat). Inward flows of younger migrants are unlikely to counter the trend. Health care will also become more expensive, as an older population draws increasingly upon it. Together, old age, sickness and health care account for nearly three-quarters of welfare spending in the EU (see Figure 11.1).

A second challenge concerns the family. The nuclear family no longer predominates. Single parent or unmarried-partner families have proliferated, as have the number of divorces. In the EU, more than 40 per cent of marriages are likely to fail and 1 child in 4 is born out of wedlock (Kazepov and Carbone 2007). This shift is partly related to the changing role of women inside and outside the home, for in the absence of an equal gender division of labour, when women enter the workforce (which they are doing in growing numbers) they often find it hard to reconcile family and professional commitments. These changes require welfare adaptation to prevent an under-investment in children and education, lower fertility rates and a more acute ageing problem (Esping-Andersen 2009).

A third challenge has to do with work and production. The transition from mass to flexible lean production has changed the nature of labour demand. In an increasingly open and knowledge-based economy, workers with low skills have become highly vulnerable 'outsiders', in terms of job security and in their access, and accrual of entitlements, to welfare benefits. They are also likely to be the first affected in a crisis: some 1.7 million temporary contract workers were hit by the 2008–9 job crunch. In many countries there is now a growing underclass of 'outsiders' alongside employment and welfare state 'insiders' on permanent contracts.

A fourth challenge is globalization and greater economic interdependence. Although the impact of globalization been greatly exaggerated (Castles 2004), the consequences of financial interdependency can be acute, as revealed by the 2008–10 crisis which triggered the 'automatic stabilizers' of higher social transfers and reduced fiscal receipts. In 2009 to 2010, the employment rate (of the 15–64 age group) fell by almost 1 per cent in the EU and unemployment rose from 8.7 to 10 per cent. Long-term unemployment rose from 2.6 to 3.7 per cent and unemployment rates for young people (15 to 24) skyrocketed from 16.9 to 21.4 per cent. The associated costs have put budgets in general and welfare finances in particular under great pressure.

These challenges are all interrelated, producing something of a vicious cycle, for unemployment and the spread of poorly protected jobs increase inequality and impede family formation, placing further downward pressure on fertility rates; and the rising welfare costs of ageing prevent a reorientation of spending towards the young and families and human capital investment. Both equity and economic efficiency are thereby undermined (Esping-Andersen 2009). Ideally, countries would be shifting resources away from elderly income support towards higher levels of support for families, children and education, thereby reducing market income inequality and growing child poverty rates. But reversing the vicious cycle is politically very difficult, given the entrenchment of welfare spending programmes and support for the status quo.

What has changed notably is the philosophy underlying welfare states, if not always the practice. The new version of social justice advocates movement from a passive and protective, to an 'active' and 'enabling' welfare state, which compensates social risk but also asks for something in return – often a 'work first' or 'work longer' commitment to employment (Gallie 2004; Serrano Pascual and Magnusson 2007). This approach has been promoted by the European Commission and the European Employment Strategy, communicated to the EU member states through the Open Method of Coordination, since the late 1990s. But although often embroidered with the rhetoric of human capital enhancement and lifelong learning, in reality there has been more 'activating' than 'enabling'. Some countries do much better than others, however, which is the topic discussed below.

Policy responses and innovations in European welfare regimes

But first a word on classification. Analysts traditionally think in terms of three 'worlds of welfare capitalism' (Esping-Andersen 1990) – the Liberal (the UK and Ireland), Conservative–Bismarckian (Austria, Belgium, France, Germany and Italy) and Social Democratic (Denmark and Sweden) – and we are no exception. Based primarily on an index of decommodification (i.e., the extent to which social policy distances the individual from dependency on the market for protection), in which the Liberal countries score lowest, the Scandinavian highest, and the Conservative somewhere in between, this framework remains useful, despite numerous challenges to it (e.g., Hicks and Kenworthy 2003).

A broad-based feminist critique (Lewis 1992; Orloff 1993) has made analysts more sensitive to the gender dimension of welfare states; and the classification has been complicated by arguments for a specifically Southern European variant given the welfare role of the family, low female employment rates, low social policy spending and uneven coverage of social risks in Spain, Italy, Portugal and Greece (Ferrera 1996; Rhodes 1997; Ferrera *et al.* 2000). That argument has been challenged in turn (e.g., by Castles 2006), especially regarding the degree of difference between Italy and the Conservative cluster. Italy is considered a member of that group for the purposes of our analysis (the decision not to treat Southern Europe as a separate cluster is also due to the fact that the cycle of policy reforms in 2000 to 2010, especially in Italy, has been very similar to the Conservative countries).

Since the 1990s, the Central and Eastern European countries, in which some social benefits are linked to work histories along Conservative–Bismarckian lines, but with family, health and social assistance much closer to the Liberal type, have generally, but not always (see Cerami 2010), been treated as new 'hybrid' category (Hemerijck *et al.* 2006). We also follow that convention below, although our indicators strongly suggest that there is too much diversity in social outcomes in the region for these countries to be lumped together in this way.

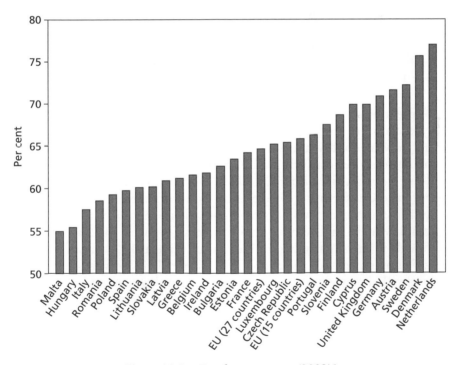

Figure 11.2   *Employment rates (2009)* *

* Note that the Lisbon employment rate target for 2010 of 70% has been achieved by only seven countries – the Netherlands, Denmark, Sweden, Austria, Germany, the UK and Cyprus.

Source: Eurostat.

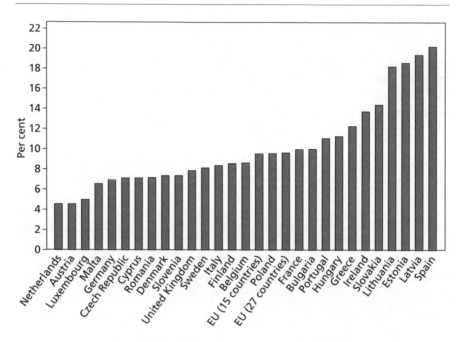

Figure 11.3   *Unemployment rates (June 2010)*

Source: Eurostat.

A preliminary set of contrasts can be drawn as follows. In the Rolls-Royce class are the big-spending, high-employment, low-unemployment, low-inequality and low poverty-risk countries of Scandinavia, which also score relatively well in their balance between spending on old age versus children and families. The Netherlands (traditionally part of the Conservative cluster) is an honorary member of this group – and in fact beats Sweden and Denmark in the 2009 to 2010 low unemployment–high employment stakes (Figures 11.2 and 11.3), although it has slightly higher inequality (Figure 11.4). Both Sweden and Denmark balance their labour market policies towards employability (with a concentration on 'supported employment and rehabilitation') better than any other countries in the EU. In terms both of the desirable policy mix, and outcomes, these countries are away ahead of their neighbours to the south and east.

The Conservative group reveals levels of social policy spending that are similar to the Scandinavian countries (and France is neck and neck with Sweden), with the exception of Italy, whose 26.7 per cent of GDP in 2007 is right around the EU-15 average (Table 11.1). On other indicators there is considerable variation. Germany and Austria are close to Sweden and Denmark in their good employment and unemployment

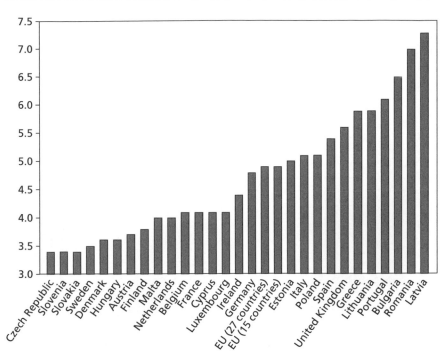

Figure 11.4 *Inequality of income distribution: income quintile share ratio**

* The ratio of total income received by the 20% of the population with the highest income (top quintile) to that received by the 20% of the population with the lowest income (lowest quintile). Income must be understood as equivalized disposable income.

Source: Eurostat.

rates, but both France and Italy score poorly: France had more unemployed than Italy in 2009, although its employment rate at 64 per cent was far superior to Italy's 57 (Figures 11.2 and 11.3). Spending on active labour market policy as against income support is lower than in Scandinavia but higher than in the Liberal and CEE groups, and Austria and Germany invest more in training than most countries. In poverty risk, Italy is again outlier in the group, while inequality is higher in both Italy and Germany than in France and Austria (the latter being close to the Scandinavians). Indeed, in spending, high poverty risk, low employment, high inequality and high spending on the elderly versus children/families (Figure 11.5), Italy is a bona fide member of the Southern European group.

The Liberal welfare states are smaller and less 'de-commodifying' than the previous two groups, but differ in their levels of social expenditure (the UK is close to the EU average at 25.3 per cent of GDP, but

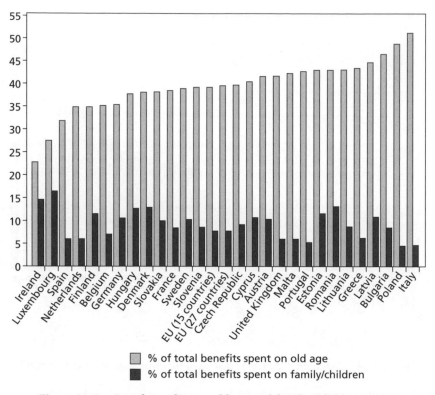

Figure 11.5   *Social spending on old age and families/children (2007)*

Source: Eurostat

Ireland's 18.9 per cent is well below it), and in employment and unemployment: Ireland fares worse than the UK on both counts in 2009, reflecting the much greater vulnerability of the Irish economy and its major banks to the financial crisis and housing price crunch. But the UK also outpaces Ireland in poverty risks and inequality (which are similar to those in the Southern European and CEE countries), while Ireland has a better balance (albeit in a smaller overall welfare budget) between old age and family/children spending (Table 11.2 and Figure 11.5). Neither does especially well in employment policy compared to the best performers (Table 11.3), although the UK invests a great deal in publicly funded services for job seekers (advice and information about jobs, training and opportunities), even if its expenditure on training as such is low.

Finally, the Central-East European welfare states combine low levels of social expenditure (16.9 per cent of GDP in Slovakia, 20 per cent in Poland and 19.1 per cent in the Czech Republic – although Slovenia has

Table 11.1   *Expenditure on social protection (% of GDP)*

	2000	2001	2002	2003	2004	2005	2006	2007
EU (27 countries)	–	–	–	–		27.1	26.7	26.2
EU (15 countries)	26.8	27.0	27.3	27.7	27.6	27.7	27.3	26.9
Belgium	26.5	27.3	28.0	29.0	29.2	29.6	30.2	29.5
Bulgaria	–	–	–	–	–	16.0	14.9	15.1
Czech Republic	19.5	19.4	20.2	20.2	19.3	19.2	18.7	18.6
Denmark	28.9	29.2	29.7	30.9	30.7	30.2	29.3	28.9
Germany	29.3	29.4	30.1	30.4	29.8	29.7	28.7	27.7
Estonia	13.9	13.0	12.7	12.5	13.0	12.6	12.3	12.5
Ireland	13.9	14.9	17.5	17.9	18.1	18.2	18.3	18.9
Greece	23.5	24.3	24.0	23.5	23.5	24.6	24.5	24.4
Spain	20.3	20.0	20.4	20.6	20.7	20.9	20.9	21.0
France	29.5	29.6	30.4	30.9	31.3	31.4	30.7	30.5
Italy	24.7	24.9	25.3	25.8	26.0	26.4	26.6	26.7
Cyprus	14.8	14.9	16.3	18.4	18.1	18.4	18.4	18.5
Latvia	15.3	14.3	13.9	13.8	12.9	12.4	12.3	11.0
Lithuania	15.8	14.7	14.0	13.5	13.3	13.1	13.2	14.3
Luxembourg	19.6	20.9	21.6	22.1	22.3	21.7	20.3	19.3
Hungary	19.6	19.2	20.3	21.2	20.6	21.9	22.4	22.3
Malta	16.9	17.8	17.8	18.3	18.8	18.6	18.2	18.1
Netherlands	26.4	26.5	27.6	28.3	28.3	27.9	28.8	28.4
Austria	28.4	28.8	29.2	29.6	29.3	28.9	28.5	28.0
Poland	19.7	21.0	21.1	21.0	20.1	19.7	19.4	18.1
Portugal	21.7	22.7	23.7	24.1	24.7	25.3	25.4	24.8
Romania	13.0	12.8	13.6	13.0	12.7	13.2	12.5	12.8
Slovenia	24.2	24.5	24.4	23.7	23.4	23.0	22.7	21.4
Slovakia	19.4	19.0	19.1	18.2	17.2	16.5	16.3	16.0
Finland	25.1	24.9	25.7	26.6	26.7	26.8	26.2	25.4
Sweden	30.1	30.8	31.6	32.6	32.0	31.5	30.7	29.7
United Kingdom	26.4	26.8	25.7	25.7	25.9	26.3	26.1	25.3

Source: Eurostat.

been close to the EU average over the last decade) with rather high current levels of unemployment, especially in the Baltic countries, whose economies, like that of Ireland, have suffered heavily in the present financial crisis (Figure 11.3). Employment rates vary considerably, though, with the Czech Republic and Slovenia at or above the EU average in the 65–68 per cent range, with Bulgaria and Estonia somewhat lower, and the others right at very low end of the spectrum (Figures 11.2 and 11.3). In inequality, the CEE countries can be found right across the spectrum, ranging from very low levels in the Czech Republic, Slovakia, Slovenia and Hungary, to the highest levels in the EU in Lithuania, Romania, Bulgaria and Latvia. At-risk-of-poverty rates are very high across the region, except for the Czech Republic, Hungary, Slovenia and Slovakia, where they are close to Scandinavian or Conservative levels (Table 11.2).

Table 11.2   *Poverty threshold (PPS*) and at-risk-of-poverty rate (%) (2008)*

		At-risk-of-poverty rate for:			
	Poverty Threshold	Total Population	Aged 0–17	Aged 65 and above	Employed
EU27	–	17p	20p	19p	8p
Belgium	10, 100	15	17	21	5
Bulgaria	2, 800	21	26	34	7
Czech Republic	5, 800	9	13	7	4
Denmark	10, 500	12	9	18	5
Germany	10, 600	15	15	15	7
Estonia	4, 700	19	17	39	7
Ireland	10, 900	16	18	21	6
Greece	7, 200	20	23	22	14
Spain	8, 400	20	24	28	11
France	9, 700	13	17	11	7
Italy	9, 000	19	25	21	9
Cyprus	11, 300	16	14	49	6
Latvia	4, 400	26	25	51	11
Lithuania	4, 200	20	23	29	9
Luxembourg	16, 500	13	20	5	9
Hungary	4, 000	12	20	4	5
Malta	7, 800	15	20	22	5
Netherlands	11, 300	11	13	10	5
Austria	11, 200	12	15	15	6
Poland	3, 900	17	22	12	12
Portugal	5, 800	18	23	22	12
Romania	1, 900	23	33	26	17
Slovenia	8, 400	12	12	21	5
Slovakia	4, 000	11	17	10	6
Finland	9, 600	14	12	23	5
Sweden	10, 400	12	13	16	7
United Kingdom	11, 600p	19p	23p	30p	9p

* The annual national at-risk-of poverty threshold is set at 60% of the national median income per equivalent adult. In order to allow comparisons between countries the threshold is in Purchasing Power Standards (PPS), an artificial reference currency unit that eliminates price-level differences between countries.

P – Provisional

Source: Eurostat Newsrelease 10/2010, 18 January 2010.

Spending on labour market policy apart from income maintenance is low (Table 11.3).

We now turn to the recent evolution of policy. For each of the four clusters identified above, we have selected one or more cases as representative of the kinds of policy innovation introduced.

Table 11.3 Labour market expenditure, by category (2008)

| | | 2 | 3 | 4 | 5 | 6 | 7 | | 8 | 9 | | |
	Total LMP services (cateogy 1)	Training	Job rotation and job sharing	Employment incentives	Supported employment and rehabilitation	Direct job creation	Start-up incentives	Total LMP measures (categories 2–7)	Out-of-work income maintenance and support	Early retirement	Total LMP supports (categories 8–9)	Total LMP expenditure
EU-27	11.8 s	11.1 s	0.1	6.8 s	4.6 s	3.8 s	2.0 e	28.4 s	54.8 p	5.0 s	59.8 p	100.0 s
EU-15	11.8 s	11.1 s	0.1	6.8 s	4.3 s	3.8 s	2.0 e	28.1 s	55.5 e	4.7 e	60.2 e	100.0 s
Belgium	5.9	4.8 e	–	13.7	3.7	10.4	0.1	32.6 e	39.0	22.4	61.4	100.0 e
Bulgaria	11.3	7.4	–	9.2	1.2	36.7	1.1	55.6	33.0	–	33.0	100.0
Czech Republic	28.7	1.7	–	3.1	16.2	3.0	0.6	24.7	46.6	–	46.6	100.0
Denmark	9.7	9.6	: n	5.6	25.2	–	–	40.3	30.1 e	19.9	50.1 e	100.0 e
Germany	14.8 e	15.2 e	0.0	4.0	1.7	3.3	3.5 e	27.7 e	54.6 e	2.9	57.5 e	100.0 e
Estonia	12.0	11.1	–	0.2	0.1	–	1.4	12.8	75.2	–	75.2	100.0
Ireland	10.1 e	12.6	–	2.0	0.5	11.0	–	26.0	60.7	3.1	63.9	100.0 e
Greece	1.8	14.3 e	–	5.8 e	0.0 e	1.4	1.3 e	22.9 e	75.3	–	75.3	100.0 e
Spain	4.1	5.9	0.3	7.5	1.0	2.6	3.7 e	21.0 e	73.0	1.9 e	74.9 e	100.0 e
France	10.3	12.9 e	–	5.1 e	3.5	7.5	1.6 e	30.5 e	58.0	1.2	59.2	100.0 e
Italy	3.1 e	14.6	0.2	12.4	–	0.6	2.0	29.7	59.6	7.6	67.2	100.0 e
Cyprus	9.4	4.0	–	7.1	1.7 e	–	0.7	13.5 e	77.1 p	–	77.1 p	100.0 p
Latvia	11.2	5.9 e	–	5.4	0.1	3.8	1.1	16.3 e	72.4 e	–	72.4 e	100.0 e
Lithuania	21.7 s	11.3	0.3	19.5	1.5	4.1	0.5	37.2	41.1	–	41.1	100.0 s
Luxembourg	5.0 e	4.4 s	–	27.6 e	1.0 s	3.8 s	0.0	36.8 s	41.0	17.1	58.2	100.0 s
Hungary	13.2	9.7	–	14.1	–	6.5	1.0	31.3	55.6	0.0 s	55.6 s	100.0 s

continued overleaf

Table 11.3   continued

		2	3	4	5	6	7		8	9		
	Total LMP services (cateogy 1)	Training	Job rotation and job sharing	Employment incentives	Supported employment and rehabilitation	Direct job creation	Start-up incentives	Total LMP measures (categories 2–7)	Out-of-work income maintenance and support	Early retirement	Total LMP supports (categories 8–9)	Total LMP expenditure
Malta	26.1	4.1	–	5.2	–	0.3	0.4	9.9	63.9	–	63.9	100.0
Netherlands	14.2 e	4.3 e	–	6.3 e	20.3	–	–	31.0 e	54.8 e	–	54.8 e	100.0 e
Austria	8.9	20.2 e	0.0	3.1	2.2	2.3	0.3	28.1 e	52.4	10.7	63.1	100.0 e
Poland	9.7 e	13.5	–	6.3 b	22.9	2.4	6.5 b	51.7 b	15.9	22.7	38.6	100.0 b
Portugal	8.3	15.6	–	8.0	1.8	1.3	0.1	26.7	59.0	5.9	64.9	100.0
Romania	12.8 e	3.3	–	13.4	–	5.4	0.3	22.3	64.9	–	64.9	100.0 e
Slovenia	19.2	5.7	–	1.4	–	9.6	4.1	20.8	60.0	–	60.0	100.0
Slovakia	15.8	1.5	–	2.2	2.4	7.7	7.9	21.7	15.4	47.2	62.5	100.0
Finland	5.4	16.9	2.8	3.6	4.0 e	3.3	0.9	31.4 e	44.9	18.3	63.2	100.0 e
Sweden	20.8 e	5.0 e	–	26.7 e	14.0 e	–	1.0 e	46.7 e	32.5	–	32.5	100.0 e
United Kingdom	51.7 s	3.2 s	–	2.4 s	2.5 s	1.1 s	–	9.2 s	39.1	–	39.1	100.0 s
NO	:	:	:	:	:	:	:	:	:	:	:	:

Key : Not available; :n Not significant; -Not applicable or real zero or zero by default; 0 or 0.00 Less than half of the unit used; e Estimated value; s Eurostat estimate; p Provisional data; b Break in series

Source: Eurostat, *Labour Market Policy – Expenditure and Participants* (Luxembourg: Publications Office of the European Union, 2010), p. 13.

The Social Democratic regime: from flexicurity to the enabling welfare state in Denmark

When the EU's European Employment Strategy (EES) emerged in 1998, with objectives based on the apparently paradoxical combination of labour market flexibility and supportive welfare benefits (dubbed 'flexicurity'), the Danish case was considered exemplary due to its so-called 'golden triangle' of easy hiring and firing by firms, generous unemployment benefits (61–75 per cent of previous earnings) and an active labour market policy (Ilsoe 2007) – although a popular metaphor in Denmark is that of an ungainly 'bumblebee' economy that nevertheless flies (Nannestad and Green-Pedersen 2008)! Other attractive features were the participation of the social partners in policy-making, the wide diffusion of welfare services, rather than just cash transfers, and the large share of public expenditure – equal to 6 per cent of GDP, or 13 per cent of total benefits (double the EU-27 average) – dedicated to child and family policies (Figure 11.5).

The Danish experience of proactive counselling and support to get the unemployed back into work has also inspired the reorganization of public placement systems across Europe. But there is a critical difference between the Danish 'enabling welfare state' or 'human–capital approach' (Dingelday 2007; Damgaard and Torfing 2010) and either the UK's 'work-first approach' or the Italian example of flexibility with little security (see below). Rather than just conditionality and the coercive use of benefits, the development and improvement of skills through education and training are the key instruments in the Danish reforms. Activation policies were already strongly promoted in the 1990s and contributed to the significant reduction of the unemployment rate from 10.5 per cent in 1993 to 5.2 in 1999.

In 1994, individual action plans were introduced via one-stop job centres that provided the full range of services to the unemployed, from vocational training to job opportunities, social care and family allowances. Between 1994 and 2001 a 'job rotation programme' allowed people to voluntarily exit the labour market for up to a year to provide a temporary job opportunity for the unemployed. And in 2001, an apprenticeship programme was introduced for adults willing to renew and update professional skills. After 2001, with a centre-right government in power, some benefits were lowered, and conditionality was tightened, but the established paradigm remained in place.

The main novelty has been a reform of labour market governance since 2006, whereby important policy responsibilities were decentralized to the municipalities – or more precisely Local Employment Councils (LECs) – to control and monitor the performance and outputs of public job centres in line with New Public Management style standards and indicators. LECs also cooperate with public offices to set up programmes and initiatives to respond to precise local needs. Welfare state reforms have therefore involved a more general modernization of the public sector, enhancing accountability, participation and user democracy.

In pensions, Denmark has been 'lucky' not to be burdened by a difficult-to-reform and heavily politicized pay-as-you-go public system as found in many European countries. The Danish pensions system has always been based on the logic of defined-contribution funded pensions, based in occupational schemes that have been gradually expanded to cover almost the entire work force under social partner management (which has *de*-politicized pension politics), backed up by a basic state pension that has become more generous over time (though it was somewhat retrenched in 1993), plus a means-tested pension supplement. With a second voluntary occupational pension pillar, and a third voluntary private pension pillar, the system resembles the World Bank three-tier model, but by accident not design (Green-Pedersen 2007).

Although a 'model' of sorts, given its specific cultural and neo-corporatist traits, the transferability of the Danish experience is far from straightforward. Along with the other Nordic countries, it has also been criticized on economic efficiency grounds (see Kautto 2010; 622, but Esping-Andersen 2009 for a counter-argument) given its high levels of public expenditure and taxation (49 per cent of GDP in 2006), the negative incentive effects of generous social protection, which may create dependency traps despite activation reforms, and the role of the social partners that can both facilitate and delay decision-making. Nevertheless, Denmark (and its Scandinavian neighbours) stands out for its best-practice mix of policies and successful 'flexicurity' innovation, although its exceptional circumstances make it very difficult to replicate (Schwartz 2001) – and most countries in the other clusters fall well behind.

The Conservative regime: activation, conditionality and 'dualization' in Germany, Italy and France

The last decade has been a period of extensive policy change in the Conservative welfare cluster. Activation policies have been introduced in all countries and placement offices have been reorganized to improve the integration of passive policies (unemployment benefits) with activation policies (vocational training and job opportunities). Pensions systems have been reformed to ensure long-term financial sustainability. Far from undermining the core characteristics of Bismarckian systems, the worsening economic conditions at the end of the decade have further accentuated their segmentation and the 'dualization' of the labour market between protected 'insider' and less, or unprotected, 'outsider' workers (Palier 2010a: 73).

In Germany, the 2000s were the decade of the four 'Harzt reforms', strongly promoted by the Schröder Social Democratic government, the first two in 2003 and the second two in 2004 to 2005. Hartz I and II focused on employability and boosting employment in the low-wage sector, while the III and IV reformed job placement offices and unemployment benefits – the latter generating protest across Germany and contributing to the Left Party's divorce from the Social Democratic Party. Regarding employability, under the 'Mini-jobs' scheme aimed at the unemployed and those with jobs but very low incomes, workers paid up to €400 per month are exempted from social security contributions and pay almost no income tax, while for employees earning up to €800 per month ('Midi-jobs'), contributions start at 4 per cent and increase linearly up to the normal rate of 21 per cent (Steiner and Wrohlich 2005).

In addition, temporary work was extended to the construction sector and fixed-term contracts were further liberalized. These innovations contributed to an increase in the share of temporary contracts to 14.5 per cent of total employment by 2009, over half of which were held by workers under 24. Beside flexibilization, The *Ich-AktienGesellshaft*, or 'Ich-AG' programme, aimed to encourage self-employment by subsidizing company start-ups, provided that the recipients' income is below €25,000 per annum. And after January 2004, companies excluded from rules of individual dismissals were expanded from those with fewer than five employees to those with fewer than ten.

The reform of job placement in 2004 was inspired by the New Public Management approach (Hood 1991), based on performance evaluation and improving public sector efficiency and effectiveness. Clients are classified into four main groups depending on employability potential: *Marktkunden* (the easily employable), *Beratungskunden Aktivieren* (clients needing general counselling), *Beratungskunden Fördern* (customers needing specific coaching and support) and *Betreuungskunden* (the least employable). As in the UK, placement offices have been turned into multitasking organizations where active and passive labour market policies are combined.

In 2005, the reform of unemployment support reduced the duration and diversity of benefits. Traditional unemployment benefits (*Arbeitslosengeld I*) were cut from 18 to 12 months and the second and third pillars of the previous system (*Arbeitslosenhilfe* and *Sozialhilfe*) were abolished and replaced by a single benefit called *Arbeitslosengeld II*, which is means tested and flat rate, and lower than those it replaced (€345 per month, falling to €331 in the East) – a level which in surveys the majority of Germans find too low. In 2010 this second pillar was extended to 8 per cent of the German population, mainly flexible workers who were suffering from the consequences of the international crisis.

In pensions, the trend, as elsewhere, is to decrease the generosity of the system by reducing replacement rates, increasing the retirement age and encouraging investment in private pensions. The 2001 Riester Reform pensions reform introduced voluntary, subsidized private pensions, reduced the replacement rate of the statutory pension system from 70 to 64 per cent, reduced the survivor's pension from 60 to 55 per cent of the deceased's benefits and introduced a means-tested social assistance minimum pension. That reform was revised in 2004 because of sustainability problems. A proposal to increase the standard retirement age from 65 to 67 by 2011 failed (the present government's plan is to achieve that increase between 2012 and 2029), the levels of social contributions were increased and indexation formulae tightened, and private pensions were further promoted using fiscal incentives for all categories of workers.

Comparing Germany to Italy reveals important commonalities, especially in the application of the 'activation paradigm' (Alti and Jessoula 2010). The key differences are the ongoing failure in Italy to reform unemployment benefits, which has been blocked since the late 1980s, and the fact that German 'flexible' workers are much less marginalized from the welfare system and the accrual of entitlements than their truly 'outsider' Italian counterparts.

The 1997 'Treu Package' (Law 196/1997) and the 2003 Biagi Law (30/2003) legalized temporary work (*lavoro in affitto*) and approved other new instruments of increasing working-time flexibility including jobs-on-call, job vouchers, job sharing and staff leasing. Project work and occasional work contracts were amended to include a more precise definition of workers' rights. The 2003 Biagi Law was especially controversial, and fiercely opposed by the largest Italian union, the CGIL, and by extreme-left parties.

The job placement system was radically transformed between 1997 and 2003, under legislative decree no. 469/1997, and Law 30/2003, legalizing private employment agencies after 50 years of state monopoly. Also introduced were conditionality rules and a commitment by the placement office to get the unemployed worker back to work as soon as possible, provided that he/she did not reject any work or training offers, in which case, as in the UK, the unemployment benefit is withdrawn. The problem in Italy is that greater labour market flexibility has not been accompanied by activation support: spending on active labour market policies was only equivalent to 0.54 per cent of GDP in 2005, half the level in both Germany and France, and just over one-quarter of that spent in Denmark. Note too that of its spending on labour market policy only a very small percentage (3 per cent) goes to placement services as against Germany's 15 per cent.

In the current crisis, additional unemployment assistance benefits have been introduced for 2008 to 2010, but they have not been sufficient to meet the increasing number of claimants. The conventional wages guarantee fund (the *Cassa Integrazione Guadagni*, CIG), has seen a massive expansion of claimants, but only permanently employed ('insider') workers get access to CIG income replacement. Italy's unemployment benefits system is as segmented as its labour market, with many workers (including young workers with no employment history) ineligible for income support (Samek Lodovici and Semenza 2008). A decree law approved by the Berlusconi government in June 2008 repealed various forms of protection for flexible workers agreed to a year earlier by the previous centre-left government.

The pension system has also been revised. Stricter rules concerning eligibility for invalidity pensions have been introduced, together with an increase in the retirement age for women in the public sector (from 60 to 65 by 2016) and the reduction of pension 'windows' in order to slow down retirement flows. After the reform of the mid-1990s, when pay-as-you-go was replaced by a defined-contribution system, a sequence of amendments and modifications have been introduced. But Italy remains a 'pensioners' welfare state. In 2007, pensions absorbed over 50 per cent of all benefits (compared with an EU-27 average of 39 per cent), as against 1.8 per cent for unemployment benefits (one-third of the EU-27 average) and 4.7 per cent for families and children (just over half of the EU-27 average, and the worst distribution apart from Poland's) (Figure 11.5). If Denmark is a best-case example of 'flexicurity' innovation, and inter-generational equity, with Germany a less well performing example, Italy is right at the other end of the spectrum.

More radical reforms have been introduced in France. As elsewhere, activation policies have been at the centre of the policy agenda. The first activation benefit – the *Revenu Minimum d'Insertion* (RMI) was in fact introduced in the late 1980s, linking income support to training and job search requirements. In 2000, the *Plan d'aide and de retour à l'emploi* introduced a series of conditionality measures and activation initiatives, including individual contracts for job seekers. In 2001 the Jospin Socialist government introduced tax credits (a negative income tax) – the *Prime pour l'emploi* – for low-paid workers, drawing lessons from the UK. Also in line with developments elsewhere, in 2009, the *Revenu de Solidarité Active* partially exempted employers from social security contributions if they hired RMI beneficiaries and provided a negative income tax guarantee to new low-wage workers, and the national employment agency was merged with the unemployment insurance fund, continuing the trend towards activation (Palier 2010a).

In pensions, the Raffarin reform of 2003 increased the contribution period for a full pension from 37 to 42 years by 2020, harmonized public-sector with private-sector contributions from 2008, and indexed public pensions to the cost of living. After a series of violent social protests, numerous concessions were made by the government; and only in 2010 under the presidency of Nicolas Sarkozy was a new reform introduced to ensure financial sustainability by increasing the normal retirement age for public pensions from 65 to 67 and early reduced pensions from 60 to 62.

The 2008 financial crisis hit France particularly hard. Bankruptcies were avoided by a quick government response to the crisis, and a package of stimulus measures was introduced, including a 'clunker' buy-back scheme, tax relief for small companies hiring new employees, tax credits for public–private partnerships, tax reductions for lower incomes and investment credit schemes, amounting to over 1 per cent of GDP (Gualmini and Schmidt 2010). A special *Revenu de Solidarité Active* was introduced for the victims of the job crunch, consisting of additional monthly payments of between €500 and €1,000.

All three countries – Germany, Italy and France – have converged on the goals of conditionality and activation – but the extent to which flexibility is backed up by security and a recalibration of social policy provision differs markedly between the cases. There is a debate as to whether these innovations have produced a 'departure' from the traditional Bismarckian regime or not. Palier (2010b) argues that the critical change has been the diffusion of a continental European variant of supply-side social policies and the dualization of welfare, labour markets and societies, creating reinforced 'insider–outsider' divides – which are especially acute in the Italian case.

The Liberal regime: a welfare-to-work approach in the UK

The UK has been a pioneer in the 'welfare-to-work' approach since 1995 when the Conservative government's Job Seeker's Allowance linked work and vocational training requirements to unemployment benefits. The goals of employability and activation became more explicit under New Labour after 1997, and were also targeted at poverty and social exclusion. In a paradoxical continuity with Victorian England where 'people who did not work should not eat' (Rimlinger 1971: 18, cited in Gualmini 1998), the mantra of New Labour became 'the best form of welfare is work'! New Labour's compromise with Margaret Thatcher's neo-liberal reforms was part of a deliberate appeal to the median voter – to attract disillusioned Conservatives as well as independents unsympathetic to old Labour-style policy (Rhodes 2000).

The consequence has been a considerable transformation of the British welfare state, and not just in the labour market. In 1997, the so-called 'New Deal' was launched. Its main target was young people in search of their first job, but it was later extended to the long-term unemployed and single parents. It included three steps: training initiatives to help the unemployed to find a job or attend an interview; an offer of a publicly subsidized job or a further training experience; and then a loss of benefits if a placement office job offer was rejected. Another form of activation – tax credits – was introduced in 1998. This 'negative' form of taxation (or fiscal discount) was targeted at working families and single parents with children to prevent voluntary exit from the labour market.

Between 1999 and 2002, the Blair government introduced a statutory national minimum wage and revised the rules on unfair dismissals and workers' rights in the workplace. In 2002, 'Jobcentres Plus' were created by merging Benefits Offices with Job Centres where the unemployed register for work opportunities. In 2007, the Freud Report – a long-term review of the Government's Welfare-to-Work strategy – presented positive outcomes: since 1998 over 1.7 million people had returned to work (Department for Work and Pensions 2007).

A major emphasis has been placed on poor families, with a pledge to halve child poverty by 2010. As part of the work place reforms, maternity rights were improved and from the late 1990s, childcare policies were linked to the New Deal and tax credits. Nonetheless, in 2005 to 2006 some 3.8 million children were living in poverty – i.e., in homes on less than 60 per cent of average income. Between 1998 and 2005, 600,000 children were lifted out of relative poverty, but in 2006 the number in poverty increased by 200,000. The government then relaunched its child support strategy in 2008 under the new Child Maintenance and Enforcement Commission (Daguerre 2006).

Nevertheless, the UK still has one of the worst rates of child poverty in Europe at 30 per cent – or 4 million children, 40 per cent of whom live in single-parent households. The high risk of poverty (among the very highest in the EU – Table 11.2) and intergenerational transmission of acute inequality has important consequences in terms of poor educational achievement and skills acquisition among a large proportion of the population (Esping-Andersen 2009)

The fight against poverty was also the goal of the 2002–03 reform of the first pillar of the pensions' system, comprising the basic state pension and the State Earnings-Related Pension Scheme, or SERPS, introduced by the Thatcher government in 1978. A new Pension Credit was introduced (providing additional weekly support for those on the lowest incomes) and SERPS was replaced by a new State Second Pension, to concentrate pensions' provision on those with the lowest and medium incomes. Two major reforms in 2007 to 2008 reduced the number of qualifying years for the basic and additional state pensions, introduced national insurance credits for people with children, increased women's retirement age, and promoted the use of private supplementary funds.

Immediately after the elections of May 2010, the new centre-right coalition government, led by David Cameron as Prime Minister, delivered a document on welfare policies ('Coalition Programme for Government, Jobs and Welfare') in which the emphasis under New Labour on conditionality and activation was deepened, alongside new austerity measures to deal with the country's budgetary crisis.

A total of £18bn in welfare cuts – the deepest since the 1970s – was announced. Benefits will become meaner and conditionality still tougher. The previously universal child benefit is being withdrawn from higher income groups. Public-sector wages have been frozen for two years, and 490,000 public-sector jobs are being cut. Job Seeker's Allowance claimants under 25 are now to be referred to a new programme within six months; all Incapacity Benefit claimants are to be reassessed for readiness to work, and those deemed capable of work are being moved on to the Jobseeker's Allowance, with a one-year time limit on their claims for employment and income support. New 'Work Clubs', where unemployed can meet, exchange information and find job opportunities were introduced, as were tax incentives (the 'Work for Yourself' scheme) to encourage business start-ups. The state pension age will be equalized for men and women at 65 from 2018 and will rise to 66 in April 2020. The pension contributions of public-sector workers are being raised by 3 per cent.

In November 2010, the government announced a radical overhaul of the entire benefit system with the aim of 'making work pay'. A new 'universal credit' is to replace the working tax credit, child tax credit, housing benefit, income support, jobseeker's allowance and other income-related allowances. Tougher penalties will be imposed on people deemed fit to work but unwilling to do so: those refusing work on three occasions will lose their benefits for three years. But people moving into and out of work will be able to retain some of their benefit (35p for each £1 they earn) – a more generous form of work subsidy than under the previous system. An already lean (some would say 'mean') welfare state will become even leaner.

From state-socialism to hybrid welfare states: reforms in Poland, Hungary and the Czech Republic

The fall of communism in the CEE countries brought fiscal crisis, the end of full employment and state subsidies, and the privatization of state-owned enterprises. A social safety net was introduced to compensate, but labour market policies became less generous, with reduced benefits and benefits duration, longer qualification periods, lower replacement rates and cuts in employers' social contributions. However, as Cook (2010: 711) puts it, over time 'the outcome shows a 'layering' of inherited communist, revived Bismarckian, and market-oriented elements that has eroded, but by no means eliminated, the solidaristic and re-distributive features of CEE welfare regimes'.

These welfare states have thus assumed a mixed nature that cuts across conventional welfare families. If pension systems have moved closer to the characteristics of the Bismarckian–Conservative welfare cluster (Cerami 2010), labour market policies which have been the object of a series of retrenchment measures, approximate developments in the Liberal countries, especially the UK. It has been argued that together Poland, Hungary, Slovakia and the Czech Republic represent a hybrid liberal–conservative model which is less generous than the average conservative welfare state but more generous than the average liberal one (Cook 2010: 723)

In the Czech Republic, the unemployment benefit replacement rate was cut from 60 to 40 per cent n the early-1990s, but increased to 45 per cent in 2004, and the minimum wage was increased from 31.2 to 39.4 per cent in 2006. In line with the UK's 'welfare-to-work approach', the 2004 New Employment Act announced new sanctions on the unemployed if they rejected a public offer of temporary work. And in 2009, the centre-right coalition implemented a one-third cut in benefits for unemployed workers who reject job offers and revealed insufficient evidence of active job search (Saxonberg and Sirovàtka 2009).

In Poland, whereas in the past there was no condition on employment benefit eligibility, from the early 2000s receipt of benefits has depended on being without a job for at least one year in the previous 18 months, but this reference period varies according to the level of regional unemployment. In Hungary, placement services were reorganized according to the philosophy of activation and support for the unemployed. In the 2000s a revision of the unemployment benefits reduced the replacement rate to 60 per cent of the individual gross income in the previous four quarters, with a reference period of 12 months. Among these three countries, Poland seems to spend least on income support (reflected perhaps in its highest at-risk-of-poverty rates in this group) and a higher percentage than the others on active labour market policies, although these are very efficiently targeted (Tables 11.2 and 11.3), and twice as much as a percentage of GDP on all labour market policies than the Czech Republic, even if both countries spend a similar amount (18 per cent of GDP) on social protection overall.

This probably reflects superior Czech employment performance (Hungary's is by far the worst of the three) (Figures 11.2 and 11.3).

In fact in none of these countries has the 'flexicurity' debate truly moved to centre stage, and even though social partner involvement is important to varying degrees in all three, neither employers, nor unions nor governments have engaged in substantial debate on linking greater investment in active labour market policies to the reform of labour market regulation. The Hungarian labour market has rather weak job protection and high levels of *de jure* flexibility. In the Czech Republic, permanent job protection (affecting approximately 91 per cent of all employees) is rather strong, while protection for temporary employment is weak by EU standards. But both countries have relatively low levels of flexible employment: in 2010, temporary employees accounted for only 8 per cent of the work force in the Czech Republic and 9 per cent in Hungary – compared with an EU-27 average of 14 per cent.

Poland, however, extensively liberalized its Labour Code in 2002, relaxing regulations on temporary employment, which led to a massive expansion of fixed-term contracts (which halved youth unemployment) to well above 25 per cent of the workforce in 2008 to 2010 (growing even after the onset of the crisis), joining Spain as the two EU countries with excessively flexible workforces. It is worth noting that while the Czechs and Hungarians have levels of in-work poverty risk well below the EU-27's 8 per cent average (at 4 and 5 per cent respectively), Poland has one of the highest risks of in-work poverty in the EU, at 12 per cent (in addition to a higher risk of poverty among the young and old than both the Czech Republic and Hungary).

All three countries have thoroughly reformed their pensions systems since the mid-1990s, with many similarities: the detachment of pension funds from the general state budget; the introduction of a Bismarckian contributory logic in traditional pay-as-you-go systems and a stricter actuarial linkage between pension benefits and earnings; increases in the retirement age and the number of qualifying years; and the revision of benefits indexation in line with inflation and wage increases (Hacker 2009; Aspalter *et al.* 2009).

The most radical reform occurred in Poland, where in 1999 a defined-benefit scheme was transformed into a notional defined-contribution scheme, based on the equivalence between contributions and provided benefits. Complementary private funds have been strongly encouraged. The result was a three-pillar system: the first is mandatory and comprises three parts (minimum public pension, defined-contributory benefits and open private funds); the second (including occupational plans) and the third are voluntary, individual and contributions related. In 2004 a new law tried to further encourage private supplementary funds (Natali 2007).

A multi-pillar system was also introduced in Hungary between 1997 and 1998: the first pillar is a Bismarckian social insurance scheme and the second a personal savings-funded scheme (although the latter was eliminated in 2010). A universal basic pension was introduced to combat increasing poverty, and, representing a 'solidaristic' element in Hungary, the gross pensions replacement rate is significantly higher (at 66.8 per cent) than in Poland (53.3 per cent) and the Czech Republic (49.1 per cent) (Senato 2007). This high replacement rate contributes to Hungary's lowest risk-of-poverty rate for the elderly in the EU (Table 11.2), despite also having a much better balance between spending on the elderly and spending on children and families than Poland which, apart from Italy, has the most imbalanced intergenerational investment ratio in Europe (Figure 11.3).

In the Czech Republic reforms have been less radical and more continuous with the past: the country still has a Bismarckian defined-benefit (or a pay-as-you-go) system, but in 1998 a contributory, earning-related element was introduced. Enrolment in private funds (following the concept of the 'individualization of risks') is not mandatory, but voluntary insurance is widespread and 50 per cent of the workforce is in occupational funds. A pension income is now composed of a basic flat-rate amount, paid monthly, monthly plus an earning-related component.

Having undergone considerable change over the last 20 years, the 2008–10 crisis has triggered yet another cycle of adjustment, with potentially profound consequences for some of the CEE countries, depending on their degree of financial stability. Poland was actually in good shape before the crisis hit, thanks to its low budget deficit, and was able to avoid recession (and significant job losses) in 2009. But Hungary was the first CEE country to go cap in hand to the IMF to deal with its alarming fiscal and financial situation, receiving $15.7 billion from the IMF in 2008, and a further $8.4 billion from the EU and $1.3 billion from the World Bank, in exchange for a package of radical austerity measures, including a freeze on wage increases and pension bonuses. Although rather sheltered from the financial crisis, public expenditure is being cut in the Czech Republic, including public-sector employment and welfare benefits, in part because of the impact of the 2009–10 recession, but also because of the need to cut its deficit for eurozone membership.

Conclusion

The analysis above allows us to highlight certain trends characterizing European welfare state development in the first decade of the 2000s. They can be summed up as follows:

- a shift of emphasis from passive income support to a proactive employment policy that seeks to 'activate' benefit claimants, in more flexible labour markets;
- attempts to remove 'perverse incentives' that allow individuals to remain on benefits and to make work an individual 'obligation';
- a higher individualization of risk, in both labour market and pensions reforms, the former placing the onus on the individual to find work, the latter increasing the private savings component of old age income support; and
- a greater attention to costs, that includes new management methods in public services, especially, but not only, in countries with low employment rates that constrain the revenue available for generous welfare provision.

In the first decade of the 2000s, welfare provisions were increasingly considered responses and solutions to individual problems and risks (the level of individual literacy, education and training, versatility and flexibility and entrepreneurship). The diffusion of a differentiated range of flexible labour contracts, the declining unionization of flexible workers and the transnational organization of business and production have made it more difficult to consider citizens and welfare recipients as a collective and homogenous category. The relationship between rights and responsibilities has been redefined, in such a way that welfare recipients have to actively cooperate in solving their own problems. These changes can be identified across all four of the country clusters, regardless of their structural differences and outcomes, in terms of employment, unemployment, the intergenerational distribution of benefits, or rates of inequality or poverty.

What is also clear, however, is that the policy outcomes of these changes are often rather poor. Not only are most countries not thereby meeting the rather basic targets set by the EU (notably the Lisbon target of a 70 per cent employment rate by 2010), but apart from a few exceptions (all in Scandinavia), nor are European countries improving their policy mix in favour of greater equity and efficiency. Ten years ago, one of the authors co-wrote an analysis of the problems facing European welfare systems (Ferrera *et al.* 2000), which focused on the employment and income security successes of certain countries (the Netherlands and Denmark), the mediocre performance of others (most countries in the Conservative group), the high levels of inequality and poverty that accompanied employment growth in the Liberal group (the UK in particular) and the severe difficulties faced by the southern European countries in reversing low employment rates, high levels of youth unemployment, and improving the level and distribution of social policy spending.

Ten years later, not a great deal has changed, at least in terms of the big picture, except that all of the Conservative countries have now joined their Southern European counterparts in developing serious divides in the labour market between protected 'insiders' and much less protected 'outsiders', only partially compensated for in some countries by undifferentiated welfare coverage. Despite their 'Third Way' innovations, the Liberal countries are still marked by large social inequalities, despite their relatively good employment performance, and are no closer to correcting their lack of investment in families and children. The Social Democratic Scandinavian countries, both then and now, combine a mix of policies that affords them high employment levels and low levels of unemployment, poverty risk and inequality, as well as a relatively good ratio between expenditure on the elderly and investment in the young.

To return to the challenges with which this chapter was introduced, despite frenetic policy activity, most countries are barely coping with societal ageing, or responding to the breakdown of traditional families, or dealing effectively with the transformation of work. The growing dualization of employment, and in many countries of welfare provision as well, is only fuelling the vicious circle identified above: more poorly protected jobs increase inequality and poverty and impede family formation, placing further downward pressure on fertility rates and aggravating the ageing of European societies; and the rising welfare costs of ageing prevent a reorientation of spending towards the young and families and human capital investment, undermining both the efficiency *and* equity of European economies.

Chapter 12

Religion-Related Issues in European Politics and Law

John T.S. Madeley

The much-discussed resurgence of the religious factor in politics across the world has not left Europe untouched. While the continent, especially in its more westerly and northern parts, has often been taken to represent the quintessence of secularity, it has also in recent decades witnessed the recrudescence of some old, as well as the emergence of some new, religion-related issues and controversies in public life (Casanova 1994; Katzenstein 2004; Taylor 2007). For some academic commentators, Europe faces nothing less than the undoing of the Westphalian settlement of 1648, which is conventionally regarded as having put an end to Europe's wars of religion, and/or a struggle to defend Western values and institutions against those in or from the rest of the world who progressively and aggressively seek to undermine them (Huntington 1996; Philpott 2004). Political commentators from the left and the right argue that Europe faces nothing short of a cultural and moral – even a civilizational – crisis (Fallaci 2002; Weigel 2005). Meantime among increasingly vocal secularists the fear is expressed that the re-emergence of religion-related issues and the political mobilization of groups along lines of religious identification represents an intolerable breach of an essential principle of keeping private religious concerns and arguments out of politics and public affairs. While Huntington's claims about 'a global revival of religion' involving 'new surges in commitment, relevance, and practice by erstwhile casual believers' cannot be sustained in the case of Europe as a whole, it is evident that major changes have undeniably occurred in the political salience of religion-related issues there as elsewhere.

The most common approach to making sense of these recent trends in Europe stresses the impact of the various epochal shifts that have occurred in recent decades, especially those associated with the end of the Cold War, the almost unprecedented surges in migration into and across Europe as a whole, which eventuated from the new world (dis-)order and 9/11 with its ensuing aftershocks, shifts which have patently had the effect of dramatically amplifying or extending the scope of religion–cultural pluralism in Europe (Byrnes and Katzenstein 2006; Banchoff 2007; Motzkin and Fischer 2008). A complementary perspective relies on the view that what Bryan Wilson called 'the inherited model' of secularization had always failed to appreciate how many of the old marks of the early-modern confessional state have survived into the late-modern period, only to emerge as newly-controversial in the context of rapid cultural change (Bader 2007; Fox 2008; Madeley 2008). Meanwhile for Eisenstadt the developments since approximately 1989 have been a matter not so much of resurgence or survival as of a 'reconstruction of religions', involving variously 'the rise of new religious (especially fundamentalist and communal-national) movements; the crystallisation of new diasporas with strong religious identities; profound transformations within the major religions, and the growing importance of religious components in the constitution of contemporary political arenas and in the constitution of collective identities' (2008: 21). The uneven incidence of these developments and their impact on European public affairs present a number of complex challenges of both description and explanation but these can perhaps only be met if the relatively stable background against which they have occurred is first properly appreciated.

State–religion relations in Europe: the comparative context

Many liberal theorists of the nineteenth and twentieth centuries argued that the avoidance of political conflict about matters of religion was a necessary prerequisite for the development of free societies and liberal democracy as they developed more or less successfully in Western Europe. In the conventional liberal account the 1648 Westphalian peace was held to have finally exorcized the demons of the Wars of Religion that had devastated early-modern Europe and was seen to stand as a monument to that achievement. The impact of the Enlightenment, which had been violently diffused across much of continental Europe in the wake of the French Revolutionary and Napoleonic wars, was judged also to have had the salutary effect of promoting a separation of church and state intended to insulate the political realm from irrational impulses issuing out of the religious sphere. It is the case that for some the wars of the twentieth century up to and including the Cold War, were seen as crypto-religious conflicts between the forces of the 'political religions' of, severally, aggravated nationalisms, imperialism, Nazism and Marxism-Leninism on the one hand and those liberals, on the other, who defended core Western values seen as deriving, in part at least, from Judaeo-Christian roots (Burleigh 2005, 2006). By the early 1990s these earlier struggles had nonetheless seemed to end with a victory for a distinctly secular model of liberal democracy twinned with an increasingly global capitalist economy. Fukuyama's version of this triumphalist tale even heralded the 'endpoint of mankind's ideological evolution' and the successful arrival of the 'final form of human government' (1992: xi).

From his very different perspective Eric Hobsbawm (1994) dated the end of his 'short twentieth century' to 1991 when the Soviet Union had ceased to exist. While that particular event appears suitably symbolic it was perhaps in 1989 that the Cold War came to a virtual end with events such as the Russian withdrawal from Afghanistan and, in Europe itself, the legalization of Solidarity in Poland (leading to the appointment of Central and Eastern Europe's first non-communist government in over four decades), the tearing down of the Berlin Wall and the revolutions, violent and non-violent, in respectively Rumania and Czechoslovakia. It happened that this year was also the bicentenary of that earlier epochal upheaval in Europe, the French Revolution of 1789, which had done so much to remake the map of Europe. As had occurred two centuries earlier Hobsbawm noted 'after 1989, dozens of new territorial states appeared without any independent mechanism for determining their borders' and, partly as a consequence, that process 'saw more military operations in more parts of Europe, Asia and Africa than anyone could remember' (*ibid.*: 559–60). Within the confines of Europe this even involved the onset of violent ethnic conflicts especially in the Balkans and the Caucasus which were partly fuelled by rival ethno-religious identities variously pitting Catholic against Orthodox against Muslim – a return it seemed to the pre-Westphalian chaos of religious war which triggered large-scale population transfers and waves of migration. In addition, even where violent ethno-religious conflicts were mercifully absent, the surge of movements of national reconstruction and reassertion, which attended the collapse of most of the Cold War structures in Central and Eastern Europe, provided opportunities for the representatives of the old mainstream religious traditions to attempt to reclaim the standing which the communist regimes had attempted to undermine or even destroy.

Coincidentally the year 1989 also saw two initially local developments in Western Europe which were to reverberate with increasing volume over the ensuing two decades: the furore, initially in Britain, over the Iranian fatwa against Salman Rushdie after the publication of his 1988 novel *The Satanic Verses*, and the banning from attendance at public school of two girls in the small northern French town of Creil on the grounds that they insisted on wearing Islamic headdress, the hijab (or *foulard*). These two events can be taken to symbolize the rather sudden eruption of new tensions across much of Europe where significant numbers of Muslims had long lived or recently settled. In the two decades since their emergence these tensions have, in Western Europe especially, periodically been both demonstrated and intensified by major civil disturbances, such as those in northern England in 2001 and France in 2005, and by dramatic events such as '9/11' in the USA (2001), the onset of the Iraq war in 2003, the jihadist attacks on Madrid (2004) and London (2005), the murder of Theo van Gogh in the Netherlands in 2004, and the Danish cartoons crisis (2005–6). The response of political and religious leaders to the disparate challenges represented by these events has varied relative to the nature of the challenges themselves as they impacted in particular national contexts and relative to the institutional and cultural traditions – in conventional shorthand the set of church–state relations – obtaining in different countries and regions. While the principal concern has become how to accommodate or integrate Muslim minorities, this has by no means been the only focus however; in the 1990s, for example, the activities of various 'new religious movements' including Scientology or the Solar Temple also became distinct objects of concern, while more traditional issues such as abortion law reform, stem-cell research, assisted dying or the teaching of religion in the public schools continued periodically to feature in the political agenda of many countries. And as with the remarkable developments in Eastern Europe where patterns of church–state relations underwent massive change in the wake of the end of the Cold War, in Western Europe the tensions generated around religion-related issues have been handled in different ways and with widely varying degrees of success.

In order to understand the variable impact of the religious factor on European politics it is therefore necessary to pay attention to the inherited frameworks of church–state – or better, religion–state – relations. While path-dependent analysis cannot explain all outcomes it is doubtful if any analysis can succeed without taking account of those inherited 'frames', as David Martin called them (Martin 1978). In describing and making sense of these contextual frameworks as they developed in different parts of Europe analysts tend to stress either communalities or contrasts. Among the latter the contrasts between rival confessional patterns of state–religion relations – those between Catholic, Orthodox and Protestant confessions in particular – have been a natural focus especially because of the dominance of these distinctive traditions in the historically mono-confessional blocs which dominated respectively the Southern, Eastern and Northern quadrants of the European continent's irregular territory through much of the early modern period (Madeley 2003b). Focusing on the confessional contrasts between the historically mono-confessional blocs also highlights the existence of the historically multi-confessional belts (which lie between the blocs) where societies have long been forced to confront the challenges arising from confessional pluralism. In these multi-confessional societies alternating episodes of religious oppression and toleration have at different times and places involved bouts of religio-ethnic 'cleansing', punitive codes of religious discipline, consociational systems of rule, local veto and varying degrees of *de jure* and *de facto* cultural–religious toleration.

It is argued by some however that focusing on the differences in state–religion relations to be found across Europe obscures the existence of common features which make Europe distinctive relative to the rest of the world including other parts of the West, such as the USA. Thus, Silvio Ferrari observes that because of the forced marginality of Jews and Muslims in the early-modern period 'religious pluralism in Europe has predominantly been intra-Christian pluralism and the religious conflicts that divided Europe after the Great Schism [between Catholicism and Orthodoxy] and above all after the Protestant Reformation did not create insuperable cultural divisions ... The unification process of Europe, for all its shortcomings, is proof that a shared notion of citizenship exists' (2008: 103–4). A decade earlier he had also claimed to identify the existence of what he called a 'common European model' of state–religion relations, contending that the differences between the principal patterns of church–state relations which have conventionally been described – in Western Europe, at least – should be seen as little more than surface features which tended to disguise the fact of underlying similarities and commonalities (1999). The traditional focus on 'outmoded' typologies based especially on the three-way distinction between separatist, concordat-based and state–church systems paid too much attention to the formal elements of institutional relationships and obscured the existence of a common 'legal substance'.

The common European model was characterized first by a commitment to recognize individuals' rights to religious liberty, something to which all West European countries – and now almost all of Europe's 50-odd states – have subscribed. Anomalies in the practical recognition of the principle of religious liberty and all its entailments – such as the constitutional ban in Greece on proselytism – were gradually being eliminated, although novel problems in connection with the toleration of several new religious movements (NRMs) or 'cults' such as the Church of Scientology or the Moonies continued to pose problems. In this the emergent European religion–state model was no different from any other – all systems confront often imponderable issues in this regard and vary in the responses made. What was distinctive and more significant about Ferrari's common European model as opposed to, say, the USA's separationist or the Soviets' exclusionist models however was its systematic privileging of religion: 'A religious sub-sector is singled out within the public sector. This may be understood as a "playing field" or "protected area". Inside it the various collective religious subjects (churches, denominations, and religious communities) are free to act in conditions of substantial advantage compared to those collective subjects that are not religious' (*ibid.*:12). This privileging of religion clearly offends against the requirements of most normative liberal theorists such as Audi (1989), for example. In Audi's terms the European model as identified by Ferrari must be seen as seriously deficient on neutrality grounds since it grants religious 'subjects' significant advantages relative to non-religious 'subjects'. Not only does this make for inequality of treatment, thereby offending against Audi's egalitarian requirement, but in many systems the offence is compounded by the effective construction of 'hierarchies of recognition' between locally favoured religions and, several gradations down, those which are denied any recognition at all, sometimes even being denied legal existence on one ground or another (Madeley 2006b).

Ferrari has not of course been alone in observing the privileged standing of religious groups in Europe, despite the continent's reputation for uniquely high levels of secularization (Monsma and Soper 1997; Rémond 1999; Stepan 2000; Bader 2003; Barro and McCleary 2005; Klausen 2005; Fox 2006; Madeley 2008). His particular contribution has been to show that this privileging has been a systematic feature underlying the most disparate particulars of state–religion linkages across Europe as a whole. One question-begging feature of the emergent model as he initially presented it however is that it was centred on what he saw as the distinctively secular nature of the modern state, in French, its *laïcité*: 'the fundamental principles of the common European model of relationships between the state and the religious communities ... are quite rigid ... [They] have been summed up in the formula "the secular state"'(1999: 11). It might be argued however that what distinguishes the European model is not so much state *laïcité* as a generalized form of state religiosity, particularly when contrasted with the US model. This is a point which emerges clearly from the analyses of Norris and Inglehart (2004), Barro and McCleary (2005) and of Jonathan Fox (2006) using large worldwide data collections for mapping religion–state connectedness. Table 12 .1 displays some of the headline results arising from the analysis of the Fox data archive for the year 2002 (the latest date currently available), arranged so as to illustrate differences and similarities within and between Eastern and Western Europe. As the note explains, Fox's SRAS (separation of religion and state) measure runs from 0.00, corresponding to complete separation of religion and state – a score represented, alone out of 175 country cases, by the USA (Fox 2006). It is constructed on the basis of six batteries of variables including measures for state support for, or hostility towards, different religions, the relative 'weight' of state regulatory practices in the field of religion, and the use of state authority to impose religious standards on different populations.

As the table demonstrates, as of 2002 no European state matched the USA's record on SRAS although the Netherlands and Estonia come close. The mean score for all 23 Western European countries is 19.17 where each whole point represents an instance of a significant derogation from, or infringement of, strict separationism. The East European mean score at 24.24 is somewhat higher, evidently as a result – as is easily noted from Table 12.1 – of the overall higher scores of the Orthodox countries. On the whole, with the possible exception of these latter, the picture is one of a broadly similar pattern across the whole continent characterized by a normal distribution of significant deviations from American separationism. However, as the other columns of the table illustrate, using a combination of Cole Durham's (1996) and Fox's typologies of state–religion regimes, there continues to be significant variety in terms of overall institutional patterns . It is notable that within Europe separationist regimes are only to be found in France and Azerbaijan where, far from conforming to the US pattern, each are found actually to score more highly than the Western and Eastern means in terms of their deviation from full SRAS. The lowest-scoring states are the ones coded as Accommodationist, a term which is taken to indicate a state's posture of 'benevolent neutrality' towards religion. The Cooperationist pattern, for which Germany can be taken as a prime exemplar, is well represented on both sides of the former Iron Curtain – in the West accounting for 8 (out of 23) cases while in the East 9 are given this designation (the same number as are listed as having Endorsed Religion). On these codings, only one Eastern country, Armenia, with the highest deviation from SRAS to be found across the whole of Europe is judged to have instituted an Official Religion regime, while in Western Europe this designation is deemed appropriate for all of 10 cases. If, following Ferrari, the *laïcité* of the state in Western Europe is to be seen as a fundamental principle of the European model of church–state relations, it would appear on this evidence to be one more honoured in the breach than the observance. And the evidence of developments in Europe East and West in the decades since Ferrari put forward his thesis is that this is more and more recognized to be the case with troubling implications for the accommodation of the 'new religious pluralism' (Banchoff 2007).

Developments in Central and Eastern Europe

The picture of religion–state relations in Central and Eastern Europe (CEE) in 2002 which emerges from the Table 12 .1 is very different from

Table 12.1 Church–state regimes in Europe: typology and degrees of separation (2002)

Quintiles	Western democracies	SRAS score	State–religious regime type	Former Soviet bloc	SRAS score	State–religious regime type
0.00 >9.99	Netherlands	1.25	Accommodationist	Estonia	3.52	Accommodationist
				Albania	7.69	Accommodationist
10.00>19.99	Luxembourg	10.50	Cooperationist	Slovenia	11.96	Cooperationist
	Sweden	12.17	Cooperationist			
	Italy	13.00	Cooperationist			
	Ireland	15.75	Endorsed Religion	Bosnia-H	16.33	Cooperationist
	Gk Cyprus	16.13	Cooperationist	Yugoslavia	16.75	Cooperationist
	Tk. Cyprus	16.96	Endorsed Religion	Latvia	17.56	Cooperationist
	Germany	19.88	Cooperationist	Lithuania	17.58	Cooperationist
				Czech Rep	18.19	Cooperationist
				Slovakia	19.88	Cooperationist
				Ukraine	19.99	Cooperationist
20.00>29.99	Switzerland	20.50	Cooperationist	Poland	22.21	Endorsed Religion
	Portugal	21.94	Endorsed Religion	Croatia	22.42	Endorsed Religion
	France	22.92	Separatist	Hungary	22.79	Cooperationist
	Andorra	23.13	Official Religion	Romania	24.50	Endorsed Religion
	Austria	24.25	Cooperationist			
	Belgium	25.50	Cooperationist			
	Malta	25.63	Official Religion			

continued overleaf

Table 12.1 *continued*

Quintiles	Western democracies	SRAS score	State–religious regime type	Former Soviet bloc	SRAS score	State–religious regime type
20.00>29.99	Norway	25.83	Official Religion			
	Denmark	26.04	Official Religion			
	Liechtenstein	27.50	Official Religion			
	UK	27.67	Official Religion(s)	Macedonia	27.17	Endorsed Religion
	Spain	28.46	Official Religion			
	Iceland	29.79	Official Religion			
30.00>39.99				Russia	30.48	Endorsed Religion
	Finland	32.88	Official Religion	Azerbaijan	31.65	Separationist
				Moldova	32.34	Endorsed Religion
	Greece	33.31	Official Religion	Georgia	32.83	Endorsed Religion
				Belarus	35.66	Endorsed Religion
				Bulgaria	36.72	Endorsed Religion
40.00>49.99				Armenia	40.36	Official Religion
Mean Scores		19.17			24.24	

Notes: Fox's SRAS index scores represent an overall measure of separation of religion and state (where 0 = full separation). It was obtained by combining six narrower-gauge measures for: (a) state support for one or more religions either officially or in practice; (b) state hostility toward religion; (c) comparative government treatment of different religions, including both benefits and restrictions; (d) government restrictions on the practice of religion by religious minorities; (e) government regulation of the majority religion; and (f) legislation of religious laws (Fox 2006). The state–religious regime type labels are a combination of those used by Fox (*ibid.*) and by Cole Durham (996: 20–22). The latter's 'Endorsed Religion' is preferred to Fox's 'Civil Religion', while Fox's 'Official Religion' is preferred to Cole Durham's 'Established Church(es)'. Source of data: Fox as detailed in Fox (2008).

the one which a similar table for 1982 would have shown. The Soviet-installed regimes had after 1945 introduced the strict state controls on traditional churches and other religious bodies which had been pioneered in Russia after the Bolshevik revolution of 1917. The ensuing repression of religious institutions, officials and adherents occurred more often than not in the context of constitutional provisions which ostensibly guaranteed religious freedom in accordance with the Universal Declaration of Human Rights of 1948 and other international legal instruments. By 1970 however all CEE 22 countries which lay behind the Iron Curtain could, despite various local relaxations of control, be designated Atheistic *de jure*, committed in Barrett's terms to 'formally promoting irreligion' (1982, 2001). This meant typically that while the state was ostensibly separated from all religions and churches, it was also 'linked for ideological reasons with irreligion and opposed on principle to all religion', claiming the right 'to oppose religion by discrimination, obstruction or even suppression' (Barrett 1982: 96). In a manner reminiscent of the penal laws which had been once used by confessional states to repress and punish dissent from official churches, the post-1945 arrangements in these states entailed the marginalization of religion, the exclusion of active religious adherents from public life, and the cutting off of most of the resources required for religious communities to flourish. 'Separation of church and state', a term ironically much in favour in the CEE countries, meant that while the religious were excluded from influence in the state, the state was not in any way prevented from interfering in the field of religious provision. On the contrary, that the state and its organs were placed in a position to exert maximum control and surveillance for the purpose of excluding religion from the public sphere. In the extreme case of Albania, finally, the attempt was openly made between 1967 and 1991 to abolish religion altogether.

In the late 1980s the so-called third wave of democratization finally washed across Eastern Europe, so putting an end to the region's communist regimes. Churches and religious groups were in some of these countries, most notably in Poland, of considerable significance in the campaigns for liberalization and democratization which – along with the withdrawal of Soviet guarantees – precipitated the shift to more open democratic regimes. By the start of the new millennium all the states which had been coded by Barrett as Atheistic in 1970 had either returned to his category of *de jure* Religious states providing support to the locally dominant religious tradition (15 cases) or had opted to be *de jure* Secular (7 cases: Russia, the 3 Baltic states, Hungary, Slovakia and Macedonia) i.e. officially promoting neither religion nor irreligion (Barret *et al.* 2001; Madeley 2008). As Table 12.1 indicates however by 2002 three of these supposedly Secular states (Russia, Hungary and Macedonia) were deemed by Fox to have installed systems of Endorsed Religion, a further three (Latvia, Lithuania and Slovakia) had opted for a Cooperationist solution, while Estonia alone had adopted an Accommodationist regime.

Initially the collapse of communism around 1989 in the CEE countries had led to a more or less rapid liberalization of the religious sphere which was promoted by the firm commitment of the Conference on Security and Cooperation in Europe (CSCE) in favour of institutionalizing full religious freedom. In the case of Russia itself a 1991 law on religion introduced a virtual free religious market overnight, with few restrictions on new entrants or terms of competition (Anderson 2003:1). In the Central European countries where the Catholic church represented the historically dominant tradition there was initially an attempt to re-establish church privileges, in particular in Poland, where it agitated both for constitutional recognition and a national commitment to Christian values (Casanova 1994: 110–13). Throughout CEE the issue was soon joined however as to how the new succession regimes should relate to the challenges of religious freedom which they had not faced during (or, in many respects, even before) the era of Soviet domination. A major shift occurred in Russia in 1997 when the State Duma adopted a new law 'on freedom of conscience and religious organisation' which introduced what can be called a hierarchy of recognition between different religious groups with regard to their symbolic status and legal rights. This involved a distinct retreat from the untrammelled freedoms of the 1991 reform on the grounds, firmly pressed by the representatives of the Russian Orthodox Church, that after seven decades of atheist repression it was ill fitted to face competition with the often well-heeled revivalist missions from the West which were – so it was claimed – flooding into Russia. The example of this 1997 retreat was arguably all the more influential because it appeared to represent an adjustment in the direction of Western European patterns with their privileging of religion – and especially of locally 'traditional' traditions. Thus, in the case of Serbia a draft religion law, first made public by the Ministry of Religions in July 2004, drew on precedents elsewhere in Europe, for example in Austria, as it proposed to allocate religious communities to separate categories with differing rights. The draft was criticized for flouting the idea of equal treatment of all religions on the grounds that it represented the creation of a virtual system of multiple state churches with special privileges on the one hand and a penumbra of other religious groups to whom those privileges were to be denied. Most privileged would be the Serbian Orthodox Church, while the six other recognized religious communities, most of them linked to historic ethno-religious minorities in Serbia (e.g. the Hungarian Reformed Church), would be accorded full recognition but fewer rights. Outside this relatively narrow circle of religious privilege, religious associations could be registered subject to special requirements and controls, while lowest in the hierarchy of recognition would be communities registered under the common law governing all civil associations. Those ostensibly religious groups – such as various sects, cults or new religious movements – which failed to gain recognition, even as civil associations, were liable to be consigned to the status of illegal groups subject to police enforcement actions (Richardson 2004).

It is noteworthy that none of the eight former CEE communist countries that joined the EU in May 2004 (in alphabetic order: the Czech Republic, Estonia, Hungary, Latvia, Lithuania, Poland, Slovakia and Slovenia) formally adopted a state church model after the end of the Cold War; nor on the other hand did any of them adopt a full separation model despite the claim of most secularist liberals that it constitutes a *sine qua non* of liberal democracy. In Slovakia, one of the countries deemed to belong to the Cooperationist category, the 2001 concordat was followed by more detailed treaties with the Vatican on Catholic education in schools, state financing of Catholic schools, and Catholic chaplains in the police and army. Indeed, all eight CEE states including those that did not have significant Catholic populations negotiated some kind of concordat settlement with the Vatican – something which is perhaps all the more remarkable since in 2004 of the 15 previous EU members only five (Austria, Germany, Italy, Portugal and Spain) had existing concordats (Schanda 2005). In Germany the fall of the Wall in 1989 had also led to a new wave of church–state treaties, as the Eastern *Länder* were again opened for free religious activity. For the Catholic church, for example, this resulted in concordats with Thuringia (1996), Mecklenburg-Pomerania (1997) Saxony-Anhalt (1998) and Brandenburg (2003). The genesis of these agreements can be seen in part as arising from Pope John Paul II's declared aim of 're-evangelising' Europe, starting first in the eastern half of the continent.

The result of all these changes was the partial re-establishment of churches which had once been locally dominant; in Central Europe the Catholic church, and further east, the various national Orthodox churches, enjoyed a restoration of sorts, symbolized by the return and refurbishment of many of the church properties which had been confiscated under communism. Many of the minority traditions which had been present on the national territories sufficiently far back in time as to be considered traditional, also benefited from this end of the religious ice age but in the case of some historic minorities, such as Ukraine's Uniates or Armenia's Muslim Azeris, negative discrimination became even more overt and oppressive than in Soviet times. In most of the former communist countries the continued existence of elements of the bureaucracy which had previously specialized in the surveillance and control of religious activities (for example, the Serbian Ministry of Religions or the Directorate of Religious Affairs in Bulgaria) have been 're-tasked' to monitor and control minority religions. The targets of these new surveillance programmes include suspected extreme Islamist groups which are presumed to threaten the very survival of particular states but they extend also to some sects or dissident movements of longstanding. In Russia, for example, Jehovah's Witnesses are still periodically involved in appealing against local bans on their activities. The decision of a Moscow judge who had imposed one such ban mentioned that, while there was no evidence that the Jehovah's Witnesses were responsible for inciting religious hatred, they did have the deleterious effect of breaking up families, flouting the equal rights of parents in the upbringing of their children, violating the Russian constitution's guarantees of freedom of conscience, encouraging suicide, and inciting citizens to refuse both military and alternative service.

Ferrari points out that the first reforms of the religion–state regimes which occurred after the end of the Cold War were strongly influenced by the example of the USA and the exhortations of international organizations like the Organization for Security and Cooperation in Europe (OSCE). The stress on separationism and the freedom of religious markets can be seen as an analogue of the enormous and rapid economic reforms which were also introduced around that time. After a few years, however, the sway of the American model can be seen to have decreased; as Ferrari observed in 2008, 'the most recent laws – particularly those on religious freedom and association – are closer to traditional European models' (2008: 107). The Council of Europe and its European Court of Human Rights (ECHR) have also been instrumental in monitoring developments in the field of the freedom of religion and have required the removal of some of the more discriminatory measures either inherited from the previous regimes or newly introduced. As Carolyn Evans argues however, '[t]he principles which [the ECHR has] developed to assist in interpreting articles relevant to freedom of religion or belief have generally been favourable to States and have given little consideration to the importance of freedom of religion or belief, both to those whose freedom is being denied, and to the development of pluralistic and tolerant democracies where the risk of serious persecution based on religion or belief is less likely to occur' (2001: 12).

Developments in Western Europe

While changes in the CEE countries can be seen as converging with a pattern already established in Western Europe, the latter has itself faced unsettling challenges. For Ferrari 'Europe is in the middle of a process of transformation which can be defined as the passage from religious pluralism to a cultural and ethical pluralism which is often characterized by a strong religious foundation' (2008: 103). He argues that one effect of this transformation is that the European model works less smoothly and has, after a period of relative stability, entered a phase of transition the outcome of which remains uncertain. The drivers of this transformation are described as twofold: increased immigration and a trend in the direction of greater individualism. Increased immigration has had the effect of broadening the range of sensitive concerns raised by religion-related issues; these have concerned not only differences of religion, 'but something larger that concerns lifestyles, beliefs, values, behaviour etc.: in a nutshell, a cultural difference' (*ibid.*). Enhanced individualism is seen in the whittling away of the historic churches' one-time control over standards relating to birth, marriage and death: 'Europe is moving towards a situation in which different ways of procreating, marrying and dying that correspond to the different ethical views of individuals exist side by side and enjoy the same legal legitimacy' (*ibid.*: 103). In support he cites the observation that the historic churches have seemingly lost the capacity to lead important contemporary debates over bioethics and recent changes in family law. Both trends, he argues, entail a shift from simple religious pluralism to a more wide-ranging cultural and ethical pluralism and this has had the paradoxical effect of actually enhancing, rather than softening, the impact of the religious factor in politics.

The presence in significant numbers of groups of immigrants from non-Christian cultures where the distinctions between the fields of politics and religion have not been traditional means that religious arguments are increasingly deployed in making claims on the host communities. A prime example is the ongoing controversies around the use of the Islamic headscarf-hijab where what 20 years ago was regarded as a matter of ethnic custom has come to be perceived more and more as a mode of religious expression which should be protected on religious freedom grounds. And within the host communities themselves a complementary shift has also occurred where disillusionment with the failing vigour of the historic churches has encouraged the emergence of revivalist groups and movements such as Pentecostalism among Protestants and Opus Dei among Catholics, which also seek to give expression to the relevance of religious values and identities across all fields of human life, including the political. These revivalist movements also tend to be considerably less tolerant of confession-blind multiculturalism than is the case with leaders of most of the mainstream churches.

These changes have not alone accounted for the increased salience of the religious factor in West European politics. The proper place of religion in the public life of liberal democracies had become an issue of intense controversy among scholars as early as the 1970s. In one corner sociologists and political scientists once again disputed the theoretical and empirical issues regarding the seeming steady progress of secularization in some parts of the world – especially in Western Europe – at a time when religious or religion-related issues seem so to be increasingly prominent on the agenda of world politics, including in other developed parts of the world such as the USA. Political philosophers also engaged in debate about the propriety of bringing religious or religion-related issues and arguments into political debate at all: the issue became newly contentious despite the fact that liberal theorists from the time of Locke have insisted that matters of religion are, or should be, no business of the state and that political debate should be conducted without reference to, or reliance upon, premises which are controversial because of their origins in religious thought and belief (Barry 2002). The neutrality of the state on the issue of what sort of life its citizens should lead had not been seen as merely one of a number of desirable features a liberal political system should exhibit; for some it was even to be regarded as 'the defining feature of liberalism: a liberal state is a state which imposes no conception of the good upon its citizens but which allows individuals to pursue their own good in their own way' (Jones 1989: 11).

Nor did the long-running 'politics of morals issues', such as those around abortion, contraception and pornography, which had exercised Christian Democrats in particular, represent the only indigenous challenge to liberalism and the modern state: 'since the end of the 1980s ... the trend towards the de-regulation of religion in some countries, disputes about what counts as religion, and attempts to devise new ways of controlling what is permitted under the label of religion have all increased' (Beckford 2003: 1). Key to these debates have been two sets of concerns, namely those affecting issues of religious freedom and religious equality. So far as Western Europe was concerned religious freedom issues had been largely settled after 1945, although troublesome questions had occasionally arisen especially in connection with various 'cult controversies' which focused on the activities of small but often very controversial sectarian movements (Beckford 1985). The position of the non-traditional religions including both relatively mainstream traditions of foreign origin and new religious movements has on occasion been made tenuous through the sometimes onerous requirements for their official registration without which their ability to operate at all is considerably handicapped. Thus, during the 1990s the recognition of the status of both the Jehovah's Witnesses, a sect with a long history, and Scientology, a relatively new phenomenon, as legitimate religious organizations has been a source of great controversy in Germany, where the granting of public law status brings considerable advantages. And since the Solar Temple suicides in 1994, in France, Belgium and Switzerland a number of public bodies have been charged with monitoring and reporting on groups that are variously described as 'dangerous sects', 'cults' or 'unconventional religious entities', an initiative which was approved and encouraged by resolutions of the Parliamentary Assembly of the Council of Europe in June 1999 (Richardson 2004).

While religious freedom issues inevitably touched on the question of equality of treatment – whether a minority religion for example is recognized by state authorities on the same basis as traditional religions or maybe not recognized as a religion at all – they do not exhaust them. In Western Europe, the cradle of Ferrari's common European model where the main religious freedoms have been relatively well established, inequalities of treatment are systemic. For secular humanists one element of this inequality is the favourable treatment which almost all religious groups get from the state whether in the form of tax relief, use of the public tax system to raise revenue from adherents, provision religious teaching in the public schools, support for private religious schools, requirements for the maintenance of public religious broadcasting, even – as in Belgium, for example – the payment of salaries and pensions to the officials of the recognized religions from the public purse. There is of course a very large number of means by which the state can and does lend support to religious groups and institutions. In Protestant Europe there are the remainders of state church establishment including those countries, which have undergone formal disestablishment while in Catholic Europe cooperative, Concordat-based arrangements are to be found and in Greece a uniquely favourable set of arrangements makes the Orthodox Church virtually, if not officially, a state church (Madeley and Enyedi 2003; Robbers 2005). All these sets of arrangements have been subject to reform and/or renegotiation in recent decades and it is an undoubted fact that there has been, and continues, a retreat from the more overt forms of church establishment despite the rearguard actions of those who continue to support some form of religious establishment (Madeley 2006a).

The relations between Sweden's national Lutheran church and the Swedish state were comprehensively remodelled after some 50 years' gestation in January 2000 (Gustafsson 2003). In Norway also the decision has been taken to follow the same path although formal disestablishment cannot be achieved until 2013 because of constitutional requirements for the passage of constitutional amendments. Meantime in Britain periodic moves to achieve disestablishment of the Church of England – or even just to repeal the anti-Catholic Act of Settlement of 1701, governing the royal succession – remain stalled despite calls from within, as well as from outside of, the church in support of such moves. Paul Weller argues that while the Church of England today does not seek the civil exclusion of other forms of worship, and in fact often facilitates minority religious contributions to British public life, nevertheless 'the public face of the CoE remains one of institutional privilege' (2005: 189). While such an arrangement can be seen as fundamentally unjust, or just irksome, it also, he claims, represents a risk: 'Where fault lines of religious difference and sometimes tension also map onto cultural and ethnic differences, the maintenance of an established form of religion that is bound up with national symbols of self-definition that were originally developed in a more "one-dimensional" context is at least potentially problematic. Under certain conditions of social crisis in which "communal scapegoating" can develop and be exploited by extremist groups, such alignments also have the potential of becoming dangerous' (*ibid.*: 191).

The single most contentious set of politically relevant issues relating to religion in the last two decades have of course been connected to the status of Islam and its 20 million-odd adherents that are found on the territory of Europe. It is in this connection more than any other that the potential for communal scapegoating and the involvement of extremist groups both among Muslims themselves and among their detractors have been most fully realized. The issues frequently have international dimensions furthermore as mention of the Rushdie and Danish cartoons affairs and the controversies surrounding 9/11 and the so-called war on terror indicates. The various jihadist terror attacks both in Europe and beyond have inevitably raised security concerns about how otherwise rather conservative Muslim communities seem provided the context for the emergence of violent terrorist insurgency, including the use of suicide bombers, and these concerns have led to the widespread engagement of state bodies, from the security agencies to local interfaith consultation groups, in religion-related affairs. In the case of Britain for example, since 2003 the government has pursued a counter-terrorism strategy which includes a well-financed set of programmes under the label PREVENT that has among its declared aims challenging the ideology behind violent extremism and supporting mainstream voices, disrupting the promotion of violent extremism, providing support for individuals who are vulnerable to recruitment, increasing the levels of resistance of communities to violent extremism and addressing the grievances which the extremists set out to exploit. As the strategy website points out: 'Protecting vulnerable individuals who might be attracted to the ideology of violence is not just a job for the police, but also for local government, schools and universities, local communities and all of us who come into contact with them, increasing the resilience of communities to violent extremism' (available at: www.communities.gov.uk; accessed 08/10/2010). Such efforts have been replicated in a number of other countries in addition to international police and security cooperation and while the reference to extreme and/or violent Islamism is usually only implicit, as in the British case, it can scarcely be doubted that this represents the principal target of such programmes.

Across Europe as a whole it has been the issue of the Islamic headscarf-hijab which has provided the most striking illustration of the communalities and differences which distinguish the treatment of religion-related issues and which place a question mark against claims such as those of Ferrari about the existence of a common European model of religion–state relations (McGoldrick 2006). As noted above it was in 1989 that the issue first rose to prominence in France in 1989 when three Muslim girls were expelled from a public secondary school for wearing the hijab in defiance – as it was interpreted by the school head – of the general rule of the *laïcité* of all French public institutions and, in particular, of the public school system. Over the ensuing 15 years a series of court decisions, declarations by the Council of State, and directives by the Ministry of Education focused on the issue without satisfactorily resolving it. This uneven process finally culminated in the recommendations in 2003 of a state commission which were adopted in September 2004 when a new law forbade public school students from wearing any ostentatious religious symbols or apparel while on school premises. In order not to be seen to discriminate against Islamic (or, indeed, any particular) religious groups, Jewish skullcaps, Sikh turbans and 'large crosses' worn by Christians, which had previously not given rise to any particular controversy and which reflected previous compromises with strict *laïcité*, were equally place under the ban.

The way the same or similar issues was treated in the different countries of Europe illustrates nicely the degree of variability which continues to exist under the supposed umbrella of a European model and at the same time challenges the limits of the model in so far as Muslims (and the adherents of other minority creeds) can in justice claim the same degree of privilege enjoyed by the traditional mainstream churches and religious groups. In Britain a generally multiculturalist approach has tended, with the support of the mainstream churches themselves, to support moderate Muslim claims for example by tolerating the hijab in state schools so long as it conforms to the colours of the school uniform. Similar exceptions are made in the application of other laws – for example, by allowing ritual slaughter for the provision of halal (just as for Jewish kosher) meat. The limit of British tolerance appeared to be overstepped however when in 2008 the Archbishop of Canterbury made the modest proposal that existing Islamic courts dispensing sharia judgments in marital and other personal matters should be regularized and conceded official recognition just as Jewish Beth Din courts had been for over a century. A media storm greeted the proposal and it was quietly shelved.

The outcome of the headscarf issue in Germany resulted in an awkward compromise which nicely reflected the maintenance of the privileges of the principal recognized religions and a studied reluctance to extend those privileges freely to other faiths. In September 2003 after a number of hijab bans had effectively been introduced for teachers in some areas, the Federal Constitutional Court ruled that the wearing of Islamic headscarves by teachers could not be banned unless the ban was supported by state legislation. The response was that some *Länder* quickly moved to introduce such legislation; thus, in November 2004 Bavaria became the third German state (after Baden-Württemberg and Lower Saxony) to proceed to ban teachers in state schools wearing 'symbols and clothing that express religious or ideological beliefs and at the same time can also be understood as an expression of an attitude incompatible with basic constitutional values and educational aims'. The target was however quite clearly the Islamic headscarf since the wearing of Christian and Jewish symbols and clothing, such as nun's habits, were excluded from the Bavarian ban, since they are taken to reflect the cultural values of the state. It is on the other hand interesting to note however that in early 2005 a Berlin court ruled that Jehovah's Witnesses were entitled to the same privileges enjoyed by Germany's major Catholic and Protestant churches, thereby bringing to a successful conclusion a 15-year legal fight about the group's status. Meanwhile, Scientology, which for long has faced attempts to have it declared an illegal fraudulent commercial organization, continues to struggle for similar recognition.

Fetzer and Soper's comparative study of state accommodation of Muslims' religious practices in Britain, France and Germany concluded that the explanation for the differences in approach lay not in the level of resources commanded by the Muslim groups or the openness of the political-opportunity structure or even in ideological considerations (Fetzer and Soper 2005). The explanation lay instead in the nature of the historically based church–state institutions or, in the terms used here, the nature of the religion–state regime obtaining in the different countries. This conclusion does not in itself undermine Ferrari's claims about a common European model although it suggests that the model is a looser one with more internal variations than might otherwise be supposed. In his most recent review of state regulation of religion in Europe Ferrari continues to maintain that 'the centre of gravity of the European system of church–state relations seems to be shifting towards a range of national systems that are distinct but which share certain common features'

(2008: 110). He lists five such common features: acceptance of the public standing of religious communities; recognition of these communities' special features; a certain degree of state control over them; and the selective cooperation of public institutions with religious communities. It is interesting to note that each of these features has however been subjected to critical scrutiny on one side or another when the question is posed as to how they might apply to Muslim communities. The suggestion that the special treatment afforded to traditional religious groups should in justice be extended to Muslim groups has met opposition not only from conservative Christian groups but, often more vehemently, from the increasingly numerous and vocal minorities of secularists. These groups insist that freedom *for* religion must also mandate freedom *from* religion for all who chose to exercise that freedom. In Europe they continue to maintain that only a radical move in the direction of some form of strict separationism can satisfy this just demand.

Despite the paranoia of some commentators from across the political spectrum, particularly in connection with issues of Muslim accommodation, the option of strict separationism seems to be the least likely to be operated in Europe short of even greater transformations than Ferrari or others have so far charted. As Fetzer and Soper observe:

> Muslims put forward public policy questions about church–state relations at the same time that secular ideas and policy models were becoming predominant in Britain, France and Germany. Muslims challenged each state's capacity to be equitable in its treatment among different religious groups, but followers of Islam also accentuated tensions between secular and religious worldviews. Church–state matters that West European states seemed to have settled long ago and that appeared to be politically peripheral were suddenly thrust to the centre of political and policy debate by Muslim efforts. (2005: 157)

If the common European model of religion–state relations is to survive it will clearly have meet demands for its ambit to be broadened to include the representatives of Muslim and other minority religious traditions – and that against a background in which any broadening will only intensify the opposition of the more militant secularists.

Conclusion

This chapter has made only the most cursory reference to the role that Europe's Christian Democratic parties have played as vehicles for projecting the religious factor into politics. While it is evidently far too soon to write off the prospects of Europe's largest single political party family, it has rarely in recent decades occupied centre stage on the most controversial issues related to religion (Broughton and ten Napel 2000; van Hecke and Gerard 2004). Instead it has tended to be the leadership of the religious communities themselves or of groups within them that have pressed the issues. And as often as not the issues themselves have been decided not via the legislative process where parties with some religion-related agenda could play a vital part but through the medium of the law and the operation of the courts. Thus, the controversial 2010 ECHR ruling in the *Lautsi* case that the hanging of crucifixes on the wall of Italian schoolrooms violated the religious rights of those children who did not share orthodox Christian beliefs was protested by the Pope Benedict XVI and his bishops and appealed by an Italian government which has only a weak connection to what is left of Italy's once dominant Christian Democratic tradition.

At the European level Christian Democracy and its political allies of the centre-right do continue to have significant impact. Of course most of the so-called founding fathers of the EU project were Christian Democrats and it was the major Christian Democratic parties of which they had been leading figures which subsequently maintained the steadiest support for the project – despite disappointment over Pope John Paul II's campaign to use EU expansion as an opportunity to press forward a re-evangelization of Europe and the patent failure of Jacques Delors' ambition somehow to instantiate a 'Soul for Europe' (Leustean and Madeley 2009). On the other hand religious actors with more fundamentalist leanings have played the roles of inveterate critics and foes of the project. They have either directly or in some cases through their activity in smaller – especially Protestant – religious parties, sustained this adversarial position, as have vigorously oppositional minorities within Roman Catholicism, Eastern Orthodoxy and European Islam. In the case of both pro- and anti-EU sentiment among religio-political actors the religious aspect has been evident and the conflict between them has had more than a suggestion of the *odium theologicum* which traditionally accompanies religious–political conflict, despite the efforts of ecumenists and others who campaign to transcend the differences (Madeley 2009b).

José Casanova claims that there is still a widespread tendency in Europe to refuse to recognize that 'the initial project of a European Union was fundamentally a Christian Democratic project, sanctioned by the Vatican, at a time of a general religious revival in post-World War Two Europe, in the geopolitical context of the Cold War when "the free world" and "Christian civilization" had become synonymous' (2006: 66; Kaiser 2007). And for George Weigel (2005) the failure to acknowledge this historical debt was rooted in a 'Christophobic' mindset committed to the denigration and progressive marginalization of Christianity in Europe's public life. As such he sees it as but one more sign that Europe is in the middle of a 'crisis of civilizational morale' which has been developing since 1914, the gravity of which was only clearly revealed by the end of the Cold War. The outcome of the controversy over whether the projected European constitution should make any reference to God or the Christian religion in its preamble was taken by such critics as a clear indication that Europe was effectively abandoning its religious heritage. Such a conclusion is hard to sustain however. First, until the Convention on the Future of Europe which drafted a Treaty establishing a constitution for Europe, overt references to religion had been conspicuous by their absence from the main documents of the European Union. The one document which had specified the position of the EU vis-à-vis religious communities most clearly was Declaration 11 on the status of churches and non-confessional organizations attached to the Treaty of Amsterdam (1997) which stated that the European Union 'respects and does not prejudice the status under national law of churches and religious associations or communities in the member states'. The fact of the debate on the insertion of religious terms in the preamble of the projected European constitution might in fact be taken as an indication of the growing presence of religious communities and their transnational influence within the EU, although the ultimate decision in 2004 to exclude an *invocatio deo* also illustrated the limits of that influence (Leustean 2007). On the other hand while the symbolic issue of the preamble was lost the draft European constitution did (in Article I-52) for the first time recognize the role of churches and non-confessional organizations in the European Union, officially designating them as partners in dialogue. And after the constitution was rejected in the French and Dutch referendums, Article I-52 was preserved in the form of Article 17 of the Lisbon Treaty. Meantime, in a manner unwelcome to even the most privileged religious organizations and communities, the governance of religious diversity in Europe is without doubt increasingly subject to continent-wide pressures making for convergence on universal standards of human rights protection, which undercut the surviving distinctiveness of inherited national patterns (Koenig 2007).

Chapter 13

European Immigration Policies: Between Stemming and Soliciting Still

Christian Joppke

A decade ago, a review of European immigration policies found them 'at the crossroads' (Joppke 2002). While previously geared towards the 'stemming' of unwanted immigrants, a new constellation of globalization and population shrinkage was pushing European states towards the 'soliciting' of wanted immigrants. But the hurdles to shifting emphasis from stemming to soliciting were formidable, not least because of mass publics who were instinctively hostile to immigration (see Citrin and Sides 2007).

This diagnosis remains true today. European states' immigration policies still hover undecidedly between perfecting the strategies for keeping out the huddled masses while laying out red carpets for a trickle of highly skilled who, most often, have better places to go. Wanted or not, the stocks of foreign-born populations across Europe have nevertheless remained high, or even further increased, in the past decade (see Table 13.1). If one considers that the foreign-born population share in the United States in 2006 was 13 per cent (OECD 2008: 324), one must conclude that a good number of European countries approximate or even exceed the immigrant share of this classic immigration country and this at a historical peak moment of the latter's immigration history.

At the same time, there is considerable variety in the size of the immigrant share, which often does not correlate with the degree of political conflict. France and Denmark, two notorious hard-liners in recent years where immigration has been consistently subject to fierce political controversy, boast relatively modest foreign-born population shares, with 8.3 and 6.6 per cent in 2006, respectively. By contrast, Sweden or Ireland, despite their relatively high immigrant shares (12.9 and 14.4 per cent, respectively), are considerably more relaxed. The same has to be said about Spain, which has seen a meteoric growth of its immigrant population, with annual inflows increasing more than fourteen-fold

Table 13.1 *Stocks of foreign-born population in selected European countries (% of total population)*

	1996	*2000*	*2006*
Austria	–	10.5	14.1
Belgium	9.8	10.3	12.5
Denmark	5.1	5.8	6.6
France	–	7.4	8.3
Germany	11.9	12.5	–
Ireland	6.9	8.7	14.4
Luxembourg	31.5	33.2	34.8
Netherlands	9.2	10.1	10.6
Norway	5.6	6.8	8.7
Portugal	5.4	5.1	6.1
Sweden	10.7	11.3	12.9
Switzerland	21.3	21.9	24.1
United Kingdom	7.1	7.9	10.1

Source: OECD (2007: 330; 2008: 324).

between 1998 and 2006 (from 57,200 to 803,000), not counting illegal immigrants (whose number is likely to be vast, considering that some 600,000 were legalized in 2005) (*ibid*.: 295). By contrast, it is Italy, with a similarly rushed, predominantly irregular immigrant intake over a short period, yet at a rate and size far below Spain's, which has seen cataclysmic political struggle surrounding immigration, recently ordering its army to patrol the country's most heavily immigrant-populated cities and making illegal entry a penal law infraction. Demography is obviously not destiny, and the policy and politics surrounding immigration often follow their own rationale, decoupled from the reality to be processed by them.

A second surprise results from a look at the major source countries for new immigrants in Europe today. In 2006, the top-three sending countries for selected European countries were as set out in Table 13.2. The interesting fact is that the top immigrant-sending countries in Europe today are mostly other European countries. This sets a stark contrast to the United States, whose major source countries are still third-world countries, most notably Mexico, China and the Philippines. This demonstrates the workings of the free market within the European Union (EU), whose mobile citizens are legally, and increasingly also socially, no longer 'immigrants' in other member states. And it shows the declining hold of Europe's guest-worker and postcolonial legacies, which had marked the great migrations after the Second World War well into the 1980s. Only 12 of the total 39 entries for top-sending countries in Table 13.2 belong

Table 13.2   *Top-three sending countries for selected European countries and the USA (2006, in 1,000s; Danish figures for 2005)*

	1	2	3
Austria	Germany (16.2)	Serbia and Montenegro (7.4)	Poland (6.0)
Belgium	France (11.6)	Netherlands (11.5)	Morocco (7.5)
Denmark	Germany (1.4)	Poland (1.3)	Norway (1.2)
France	Algeria (25.4)	Morocco (19.2)	Turkey (8.3)
Germany	Poland (152.7)	Turkey (30.7)	Romania (23.7)
Ireland	United Kingdom (9.9)	United States (1.7)	Other countries (77.3)
Luxembourg	Portugal (3.8)	France (2.5)	Germany (0.9)
Netherlands	Germany (7.2)	Poland (6.8)	United Kingdom (3.6)
Norway	Poland (7.4)	Sweden (3.4)	Germany (2.3)
Portugal	Brazil (11.4)	Ukraine (7.7)	Cape Verde (4.1)
Spain	Romania (111.9)	Bolivia (69.5)	Morocco (60.8)
Sweden	Iraq (10.9)	Poland (6.3)	Denmark (5.1)
Switzerland	Germany (24.8)	Portugal (12.5)	France (7.6)
United States	Mexico (173.8)	China (87.3)	Philippines (74.6)

Source: OECD (2008: 297–310).

to the guest-worker or postcolonial nexus. An exception to this is France, whose three top-sending countries in 2006 are Algeria, Morocco and Turkey, that is, a former colony, a protectorate and a guest-worker-sending country, respectively. This helps explain the particularly harsh and politicized immigration debate in France today.

By the same token, if Britain has recently experienced what *The Economist* (30 August 2008: 33) called the single 'biggest influx in British history', the main source country for this has not been Pakistan or Bangladesh – but Poland. Being one of only three EU states to immediately grant free movement rights to the citizens of new Eastern member states in 2004, Britain received one million Eastern migrants in just four years, Poles making up two-thirds of these newcomers. Most of them were easily absorbed in Britain's flexible and – until the recent financial and economic crisis – insatiable labour market (especially the hospitality and construction sectors), which positively distinguishes Britain from continental Europe (whose immigrants are at a minimum twice as likely to be unemployed as natives). A second feature of the East European influx is its wide geographic dispersal, only one-fifth settling in London (where over 40 per cent of other foreign nationals reside). Overall, the Polish influx helped in 'decoupling the issue of immigration from that of race' and led to viewing the matter in 'more purely economic terms' (*ibid.*). Finally, reflecting that at the sudden end of Britain's economic boom at least half of the Polish newcomers have packed and returned, these newcomers are commonly referred to as 'migrants', whereas the 'immigrant' label is reserved for the less mobile non-European folk of old. A recent comparison of ever swinging London and museum-style Paris concluded that much of London's energy and inventiveness had to do with Britain's new source countries, and its capacity to draw predominantly high-skilled immigrants, while Paris's sluggishness was also due to its much smaller and predominantly lower-skilled immigrant intakes of mostly postcolonial extraction (see 'The rivals – London and Paris', *The Economist*, 15 March 2008).

While the Polish influx did much good to Britain's economy and society, an influx of Romanians, many of them Gypsies, created Italy's 'first big race-relations crisis'. Since the early millennium, Romania has become Italy's major immigrant-sending country, with 62,300 newcomers in 2004 (which is more than double the figure that year of the second-most important sending country, Albania, with 29,600 newcomers) (OECD 2007: 309). The reason is that consecutive conservative and leftist governments first lifted visa restrictions on Romania, even before the country would join the EU, and, upon Romania's EU accession, granted immediate entry rights to Romanian workers. The open-arms policy, which was notably not accompanied by providing housing or any other infrastructure for the newcomers, was in the expectation that the Romance-language-speaking newcomers would be easy to integrate. However, the brutal killing of a 47-year old middle-class woman in the outskirts of Rome, presumably by a Romanian Gypsy camping in the forest, triggered a government response that *The Economist* (10 November 2007), not known for its hyperbole, characterized as 'opportunistic, histrionic, irresponsible and, perhaps at best, insensitive': a decree was passed that gave local prefects, if backed by a judge, the power to expel EU citizens. Amounting to unprecedented national-origin discrimination, the decree targeted Romanians explicitly, because 'the proportion of crime committed by foreigners has increased, and those who commit most crime are the Romanians' (*ibid.*). True, according to police statistics one-third of all thefts, rapes and murders in Italy are committed by 'foreigners' (which is over three times above their population share) (*The Times*, 29 May 2008). But this emergency-style response, curiously by an otherwise moderate centre-left government under Romano Prodi, did its share to fan the flames of xenophobia that were already high. No wonder that a right-wing government under Berlusconi, which followed upon Prodi's in 2008, has held high 'the right of Italians not to be afraid', deploying troops in Italian cities, bulldozing unauthorized Gypsy encampments, and making illegal entry a crime under penal law. However, as much as it might try to please a xenophobic public, with its in-house transmission belt, the Lega Nord, the Italian government's hard-lining also shows the tight limits that are set to any such manoeuvre by EU law. In particular, there is little the Italian government can do to deter the unwanted Romanians: a provision to automatically expel EU citizens without adequate means of subsistence, which was part of the original proposal for a tough new immigration law, had to be withdrawn because of its incompatibility with free movement rights within the EU.

One sees that European immigration realities are multiple and often contradictory, making any attempt to identify common trends a daunting task. The South of Europe is mired in a chaotic reality of largely undocumented inflows for which no adequate governance structures exist nor seem to be in the making (see Calavita 2005). Instead, the most important policy innovations over the past decade or so have originated in North-Western Europe, thus returning the focus to Europe's earliest and classic immigration sites after the Second World War.

In the remainder of this chapter, I will focus on two of these innovations. First, the trend of Europeanizing not just intra-European migrations by European citizens but also external immigration by non-Europeans, that is, 'immigration' proper, which had started with the Amsterdam Treaty of 1997 (coming into force in 1999), has increased to a dramatic extent, with new Council directives on minimum standards for receiving asylum-seekers, family reunification, the long-term residence status of third-country nationals (all three passed in 2003), and most recently on high-skilled immigrants (in terms of the 2009 Blue Card directive, discussed below). In addition, there has been a host of operational measures, such as the establishment of sophisticated information and identification systems (Schengen Information System, Visa Information System, EURODAC, etc.) and the creation of a joint border patrol (FRONTEX). While the spirit of most of these measures is to facilitate member state attempts to control immigration, especially of the unwanted kind, they have subtly placed constraints on this, often in unforeseen and rights-protecting ways.

Second, there has been a wholesale attack on unwanted family migration, which now constitutes by far the largest category of migrant intakes. This replaced an earlier emphasis on reducing asylum-seeking, which was the main target of stemming unwanted immigration throughout the 1980s and 1990s, and which turned out largely successful. At the same time, there has been a foray towards soliciting new legal immigration, but only of a small number of the highly skilled. The connection between both movements is best expressed in French President Nicolas

Sarkozy's logo to shift from 'suffered' to 'chosen' immigration. This section closes with a brief look at the contours and limitations of this project, with a focus on Germany and Britain, which represent extremely unsuccessful and successful variants of it, respectively.

Ongoing Europeanization of immigration policy

It used to be the wisdom that there are 'two European migration regimes' (Joppke 1999: 277): a rights-focused free movement regime within the boundaries of the EU, in which EU law trumped national law; and a security-focused immigration regime proper for moves across these boundaries, which remained under the authority of member states. This neat division, already heavily dented by 1999, has almost collapsed one decade later. When commenting on the limited scope of Germany's new immigration law passed in 2004, Günter Renner (2005: 19) noted the 'preponderance of European Union law' in this domain, so that 'the function of German law was little more than implementing and filling gaps, with the exception of legal labour migration'. Indeed, legal labour migration is by now the last bastion of state sovereignty in Europe, though an end to this is nearing also. By now thoroughly Europeanized are all the other elements of the immigration function, including the distribution of visa, asylum determination, the long-term residence of third-state nationals, family reunification, the entry and residence of students and researchers, and anti-discrimination policies. Considering this successive Europeanization, a separate treatment of immigration policy at state level and at European level is no longer possible. Any consideration of state-level trends must first draw the EU framework that constrains, triggers or gives shape to the state-level trends.

The logic of the successive Europeanization of the immigration function is simple, and it combines elements of intergovernmentalism and functionalist spill-over, the two rivalling paradigms of Euro politics. States always first concede authority over immigration in the interest of maximizing control and security. However, as it is sucked into the ambit of supranational actors within the EU, immigration becomes infused with the liberal rights logic of free movement that, in turn, further restricts state authority in this domain, in often unexpected and surprising ways. The inevitable end point of this development is the Europeanization of legal labour migration from outside the EU.

This logic is very evident in the development and impact of the long-term resident and family reunification directives, both passed in the second half of 2003, which regulate the intra-European movement of settled immigrants and family migrants, respectively. Combined, both movements cover about half or more of all legal migration by third-state nationals in the EU. The tracks towards the long-term resident directive were laid at the European Council meeting in Tampere, in October 1999, which declared that the legal status of third-country nationals should be 'approximated' to that of member state nationals, providing the former with a 'set of uniform rights which are as near as possible to those enjoyed by citizens of the European Union'. It would thus amount to a kind of quasi-European citizenship for immigrants, without the need for acquiring a member state nationality first. For years, this had been one of the major demands of the immigrants' lobby in Brussels. Yet the logic behind this was less that of a rights-focused, pro-immigrant stance than of completing the internal market, which was not achieved as long as the labour market mobility of Europe's 23 million third-country nationals remained restricted. As the introduction to the 2003 long-term resident directive put it, this measure 'should contribute to the effective attainment of an internal market as an area in which the free movement of persons is ensured'. The directive that was passed four years later naturally fell short of the goal of a quasi-European citizenship for immigrants, but it still exceeded the residence rights granted to immigrants in a number of member states, on which it thus exerted an upwards-adjustment pressure. Its key provision is to force member states to grant long-term residence status after five years of legal residence.

Paradoxically, a prerequisite for getting the long-term residence directive passed was its undercutting of more generous residence rights and entitlements in some member states. The latter would thus support the directive, in order to find an external justification for imposing more restrictive immigration laws at home. France and Belgium, for instance, two strong supporters of the directive, offered a far more generous residence status in their domestic laws (see Luedtke 2008: 9): long-term resident status was available after three years, not five; there was the automatic right to bring one's family members, which was not given by the directive; long-term residents had free access to the labour market, while the directive allowed governments to prioritize their nationals; social security and assistance was to be on equal level with that for nationals, while the directive allowed discrimination in this respect; and, among many more advantages, immigrants under Belgian and French law could not lose their status when unemployed, while the directive would make this possible. All these entitlements were nationally entrenched and backed by the legal systems and autonomous courts in these states; 'Europe' would allow rolling them back.

By contrast, for other member states, such as Austria, Greece, Italy, Germany, Luxembourg, Portugal and Spain, the long-term residence directive exceeded the rights granted under domestic law, and consequently these member states would try to make the directive more restrictive. Their relative success at that is revealed by the frequent appearance of the word 'may' instead of 'shall' in the text of the directive, which minimizes the legal obligations. But the most important victory, at the behest of Germany, was to make the free movement of settled immigrants dependent on their meeting the 'integration conditions' of the receiving member state. This obliged the mobile immigrant to pass a language test, which in a number of European states is now a requirement for being granted a long-term residence permit. Such 'civic integration' requirements, of course, do not exist for European citizens. Including them in the long-term residence directive amounted to a significant hurdle to intra-European mobility, and it signals the defeat of the exuberant Tampere promise of 'approximating' the rights of settled immigrants to that of European citizens.

However, it has to be equally stated that in other respects the long-term residence directive forces the more restrictive states to adjust in a liberalizing direction: if some of them had previously granted long-term residence status after as many as 15 years' residence, they were now forced to grant such status after only five years. And, most importantly, in supranationalizing the conditions of permanent residence the European Court of Justice was brought into the game, which might find fault with certain deficiencies of the directive, such as 'the removal of the word "right" (of residence) from the final draft' (*ibid.*: 11).

A very similar dynamic can be observed in the making and impact of the family reunification directive. Considering that family migration constitutes 40 to 60 per cent of new legal admissions across European states, even as much as 70 per cent of legal immigration in France, the establishment of supranational authority in this domain amounts to a huge gain of immigration control authority on part of the EU. The origin of the family reunification directive is again the 1999 European Council declaration on immigration at Tampere, which included the call for a common European immigration and asylum policy. A rather liberal proposal by the European Commission that followed shortly upon Tampere was subsequently made more restrictive, until the final version of the family reunification directive was passed in September 2003.

At the behest of the restriction-minded usual suspects, most importantly Germany, Austria and the Netherlands, the text is again littered with the word 'may' that duplicates at European level their restrictive domestic agendas. Inserted at the behest of Germany (whose *Zuwanderungsgesetz* of 2004 interestingly abstains from invoking it), Article 4 allows states to impose certain integration conditions to children over 12 years who wish to join their parents in a member state; and it allows states to impose the age limit of 21 years on the sponsor. Article

7 allows states to require 'third country nationals to comply with integration measures, in accordance with national law'. Article 8 allows states to require two years of legal residence on part of the sponsor, as well as erecting a waiting period of maximally three years between the application and the granting of a residence permit for family members. Article 12 allows states to deny spouses' access to the labour market for one year. Article 15 stipulates that after maximally five years an autonomous residence permit, apart from that of the sponsor, has to be given to family members.

As the frequent use of the word 'may' in the family reunification directive suggests, this was more a catalogue of possible restrictions on the part of member states than the granting of family rights for immigrants. And in important respects its provisions undercut the family rights established in the more liberal member states, especially, and again, France and Belgium. Hence 'the utility for these governments of supporting a binding, strong directive: it would allow them to lower immigrant rights at home', as Adam Luedtke writes (*ibid*.: 15). In Belgium, for instance, one of Europe's most liberal countries on family reunification (as on many other aspects of immigrant integration and citizenship), same-sex reunions were allowed, about which the directive said nothing; instead of allowing three years of waiting time (as in the directive), Belgian law allowed only one year; and an autonomous residence permit for a family member was available in Belgium after only 15 months, instead of five years, as stipulated by the EU directive. And so on. The French government, under Interior Minister Sarkozy, has promptly used the 'European alibi' to whittle down its generous family rights in a new domestic immigration law that followed barely three months upon the issuing of the family directive in autumn 2003 (Barbou des Places and Oger 2005: 362).

However, an influential initial critic of the family reunification directive, the legal scholar Kees Groenendijk, who headed the Standing Committee of Experts on international migration, later confessed to be 'glad' that his committee's demand to 'withdraw' the measure because it violated the family rights granted by Article 8 of the ECHR, was not followed (2006: 221). As Groenendijk submits, everyone involved in negotiating the directive, including the immigration lawyers delegated by member states, 'underestimated' (*ibid*.: 220) the effects that EU law would have on national immigration laws. For one, EU law principles such as 'proportionality', 'effectiveness' and 'effective legal remedies' now inevitably applied. Moreover, central concepts of the directive, such as 'public order', 'sufficient income' or 'integration measures', would have to be influenced by the meaning of these or related concepts in other directives on migration or even in other fields of Community law. To guard and propel this process is exactly the function of the European Court of Justice. Accordingly, the most drastic elements of ever tighter family reunification rules passed by the Dutch government in recent years are, in Groenendijk's view (*ibid*.: 221–5), in violation of the directive and likely to spur an ECJ intervention, such as 'disproportional' visa and residence permit fees, high income requirements for sponsoring family migrants, a categorical one-year waiting period before the granting of access to employment, or even the entire new policy of 'integration from abroad'. With respect to the latter, there was an arcane legal battle over making newcomers comply with integration 'measures' or integration 'conditions' as set by the receiving state. The first alternative ('measures') would entail a loose effort on the part of the migrant to participate in integration courses, while the second would impose on her the need to pass a formal test. As the family reunification directive, in Article 7, mentions only 'integration measures' (but not the stricter integration 'conditions', in contrast to the long-term resident status directive), Groenendijk (*ibid*.: 224) concludes that imposing an integration test abroad for family migrants is in violation of the directive. This is the 'legaleeze' out of which 'Europe' is made, and the immigration function is no longer an exception to this.

With respect to family reunification, the teeth of the European Court of Justice were first felt when the latter enforced a later directive, passed in April 2004, which protects the free movement rights of EU citizens and their family members. One must know that, with the rise of a second or even third generation of immigrants in Europe, the frontier of states' fight against unwanted family immigration has increasingly moved towards restricting the family rights of *citizens*, because many a young person of immigrant extraction is by now a European citizen (see Joppke 2008: 136–8). The avant-garde of that fight has been Denmark, which since 2002, under a conservative government led by Prime Minister Anders Fogh Rasmussen, who is dependent on support by the rabidly anti-immigrant Danish People's Party (DPP), has implemented Europe's harshest family reunification rules for immigrants and citizens alike. These rules require that both partners are at least 24 years of age, that the couple has a greater attachment to Denmark than to other countries, and that the Danish partner is self-sufficient, plus putting up almost €8,000 collateral as guarantee that the couple won't fall destitute and dependent on state support.

After having been successively hollowed out in a string of ECJ rules, Denmark's harsh family reunification rules for its own citizens received the final blow in the famous ECJ decision in *Metock*, of 28 July 2008. Here the court held that an EU citizen had the unconditional right to be joined by his or her spouse when moving across member state borders, even if the couple had resided abroad for only a few weeks (perhaps not even in employment), and even if the spouse had never had a legal residence permit in any European country. This meant that several thousands of mixed couples who had taken up residence in neighbouring Sweden, which is rather more relaxed about immigration, were free to move back to Denmark instantly. In fact, as the leader of the DPP, Pia Kjaersgaard, put it, the European Court rule had 'capsized' Denmark's tough immigration policy. Even the leader of the opposition Social Democratic Party, Helle Thorning Schmidt, fumed that 'The European Court of Justice must not be allowed to determine Denmark's policy on foreigners', and he urged the government to boycott the decision. However, the call to 'Give Denmark back to us', which the DPP (not differing in this from the political mainstream and more than half of the polled Danish population) issued in full-page newspaper advertisements, was too late. Short of leaving the EU, Denmark will have to accept that the family rights of its immigrants and citizens alike are now firmly under the reign of EU law.

The last bastion of state sovereignty is legal labour migration. This is the one (though, of course, core) area of immigration where not much progress has been made since the Amsterdam Treaty and its Tampere sequel had mandated the crafting of a common immigration policy. Following the logic of the long-term residence and family reunification directives, the reason for this is simple: there are no strong legal entitlements for labour migrants that member states might have an interest in to underbid with the help of 'Europe' (see Luedtke 2008: 17–22). While after entry a migrant is protected by the strong rights provisions entrenched in and protected by the autonomous legal systems of constitutional states, there is nothing that commands European states to issue work and entry permits to new immigrants whose sole intention is to take up work. As Luedte aptly formulates the paradox, labour migrants 'are better off immigrating *illegally* and then fighting their deportation, rather than fruitlessly applying for a work visa' (*ibid.*: 18). Incidentally, as long as the supply of especially low-skilled labour migrants exceeds the demand for them, which seems to be inevitable in a world divided between a poor South and a rich North (see Bhagwati 2004), even a more open system for legal labour migration may perhaps soften but can never eradicate this structural source of illegal immigration.

Despite the absence of a strong 'underbidding' incentive to Europeanize labour migration, similar to the one in place with regard to rights-based (asylum and family) immigration, there is still a functional logic pushing towards Europeanization. This is that a single labour market is not in place as long as there is not a system of harmonized labour migration. As long as the latter does not exist, one member state's immigration policies inevitably affects the labour market of other member states – especially since the granting of free movement rights for settled immigrants after 2003. This is why especially France, known to be highly reticent to legalize even a trickle of *sans papiers* (undocumented workers), was outraged when Spain legalized some 600,000 of them in 2005, who, it was feared, would simply move north and undercut France's opposite approach on this matter. Incidentally, since the Spanish mass legalization France has become a staunch advocate of Europeanizing legal labour migration. In addition, the Europeanization of most other aspects of the immigration function, including family migration, cross-border moves of settled immigrants, students, researchers and tourists, makes still-nationalized labour migration appear ever more an anomaly that stands to be removed. Adam Luedtke (2008: 21) quotes a French negotiator in Brussels as saying that: 'I think it's the most delicate subject, but also the most important for legal immigration in the coming years, because all the rest we have done. We have done students, researchers, family reunification, so only economic migration is left'.

After a first proposal for a directive on economic migration quickly failed in 2001, a second, much better received Commission foray, which was launched with its 2005 Green Paper on an EU Approach to Managing Economic Migration (European Commission 2005a), mentions three reasons in favour of a common immigration policy: the fact of 'demographic decline and ageing' (p. 3), international 'competitiveness' in the context of the so-called Lisbon objectives of turning Europe into the 'most competitive and dynamic knowledge-based economy in the world', and the fact that immigration decisions of one member state inevitably 'affect others' (p. 4).

However dramatic and urgent the demographic rationale may be, it is not one that is persuasive to democratically accountable governments, whose leaders are unlikely to maximize votes by advocating large-scale migration. Reference to population ageing and shrinking has featured in all Commission migration proposals for over a decade now, but it cannot be found in domestic immigration debates. As if aware of this, the 2005 Green Paper and subsequent proposals stress that 'decisions on the numbers of economic migrants' will remain 'a matter for the Member States' (European Commission 2005a: 4).

When four directives were proposed in late 2005 under the European Commission's 'Policy Plan on Legal Migration' (European Commission 2005b), as result of the 'consultation' process opened up by the 2005 Green Paper, the first to be put on the table was the one dealing with 'the entry and residence of highly skilled workers' (not the ones on 'seasonal workers', 'intra-corporate transferees' or 'remunerated trainees') (see *ibid.*: 7–8). This is simply because admitting high-skilled workers resonated best with the Lisbon objectives. This was the one type of immigration that European states had recently courted each for itself, in attempts that often – like the German 'Green Card' scheme of 2000 – ended as dismal failures. In 2005, the Mediterranean Migration Report (CARIM 2005: 21) published the alarming figure that more than half of Med-MENA (North-African/Middle Eastern) first-generation immigrants (54 per cent) with a university degree preferred North America, whereas the overwhelming majority (87 per cent) of Med-MENA immigrants with less than a secondary-level education ended up in Europe. The EU as a whole did '(not seem) ... to be considered attractive by highly qualified professionals in a context of very high international competition', as the October 2007 European Commission 'Blue Card' proposal put it (European Commission 2007: 3). Considering the relative failure of the 10 European member states that had specific schemes for admitting highly skilled workers at the time, the EU's 'main attractiveness compared to its competitors' might exactly be 'the possibility of accessing 27 labour markets' simultaneously, by means of one entry and residence permit (*ibid.*: 7).

The Commission's 2007 Blue Card proposal, like its German 'green card' predecessor, fell significantly short of the model that was being copied here, the American Green Card. The Blue Card was to be limited to two years, though renewable, and in this period its holders would be impeded from moving to another member state. Furthermore, the Blue Card was to be contingent on presenting a 'valid work contract or a binding job offer' (for a minimum of one year), at a salary level 'at least three times the minimum gross monthly wage as set by national law' (*ibid.*: 21), and subordinate to the 'principle of Community preference' (that is, of preferring EU or permanent resident citizens for a job vacancy) (*ibid.*). Moreover, after three months of unemployment, the Blue Card permit could be voided. Overall, this proposal left in place the typically European approach to legal immigration, according to which the rights of immigrants grow incrementally with the length of stay (*ibid.*: 10), rather than being set from the start in terms of a permanent residence guarantee with the final destination of acquiring citizenship, which is the classic settler state demarche on legal immigration.

If one considers that in the case of highly skilled migrants demand exceeds supply, such measure was unlikely to boast Europe's competitiveness in the global competition for the best and brightest. Certainly, a wager on the sovereignty front was that the Blue Card would prevent member states from outbidding one another in offering more advantageous rules to attract the highly skilled. But this deflected from the demand–supply asymmetry and the fact that 'European countries increasingly compete with each other' for this type of migrant (Collett 2008: 2). In particular, a country such as the United Kingdom, already more capable than others of attracting high-skilled workers, would gain little from a Blue Card scheme thus conceived. And a country such as Germany, which in its 2004 *Zuwanderungsgesetz* shied away from instituting a points-based regime for high-skilled immigration, would not support the Blue Card either, arguing that in the face of high domestic unemployment 'skills can still be sourced domestically' (*ibid.*: 3). Accordingly, the Blue Card seemed destined, like all Commission forays into legal labour migration since 2001, to end in the wastebasket.

It didn't. But the Council Directive 2009/50/EC of 25 May 2009 implementing the Blue Card still appeared to a well-travelled business observer from India as 'unlikely to surpass the US green card in appeal' (Pallavi 2009). After two years of controversial discussion, some of the more unappealing features of the original proposal could be remedied, a bit: member states were free to grant the initial permit for up to four years (though it could also be as short as one year), free movement was made available after only 18 months of stay, and the minimum salary was lowered to just 1.5 times the average gross salary in the respective member state. However, as if to compensate for such liberality, new sand was thrown into the gears of the system. Most importantly, the sovereignty crunch was revoked, so that member states remained free 'to maintain or to introduce new national residence permits for any purpose of employment'. This could cut both ways, as member states were free to offer more generous conditions than those offered by the Blue Card, or not to grant any permit at all. Especially galling, member states retained the right to deny free movement of a Blue Card holder from another state, so that the one competitive advantage of the Blue over the Green Card, to offer access to 27 national labour markets simultaneously, was effectively voided. Considering that the UK and Ireland (as well as Denmark) opted out of the Blue Card anyway, thus reducing the attractiveness of 'Europe' for high-skilled English-speaking migrants, it is no wonder that our Indian business observer foresees that 'blue is likely to flounder in its battle with green' (Pallavi 2009).

The Blue Card is nevertheless a first and significant crack in Europe's still-nationalized control of economic migration (a proposal for a directive on seasonal workers was presented by the European Commission in July 2010). That the future cannot but be more European is obvious in the 'European Pact on Immigration and Asylum', passed by the European Council under the French Presidency in September 2008. Considering that it was pushed through by a Gaullist French government, whose 1990s predecessor, under Interior Minister Charles Pasqua, had still acted under the maxim of realizing 'zero immigration', the new

European mindset expressed in this document is nothing less than revolutionary: 'The hypothesis of zero immigration is both unrealistic and dangerous' (Council of the European Union 2008: 2). Now it is recognized that 'international migration is a reality that will persist as long as there are differentials of wealth and development between the various regions of the world' (*ibid.*: 2), so that the option could never be to stop it but to better 'manage' it (*ibid.*: 2f.). Hence the 'new impetus' for a 'common immigration and asylum policy', whose need not even the sovereignty-guarding governments of member states of Europe (assembled under the European Council) any longer deny. As *The Economist* summarized the gist of the immigration pact: 'given free movement of people around the EU, different national policies no longer make sense'. Moreover, considering that immigration has by now become a policy area that produces up to one-third of new EU legislation (Collett 2008: 4), a fully Europeanized immigration policy is only a question of time.

From family to high-skilled immigration

In the 1990s asylum-seeking constituted the main target of European states' attempts to restrict unwanted immigration. By contrast, today's major preoccupation is with restricting family immigration. The successes on the asylum front, by means of EU rules on 'safe third countries' and 'safe countries of origin' and of state-level policies to tighten legal procedures and reducing material benefits, incidentally show the capacity of states to control unwanted immigration. If in 1992 there had been 675,460 asylum applications in the old EU-15, the number of such applications was down to 384,530 in 2001 (*Financial Times*, 11 June 2002). By 2006, the inflow in the enlarged EU-25 (including Norway and Switzerland) was further down to 209,391 (OECD 2008: 315). Britain, which was particularly drastic in cutting appeal procedures, reducing benefits, and detaining and expelling failed applicants, managed an over 70 per cent reduction in new asylum seekers between the peak year 2002, when the UK was Europe's most popular asylum destination, and 2006 (from 103,080 to 28,320) (*ibid.*).

Family migration now constitutes by far the largest category of legal inflows in all but a few European countries – if one exempts 'free movement' under regional mobility regimes (such as the EU), which is staggeringly strong in some West European countries (see Table 13.3). Table 13.3 shows considerable variety in the distribution of inflows across legal entry categories, both within EU countries and between the EU combined and some classic immigration countries. Astonishingly, the country with the smallest family inflow of all and with only a trickle of

Table 13.3 *Permanent-type immigration by category of entry, selected OECD countries (2006, percentage of total inflows)*

	Work (%)	Accompanying family of workers (%)	Family (%)	Humanitarian (%)	Free movement (%)
Austria	1	1	40	11	46
Belgium	8	0	35	7	50
Denmark	15	6	18	5	50
France	6	0	59	4	20
Germany	6	0	23	3	64
Italy	31	2	40	3	22
Netherlands	5	0	47	24	24
Portugal	29	0	62	0	9
Sweden	0	0	37	28	35
United Kingdom	29	14	18	9	24
Non-EU: USA	6	7	63	17	0
Non-EU: Australia	26	26	25	7	15
Non-EU: Canada	22	33	28	17	–

Source: OECD (2008: 36; http://dx.doi.org/10.1787/427163172430).

work inflows is the United States. The United States shifted to a family-focused quota system in 1965, in order to retain European-dominated immigration within an ethno-racially neutral immigration regime, and this proved immune to revision even when the system came to be dominated by Mexican and Asian immigrants in the following years. This has not really impaired America's capacity to attract high-skilled immigrants, as they have been processed outside the quota system, in terms of a temporary high-skilled workers visa ('H1b') that is convertible to permanent residence.

The inspiration for Europe's current turn to high-skilled immigration has been less family-oriented US than Canada and Australia, in terms of their fabled points systems. However, it is often overlooked that even in Canada and Australia family inflows, including the family that directly accompanies new labour migrants, constitute more than half of total legal inflows. And, if in Europe the discrepancy between worker and family inflows is particularly drastic in France, this is *also* because even accompanying family members of labour migrants are counted here within one combined 'family' category. Still, with only 6 per cent France exhibits a relatively small share of labour migrants among European countries. The contrast with the massive family figure (59 per cent of all legal inflows in 2006) makes President Sarkozy's campaign to move from 'suffered' to 'chosen' immigration rather understandable. And if there is one European country where such a move has already happened, that is Britain. Its share of labour migration even exceeds that of Canada and Australia, whose points systems are now emulated everywhere, including by Britain itself. Conversely, Britain has managed to drop non-accompanying family migration below the 20 per cent mark, which is (with Denmark) the smallest share in Europe today.

If one seeks to understand the current European dynamics surrounding family and high-skilled immigration, a comparison with the United States is again instructive. In the debate leading up to the 1990 Legal Immigration Act in the United States, there was a strong Republican Party attempt to cut quota immigration of extended family members (the fabled 'Fifth Preference' for siblings, dubbed the 'brothers and sisters clause', heavily used by Asians), which was criticized for its low skill levels. In turn, there was an attempt to increase the quota for high-skilled immigration. This quid pro quo was rejected by the entrenched ethnic lobby on Capitol Hill, and the eventual solution was to increase total annual intakes in order to create space for an enlarged high-skilled quota while retaining the extended family quota. The logic of this was to '(avoid) choices by expanding the pie' (D. Papademetriou, quoted in Joppke 1999: 38f.).

In a Europe plagued by right-wing populist parties and movements that thrive on an anti-immigrant stance, and further considering the absence of anything akin to an 'ethnic lobby' that could entrench family immigration, there is no political space for an additive rather than substitutive solution to the family–high-skilled immigration conundrum, however rational an additive solution might appear in light of Europe's demographic needs. Accordingly, the European logic is one of substitution, that is, of reducing presumably low-skilled family inflows in order to create a space for high-skilled worker flows. The limit to this move is less entrenched group interests, as in the United States, as rights on the part of settled immigrants. This is because family immigration in Europe has always been processed, not as wanted quota immigration, but as as-of-right immigration that has to grudgingly accepted, because of international conventions and domestic constitutional clauses that protect family life.

Interestingly, however, the European Court of Human Rights, watching over the European Convention for the Protection of Human Rights (ECPHR), has so far been unwilling to invoke the family clause (Article 8) for reining in on restrictive state practices in this domain, arguing that states have a wide 'margin of appreciation' (read: sovereignty) in dealing with immigration matters (de Hart 2006: 259). Even a harsh, and heavily criticized clause in the 2003 EU Family Reunification Directive, which allows restricting the family migration of children above 12 years, was deemed acceptable by the European Court of Justice, in conformity with ECPHR (Franz 2006: 51). And the fact that across Europe states have had a free rein, largely unimpeded by domestic courts, to raise the required minimum age of both spouses, to impose duration-of-marriage conditions, and to raise the minimum income threshold and related material conditions (such as sufficient housing), shows that previously granted 'rights' in this respect are better conceived as 'privileges' or 'concessions' that may be easily revoked. If there is legal opposition, it is increasingly invoking EU law, reflecting the thorough Europeanization of family migration that has occurred in the past five years. So a Dutch court recently objected to a domestic immigration rule that required at least 120 per cent of the minimum wage on part of the resident spouse, but which – contrary to the EU Family Reunification Directive – applied only to marriages conceived *after* the settlement in the Netherlands of the resident spouse (EU law does not recognize this distinction) (*Migration News Sheet*, August 2008: 6), and so on. But by far the biggest impact is likely to result from the recent European Court of Justice rule on *Metock* (discussed above), which does nothing less than derail member state efforts to fight against marriages of convenience, and which has been criticized as 'family reunification rules hijacked (by the ECJ)' (Danish Prime Minister Anders Fogh Rasmussen, quoted in *Migration News Sheet*, September 2008: 3). While this decision concerned marriages whose genuineness was affirmed by the court, the mere fact that the residence status of the spouse of EU citizens is now irrelevant for invoking the latter's free movement right opens the door for a massive abuse of the system.

In calibrating Europe's fight against family immigration, one has to realize that one of its main targets is indeed marriages of convenience, which are deemed to be concocted for immigration purposes only. The increasingly restrictive policies in the past few years thus home in on resident immigrants or citizens who seek to be joined by spouses from abroad. The new policies do not apply to new immigrants, directly (or not) accompanied by their nuclear family. For new immigrants, the rules are clear and have little changed over the years: high-skilled immigrants are always entitled to be immediately joined by their spouses and children, otherwise a country could not be competitive in attracting people for whom demand is larger than supply; by contrast, low-skilled, seasonal immigrants, where supply vastly exceeds demand, are always denied this privilege.

With respect to marriage of convenience, up to 80 per cent of the mixed-nationality or immigrant marriages in the Netherlands are deemed to fall in this category (de Hart 2006: 251). The EU Family Reunification Directive of 2003, in Article 16, clearly outlaws such marriages, which are defined as those where the 'sole aim' is acquiring the residence of the member state. A weaker prohibition (that has to respect the principle of 'proportionality') can be found also in the EU Free Movement of Citizens Directive of 2004. The number of such marriages still seems to be high. A British source claims that in 1999 76 per cent of those granted marriage status had first been admitted under a different status, and that 50 per cent of those switching to marriage status did so within the first six months of stay (Home Office 2002: 101). Such a rush to marriage, one must assume, is connected to immigration purposes. And in the context of the ECJ's *Metock* ruling, Irish officials pointed to an 'unusually high number of Latvians who marry Pakistanis', a rather unlikely attraction from an ethnic point of view, and there were media reports that Polish and Bulgarian women are contracting marriages of convenience for as little as €800 (*Migration News Sheet*, October 2008: 4).

Apart from France, where Sarkozy's slogan of moving from suffered to chosen immigration suggests there is intention in this substitution, in most other countries this is not so clear. While the coincidence of fighting family immigration and pushing for high-skilled immigration is conspicuous, one also has to consider that there are sector-specific considerations at play, such as fighting an obvious abuse of the system. In addition, there are integration concerns with respect to a widespread practice among second- and third-generation Turks and Moroccans to look for marriage partners abroad, which is the backdrop to the new 'integration from abroad' schemes invented by the Netherlands but now also practised in France and Germany (though there are important variations in the harshness of these policies; see Bonjour (2009)). Even where there is intention at play as in France, the declared objective to increase the share of economic migration from under 10 per cent to 50 per cent is, indeed, 'absolutely unrealistic', as Patrick Weil (*Le Monde*, 10 July 2007) pointed out in a furious critique of the French president's policy, because family immigration, as unwanted as it might be, is still as-of-right migration, protected by domestic, international and – most importantly – European law.

While there is now no Western European country that does not provide a privileged route of entry for high-skilled immigrants, the degree of moving to a soliciting immigration policy is still highly uneven across Europe. Opposite extremes are Germany and Britain. Germany, Europe's early pioneer in this respect (see Joppke 2002: 275–6), is now its rearguard. A new Immigration Law in 2004, tellingly entitled Law for the Steering and Limitation of In-migration (*Zuwanderung*), rejected the earlier proposal for a Canadian-oriented points system. The main innovation of the new law is procedural, moving from a complex system of multiple residence and separated work and residence permits to a simplified system of just two residence titles (temporary and permanent) and 'one-stop government' that combines work and residence permit. But the 1973 recruitment stop remains formally in place, and an exception allowed for high-skilled immigrants is rather timid and difficult to meet. Certainly, high-skilled immigrants are now granted an immediate permanent residence permit (*Niederlassungserlaubnis*), which breaks the European pattern of a gradual move from temporary to permanent residence (that even a country as open as Britain is still adhering to), and the Federal Labour Office does not have to agree. However, except for scientists and academics, the required minimum income was initially set at the absurdly high level of €84,600 (later reduced to €63,300). And a job offer at hand is a prerequisite for even being considered, which constitutes a further obstacle. No wonder that by summer 2005, that is, about half a year into the new policy, 'not a single highly qualified person has immigrated to Germany for work reasons' (Schmid-Drüner 2006: 208), and in the entire year of 2007 as few as 466 highly skilled immigrants arrived on this ticket (*Migration und Bevölkerung* no.7, September 2008). The only true innovation of the 2004 immigration law is to no longer require foreign students to return home after completing their degrees, but to allow them one year to find work and then to move towards permanent residence in Germany. Considering the pending internationalization of the German university system, which was recently boosted by federally funded clusters of 'excellence', the student route seems at this point Germany's main bid for entry in the global 'race for talent' (Shachar 2006).

By contrast, Britain is today Europe's most advanced and competitive participant in the race for talent. Already in 2002 it launched a Highly Skilled Migrant Programme, in order to 'compet(e) for highly skilled workers with other countries' (Home Office 2002: 42). It granted a one-year visa, without employment at hand and allowing immediate family unification, convertible after four years into permanent residence. It was replaced in 2008 by a new points system covering the entire (high- to low-skilled) economic migrant spectrum, dubbed by the responsible minister as 'the most significant change to managed migration in the last 40 years' (Home Minister Charles Clarke, in his foreword to Home Office 2006). High-skilled immigration figures here as the first of five 'tiers' (next to tiers for skilled, low skilled, students and temporary workers), geared to doctors, engineers, finance and IT specialists, and defined by meeting a minimal number of points for qualifications, previous earnings and age.

There is a nominal tier for 'low-skilled' workers, but it would not be used as long as there are sufficient numbers of 'workers available from the newly enlarged EU' (*ibid.*: 29). Should a need for non-EU workers arise in the future, there is a list of strings attached that reads not unlike those for prisoners on leave: there would have to be 'effective returns arrangements' with the country of origin, entry would be limited to 12 months with no dependants and without the right to switch to another status later, and 'we are considering options such as compulsory remittances, requiring open return tickets, and biometric capture to ensure that workers return at the end of their stay' (*ibid.*: 30). Considering innovative moves on the front of immigrant integration also, with a new policy that favours citizenship over legal permanent residence (Home Office 2008), even introducing a point system for the acquisition of citizenship (Home Office 2009), Britain is now Europe's laboratory for a new migration world in which not just the opposite logics of stemming and soliciting, but immigrant selection and immigrant integration are meant to be integrated into one coherent system. But this appears too neat on paper to ever match a messier, patchworked reality.

Chapter 14

Resource Politics: The Rapidly Shifting European Energy Policy Agenda

Christian Egenhofer and Arno Behrens

European Union (EU) energy policy has been confined to the narrow fields of coal and nuclear energy for decades, deriving its authority from the treaties on the European Coal and Steel Community (ECSC) and on the European Atomic Community (Euratom). Periodic attempts to extend the EU's jurisdiction in times of real or perceived threats to energy supplies remained unsuccessful. Outside these two sectors, EU policy has been limited to a series of broad horizontal policy goals, such as promoting the rational use of energy and reducing Europe's oil import dependency. Member states were not able to accept an energy chapter in the EU's most important treaty, the Treaty on the European Community (TEC), most recently in Maastricht (in 1992) and Amsterdam (1997). Although the Maastricht summit agreed on a new article (Article 3(u)), which added 'measures in the field of energy as legitimate Community activities', this by no means constituted an EU competence or authority in the field of energy. Despite strong support from the European Commission and the European Parliament, the majority of member states were reluctant to lose their real or perceived autonomy over energy policy. The main reasons have been differences in interests between producer and non-producer countries as well as the different structures of national energy sectors, best exemplified in the organization of network energy industries. For the same reason, the creation of a single energy market was originally neither part of the European Commission's 1995 White Paper on the internal market nor of the Single European Act (SEA), the treaty revision of 1986 that led to the implementation of the internal market. This anomaly was, however, rectified already in 1988 by including energy in the internal market programme.

In parallel to its efforts to introduce a chapter and thereby authority in the field of energy, the European Commission attempted to improve coordination between member states and even to introduce a coordination mechanism. As early as 1995, the Commission tabled a White Paper (European Commission 1995) after extensive consultations with member states and European industry, which argues that European energy policy lacks coherence due to the fragmentation of its legal basis into different areas such as regulation, competition and environmental and foreign policy. One of the Commission's key concerns has been the absence of EU authority (competencies) to safeguard security of energy supplies. This approach was further developed in the Green Paper of 2000 (European Commission 2000), which was aimed at initiating a debate about reducing the risks associated with increasing European dependency on energy imports. In addition to the focus on coherence and better coordination, this debate has introduced the concept of security of supply as a *hedging strategy* to address risks from energy *use, production, transport* and *imports* (Stern 2002; Luciani 2004; Egenhofer *et al.* 2004). There has been a growing realization that energy security exhibits different risks including political, economic, environmental and technical ones (Checchi *et al.* 2009). They all necessitate different responses. The 2000 Green Paper prescribed energy efficiency, less polluting energy sources (including renewables and nuclear) and the better management of relations with producer countries as solutions.

More recently, there has been a change of mind. EU member states have started to realize the possible benefits or even the need for a more integrated EU energy policy. New challenges such as climate change, but also the resurfacing of old ones such as security of supply or the need to face up to increasing global competition for resources have triggered this new thinking. In addition, the gradual integration of energy markets through three successive legislative packages and other market developments, have led to some convergence of member states' policies, mixes and interests.

In fact, it could even be argued that EU climate policy has severely reduced the scope for national energy policies by limiting EU member states' autonomy regarding their energy mixes. On the one hand, some 40 per cent of EU greenhouse gas (GHG) emissions (i.e. power and energy-intensive sectors) are subject to the EU Emissions Trading Scheme setting a cap to CO_2 emissions. On the other hand, the energy and climate package as adopted in 2009 sets binding targets for the use of renewables in energy consumption as well as for the overall reduction of GHG emissions in the EU (i.e. also for sectors not covered by the European Union's emission trading system (ETS)). The long-term energy mix will thus increasingly be determined by EU policies aimed at decarburizing the EU economy and thus at phasing out carbon intensive fuels. In addition, long-term targets to reduce GHG emissions by 80 to 95 per cent by 2050 (compared to 1990 levels) point to a large-scale increase of low-carbon fuels such as renewables, fossil fuels with carbon capture and storage and nuclear (in some member states). Technology development and market forces will largely determine the mix of these, further decreasing governments, influence on their energy mix.

There is now agreement about the value-added of EU-level energy policy. However, many aspects of this policy will need more time to develop. While climate change policy has led to some harmonization of energy policies and a stronger role for the EU, several member states continue to build on bilateral relationships with supplier countries in the context of securing their energy supplies. National responses to energy supply risks may not always be compatible with the security of supply interests of other member states or the EU as a whole. The pursuit of different national policies and interests is mainly related to the hetero-geneity and the different starting points of the 27 EU member states, such as the degree of energy market liberalization, differences in the energy mix or levels of diversification, geographical location or even differences over foreign policy objectives. A 'European concept of security of supply' against which to assess member states' energy policies could overcome such inconsistencies, as well as the increasing harmonization of EU exter-nal energy policy.

After an introduction to past energy policy, this chapter will identify and assess the driving forces for this new dynamism in EU energy policy. It will then discuss some of the implications to outline future prospects.

The changing global and European energy landscape

Recent decades saw the EU in a rather comfortable energy supply situa-tion. Domestic resources from the UK, the Netherlands and other coun-tries and quasi-domestic ones from Norway enabled the EU to limit import dependency. Oil markets generally were efficient and liquid with some but not excessive government interference. Oil has been abun-dantly available and the International Energy Agency (IEA) crisis mech-anisms a comfortable buffer in case of supply problems. Even more assuring has been the fact that the crisis mechanisms never had to be used. As to natural gas, possibly the most risky source due to rigidities in transportation, some 80 per cent of the world's gas reserves are in an economically transportable distance from Europe. In addition, the EU enjoyed a near monopsony with Russia, home to the world's largest gas resources. Other supplies such as those from Northern Africa were also considered secure as these countries depend in many cases exclusively on oil and gas for foreign exchange revenues. Furthermore, massive invest-ments in nuclear energy in the 1970s and 1980s allowed nuclear power to play an important role in the energy mix, with a positive effect on overall import dependency (albeit associated with other security of supply risks). The EU thus generally enjoyed a healthy diversification as regards both energy sources and geographical origin. There have been a number of member states for which this has not been true to the same extent, e.g. Finland, Spain or Portugal. But for most member states, the security-of-supply position has been rather comfortable. Especially those countries with domestic sources such as the UK or the Netherlands or those with a healthy diversification such as Germany did not see a need to act.

This situation has been changing over the last decade with a worsening international long-term outlook.

- European energy demand is increasingly rivalled by demand from emerging economies, especially in Asia. Without new developments on the supply side, increasing world energy demand will lead to significantly higher prices in the medium and long term. The IEA concludes that 'ensuring reliable and affordable supply will be a formidable challenge' (IEA 2007).
- Conventional oil and gas reserves in the EU are dwindling (BP 2010). In some countries, which could fill the gap, EU industries have little or no access to reserves. Access to energy reserves becomes a critical issue for the EU and other consumer countries.
- Energy industries in supplier countries are subject to extensive government interference, and do not function in a competitive market framework. To a large extent, energy production and export companies are state-owned monopolies. This adds to the fears that energy will increasingly be used as a political weapon. Government-regulated investment policies also raise doubts about the level of future investments and their effects on production and price levels. In the past, many supplier countries have proved unable to increase production, adding to the pressure on market prices (e.g. Riley 2006). In addition, security of supply is threatened by the political instability of exporting regions.
- Many reserves will take years to develop due to problems of access, investments and physical conditions. A prolonged tight market might increase political tensions and foster a form of 'resource nationalism'. On top of this, the absence of visible progress towards a global climate regime increases uncertainty for investors.
- The EU internal market for electricity and gas, which currently consists of different national or regional markets, is still developing and is far from functioning smoothly. Without an efficient internal market, the EU/European Economic Area (EEA) response is likely to

lack efficiency, which is normally imposed by market discipline, and competitiveness, and member states will feel compelled to resort to national solutions, further undermining the internal market. The lack of transparency in the price formation mechanisms – which is also a crucial condition and an indicator for the functioning of the internal market – inhibits new entry, at least in some member states.

- The recent economic crisis has led to a reduction of European energy demand and related GHG emissions. However, this impact is likely to prevail in the short term only, with demand picking up as European economies recover.

In addition, the following sector-specific challenges can be identified:

- The supply of oil in the EEA and Organization for Economic Cooperation and Development (OECD) countries has largely been secured by existing infrastructure, reinforced by security measures such as the IEA strategic stocks and demand restraint measures. However, Europe and all other major consumer regions are faced with declining domestic oil extraction rates, leading to increasing import dependency and stronger competition between oil importers. At current production rates, the EU-27 will have exploited all its proved reserves in the course of the year 2019 (BP 2010). On the other hand, global estimates of how much recoverable oil remains have consistently increased over time. BP (*ibid.*) estimated global oil reserves to amount to 1.5 trillion barrels at the end of 2009. At the current rate of global production, these remaining reserves would last for another 46 years. This reserves-to-production (R/P) ratio has remained more or less constant at around 40 years until 2007 but increased sharply since then, probably due to reduced world oil consumption related to the economic crisis. However, appropriate investment is the key if future production is to succeed in matching demand. In the long run, non-conventional oil resources (e.g. oil sands, gas-to-liquids, coal-to-liquids, oil-shale, etc.) will play an increasing role in global oil supplies. With estimated reserves of at least 1 trillion barrels, they are expected to contribute about 8.5 per cent to global oil supplies by 2030 (IEA 2007). Moreover, these resources are mostly located outside the current oil-producing countries. Whether non-conventional alternatives will be commercially available will depend on world oil prices and technology/infrastructure development.
- As for natural gas, the pre-economic crisis outlook – i.e. projections used for the EU energy and climate change package (see below) – the assumption has been that irrespective of the projected increase of the

liquefied natural gas (LNG) market, the EU and EEA will increasingly depend on gas pipe supplies coming from very few countries. Whereas over 80 per cent of the global natural gas reserves of 187 trillion m? (BP 2010) are located close enough to Europe to allow for pipeline transport (Müller 2007), Europe lacks the infrastructure to tap resources in the Middle East, which has the largest proven reserves (over 40 per cent of global reserves). Almost 85 per cent of Europe's natural gas imports come from three countries (European Commission 2010), where the gas market is tightly controlled by governments. In this respect, fears of 'gas cartels' or of energy being used as a political weapon do not seem unfounded. However, following the economic crisis and the rapid growth of US non-conventional gas production freeing up additional LNG exports to the EU, the prospect of a tight market has somewhat been altered and the IEA (2009) now even predicts a gas glut. If the IEA projections prove to be right, gas cartel and political exploitation will become far less likely. On the other hand, the economic crisis has aggravated the risk of a lack of investment in exploration, production and transportation, despite reserves being abundantly available in areas surrounding Europe. Be it as it may, the assumption leading the adoption of the EU energy and climate change package has been that if gas were unable to take a larger share in power generation, it would not be able to live up to the expectation that it could serve as a 'bridge' to a low-carbon economy and might even become a 'sunset' industry (Stern 2006). The future carbon price will also have an impact on future gas markets.

- Issues for the electricity sector are continuity and reliability of supply. Risks include electricity blackouts due to ageing infrastructure and a lack of investment in networks, especially cross-border capacity, erosion of reserve capacity, public opposition to new investment projects in generation and transportation, bad regulation and increasing the market share of incumbent companies in domestic generation. A particular aspect is the slow progress in liberalization and integration of the European electricity market. Markets in 'transition' create their own risks such as erosion of reserve capacity. Such issues are likely to disappear, once the market functions properly. A major issue in the electricity sector is the ageing nuclear capacity, which is coming to the end of its lifetime with only limited prospects for replacement. Even though some member states have announced new projects, without massive investment to replace ageing facilities and build new plants, Europe's nuclear generating capacity is in fact expected to shrink rather than grow. Accordingly, the IEA forecasts that electricity generation from nuclear power will decrease from 31 per cent to 21 per cent by 2020 (IEA 2008). This expected trend is due to a number of risks that investors have to face when operating in the nuclear sector. More specifically, the main reasons for the possibly stagnation and decline of nuclear power generation are costs, safety, public opinion, waste and proliferation (MIT 2003). A challenge for European electricity systems will thus be to replace the declining share of nuclear with other low-carbon energy sources.

On top of this, the EU (together with the rest of the world) faces the long-term climate change challenge. Given that energy-related emissions account for about 80 per cent of all greenhouse gas emissions in the EU, climate change policy based on the recently agreed EU targets (20 20 by 2020, see below) and on the vision of a long-term decarburization of the EU economy will require profound changes in European energy systems. Climate change thus plays an important role in energy policy making and the value of considering interactions between global warming and energy security is increasingly recognized (Behrens 2010). The absence of a global agreement and the lack of a firm perspective for such an agreement is heightening uncertainty and holding back energy sector investment in the EU and worldwide.

The member-state level: a diverse EU energy map

The debate about an EU response to these challenges must take into account the energy situation of various member states and thus differing costs and benefits of a common EU energy policy. Geographical location, availability of domestic resources and political preferences play an important role in determining the energy challenges and policy responses in different member states, in addition to varying historical contexts, which may limit diversification options due to (often unjustified) public concerns. Similarly, member states have made mixed progress in terms of competitiveness, supply security and environmental sustainability of their energy systems. Röller *et al.* (2007) have developed a relatively simple so-called 'energy policy index' (EPI) to assess the performance of member states against these three EU energy policy objectives. They find great heterogeneity among different member states, concluding that 'the EU's energy map is diverse'. One group of countries scores well in terms of both competitiveness and security of supply (including Austria, Czech Republic, Denmark, Netherlands and UK) while another scores well in terms of environmental sustainability (Finland, Latvia, Sweden). A third group of countries lags behind in terms of competitiveness but has a relatively high level of supply security (Germany, Estonia, France, Greece, and Poland). Finally, there is a host of countries that score around the EU average (Hungary, Italy, Lithuania, Portugal, Slovenia and Slovakia) as well as Belgium and Spain who lag behind in all three criteria.

This analysis shows that member states are at different points on the playing field, facing different energy challenges. There is little common ground in terms of geography, size or time of EU accession. According to the EPI, the level of domestic competition and exposure to foreign competition is highest in Slovenia, Luxembourg, Denmark and Lithuania. The highest levels of security of supply (taking into account import dependency and generation adequacy) have been found in Poland, Denmark and the UK). Furthermore, countries in the north of Europe generally score better in terms of environmental sustainability (Latvia, Sweden and Finland). When looking at the energy mix on the member state level there are more common conclusions to be drawn. While the EU-15 are more reliant on oil and gas, new member states in general have a considerably higher reliance on coal and – to a lesser extent – nuclear. On the other hand, some of the highest dependencies on nuclear power are found in Western European countries such as France and Sweden.

To illustrate different national policy responses to energy and climate challenges, we present three short case studies of countries which recently presented their long-term energy strategies: the UK, Poland and Sweden.

The UK aims to reduce GHG emissions by some 34 per cent by 2020 (compared to 1990) with a self-set binding target to achieve a reduction of at least 80 per cent by 2050 (Crown Copyright 2009). Similarly, the UK intends to meet its EU obligation of producing 15 per cent of all energy from renewables by 2020 (see Table 14.1). About half of the annual emissions cuts between 2009 and 2020 are to be achieved in the power sector through the EU ETS and by increasing the share of low-carbon electricity to 40 per cent. The main focus will be on renewables (mainly wind but also wave and tidal power, biomass and geothermal), which are expected to deliver 30 per cent of electricity in 2020. The rest (another 10 per cent) will be based on nuclear and clean coal. It is interesting to note that this would represent a considerable drop in the share of nuclear, which in 2007 added about 16 per cent to UK electricity generation (European Commission 2010). By 2050, the UK government aims for a carbon neutral electricity sector – which will include new nuclear power plants starting from 2025. Given that electricity demand is expected to increase due to a larger role of electricity in heating and transport, the electricity grid will be expanded with a focus on 'smart grids'. Renewable energy will also play an increasing role in reducing emissions from homes and communities, together with energy efficiency.

In terms of transport, the UK government focuses on new vehicle CO_2 policies (e.g. for electric and plug-in hybrid cars) as well as the introduction of additional renewable fuels.

Although Poland has the same target as the UK for the share of renewables in its energy mix in 2020 (15 per cent), the preliminary Polish energy strategy for 2030 is considerably less pronounced on renewables, and instead focuses more on the use of other domestic resources to increase supply security, particularly on coal. One of the biggest challenges of the country is its reliance on coal in the electricity sector (almost 92 per cent) and related GHG emissions. At the same time, there is a reluctance to increase dependency on gas imports, especially from Russia. To allow for the continued use of coal, Poland intends to support the development of technologies 'whereby it will be possible to acquire liquid and gaseous fuels from domestic resources' (Polish Embassy 2009). Coal gasification and carbon capture and storage (CCS) will be at the heart of this strategy. Similarly, natural gas is intended to play an increasing role through an increase in the domestic production, better pipeline infrastructure and a new port for LNG. Furthermore, Poland intends to build its first two nuclear power plants to decarbonizes its electricity sector. These could be operational by 2025 and supply some 20 to 25 per cent of domestic electricity demand. In terms of renewables, the government intends to achieve a 15 per cent share in final energy consumption by 2020 and a 20 per cent share by 2030. Main potentials lie in biomass from forestry and agricultural waste and geothermal waters, as well as in hydroelectric stations and offshore wind farms. A plan by the ministry of economy aims for the construction of at least one agricultural biogas plant in each commune.

The most ambitions decarburization policy can be found in Sweden, which aims to be a carbon-neutral country by 2050. In 2006, 97 per cent of Sweden's electricity generation came from low-carbon sources (50 per cent renewables and 47 per cent nuclear) and the share of renewables in final energy consumption was over 41 per cent – by far the highest in Europe, essentially based on hydropower. The only main fossil fuel in use is oil, all of which needs to be imported (European Commission 2010). Since oil is largely used in the transport sector, the country aims to make its vehicle stock independent of fossil fuels by 2030 while the use of fossil fuels for heating will already be phased out by 2020 (Regeringskansliet 2009). Sweden considers natural gas as an important option in the transition period and supports the development of infrastructure that may also be used for the gradual introduction of biogas. To reduce the 'dependence on nuclear power and hydropower' (*ibid.*), Sweden aims to significantly increase the share of cogeneration, wind power (on land and offshore) and other renewables in electricity production. Sweden has annulled its Nuclear Phase-Out Act and has extended the 'transitional period during which nuclear power will be in use' (*ibid.*) by allowing new nuclear power plants to be built on existing sites, albeit without the support of central government subsidies. Energy efficiency plays a role in all three countries and will be essential to counteract increasing costs associated with new investments in energy systems.

More EU energy policy

Changing geopolitics, climate change and market liberalization have made member states accept the logic of granting further energy competencies to the EU. Going beyond the Maastricht Treaty (1992), which introduced 'measures in the sphere of energy' to the list of 'activities of the community' (albeit subject to unanimity), member states agreed to add an energy chapter in the Lisbon Treaty. With the ratification process of the Treaty of Lisbon completed in November 2009, the reform treaty entered into force on 1 December 2009. It amends the Treaty on European Union (TEU) and the Treaty establishing the European Community (TEC), the latter of which is renamed Treaty on the functioning of the European Union (TFEU). By assigning new competencies to the EU, the treaty creates a legal basis for European energy policy, which is elevated into an area of shared competence between the Union and the member states (Article 4 TFEU). This means that member states can only regulate energy issues when the Union has not exercised its competence. Similarly, member states lose their competence when the EU does decide to regulate. In that case, EU law would override member states' existing legislation and their right to legislate in this area.

A separate chapter on energy (Article 194 TFEU) mandates overall EU energy policy to focus on the establishment and functioning of the internal market and on preserving and improving the environment. Within this context, EU energy policy should aim at four explicitly mentioned goals: (a) functioning of the energy market; (b) security of energy supply in the Union; (c) the promotion of energy efficiency and energy saving and the development of new and renewable forms of energy; and (d) the promotion of the interconnection of energy networks. The Treaty of Lisbon greatly extends the application of the ordinary legislative procedure, thus enhancing the European Parliament's powers of decision. This procedure will also apply to measures aimed at achieving the above objectives. They will be adopted jointly by the European Parliament and the Council, acting by qualified majority, and after consultation of the Economic and Social Committee and the Committee of the Regions.

There will, however, be two notable exceptions to these new provisions. First, the Treaty of Lisbon leaves to member states the right to determine the conditions for exploiting its energy resources, as well as the critical choice between different energy sources and the general structure of their energy supplies. Second, fiscal measures (e.g. energy taxes) will continue to be subject to unanimity. These two provisions can be regarded as safeguards for national sovereignty in the field of energy.

Taking into account the security of supply concerns by some member states, the Lisbon Treaty also includes a reference to solidarity among member states in case of difficulties in the supply of energy (Article 122 TFEU). However, what this article means in practice remains to be seen. It provides for the Council to take appropriate action in case of serious supply disruptions. However, the Treaty does not go beyond this rather generic formulation, due to the resistance of some member states fearing wrong incentives for national energy policies, referred to as 'moral hazard': member states partly insulated from supply risks by the solidarity clause may adopt a more risky energy policy (i.e. under-invest in security of supply), because they know that they will be 'bailed out' by the EU in case of a crisis. Nevertheless, the issue of solidarity has been taken up by the European Commission in its Second Strategic Energy Review of November 2008, the European Economic Recovery Plan in 2009 and the Regulation on Gas Supply Security. The first puts forward a five-point EU energy security and solidarity action plan, including energy infrastructure, external energy relations, oil and gas stocks, energy efficiency and optimizing the EU's indigenous energy resources. The European Economic Recovery Plan will support energy infrastructure projects with some €4 billion until 2011, focusing mainly on gas and electricity infrastructure, carbon capture and storage (CCS), and offshore wind energy. Both of these initiatives will help in the creation of well-interconnected and flexible European gas and electricity markets, thus increasing de facto solidarity among all consumers and reducing risks associated with external energy security challenges. The Regulation on Gas Supply Security imposes minimum security of supply obligations including contingency plans for the failure of the principal gas infrastructure of each member state. This so called N-1 approach (this indicator refers to the breakdown of the largest regional gas supply infrastructure – either an import pipeline or a production facility – in which case the remaining infrastructure (N-1) would need to be able to supply sufficient quantities of gas to satisfy total regional gas demand for a period of 60 days – whereby total gas demand is calculated on the basis of exceptionally cold winters statistically occurring every 20 years) is important in two respects. It potentially increases the resilience of the EU gas supply system, which is a function of the security of member state systems. At the same time, imposing obligations addresses the risk of 'moral hazard' as outlined above.

The central role of EU energy and climate package

In an effort to come up with a comprehensive and ambitious response to European energy and climate change challenges, European heads of state and government met during the German Presidency of the EU on 8/9 March 2007 to agree on binding targets to reduce GHG emissions and to increase the share of renewable energy sources in the EU's energy mix. Based on the European Commission's proposal of January 2007 entitled *Energy Policy for Europe* (European Commission 2007a), which was accompanied by its twin communication *Limiting Global Climate Change to 2° C* (European Commission 2007b) as well as by a number of sectoral policies such as those on renewables or carbon capture and storage, the agreed targets included the following elements:

1   A binding absolute emissions reduction commitment of 30 per cent by 2020 compared to 1990 conditional on a global agreement, and a 'firm independent commitment' to achieve at least a 20 per cent reduction by 2020. At the same time, the EU advocated that industrialized countries reduce their emissions collectively by 60 to 80 per cent by 2050 compared to 1990.
2   A binding target of 20 per cent renewable energy sources in the EU's final consumption of energy by 2020 (because of the binding nature of the GHG reduction and the renewables targets, they are often referred to as the '20 20 targets').
3   A binding minimum 10 per cent share of biofuels in each member state's transport energy consumption by 2020, which will also count towards the overall 20 per cent renewables target. This target was later broadened to include all forms of renewable energy sources in transport.
4   A 20 per cent reduction of primary energy consumption by 2020 compared to projections (non-binding).
5   A commitment to enable the construction of up to 12 large-scale power plants using carbon capture and storage (CCS) technology.

The implementation of the overall targets has been based on the 'climate-energy legislative package', which was adopted by the Council of the European Union on 6 April 2009 (www.consilium.europa.eu/uedocs/cms_data/docs/pressdata/en/misc/107136.pdf). This package contains six principal elements, including a directive for the promotion of renewable energy sources, a revised Emissions Trading System (ETS) starting 2013, an 'effort sharing' decision setting binding emissions targets for EU member states in sectors not subject to the ETS, a regulation to reduce CO_2 emissions from cars, new environmental quality standards for fuels and biofuels, and a regulatory framework for carbon capture and storage.

The main innovation about this package is the attempt to increase the coherence of different policy objectives, especially energy security and climate change, and thereby to align domestic policy objectives with the EU external policy and to create the necessary procedures and mechanisms. The package sets out three principal long-term EU energy policy objectives: (a) security of supply, especially reducing import dependency; (b) the need to drastically reduce GHG emissions; and (c) the EU international competitiveness.

Additional advantages of the EU package include (Jansen *et al.* 2005: 3–6; Egenhofer 2009):

- the renewable energy policy can provide technological leadership in sunrise technologies;
- renewable electricity can reduce long-term electricity price and price volatility;
- substitution of fossils combined with renewables may reduce pricing power by Russia (notably on gas); and
- finally, the introduction of the EU CO_2 Emissions Trading System is effectively retaining economic rents from hydrocarbon producer countries, redirecting these rents to EU governments via auctioning of EU allowances (the appropriation of rent is most pronounced for coal where already a price of $30 per tonne of CO_2 leads to a price increase of 88 per cent. The corresponding figures for oil and natural gas are rather low compared to gas with 17 per cent and 18 per cent, respectively. To date only half of the EU ETS allowances are auctioned but this figure should increase progressive).

To offset the higher prices both for industry and domestic customers, energy efficiency is a central piece, certainly for the transition period until new technologies and new fuels become available. Reducing consumption while prices increase gives a reasonable prospect for keeping the energy bill constant. Unlike for GHG emissions and renewables, however, there is no binding target on improving energy efficiency in the EU. Given the sluggish improvements of energy efficiency in member states, there seems to be increasing momentum for the European Commission to table a proposal for a binding 20 per cent target in the context of the revised Energy Efficiency Action Plan. There is thus a chance that the currently indicative target of saving 20 per cent of Europe's energy consumption compared to projections for 2020 could turn into a binding target in the future.

The interaction of energy policy and climate change

While there is sufficient reason for an EU energy policy, this dramatic reorientation would not have been possible without climate change. Tackling climate change has been identified by the EU as one of the world's greatest challenges, recognizing that climate change is likely to have major negative consequences for the environment, the economy and societies at large. The EU has repeatedly confirmed its position that an increase in the global, annual, mean surface temperature should not exceed 2°C above pre-industrial levels. After the US withdrawal from the Kyoto Protocol, the EU found itself being catapulted into global leadership on climate change. While it looked unlikely that the Kyoto Protocol would survive, Japan, Canada and Russia ratified the Protocol – not least due to active EU diplomacy – to bring it into force in 2005. To prepare for this, the EU has adopted numerous laws to fulfil its commitments and prepare the path for a new follow-up post-Kyoto agreement, when commitments expire in 2012. Among them have been a host of policies to support renewable energy, improve energy efficiency in buildings and transport. However, the centrepiece of EU climate change policy has been the EU Emissions Trading Scheme (EU ETS) that started in 2005. The EU ETS covers about 40 per cent of EU GHG emissions and about half of all European CO_2 emissions.

Origins and the political context of the EU ETS

Prior to adoption of the EU ETS, experience with tradable permits has largely been confined to the United States, which has operated such schemes since the 1970s. Among them was the successful US SO_2 trading programme, which has become the reference point of emissions trading globally (e.g. Klaassen 1996). While there is little doubt that the EU ETS has strongly been influenced by the US SO_2 trading programme and the NOx Budget Trading Program, EU and US schemes differ in several important aspects. The principal difference is the high level of decentralization in the EU and the significant degree of discretion for member states in the implementation phase, even if compared to the NOx Budget Trading Program.

Increasing use of market-based solutions

Market solutions have in many instances proved easier than harmonization across 27 or more national jurisdictions, which display major differences in legal systems, enforcement cultures and administrative capacities. In the case of the EU ETS, EU legislation has been initiated by nationally proposed legislation. European Commission action towards an emissions-trading scheme has – at least – partly been triggered by the establishment of national emissions-trading schemes in Denmark, the UK and the associated risks of 'proliferation' of such schemes in other member states (see e.g. Zapfel and Vainio 2002). At the same time, companies such as BP and Shell, the EU electricity sector and industrial associations such as Entreprises pour l'environnement started to promote emissions-trading schemes for GHG (e.g. Egenhofer 2003; Philibert and Reinaud 2004).

Ultimately, the EU ETS has been promoted on the basis of a mixture of economic, environmental and EU internal market arguments (see Delbeke 2006). Another strand of the literature associates the rise of emissions trading with the 'entrepreneurial role' that the DG Environment of the European Commission has played (Skjærseth and Wettestad 2008).

Under the EU ETS cap-and-trade scheme, the covered sectors must monitor and annually report their CO_2 emissions, and are obliged every year to surrender an amount of EU emission allowances (EUAs) to the government that is equivalent to their CO_2 emissions in that year. The scheme covers electricity and heat generation, cement, pulp and paper, refining, coke ovens, iron and steel, glass, ceramics and paper and board, which together represent approximately 40 per cent of total EU GHG emissions. For an authoritative overview on the design of the ETS, see Meadows (2006) and Vis (2006). Credits from the Kyoto Protocol's project mechanisms, the Clean Development Mechanisms (CDM) and Joint Implementation (JI) can be used for compliance within limits (Lefevere 2006).

The EU ETS has been the result of rigorous consultation on the part of the European Commission with stakeholders before, during and after the European Climate Change Programme, followed by intensive discussions within and between the Council of Ministers and the European Parliament. The EU ETS was adopted unanimously by the Council of Ministers and by a very large majority in the European Parliament. In general, business was favourably disposed to the scheme, as were environmental NGOs.

In order to ensure support from member states and industry to ensure fast adoption the European Commission had to offer a number of concessions. One such concession was free allocation of allowances of up to 95 per cent for phase 1 (2005–7) and up to 90 per cent for the second phase (2008–12). The principal reason for free allocation was to 'buy' industry acceptance. As long as allowances are given for free, companies receive additional revenues to partly or entirely offset higher production costs as a result of the EU ETS.

Another necessary concession – this time to member states – has been to leave the allocation *process* in the hands of member states. Although this is in line with general EU practice of leaving implementation to member states, the high degree of decentralization was the price to pay for both member state and industry support. Member states are reluctant to cede influence on the energy and energy-related industries. And most of the industries felt more comfortable with allocation undertaken at member state rather than at EU level.

As a result, the original EU ETS Directive and its implementation in the first phase had a number of deficiencies including notably over-allocation, distorting allocation between member states, windfall profits for the power sector and the risk of deferred investment (for details, see Swedish Energy Agency 2006; Egenhofer 2007, 2009; Ellerman *et al.* 2010).

Over-allocation in 2006 finally triggered a CO_2 price collapse. In their National Allocation Plans (NAPs), member states pitched their caps somewhere between 'less than business-as-usual' and moving towards a 'path consistent with the Kyoto Protocol'. Most NAPs foresaw modest caps and high dependency on projections. It turned out that most if not all projections were considerably inflated (LETS Update 2006). This combination of modest cuts, close to actual emissions and inflated projections has led to over-allocation of as much as 97MT of CO_2 out of a total of about 2.2 billion annual EU allowance, i.e. almost 5 per cent of total annual allowances (Kettner *et al.* 2007).

The second round of NAPs in the period from 2008 to 2012 has seen some improvements in the implementation by EU member states and the EU. Renewed over-allocation has been avoided when the European Commission could impose a formula to assess member states' allocation plans and thereby de facto impose an EU-wide cap. For NAPs-2, the European Commission has used explicit 'objective' projections based on 2005 verified emissions across the board for all member states (i.e. verified 2005 ETS emissions x GDP growth rates for 2005 to 2010 (based on the PRIMES model) x carbon intensity improvements rate for 2005 to 2010 + adjustment for new entrants and other changes (for example, in ETS coverage)). As a result, the European Commission could shave off 10 per cent of member states' proposed allocation, leaving the ETS sector short of around 5 per cent for the second period. While the price for the allowances was expected to be in the region of €20–25, the actual prices were much lower due to the economic crisis.

The most important effect, however, has been that experience from the initial phases and design flaws have greatly helped the European Commission to propose radical, one could even argue revolutionary, changes to the EU ETS. Principal elements of the new ETS include a single EU-wide cap, decreasing annually in a linear way of 1.74 per cent, starting in 2013, to reach around 1.720 million tonnes of CO_2 in 2020. This translates into an overall cap of 21 per cent lower than compared to 2005 verified emissions. This linear reduction continues beyond 2020 as there is no sunset clause. In addition, there are EU-wide harmonized allocation rules; full auctioning to sectors that can pass through their costs, e.g. the power sector, partial free allocation to industry based on EU-wide harmonized benchmarks. Overall, this would translate into 60 per cent auctioning, which would equal about €33 billion auctioning receipts per annum at a price of €30 per tonne of CO_2 (see Behrens *et al.* 2008).

The ETS in the context of the '20 20 targets'

The adoption of the energy and climate package has a major steering role for the energy sector. Although decisions that affect the energy mix remain subject to unanimity under the Lisbon Treaty, in reality the long-term energy mix will be determined by EU policies. In addition to the legally binding renewable targets, member states have also agreed on legally binding GHG emissions reduction targets (see Table 14.1). This together with the EU ETS will gradually phase out high-carbon fuels such as unabated coal. While in the non-ETS sectors, member states are free to decide on how to achieve the target, EU policy is harmonized by EU-wide rules within the sectors covered by the EU ETS (i.e. in the industry and power sectors, which cover about 40 per cent of EU GHG emissions). Abatement is dictated by the market logic rather than by (member states') governments.

Such centralization, i.e. hard caps and binding renewable obligations has only been possible as a result of a complex burden sharing, which essentially has been based on a mixture of efficiency and equity considerations. Hard targets for the EU ETS and the non-ETS sectors as well as for renewables have been set on the basis of an 'efficiency approach', i.e. reflecting a least-cost approach for the EU as a whole, however with some adjustment to ensure that in per capita terms, costs for member states remain roughly similar.

- GHG reduction target: countries with a low GDP per capita are allowed to emit more than they did in 2005 in non-EU ETS sectors,

Table 14.1   *National targets for renewable energy use and greenhouse gas emissions*

Member state	Share of energy from renewable sources in final consumption of energy, 2005 (%)	Target for share of energy from renewable sources in final consumption of energy, 2020 (%)	Member state GHG emission limits by 2020 compared to 2005 GHG emission levels for sources not covered by ETS (%)
Austria	23.3	34	−16
Belgium	2.2	13	−15
Bulgaria	9.4	16	20
Czech Republic	6.1	13	9
Cyprus	2.9	13	−5
Denmark	17	30	−20
Estonia	18.0	25	11
Finland	28.5	38	−16
France	10.3	23	−14
Germany	5.8	18	−14
Greece	6.9	18	−4
Hungary	4.3	13	10
Ireland	3.1	16	−20
Italy	5.2	17	−13
Latvia	32.6	40	17
Lithuania	15.0	23	15
Luxembourg	0.9	11	−20
Malta	0	10	5
Netherlands	2.4	14	−16
Poland	7.2	15	14
Portugal	20.5	31	1
Romania	17.8	24	19
Slovak Republic	6.7	14	13
Slovenia	16.0	25	4
Spain	8.7	20	−10
Sweden	39.8	49	−17
UK	1.3	15	−16

Source: European Commission.

reflecting projected higher emissions due to higher economic growth mainly in transport. According to European Commission modelling, this increases overall EU compliance costs for the 20 GHG reduction target increases by 0.03 per cent total EU GDP.
- Renewables targets: half is calculated on a flat-rate increase in the share of renewable energy and the other half weighted by GDP, modulated to take into account national starting points and efforts already made.
- In the EU ETS sector, where the cap would be set through a uniform (across member states) cap and allocation would be based on EU-wide

allocation methodologies, 10 per cent of the overall auctioning rights will be redistributed to lower per capita member states.

According to assessments by the European Commission (European Commission 2008a, 2008b), the total direct costs of implementing the two binding 20 per cent targets could be as high as 0.6 per cent of the GDP in the year 2020, or some €90 billion. However, through access to the Clean Development Mechanism (CDM) and Joint Implementation (JI) costs are expected to be as low as 0.45 per cent of GDP in 2020 or roughly €70 billion (European Commission 2008b). Rising oil prices would also contribute to lower costs. Annual GDP growth is estimated to decrease by approximately 0.04–0.06 per cent between 2013 and 2020, which would lead in 2020 to a GDP reduction of 0.5 per cent compared to the 'business as usual'. These calculations do not take into account possible macroeconomic benefits (in the estimated magnitude of +0.15 per cent of GDP) from the reinjection of auctioning revenues back into the economy.

External energy policy

In parallel, there have been important developments in external energy policy. The 2006 Green Paper identified a 'coherent external energy policy' as one of the six EU energy policy pillars. It has taken a procedural approach and is putting its faith in the Strategic EU Energy Reviews to serve as the basis for establishing a common EU vision, which will gradually become a common external voice very much in line with traditional EU thinking. It is interesting to note, however that the European Commission proposed to go beyond the existing policies and prescriptions – e.g. energy partnerships, producer–consumer dialogue, integrating energy into other external policies or support for energy markets – by calling ambitiously for a 'clear policy on securing and diversifying energy supplies' and an effective crisis response mechanism. The European Council of 7/8 March 2007 did not agree on the Commission developing this 'clear policy on securing and diversifying energy supplies'. Instead it developed an action plan that essentially focuses on better coordination and coherence, i.e. following the traditional approach of improving coordination and coherence between different energy policies rather than being a template for a new foreign energy policy. Effectively, the European Council stripped the European Commission of its more ambitious aspirations beyond better coordination.

A somewhat in-between solution has been found when the June 2006 European Council – i.e. already ahead of the crucial 2007 Spring European Council – adopted a legal framework for the external energy policy on the basis of the joint paper by the European Commission and the High Representative. Among others, it foresees the creation of a network of energy correspondents (consisting of representatives by member states and the General Secretariats of both the Commission and the Council) to set up an early-warning system and to improve the reaction in case of a crisis. Such 'organic' integration of external energy policy – typical for integrating external aspects in EU policy-making – is likely to continue in the foreseeable future. A first step has been the Second Strategic Energy Review with its energy security and solidarity action plan.

Beyond this institutional progress, further impacts can be expected of the Lisbon Treaty. In addition to the new energy chapter, other institutional changes such as the Permanent Council President, the High Representative with new powers under the Lisbon Treaty or the External Action Service might strengthen EU-level external energy policy-making over time. However, implementing the new provisions will take time, partly also due to the ambiguity of many of the new Lisbon Treaty provisions.

Conclusions

For many years, member states have denied the need for a meaningful EU energy policy. Reasons included differences of interests between energy-producing and non-producing member states, different political choices for the energy mix or diversity as regards market regulation. Since around 2000, this situation has changed mainly due to the changed geopolitics (i.e. increasing import dependency on a number of politically unstable and/or hostile countries with growing government intervention in the energy sector), increasing energy market integration with the gradual completion of the internal energy market and finally the need for a response to climate change.

However, it was the climate change challenge and the EU's response that acted as a catalyst for this 'sea change'. Catapulted into global leadership after US President Bush's refusal to put the Kyoto Protocol before Senate for ratification, the EU seized the opportunity to strengthen its role and appeal internationally. At the same time it developed an international standard with the EU Emissions Trading System, a domain previously reserved for the US. This leadership role fed back into the domestic agenda and allowed the European Commission to design and ultimately get agreed an ambitious climate change package. The EU ETS – implemented at record speed documenting the political will for EU-level action – laid to rest the myth of EU member states' autonomy regarding their energy mixes. By putting around 40 per cent of EU GHG emissions (i.e. power and the energy-intensive sectors) under a CO_2 cap, member states by and large accepted EU control. The review of the ETS, coming into operation in 2013, will reinforce this. Even more influence on the energy mix has been transferred to the EU by the successive renewables directives, which now mandate a 20 per cent share of renewables in total energy consumption by 2020.

In light of these developments and the need for further GHG emissions cuts (up to 80 to 95 per cent by 2050), member states have started to reconsider how much value is actually added by conducting energy policy at the EU level. On the one hand, it is hard to see how the EU can meet its energy challenges and ambitious targets without some element of EU-wide policies. On the other hand, it is even harder to imagine how this could be done at member-state level without seriously jeopardizing the internal market. The centralization of the EU ETS was a first step, followed by an EU-wide renewables policy with mandatory national targets. As a consequence, a considerable part of the energy sector is now subject to EU-wide policy and regulation, leaving increasingly less autonomy to member states regarding fuel mixes. The remaining autonomy – mostly in sectors outside of the EU ETS – is largely reduced by the need to reduce GHG emissions. Targets to reduce GHG emissions by 80 per cent to 95 per cent by 2050 de facto prohibit the prospective expansion of carbon intensive fuels (such as unabated coal) and point to the future increase of low-carbon fuels, i.e. renewables, nuclear or fossil fuels with carbon capture and storage. Choices among the three will ultimately depend on technology development and market forces, both of which can partly be influenced by member state policies in an EU internal market. Even regarding energy efficiency – presently left to member states – member state autonomy is somewhat constrained. Better energy efficiency will be required to offset higher energy prices as a result of the massive deployment of new and more expensive low-carbon technologies. It is only through lower consumption that the energy bill can be kept constant in a period where prices increase.

This energy policy integration drive has also raised member states' interest in the EU's added value in external energy policy. As a result, the EU has further deepened energy cooperation and put in place important new external energy partnerships in recent years. Energy security now forms part of foreign policy in a way it did not only a few years ago. However, this integration does not go beyond the familiar notion that the EU's internal market constitutes the basis of Europe's external projection and influence. While fostering markets outside of the EU presents a useful foundation from which a more effective energy security strategy can be coordinated, the question on whether there is a need for a more government-led approach to energy security in the context of the external strategy remains unanswered.

Chapter 15

The Foreign Policies of Europe and its States

Richard G. Whitman and Emma J. Stewart

The early twenty-first century has been a period of change and transition in international relations to which European states are still adjusting. Individually and collectively, European states face foreign policy challenges in connection with the forging of relations with other key global powers such as the United States (US) and the new 'rising powers' of China and Russia. These relations are developing in the context of an ongoing process of globalization, alongside the *relative* decline of the US as the Asia-Pacific region accounts for a greater share of global economic activity, levels of US indebtedness increase, and US military power appears diminished as a consequence of the difficulties encountered by interventions in Iraq and Afghanistan.

Additionally, European states face ongoing foreign policy challenges related to their responses to a number of contemporary conflicts and crises that have elucidated differing national responses: the most significant of recent years being the US-led interventions in Iraq and Afghanistan; the question of the independence of Kosovo from Serbia; the ongoing civil war and humanitarian crisis in Darfur (Sudan); the Russian intervention in the breakaway region of South Ossetia (Georgia); and Israel's military incursion into Gaza ('Operation Cast Lead').

During the decades of the Cold War European states' foreign policies were heavily conditioned by which side of the Cold War divide they were aligned to – or by attempting to stand aside from superpower conflict by pursuing policies of neutrality. The situation was transformed after the fall of the Berlin Wall in 1989 and the dissolution of the USSR in 1991. As argued by Christopher Hill (2003), the removal of the ideological 'straitjacket' of the Cold War, that had constrained the foreign policies of European states for many decades, led to dramatic changes in both the domestic and foreign policies of states. Post-Cold War Europe was characterized by economic and political disparity between the wealthy West (underpinned by institutional membership of the European Union (EU) and the North Atlantic Treaty Organization (NATO)) and the struggling new democratic states in the East. European integration acted as a new conditioning factor on states' foreign policies by transforming intra-European states' relations through the progressive enlargement of the EU and by the attempt to build a collective foreign policy through the EU.

West European countries first developed new forms of foreign policy cooperation under the shadow of superpower confrontation; these mechanisms were developed into the Common Foreign and Security Policy (CFSP) after the end of the Cold War and then extended first to countries that had taken a neutral stance during the Cold War (with the accession of Austria, Sweden and Finland to the EU in 1995) and then to Central and East European countries with the 2004 and 2007 EU enlargements.

All European states continue to pursue national foreign policies, but a distinction can be drawn between the 27 counties that have joined the EU and those who are not members. For member states of the EU their national foreign policies are characterized by intensive bilateral and multilateral relationships with other EU member states and cover a wide range of issues that straddle domestic and international politics, a variety of national and European institutions, sectoral ministries and sub-national actors. Whether this *intra-EU* diplomacy has now gone beyond diplomacy as relationships between member states have been 'domesticated' is a matter of debate (Hocking 2004). Alongside this *intra-EU* diplomacy European states continue to pursue international politics individually, but also increasingly collectively, beyond the EU. For European states that are not members of the EU their foreign policies are often determined by whether they aspire to membership of the EU, or have close contractual relations with the EU under the European Neighbourhood Policy (ENP). Even for those European states that are not membership candidates (whether Switzerland in the West, or Ukraine in the East), the political and economic policies of the EU impact significantly on their national foreign policies. This chapter first examines how European integration has shifted and shaped European nations' responses to the outside world. It then goes on to analyse contemporary foreign policy challenges by addressing how European states are responding to the following key developments: counter-terrorism and the transatlantic relationship; the emergence of new global powers; and contemporary crises and conflicts.

European integration and national foreign policies

Europe is a significant part, or subsystem, of a wider international politics from which it cannot be analytically separated. European states contribute to over a quarter of global economic activity and are significant in the global political economy and the politics of the global environment. Europe is affected by the transnational and transborder phenomena identified in the other chapters in this volume on migration, crime and security that have widened the range of issues that are now the subject of international politics and with which states need to grapple. The shift to the 'war on terror' since 9/11 has also caused European states to accommodate to this new focus of the US as a key actor in international politics. European states are also significant actors within international political and economic institutions, with membership of institutions such as the United Nations (UN) Security Council and the G-8.

Europe itself is characterized by the unique density of international institutions covering the region. The 56-member state Organization for Security and Cooperation in Europe (OSCE) includes the United States, Russia and Central Asia and demonstrates that the security boundaries of Europe extend beyond its geographical boundaries. The Council of Europe has the purpose of 'benchmarking' the democracy, human rights and the rule of law in Europe and opens membership only to those who conform to a set of established European norms. A majority of European states are also in a military alliance with the United States through NATO. These pan-European institutions operate alongside a significant number of sub-regional organizations in Europe, such as the Nordic Council. The EU straddles the activities of all of these organizations and, in addition, organizes and regulates economic activity between its members, neighbouring states and beyond Europe.

European states operate within this dense institutional network which constrains and conditions the conduct of national foreign policies. Where such constraints and conditioning generates a process in which national policies converge through the increase in shared norms and interests in foreign policy is defined as processes of 'adaptation' (Manners and Whitman 2000) or 'Europeanization' (Wong 2005a). This is not to suggest that national foreign policies in Europe are becoming homogenous but rather there is a distinctive 'system' of European international relations, which includes both the European and the national level (White 2001; Hill 1993: 322–3). The most salient element of the system is represented by the framework for coordinating foreign policies and producing common policies between EU member states, the CFSP. Reforms to the CFSP have been almost continuous, occurring also as the framework has been stretched to over four times the original number of member states involved in it. As a result, European foreign policy has expanded in scope and in depth: the original character of consultation among member states has developed into a 'coordination reflex' (de Schoutheete 1980) and an increasing capacity to act collectively in certain areas and on given topics, including in military and civilian crisis management missions under the Common Security and Defence Policy (CSDP). However, European states continue to display a capacity to act on a national basis, along the lines of well-established foreign policy traditions, to which we turn to below.

National foreign policies

All European states retain the foreign policy-making and diplomatic infrastructure to pursue national foreign policies in international politics. States do, however, have differing resources at their disposal and differing levels of ambition in international relations. 'Large' Western states such as the UK and France, with extensive diplomatic networks and foreign policy-making infrastructure, pursue foreign policies which are global in extent and aspire to be first-order international actors active on all issues on the international agenda. These two states are the only permanent European members of the UN Security Council (an anachronism that reflects the balance of power in 1945 rather than in 2011). By contrast, other European states seek 'role specialization' by making a distinctive contribution to international politics. Norway has adopted such a strategy of role specialization by acting as a neutral party in conflict resolution in the Middle East and Sri Lanka; Ireland has been a significant contributor to UN peacekeeping missions.

Studying the foreign policies of European states presents the same problems as the study of national foreign policies in general. How do we assess the impact of a changing international politics upon states in which distinctions between domestic and international politics are increasingly difficult to draw (and commonly referred to as processes of globalization) and in which international politics increasingly involves the actions of non-governmental actors as much as those of governments? What constitutes 'foreign policy' is becoming increasingly difficult to assess and raises challenges for foreign policy analysis (FPA), a sub-discipline of International Relations that purports to understand and explain public policy projected beyond the nation-state (Webber and Smith 2002; Hill 2003).

Whether the EU represents a constriction or an opportunity for the foreign policies of its member states is a key question. Does EU membership have a determining impact on a state's foreign policy and/or does it provide a vehicle through which countries can pursue essentially national foreign policies? It is possible to talk about patterns of external relations that shape the way in which membership impacts on foreign policy actions (Manners and Whitman 2000: ch. 1). A first discernible pattern is seen in member states which have an extensive network of external relations outside the EU with this affecting foreign policy behaviour and the way in which these states interact with the EU and with other member states. The two premier examples of this pattern are to be found in the British and French cases, although it is far too simplistic to argue that this represents the only, or most determining, factor in explaining their foreign policies. For these two states the EU is more often perceived as a constriction on national foreign policy or simply as a means to amplify national foreign policy. Britain and France are also often bracketed with Germany as three members of an informal EU foreign policy *directoire* between whom there needs to be agreement in areas of foreign policy if the EU is to have a coherent collective position. The agreement between this EU3 driving EU policy towards Iran's uranium enrichment programme is contrasted with their disagreements over the war in Iraq and, consequently, for the failure of the EU member states to agree a common position.

A second pattern apparent among European states are those that have a less extensive network of foreign policy relations than Britain and France, and which tend to work through the EU. In this pattern the countries involved often seek to work with the EU or defer most foreign policy prerogatives to the Union. It might also be argued that the EU presents an opportunity within which to hide difficult decisions, or the absence of any preconceived policy. Within this pattern of external relations are two types of states – smaller states without the capacity or desire to engage in extensive external relations, and states which for historical reasons wish to enmesh themselves in a European rather than national system of foreign policy making. Examples of the smaller state can be found in Portugal or Ireland. Examples of the 'European' state include Italy and Belgium, both of whom find EU solutions to difficult historical and domestic problems. An important additional point here is whether the EU can provide a balance between 'Europeanist' or 'Atlanticist' foreign policy trends which satisfy internal tensions. As has been the case for Spain, Italy, Greece and to a certain degree Denmark, this second pattern of foreign policy can be viewed as a solution to the tensions between pro-European (read 'EU' or 'anti-US') and pro-American (read 'NATO' or 'anti-EU') forces within these countries. Clearly in this pattern of external relations, the EU is more often perceived as an opportunity for foreign policy action (or perhaps as an excuse for national foreign policy inaction).

A third pattern can be observed in those states which may not have an extensive network of foreign policy relations, but tend to work through other international organizations such as the UN, NATO or OSCE. Within this pattern a state may seek to act independently, or in concert with the EU in order to assist their foreign policies. Thus not all states feel constrained to participate solely in EU foreign policy activity, and may well seek to avoid doing so because of the implications for further integration. This pattern of international rather than European foreign policy relations may also be related to the Cold War experience of a country, in particular its status as neutral or non-aligned. Additionally, this pattern of activity might be directly related to a multilateral foreign policy orientation within a state. Examples of the 'international' pattern may be found in the cases of Austria, Finland and Sweden, all of which are actively engaged participants in the OSCE and UN. Examples of the 'multilateral' pattern may be found in the case of Germany which, through its *Sowohl-als-auch* approach pursues its foreign policy through the EU, NATO, OSCE and UN. In this type of pattern EU membership represents not so much an opportunity or a constriction, but merely another forum for its foreign policy (as traditionally conceived).

For the EU member states participation in the Union represents a mixed blessing for their foreign policy activities. On the one hand it forces them to confront the rigidity or flexibility in their foreign policy-making within a European framework, while on the other hand it tends to underline the paramount role which non-traditional foreign policy (external or economic relations) has come to assume in the twenty-first century.

What is clear is that EU membership involves asking some difficult questions of foreign policy practices, or the absence of them. The challenges and responses this presents can be considered through looking at notions of the 're'-formulation of foreign policy in terms of 'remove', 'rescue', 'retreat' and 'renationalise' (Manners and Whitman 2000). The first response is the attempt by member states to 'remove' many of the activities of foreign policy-making from state capitals to Brussels. It is important to note that this 'Brusselization' of foreign policy does not mean the wholesale communitarization of foreign policy-making and implementation within the European Union. Rather it has been argued, the Brusselization of foreign policy-making is facilitated by the 'steady enhancement of Brussels-based decision-making bodies' such as the Political and Security Committee of the Council of Ministers, although some might wish to include decision-making within the NATO Headquarters also located in Brussels (Allen 1998).

The second response goes further than simple 'removal' by attempting to 'rescue' the foreign policies of member states by using membership of the EU as 'the means by which member states made their positions less rather than more vulnerable' (Allen 1996). In broad terms this second strategy goes far beyond the strategy of simple removal by Europeanizing a member state's foreign policy in an attempt to improve or strengthen its relations. From this perspective, the European Union is often presented as an intergovernmental mechanism for rescuing and strengthening the state and its foreign policy (Laffan *et al.* 2000). However as has been made clear by other commentators, the extent to which Europeanization can 'rescue' foreign policy from the pressures of the supranational, the subnational, and the transnational needs to be questioned (Spence 1999).

Another response to any perceived 'retreat' of states' foreign policies is more recent and for some reflects the crisis moments for CFSP, particularly in light of the embarrassing failures (shared with the most powerful state in the world) in the Balkans and over the Iraq war. This response would appear to be the 'renationalization' of foreign policy as a means of dealing with the 'failure to progress' through the reassertion of 'traditional national foreign policies' (Hill 1998). It is important to note, as they do, that even though 'renationalization' is 'freely discussed' and a 'drift apart' has been noticed by some, 'vested interest' in the still early stages of CFSP makes this argument questionable.

The contrasting benefits of 'removal', 'rescue' or 'renationalize' in response to a perceived 'retreat' depend on the viewpoints of those engaged in the foreign policy processes under discussion. For post-colonial states such as France, Britain, the Netherlands, Belgium, Spain and Portugal the use of development policy and external relations provides a convenient conduit for a 'rescue' of these relationships in the guise of a less historically 'loaded' EU policy. For smaller states such as Denmark, Ireland and Greece the EU can represent a rescue of their non-security policies, but the pressure to 'remove' security interests to Brussels is fiercely resisted. For the (post) neutral states of Austria, Finland and Sweden, the removal of aspects of their Cold War security stance to Brussels provides a means for overcoming domestic resistance, as well as seeing the human rights and development policies of the EU as a means for rescuing, or at least advancing, these issues on a larger stage. For the newest members of the EU in Central and Eastern Europe EU membership is about 'renationalizing' foreign policy after the constraints on foreign policy action that existed as the consequence of being Soviet satellite states.

The foreign policies of European states that are not members of the EU or NATO are very much conditioned by whether they are candidates for membership of these organizations (e.g. Croatia, the Former Yugoslav Republic of Macedonia, Turkey), or aspire to be (e.g. Ukraine, Georgia). Candidate countries are invited to 'align' their positions with the common EU position (when there is one), and to participate in EU military and civilian crisis management missions under the ESDP. In the NATO context, cooperation occurs under the Partnership for Peace Programme. For post-Soviet countries that are not candidates for EU/NATO membership, their relationship with the Russian Federation is fundamental to their foreign policy and, in some cases has led to conflict.

The beginning of the twenty-first century has been a particularly challenging time for foreign policy-making in Europe. The aftermath of the 9/11 terrorist attacks in the US resulted in military action in Afghanistan and Iraq for NATO members in the former and a 'coalition of the willing' with the US in the latter. The continued instability in Iraq and resurgence of the Taliban in Afghanistan suggest that these crises will be on Europe's agenda for some time to come. In the Iraq crisis of early 2003, the internal divisions between European states over foreign and security policy were laid bare for the entire world to see: one recent spectacular example of the extent to which EU foreign policy does not constrain European states. The failure of European states to agree on fundamental reforms to the UN Security Council in 2005 was another, less dramatic case: neither France nor the UK will contemplate giving up their permanent seats in favour of an EU seat, and Italy assertively countered Germany's attempts to become a permanent Security Council member. Disagreements about how to manage relations with Russia after the Russian–Georgian war, in August 2008, and different national responses to other contemporary challenges and crises provide further examples of European foreign policy disunity in the face of crisis.

Europe's foreign policy challenges

European states face a number of pressing contemporary foreign policy challenges and priorities, which include climate change, nuclear proliferation, global poverty and violent conflicts. The following section identifies a number of interrelated foreign policy challenges that have had the greatest impact on the shape of foreign policy at the national level: counter-terrorism and the transatlantic relationship; relations with emerging global powers; and responding to crises and conflicts. We address these themes in turn below.

Counter-terrorism and the transatlantic relationship

Europe's relationship with the United States remains of key importance for international cooperation across a wide range of issues. The counter-terrorist policies of the Republican Bush administration (2000–8) in Afghanistan (2001–) and Iraq (2003–) following the 11 September 2001 terrorist attacks precipitated a particularly turbulent time in Europe–US relations. Transatlantic discord during this period also derailed international agreements on climate change and chemical and biological weapons.

US policy under the 'war on terror' rubric was controversial with

European citizens, and divided European leaders. Nevertheless, the NATO invasion of Afghanistan in 2001 garnered support from most European states. The conflict accelerated US relations with several unlikely pan-European partners. The post-Soviet state of Uzbekistan became a strategic ally of the US when it allowed a military base for US incursions into Afghanistan to be sited on its territory. Despite Central Asia's dubious record on human rights, the US partnership with several regional states has continued as stability in Afghanistan has remained elusive. Kyrgystan agreed with the US in January 2009 to keep an air staging post open in the wake of Taliban attacks on the US military supply route through Pakistan. However, the resurgence of the Taliban in Afghanistan has strained US relations with fellow European NATO members as American calls for more troops have met with a lukewarm response.

The Iraq crisis of 2003 caused great disunity within Europe, and only a handful of European EU/NATO members joined the US coalition to invade Iraq (UK, Poland, Czech Republic, Denmark, Bulgaria, Romania and the Baltic states). The coalition also included a number of non-EU/NATO members – Albania and several Balkan, Central Asian and South Caucasus states. Unlike the case of Afghanistan, EU member states failed to agree on a collective response to the Iraq war: states retreated to national positions, with the damaging split described by the Bush administration as a rift between 'old' (i.e. France and Germany) and 'new' (i.e. eastern Europe and the UK) Europe. However, despite limited support for US foreign policies, European states, as members of NATO, the EU, and bilaterally continue to be involved in the stabilization and reconstruction of both Afghanistan and Iraq. This follows the trend of collective European action in the *aftermath* of crises that is evident in the case of other crises and conflicts (see below).

The Bush premiership was marked by protests during his many European tours, particularly as a result of the controversial intervention in Iraq, and associated 'war on terror' policies such as the CIA's 'extraordinary rendition' of terror suspects and the Guantánamo Bay terrorist detention centre in Cuba. The practice of extraordinary rendition, involving the abduction of terrorist suspects and their removal to third states for interrogation, caused domestic outcries in several European states. The UK government, having previously denied that rendition flights landed in UK airports, admitted in February 2008 that several such flights refuelled on the UK dependent territory of Diego Garcia in the Indian Ocean in 2002. An Amnesty International report in June 2008 accused European governments, particularly the UK and Ireland, of complicity and inaction over these US 'torture flights'.

The election in November 2008 of Democrat Barack Obama as US

President represents a turning point in Europe–US relations. Obama's first action after his inauguration in January 2009 was to order the closure of the Guantánamo Bay prison camp and Central Intelligence Agency (CIA) secret prisons, as well as to ban rendition and torture. These actions, widely welcomed in Europe, suggested that a new era of cooperation between the US and Europe could lead to enhanced international cooperation to address pressing international issues such as climate change, nuclear proliferation, conflict in the Middle East and the global financial crisis. Initial optimism, however, has been tempered by the growing realization that the Obama administration's foreign policy priorities are focused more on US relations with the Middle East and the Islamic world, rather than on US–European relations. Additionally, Obama's ability to shape both domestic and foreign policy agendas has been slowly eroded by economic crisis and the Democrats' loss of power in the US Congress.

Emerging global powers

European states have also been responding to the rise of several new global powers on the international stage. The 'BRICs' countries – Brazil, Russia, India and China are particularly significant: in 2007, foreign direct investment (FDI) from the 27 EU countries to the BRICs more than doubled to a total of €43 billion (Petridou 2008). The growing economic strength of these states has gone hand in hand with increasingly prominent political profiles at the international level, and has led to an acceleration of relations between the BRICs and European states. While the international profiles of Brazil and India are on the rise, it is European states' relationships with Russia and China that have impacted most on contemporary foreign policy developments, and we therefore focus on these two states.

China is Europe's largest trade partner, and with its membership of the UN Security Council, it is influential in global politics. However, China does not conform to Western norms, and is wary of the extension of Western power close to Chinese borders (Holslag 2006). The Chinese government's close relationship with the oppressive regime in Burma/ Myanmar, arms sales to oppressive African regimes in Zimbabwe and Sudan, and domestic human rights violations have been particular points of contention, and European states' efforts to invite China to play a more constructive international role in world affairs have more often than not fallen on deaf ears.

The UK is Europe's main investor in China, and continues to establish cultural and educational links with the country. However, this influence rarely extends to criticizing Chinese human rights abuses in Tibet and elsewhere: in May 2008 the UK Prime Minister, Gordon Brown, decided not to receive the spiritual leader of Tibet, the Dalai Lama, at Downing Street in order to avoid a diplomatic spat with the Chinese leadership. The UK government correctly anticipated the Chinese response: the French President's meeting with the spiritual leader in Gdansk seven months later led to China abruptly cancelling the upcoming EU–China Summit in December 2008. China has skilfully exploited European states' differences and the tensions within European states between business interests and human rights concerns. While some European states such as Austria, Belgium and Ireland are content to 'remove' their national policy on China to the EU level, Germany, France and the UK have retreated to national positions at the expense of a united EU policy. The latter three states are therefore particularly responsible for Europe's disunited policy towards China (Fox and Godement 2009). Disagreements about the proposal to lift the arms embargo to China (in place since the 1989 Tiananmen Square massacres) are a case in point: the UK government (and others) backtracked in 2004 in the face of aggressive Chinese rhetoric towards Taiwan and American criticism of the proposal, while the French administration argued for the unconditional lifting of the ban. The EU was exposed as indecisive and divided, and the decision on the embargo was postponed. Neither has Germany's middle-ground approach, which attempts to separate trade issues from human rights, borne any fruit: the Chinese government has simply ignored Chancellor Merkel's concerns. Clearly, Europe's dealings with China are more constructive when a coordinated policy can be agreed on – for example, in gaining Chinese support in the UN Security Council for the EU's position on Iran's uranium enrichment programme (*ibid.*). Moreover, the challenge of the global economic crisis requires greater consensus and common action at the European level, especially given the €169 billion EU trade deficit to China in 2008, which points to the strengthening of Chinese economic influence in the face of European economic decline.

The emerging power with arguably the most divisive political impact on the foreign policy of European states is Russia, despite being the main recipient of EU FDI in 2007, and EU states' third largest trade partner. Relations between European states and Russia have been strained by the parallel expansion of the EU and NATO in 2004 and by Russia's robust policy in its former Soviet neighbours – particularly Georgia and Ukraine, both aspiring EU/NATO members. Russia has shown little enthusiasm for the EU's Neighbourhood Policy framework, and the EU and Russia are still striving to define priorities and actions for a complex bilateral economic and political relationship.

Russia's ascent from a weakened power in the 1990s to a robust economic and political actor in recent years has had a major impact on Europe–Russia relations. Disagreements between European states on how to deal with Russia have strained foreign policy-making, particularly in the aftermath of Russia's refusal in the UN Security Council to endorse independence for Kosovo in 2007, and the Russian–Georgian conflict in August 2008 (see below). As with Europe–China relations, there is a tension between business and economic interests on the one hand and concerns about the lack of democracy and human rights in Russia on the other. The relationship is complicated by a crossing over of interests in the post Soviet space, and Europe's reliance on Russian gas and oil supplies.

Western European states' approaches to Russia are shaped by history and geography, and cross the full spectrum from full support (Greece and Cyprus) to total hostility (Poland and Lithuania). The majority of Western European states take a pragmatic approach, but broadly fit into two camps: those seeing themselves as non-critical, 'special' partners (France, Germany, Italy and Spain); and those regarding themselves as occasional partners that are more willing to be critical of Russian policy (Denmark, Czech Republic, Estonia, Ireland, Latvia, the Netherlands, Romania, Sweden and the UK) (Leonard and Popescu 2007). This diversity of approach precludes a common EU policy towards Russia. The pattern of retreat to national positions and interests is particularly stark in this case.

The external policies of non-EU/NATO post-Soviet European states towards Russia are very much conditioned by their relationship with their neighbour: some align themselves closely with Russia (e.g. the Central Asian states and Georgia's separatist territories), others are in regular conflict with Russia as a result of their West-leaning tendencies (Georgia, Ukraine), while others weave a complex path between Russia and the West (e.g. Armenia, Azerbaijan, Belarus). Russia's August 2008 intervention in Georgia and the gas dispute with Ukraine in 2009 (during which Eastern Europe suffered reduced gas supplies), indicate that the Russian Federation is not likely to divert from its current robust foreign policy path. In fact, Russia can be seen to be leading a group of countries that reject the norms espoused by the majority of Europe, and that continue to criticize the democratic and human rights efforts of the only pan-European security organization, the OSCE. Cooperation within the OSCE is waning as the organization is undermined and as long-term field missions are closed (for example, in Georgia, where the Russian government vetoed the extension of the mission in December 2008). The continued failure of the EU and individual European states to forge a constructive policy towards Russia will accelerate this uncooperative trend, and lead to greater insecurity in Europe.

The power of emerging powerful states to resist a 'Western' agenda characterized by the promotion of liberal democratic norms and humanitarian intervention has arguably increased in a climate of global economic crisis (Cottey 2009). Russia and China have been influential in conditioning how European states respond to emerging and ongoing crises and conflicts across the world, and this shifting trend in the balance of global power is unlikely to wane in the foreseeable future.

Responding to crises and conflicts

The following review of European responses to contemporary crises and conflicts is not intended to be a comprehensive account, but more an illustrative global selection demonstrating significant trends and divisions in European foreign policies. While European states tend to act through international institutions (EU, NATO, UN), as we have already seen in the cases of Iraq and Afghanistan, there is more consensus in the aftermath of conflict (i.e. for post-conflict reconstruction) that in initial responses to crises. We focus on the question of the independence of Kosovo from Serbia; the conflict in the Darfur region of Sudan, East Africa; the conflict in the South Caucasus breakaway territory of South Ossetia; and the 2008–9 Israeli–Palestinian conflict in Gaza.

Kosovo

The crisis over the independent status and international recognition of Kosovo in 2007 to 2008 highlighted clearly that post-Cold War uncertainty over rules and norms continued to challenge the foreign policies of European states (Hill 2003). The initial humanitarian intervention by NATO states in 1999, without sanction by the UN, challenged the established international convention of non-interference in the internal affairs of states (in this case, Serbia), and the recognition crisis confronted the precedent of the territorial integrity of states and the rights of self-determination. The Kosovo case has therefore had implications for the making of foreign policy in Europe and beyond.

Kosovo was internationally administered under the leadership of the UN in the aftermath of NATO's aerial bombardment (Operation Allied Force) of Serbia in support of the oppressed Kosovo Albanian population. International discussions pertaining to the former Yugoslav province's final status began in 2005, and culminated in 2007 with the publication of UN Special Envoy Martti Ahtisaari's report recommending a process of 'supervised independence' for the territory. The plan was supported by the US and most European states, but was vetoed in the UN Security Council by the Russian Federation. Despite the lack of international consensus, Kosovo declared independence in February 2008, and has since been recognized by more than sixty states, including the majority of states in Europe (with Spain, Greece, Cyprus, Romania and Slovakia the exceptions).

The Kosovo conflict and recognition crisis demonstrated the continuing divisive impact of Balkan politics in Europe and globally. The conflict in 1999 did not elicit a common response from European states, with military intervention in the absence of a UN mandate proving to be a divisive issue. For the UK, it showcased Prime Minister Tony Blair as a champion of human rights, promoting a new doctrine of humanitarian intervention. For Germany it was a watershed in the country's foreign policy, since it was the first external use of force by the state since the Second World War. The possibility of granting independence to an autonomous province within a sovereign state raised issues for the viability of the Muslim-Croat Bosnian state created in 1995, and new expectations for breakaway territories in post-Soviet states, as well as objections from countries such as Spain, with domestic separatist groups of their own demanding territorial autonomy. European states were pitted against a recalcitrant and resurgent Russia state, angry over the NATO aerial campaign and eager to support its Serbian ally. In short, the unsatisfactory conclusion of the Kosovo issue in 2008 reflected a decade of international discord and set some difficult international precedents. The repercussions are likely to create further foreign policy challenges for European states in the future.

Darfur

The ongoing humanitarian crisis in the Darfur region of Sudan has failed to illicit a unified response from Europe, and highlighted the selective nature of the so-called doctrine established by the Kosovo precedent (and reinforced by the UN's 2005 'responsibility to protect' principle). The African country has been in the throes of its latest civil war since 2003, when rebels first attacked government targets in the Darfur region, and government forces and militias targeted the civilian population. The humanitarian crisis has been acute, and escalated in 2009 with the expulsion of aid agencies in the wake of the International Criminal Court's arrest warrant for President Omar al-Bashir on the grounds of war crimes and crimes against humanity.

Action by the international community was constrained by Chinese opposition in the UN Security Council, as well as by French objections to sanctions and to a proposed role for NATO in the conflict. European states were criticized for making numerous statements condemning the violence without being prepared to take a stronger stance towards the Sudanese government. The French government's resistance to strict sanctions (favoured by the US) came under fire, and the presence of Western oil companies in Sudan (the Franco-Belgian company Total, for example) opened European states up to accusations of putting business interests before humanitarian concerns.

EU states initially preferred to offer financial support rather than to commit troops, and used the 2004 'African Peace Facility' funding instrument to support a peacekeeping mission by the African Union (AU) in Darfur (replaced by a joint UN–AU peacekeeping force in January 2008). After much discussion and delay, the EU eventually launched an ESDP military mission to the neighbouring states of Chad and the Central African Republic, which operated from 2008 to 2009 until it was passed on to the UN as part of a larger civilian/military mission. The French government, long pushing for an EU conflict management role in Africa, was the driving force behind the EU initiative. French motives for intervention were, however, questioned by other member states because of French national interests in Chad (a former French colony, and France retains a military base and task force in the country), and neutral states in particular were wary. Nevertheless, France succeeded in 'amplifying' its national foreign policy at the EU level and gained agreement from the other member states. The conditions of engagement were important, nonetheless: a commitment to impartiality in the mandate and the limited duration of the mission were crucial in this regard. It is also significant that Germany and the UK, despite being vocal advocates of international action in Darfur, were only willing to provide personnel at the headquarters level, citing existing commitments in Afghanistan as the limiting factor (Mattelaer 2008).

Europe's limited role in the Darfur conflict reflects the scale, complexity and volatility of the conflict(s) as well as the military commitments of the key military powers elsewhere. European states' roles also demonstrate that while they may (with leadership) be willing to support UN efforts with short-term military operations on the African continent, the will for longer-term commitment is lacking – unlike in the case of Kosovo, and in spite of the crisis in Darfur being compared to the 1994 Rwandan genocide.

South Ossetia
The brief military conflict between Georgia and Russia over the breakaway Georgian territory of South Ossetia in August 2008 illustrated the extent of animosity between Russia and the West, and can be seen as directly linked (at least in Russian minds) to Western intervention in, and recognition of, Kosovo in the preceding years. Georgia's de facto states of Abkhazia and South Ossetia broke away from Georgian rule in the early 1990s when the Georgian state gained independence after the fall of the USSR. Long relying on Russian political and economic support, South

Ossetian troops were immediately backed up by overwhelming Russian force when the Georgian leadership launched an ill-judged assault in the territory.

EU member states responded quickly and collectively to the conflict, and a ceasefire between the parties was negotiated by the EU Presidency, held at this time by France. The EU subsequently sent a civilian team to monitor the ceasefire and pledged increased aid to the Georgian state. The swift action from the EU followed years of indecision about the extent of EU involvement in Georgia, underpinned by member state disagreements about practicing foreign policy in the post-Soviet space. Central and Eastern European states favour deeper involvement, while states such as Germany and France tend to prioritize EU–Russian relations. The conflict brought Europe–Russian relations to the fore, and demonstrated the extent of Russian's non-cooperative foreign policy in its sphere of influence. This was further underlined by Russia's subsequent recognition of the breakaway territories as independent states, an action that had been threatened since Kosovo was recognized in 2008 by most European states. The Russian Federation is also striving to limit the presence of international observers in both of Georgia's breakaway territories – as already mentioned, the extension of the OSCE Georgia mission was vetoed by Russia in December 2008, and the UN's monitoring mission in Abkhazia was vetoed in June 2009. Russia's hold over the de facto regimes has been consolidated, yet it has so far not persuaded other post-Soviet allies to recognize the territories as independent states.

As well as further straining relations between European states and Russia, the South Ossetian conflict had a destabilizing effect on other post-Soviet states, particularly Ukraine, whose coalition government collapsed in September 2008 after it failed to find consensus regarding the Georgian crisis. The fallout from the short conflict in South Ossetia is likely to cause further foreign policy headaches for European states in the future.

Gaza
Unlike in the case of South Ossetia, Europe's response to Israel's incursion into the Gaza Strip in late 2008/early 2009 (Operation Cast Lead) was not instrumental in bringing about a ceasefire. Despite attempts by the French Presidents and Czech Foreign Minister to negotiate a ceasefire (under EU auspices, and alongside Egypt, Turkey and Syria), Israel ceased its offensive only after signing a memorandum of understanding with the US on the 17 January 2009.

European states have long been overshadowed by the US in their efforts to mediate in the Israel–Palestinian conflict, despite committing civilian monitors to the region (European personnel comprised the majority of the enhanced UN monitoring team in Lebanon (UNIFIL) after the Israeli assault of 2006, for example). European states also provide the bulk of the aid sent to the Palestinian territories. The European strategy of isolating the Palestinian Hamas party after its election victory in the Palestinian territories in 2006 has, however, served to further reduce European influence in the Middle East and, with the reduction of humanitarian aid, to increase the suffering of Palestinian civilians.

Gaining legitimacy in the eyes of Israel has been particularly problematic due to the different foreign policy approaches of European states towards Israel. There is a deep division within EU states about whether EU–Israeli relations should be linked with progress in the peace process: Ireland, Greece and Belgium continue to favour this approach, while it is resisted by the new member states of Poland and the Czech Republic in particular. More generally, the Southern European states are perceived as being more critical of Israel than Germany, the UK and the Central and Eastern European states.

European divisions were evident during and after Operation Cast Lead, with some governments (e.g. France) vocal in their condemnation of Israel, and others (e.g. Czech Republic) supporting Israel's right to self-defence. The bombing of UN buildings during the campaign caused anger in Islamic states, and protests in many European cities. The EU's planned upgrade of bilateral relations with Israel was delayed as a result of its military incursion in the Gaza Strip, largely as a result of pressure from Belgium, Sweden, Ireland and Portugal. Europe's relations with Israel will continue to divide states, and, without a common approach Europe's role in the Israel–Palestinian conflict will continue to consist of aid and post-conflict reconstruction in the wake of American-led mediation.

Conclusion

European states are inseparable from the international environment that impacts upon their foreign policies and through which they seek to have influence individually and collectively. The preservation of the means to conduct national foreign policies alongside the evolving collective EU foreign policy arrangements creates the need to understand developments within, across and between European states if the role of these states in international politics is to be fully comprehended.

This, however, is a complex task, and while the foreign policies of EU member states are distinctive because of the additional impact of the structures and processes of European integration, it is clear that the CFSP does not always constrain national foreign policy-making when national interests or alliances are at stake. Further integration in Europe could result in the emergence of a true common and collective foreign policy, but the retention of national control over foreign and defence policies in a wider, rather than a deeper EU, is a trend that looks likely to continue in the foreseeable future.

European states face significant foreign policy challenges in the face of early twenty-first century international developments. Rebuilding the transatlantic relationship after close to a decade of discord will be a priority in coming years, as will dealing with the fallout from the US 'war on terror' policies in Afghanistan and Iraq. A renewal of the relationship under the new American administration could yield significant results in the mitigation of climate change, nuclear non-proliferation and conflict resolution in the Middle East and elsewhere.

Relations with China and Russia will continue to impact on European foreign policies. China's economic power sits uneasily alongside its repressive domestic policies and increasingly confident (and not always constructive) role in international politics. Relations with the emerging power will continue to top the agenda of many foreign ministries across the pan-European area. The external policies of the Russian Federation will have a deleterious impact on pan-European security until a constructive relationship that accommodates both the interests of the Russian Federation and those of European states, can be forged. The revival of the OSCE as a pan-European organization representing all states equally is the best platform for this long-term rapprochement, but above all, European leadership and foreign policy unity is a prerequisite, and may not be forthcoming in an era of economic decline.

When it comes to responding to crises, European states often retreat to national positions rather than striving to agree on a collective response. This trend undermines attempts to forge a common EU foreign policy, notwithstanding the rapid development of EU-level security and defence policies. Cooperation between states takes place more often in the aftermath of conflict, illustrating at any rate a commitment from most European states to work through international organizations for reconstruction purposes. The can of worms relating to intervention and sovereignty opened up as a result of states' responses to the Kosovo crisis has already resonated through the crises in Darfur and South Ossetia, and will continue to impact on foreign policy choices in future.

While states that belong to the EU/NATO group have struggled to agree on foreign policy actions, the gap between this group and the foreign policy cultures and priorities of the post-Soviet states is even more pronounced. A significant number of these states are following a dictatorial path far removed from the democratic norms espoused by their institutionalized neighbours. This is an anomaly that EU/NATO states will have to address, sooner or later. Meanwhile, the foreign policies of states across Europe are likely to continue to remain diverse and convergent, and marked by both conflict *and* cooperation across a wide range of international issues.

Chapter 16

'Old' and 'New' European Counter-Terrorism

Alexander Spencer

After the attacks on September 11, 2001 governments around the world rushed to implement new counter-terrorism measures to deal with this apparently new danger. Although the terrorist attack now commonly referred to as 9/11 was condemned by almost all countries, the initial harmonious relationship in the fight against terrorism quickly evaporated thereafter. It is generally accepted that the United States and Europe see the problem of terrorism very differently, but even within Europe there are differences. This chapter seeks to examine some of the recent European counter-terrorism measures implemented in the aftermath of 9/11 and the bombings in Madrid on 11 March 2004 and London on 7 July 2005, and discusses the theoretical advantages and disadvantages of these policies. In order to draw out some of the similarities and differences in responses to counter-terrorism across European countries, and to examine their impact on civil liberties, the key focus will be on a comparison between the national policies of both 'old' and 'new' members of the European Union (EU) rather than on the policies of the EU itself. Due to the large number of European states it should be stressed that this chapter can only offer a very brief overview of European counter-terrorism.

In pursuit of this aim the rest of this chapter will be structured as follows. The first section will examine anti-terror legislation after 9/11 and its implication for civil liberties in Europe. The second will investigate the role of European intelligence agencies and organizational structures against terrorism while the third will focus on internal security and defence measures. The fourth part will outline Europe's military role in the 'war on terror'. Throughout, the chapter will draw on examples from a variety of European countries to indicate a number of European trends in an otherwise very diverse policy area influenced by different historical experiences with terrorism.

Anti-terror legislation and civil rights in Europe

The central idea of the legislative approach to fighting terrorism is that terrorism can be countered with the help of traditional criminal justice tools such as law enforcement, police investigations and special anti-terrorist legislation. As Paul Wilkinson (2000: 113, emphasis in original) points out, 'Much anti-terrorism legislation is designed to increase the level of protection of life and property by *providing law enforcement authorities with the powers needed to assist them in the apprehension and conviction of those who commit crimes of terrorism*'. Finding and arresting terrorists using police investigations, prosecuting them in a judicial court and placing them in prison will evidently mean that the terrorist is stopped from committing further terrorist acts while in custody. The imprisonment of those who are responsible for planning attacks, organizing the group, arranging finances and needed resources and giving the group the spiritual and charismatic face so important for recruiting new members, can result in the disruption of the terrorist network and can suppress and delay further attacks due to the time needed to reorganize (Pillar 2001: 81).

The central problem, however, of using a criminal justice model of counter-terrorism in a democracy is the difficulty of balancing security with liberty. It is generally assumed that policies such as greater police powers aimed at increasing the countries' security will reduce the freedoms and civil liberties of the population. It is considered vital to strike the right balance, as an overemphasis on security and the implementation of excessive counter-terrorism powers can endanger the democratic state these measures are supposed to protect in the first place. Legislative measures such as powers to indiscriminately intercept communications, to indefinitely incarcerate suspects and to create special terrorist courts in which normal standards of proof are watered down, or sanctioning the use of brutal interrogation techniques, can all be considered a first step on the slippery slope of authoritarianism. Using such powers and restricting freedoms, civil liberties and human rights may be like opening Pandora's box, as, once implemented, such policies to stop terrorism lead to the erosion of democracy and the creation of an authoritarian regime in which a terrorist becomes a synonym for individuals, groups and communities which disagree with a state's leadership. Thus, winning against terrorism can mean losing democracy. There are a number of examples such as Chile, Uruguay, Argentina and Brazil, where the use of the excessive powers in the name of 'counter-terrorism' has ultimately led to the retreat or downfall of democracy and the disappearance and death of thousands of civilians (Gearty 1997: 32). As Grant Wardlaw (1989: 69) points out: 'To believe that depriving citizens of their individual rights and suspending the democratic process is necessary to maintain "order" is to put oneself on the same moral plane as the terrorists who believe the "end justifies the means"'.

Apart from this difficult balancing act, however, the use of a criminal justice model against terrorism poses a number of other practical problems. For example, it is questionable how far terrorists would be deterred by new anti-terror laws and tough prison or even death sentences. Fanatical sections of any terrorist group will generally disregard the judicial consequences of their terrorist attacks due to their motivation and passion for the glorious cause as well as their rejection of the legitimacy of the court trying them. Even more apparent is the fact that harsh terrorism laws, long prison sentences or even the death penalty will not deter a terrorist who is prepared to sacrifice his or her own life in a suicide attack (Heymann 2001/2002: 29).

Apart from the actual problem of finding terrorists, their prosecution faces even more difficulties, as the involvement of many senior terrorist leaders and their connections to an attack are extremely hard to prove, especially when considering the inherent tension between the prevention of terrorism and the prosecution of terrorists. Intelligence agencies are unwilling to identify sources and use their secret agents or informers as prosecution witnesses or reveal their sources of information, for the revelation of sources would lead to them drying up (Steven and Gunaratna 2004: 106). As Pillar (2001: 84) notes, 'some of the individuals about whom the strongest criminal cases could be made – because they have significant, known roles in the group – are, for the same reason, among the best sources of intelligence (as either witting informants or as people whose activities and contacts can be secretly monitored)'. Therefore it is necessary to consider whether it is worth prosecuting a terrorist or whether it is better to guard one's intelligence sources in order to be able to prevent future attacks. Prosecution is made even more difficult by the fact that most attacks on Western targets and planning by the groups' leaders occur abroad. This makes it hard for the perpetrators to be brought to justice quickly as governments have to then arrange for the suspects to be apprehended by their host nation and initiate extradition proceedings. And extradition has proved to be very difficult even among the closest of allies, especially when the accused faces the possibility of the death sentence (Sandler 2003: 796). The fact that judicial standards and national legislations regulating a nation's criminal justice system and issues such as the arrest, interrogation and the prosecution of a suspect, as well as the interest in doing so, vary greatly from country to country, makes international cooperation in the fight against terrorism extremely difficult (Bensahel 2006).

The legislative response to 9/11 and the bombings in Madrid and

London in Europe varied greatly and depended strongly on the individual judicial traditions as well as on the historical experiences with terrorism. Probably the easiest way of giving a brief insight into the overall trends is to divide the European approaches into two groups: countries which had extensive prior experience with terrorism and those which did not.

Countries with experience of terrorism

The first group is predominantly made up of 'old' EU member states. France for example has faced a number of left-wing terror groups such as Action Directe but also separatist groups such as the FLNC in Corsica and radical Islamic groups such as the GIA in Algeria. Similarly, Italy confronted the left-wing Red Brigades and right-wing terrorist groups in the 1970s and 1980s and Spain has continuously struggled with the Basque terrorist group ETA. However, altogether only six European countries (France, Italy, Spain, Portugal, Germany and the UK) had specific anti-terrorism legislation prior to 9/11.

In France, for example, much of the legislative response to 9/11 was based on the 'Act of September 9th of 1986' and the *Vigipirate* plan of 1978 and, interestingly, in Spain fighting terrorism is explicitly part of the Spanish Constitution from 1978 (Beckman 2007). Similarly, the United Kingdom with its experience of colonial terrorism and its struggle with the Irish Republican Army, was from a legislative point of view very well prepared for the events of 9/11 as it had passed the new Terrorism Act of 2000 only a couple of months prior to the attacks in New York and Washington. The act represented the first permanent nationwide anti-terror legislation (Taylor 2002). After 9/11 and despite this fairly new legislation the British government introduced the Anti-terrorism, Crime and Security Act 2001 to supplement and partly replace the Act of 2000. The new act includes among other things legislation on the freezing of terrorist property and cash, the security of the nuclear and aviation industries, immigration and asylum matters and most controversially the detention without trial of foreign persons denied asylum on the ground of national security (Walker 2003). This was followed by the Prevention of Terrorism Act 2005 which further strengthened the tools of law enforcement. However, while there was some protest against the first two acts by civil rights groups such as Liberty, the third legislation met with more scepticism as concerns about increasing police powers to the detriment of civil liberties started to grow. Especially controversial here was the issue of 'control orders' which placed suspects under a kind of house arrest for which the burden of proof was a lot lower than that required for normal incarceration. Not only was the act opposed by a number of human rights organizations such as Amnesty International, Human Rights Watch and JUSTICE, but it was also heavily criticized by High Court judge Justice Sullivan who considered it 'an affront to justice' and incompatible with the right to fair proceedings under Article 6 of the European Convention on Human Rights (Dodd and Bailey 2006).

Following the London bombings in 2005, the UK government introduced even more draconian legislation. This included, for example, new criminal law offences relating to terrorism, new rules on immigration detention and controversially the act made the glorification or encouragement of terrorism a crime which has clear implications for the democratic notion of free speech. The government also tried to introduce new laws which allowed the authorities to hold suspected terrorists for three months without charge. This provoked strong opposition not only by senior judges, lawyers and civil rights groups but also by Conservative, Liberal and rebel Labour MPs. This ultimately led to the defeat of the government on the 90-day detention matter and a reduction to 'only' 28 days. Nevertheless, the Labour government again tried to increase the number of days in detention without charge to 42 in the Counter-Terrorism Bill 2008. Even though this counter-terrorism initiative was voted down by the House of Lords in 2008, the implications of this measure on the civil liberties and human rights in the country have been continuously stressed by human rights groups such as Amnesty International and Human Rights Watch. And the conflict between counter-terrorism and civil liberties has led to a number of conflicts between the UK government and the European Court of Human Rights including in February 2009 the case A and Others v. the United Kingdom in which 11 foreign individuals received compensation for the violation of the right to liberty and security and to have lawfulness of detention decided by a court. In June 2010 the UK Supreme Court ruled that the control order introduced under the 2005 anti-terror legislation breached the human rights of a terror suspect forced to undergo a 16-hour curfew in the Midlands while his family lived in London

Interestingly, despite this opposition within the government and legislature as well as human rights organizations the majority of the British population does not consider many of the new laws and police powers to be overly intrusive. In fact opinion polls seem to indicate that large parts of the population believe that civil liberties are a hindrance to the security of their country and that these should be curtailed for the benefit of a safer Britain.

Apart from France, Spain, Italy and the UK, Germany also has had first-hand experience with terrorist groups such as the Red Army Faction or the Movement 2 June. Interestingly, similar to France, Germany does seem more concerned with the infringement of civil liberties in the name of security than Britain. Yet similar to the UK, Germany was very quick to respond to the events of 9/11. It implemented two so-called security packages (*Sicherheitspakete*) which both include a large number of anti-terror laws and alterations to existing legislation. While the first package is considered predominantly repressive in nature and includes, similarly to Spain, the abolition of the privileged role of religious associations under German law, the second package, with more than 100 regulations in 17 laws and five decrees, has a more preventive character (Beckman 2007). It included diverse measures such as increased air traffic security, stricter asylum regulations and the reintroduction of the controversial measure of profiling (*Rasterfahndung*) used in the 1970s to fight the Red Army Faction. Germany has also introduced a number of financial measures and adopted international Financial Action Task Force's (FATF) special recommendations aimed at preventing the financing of terrorism. Despite the renowned importance Germany places on civil liberties and human rights the partly controversial measures of the first two security packages were passed surprisingly without much protest. However, as the shock of 9/11 started to dissolve, protest against the infringement of civil liberties grew stronger. Especially, the recent introduction of online computer searches has caused judicial and political protest and opposition by privacy advocates as it stands in stark contrast to the Germany's traditionally very prominent data privacy laws.

Other controversies include the debate about the use of the Bundeswehr within Germany in the case of a major terrorist attack and the controversy around the involvement of the German government in CIA flights and the abduction of suspected terrorists such as Murat Kurnaz to Guantànamo Bay. One of the rare examples where human rights to have triumphed with regard to counter-terrorism is the controversial 2005 Aviation Security Act. In response to 9/11, part of this law authorized the armed forces, as a last resort, to shoot down aircraft used as weapons against human lives. There was a heated debate in Germany among the government and the opposition about whether such a measure was appropriate and in 2006, following a constitutional complaint by former liberal (FDP) politicians Burkhard Hirsch, Gerhart Baum and four others, the Federal Constitutional Court revoked the law in cases in which a hijacked plane had passengers on board who were not participants in the crime. It argued that the act was incompatible with the fundamental right to life and with the guarantee of human dignity enshrined in German Basic Law. As Victor Mauer (2007: 69–70) points out, this decision 'has put an end to a tendency that appeared to run rampant in the aftermath of the 11 September 2001 attacks – the fundamental primacy of the state's "national security" paradigm over the legal right to liberty'.

Countries without experience of terrorism

In contrast to this first group of countries, the second group did not have extensive experience of terrorism and did not have explicit anti-terror legislation prior to 9/11. While a number of European states such as Estonia, Latvia, Lithuania and the Czech Republic (Spencer 2006) drafted national action plans against terrorism, others such as Slovakia and Hungary adopted a number of individual resolutions and laws to confront terrorism. For example, the government of Slovakia adopted a resolution approving 'The Set of Preventive Measures for Combating Terrorism in the Territory of the Slovak Republic', which provides for the implementation of a preventative counter-terrorism measures by individual bodies of central administration, municipal authorities, and major production facilities and institutions (Slovak Ministry of Foreign Affairs 2001). For example, financial institutions have to identify any person who is preparing to carry out a financial transaction exceeding US$2,000, and they have to report any suspicious transactions. Furthermore, funds of a sponsoring state can be frozen if the UN Security Council or the Council of the European Union imposes sanctions, or if there are judicial criminal proceedings underway. Other laws include the extension of detention of an accused person and the restriction of personal freedom of a suspect person. In addition, new laws have also eliminated existing gaps which allowed the importing and exporting of military material and weapons without any licence. Slovakia has also taken measures to prevent recruitment of terrorists and supplies of weapons to terrorists by passing new laws that criminalize such acts. Slovakia has signed all 12 UN conventions and protocols relating to terrorism and has implemented all obligations into domestic legislation arising from the anti-terrorist conventions (Tomka 2001). When examining the dates of ratification of the UN conventions and protocols it becomes clear that Slovakia is the only new EU member state which has ratified all conventions except the International Convention for the Suppression of the Financing of Terrorism prior to 9/11.

Similar to Slovakia, Hungary was also very quick to ratify all the UN conventions and protocols relating to terrorism and had mostly done so prior to 9/11. Hungarian law has firmly established that terrorism, including making available funds for terrorist acts, is a crime. And Hungary has been relatively active in combating the financing of terrorism as it has introduced a number of different countermeasures that bring it into full compliance with EU and Financial Action Task Force norms (Bárándy 2003).

Interestingly, the topic of civil rights and the balance between liberty and security is something that many of the 'new' EU member states seem not very bothered about. For example, in contrast to the United Kingdom and Germany the issue of civil liberties with regard to counter-terrorism in Hungary is not a major topic. Despite the experience of a repressive national intelligence apparatus during the communist rule of the country, the Hungarian public does not seem particularly sensitive to civil liberties and human rights violations in the name of counter-terrorism (Rihackova 2006: 4). Nevertheless, there are a number of issues concerning national security and civil liberties which are reminiscent of the communist era. For example, many secret information gathering methods can be used without a warrant and those effected may never find out that they have been investigated as the conduct of such activities is deemed a state secret (Szikinger 2003). Still, in an opinion poll conducted by the EU, 62 per cent of Hungarians considered that access to personal information by law enforcement authorities in the fight against crime and terrorism is not an intrusion into citizen's privacy or only a minor inconvenience (Standard Eurobarometer 2007). This situation is similar to that of many of the other Eastern European countries such as Slovakia. Although there are a number of human rights issues such as the rights of the Roma (Gypsy) minority in the country, there are few known cases of civil liberties violations in the name of counter-terrorism as such. There are nevertheless concerns about the involvement of the secret service in illegal acts such as kidnapping, torture and unwarranted surveillance. For example, the former head of the SIS, Ivan Lexa, has been implicated in the kidnapping and torture of a former president's son in 1995 and in 2003 it was revealed that the SIS had illegally wiretapped the editorial offices of one of the country's leading newspapers (Forlong 1999; US Department of State 2004).

Intelligence and counter-terrorism organization

It is frequently argued that the key to fighting terrorism is good intelligence work. National intelligence agencies are supposed to identify possible threats, gather data on these threats, analyse it and then react or distribute the extracted information to the appropriate agencies responsible for acting. Although this may sound a good idea, such intelligence work has a number of traditional problems. For example, one has to consider the indirect, fragmentary and ambiguous nature of information gathering, which is further exacerbated by the fact that gathering intelligence has become more difficult due to the looser operational linkages between terrorist cells. The smaller these network cells are, and the more the members know each other personally, the more difficult it will be to infiltrate such groups. Apart from the problem of getting close to terrorists and cultivating personal relationships or trying to recruit members as informers, there is the problem that those who are in close contact with decision-makers, and are therefore more likely to have knowledge of the next terrorist operation, are the most loyal and least likely to betray their group (Pillar 2004). This difficulty is compounded even further by the current lack of human intelligence resources, which some say is due to Western obsession with technology such as spy satellites or intercepting communication, the over-regulation of intelligence agencies, or their inability to recruit suitable staff willing to engage in such dangerous activities (Berkowitz 2002).

If there are difficulties in collecting terrorist intelligence, there are also significant challenges in analysing it (Pillar 2001: 112). There is simply too much information to allow an analysis of everything concerning all the known terrorists groups in the world, including those groups who are still considering the use of violence, and those who have not yet formed or joined a group at all. Without exactly knowing the terrorists plans and their whereabouts, it is almost impossible to precisely identify targets, and connections between groups who might strike some time in the future as they often only become apparent after an attack has occurred (Hoffman and Morrison-Taw 2000). Focusing on certain specific profiles, such as for example young Middle Eastern men, is both under and over-inclusive at the same time. For one it is under-inclusive because there are US or European nationals who may also be terrorist threats. Treating such a large group as suspicious means that government authorities could miss genuine terrorists who do not fit the profile. At the same time it is over-inclusive because the vast majority of young males from the Middle East have no involvement in terrorism what so ever. Youthfulness, the male gender and a Middle Eastern origin is dangerously inaccurate with probably 99.9 percent being totally innocent (Romero 2003).

Although the intelligence and organization of counter-terrorism is different in every European country, one trend seems to have prevailed: in contrast to the United States, European countries did not respond to 9/11 by creating a huge organization along the lines of the Department of Homeland Security to improve their intelligence and organizational struggle against terrorism. The European emphasis has been predominantly on cooperation and information sharing between existing institutions without creating a large overarching new bureaucracy to control those agencies already in existence. The United Kingdom for example has, apart from various branches of the police force, three major national intelligence and security services responsible for fighting terrorism: MI6, the nation's external intelligence agency; MI5 the country's internal intelligence service responsible for gathering information on and assessing internal threats such as terrorism; and the Government Communication Headquarters (GCHQ), which intercepts and decodes communication to create intelligence information (Chalk and Rosenau 2004). Although the government placed more importance on information sharing between departments and established a new Joint Terrorism Analysis Centre after 9/11 and the Bali bombings, the overall intelligence structure remained largely unchanged (Donohue 2007).

Germany also has no single central agency which could coordinate the country's counter-terrorism activities. A total reorganization of the German security and intelligence apparatus and the creation of an over-arching central organization responsible for fighting terrorism such as the US Department of Homeland Security were made impossible by the federal nature of the state and the country's historical experience as enshrined in the German Basic Law. There are numerous agencies involved in the fight against terrorism, including the Federal Bureau of Criminal Investigation, the Federal Police, the Federal Intelligence Service, the Federal Bureau for the Protection of the Constitution and the Federal Border Guard to name but a few. Security package two, and further institutional innovation such as the Joint Counterterrorism Centre in Berlin in 2004, have improved cooperation between the different agencies (Mauer 2007). Despite the constitutional restrictions, Germany has increased the competencies of its security and intelligence services in a number of ways, including increased powers for the Federal Criminal Police Office (BKA), for example, which no longer has to rely on the *Länder* for data collection. In 2008, the BKA received controversial responsibilities in the fight against terrorism which allow members of the agency to bug the homes of terror suspects with cameras and microphones, and conduct online searches of their computers. Although these new powers proposed by Interior Minister Wolfgang Schäuble, were heavily criticized by some SPD politicians and large parts of the opposition at that time including the FDP and the Greens, these online computer searches were declared constitutional by the Federal Constitutional Court in February 2008 under strict conditions and only if they are warranted by a concrete danger and sanctioned by a judge.

Many of the 'new' Eastern European EU members such as the Baltic States, the Czech Republic and Hungary responded to 9/11 with institutional measures to improve cooperation between security and intelligence agencies. In Hungary, for example, the government focused on measures in the field of judicial and police cooperation, the fight against terrorist financing, border control, and aviation and political cooperation. The plan establishes which authorities are in charge: traditionally, the detection and investigation of terrorists and their activities is the responsibility of the anti-terrorist unit of the Hungarian National Police

HQ. However, after 9/11 the government decided to set up an Anti-terrorist Coordination Committee (TKB). The committee meets once a week and consists of representatives from the National Security Office, the Information Office, the Military Intelligence Office, the Military Security Office, the National Security Special Services, the National Police Headquarters and the Border Guards. The main role of the TKB is to raise the level of cooperation between the different agencies as well as coordinate specific operational counter-terrorist measures (National Security Office 2003). In comparison to many of the other new EU member states, the TKB is a considerable step towards a coordinated intelligence structure (Spencer 2006). However, the fact that the TKB's relationship with other agencies involved in counter-terrorist measures is outlined in individual bilateral agreements between them, rather than set in law, shows that there is still no formal and indisputable chain of command.

Other Eastern European states such as Czech Republic, Slovenia and Poland created coordinating centres and committees to enhance information exchange between agencies and therefore improve their capabilities against terrorism. Slovakia established the Counter-Terrorism Crisis Management Unit at the Ministry of the Interior to coordinate the action of the police force in case of a crisis caused by a terrorist act. In addition, a specialized organization for the fight against terrorism has been set up within the Police Force Presidium with responsibility for the detection, documentation and prosecution of terrorist acts. However, at the same time, the general Police Force, the Slovak Intelligence Service (SIS), the military defence intelligence and the Railroad Police also take part in the fight against terrorism (Slovak Ministry of Foreign Affairs 2001). So, although there have been efforts to establish new institutions and organizations to deal with the threat of terrorism, there is no coordinated intelligence structure in the form of a central body to manage all the elements central to the fight against terrorism. As Kulich and Rybár (2002: 71) point out, '[i]n our controlling structures, an agency is missing, which would gather and analyse information from individual departments and would be able to "warn" the competent bodies of the possibility of terrorist attacks on the Slovak Republic'.

Internal security and defence measures

A common response to the threat of terrorism around the world has been the tightening of internal security and defence measures. On the one hand this can involve making access to potential targets more difficult for terrorists. So for example this would include enhanced security checks at national borders, airports, train stations, public events, government buildings or critical infrastructure with the use of technology such as X-ray scanners, closed-circuit television (CCTV) surveillance or simply more security staff and more barbwire. On the other hand this also involves hardening targets to make them more resistant to a terrorist attack. So, for example, this would include the fortification of embassies with blast-proof glass or the development of bomb-proof luggage compartments on planes.

Although these measures seem to make sense, they do face a number of difficulties (see Chapter 13, in this book). First of all, considering the issue of border security one has to note the sheer impossibility of making a national boarder utterly impervious to terrorists, however tight border controls may be. Second, increased security at one potential target can lead to a deflection of the attack to another less well protected target. So terrorists may shift their attacks from traditional targets, which have now become too well defended, to new soft targets which lack such protection (Sederberg 2003: 279). This could mean a move away from assaults on military bases, such as those on US and French barracks in Lebanon in 1984, to attacks on tourist resorts in Bali, public transport in Madrid and London, or schools in small towns in North Ossetia. It is therefore unclear what targets and resources should be protected (Heymann 2001/2002: 31). Just as it is impossible to create a 'Maginot Line' at one's border (Bigo 2002), it is impossible to protect all potential targets, as there are far too many to consider protecting all. If the entire population is considered a valid target, then the majority will remain vulnerable and it is easy for terrorists to find targets.

Apart from the substitution effect, there is also the danger of 'terrorist innovation'. So rather than shifting to a different target the implementation of internal security and defence measures may 'invite the terrorists to invent novel circumventions' (Sandler 2003: 795). In the past terrorists have proved to be very ingenious in adjusting to and trouncing new security and defence measures (Faria 2006). For example, the Irish Republican Army continuously changed its way of detonating bombs with the help of radar guns or photographic flash equipment to circumvent security measures to prevent and jam the detonation remotes (Pillar 2001: 39). Other such terrorist innovations have included the use of aeroplanes as guided missiles, shoe bombs and more recently the attempted use of different liquids which would pass through security undetected to make a bomb on board a plane. Following this line of argument, one could go as far as claiming that when traditional methods of terrorism such as conventional bombing cease to work due to the enhanced security and defence measures, terrorists could be tempted to use unconventional weapons of mass destruction out of desperation (Quillen 2002: 290).

Despite the unanimous condemnation of the 9/11 attacks by all European countries, the individual threat perception in each European state was very different. While some of the older EU member states such as Germany, France the UK, Italy, the Netherlands and Spain were more concerned about being a potential target for terrorism the newer members such as Poland, Slovenia, Cyprus and Malta were far less worried. This is clearly also reflected in the vigour with which the different countries implemented different internal security and defence measures in the name of fighting terrorism.

Both 'old' and 'new' Europe tightened their boarder security. For example, Hungarian border security has been improved by modernizing the infrastructure, introducing infrared surveillance equipment, passport checking computers, carbon monoxide meters and drug identification equipment. In addition, more border guards have been recruited, their training has been enhanced and they have merged with the National Police which has further enhanced its ability to monitor the border (US Department of State 2007). Similarly, Slovakia also increased boarder security after 9/11 by introducing new technologies, special equipment and completing technical infrastructure. In addition, soldiers have been drafted in to bolster the protection of the state border, and training available to the border police and customs service has been improved. Furthermore, checks on passports and visas have been intensified in order to detect forged documents. Although this increased security at Europe's borders seems to be a pan-European trend, one should consider whether these enhanced boarder measures are a direct result of a terrorist treat, or whether the looming accession to the European Union and its entry requirements had something to do with the 'enthusiasm' of 'new' Europe.

Similarly, all European states improved their security procedures at airports after 9/11, but only some, including Germany, Austria, France, Italy, Spain and the UK, have resorted to using sky marshals on planes. Similarly only a handful of countries, including France and the UK, implemented substantial security measures in other transport systems such as the London underground or the metro in Paris. Physical protection of infrastructure and prominent buildings such as the placement of barriers around the British Parliament building (Bamford 2004) also varies considerably among European states as internal security measures are considered of varying importance across Europe. The same can be said of disaster management. While, for example, some European states such as Germany, the UK, France and Hungary have more or less elaborate national systems for dealing with possible catastrophic terror attacks, other states such as Malta, Cyprus or Slovakia do not. In Hungary for example, the National Directorate General for Disaster

Management has been given the task of issuing a disaster plan, an emergency communication plan, safety actions in the case of a terrorist attack and dealing with the consequences of such an attack and fire service plans (Zsohar 2004). Hungary has also taken several steps to prevent and prepare for the threat of biological terrorism, including the examination of existing stockpiles of vaccines, antidotes and antibodies, as well as the preparation of measures to be taken in the event of an anthrax or smallpox outbreak (National Security Office 2003).

Military responses in Europe

Although the idea of using the military to combat terrorism is generally considered problematic, there are a number of arguments for why a military response can in fact be a viable defensive and offensive option for confronting terrorism, both on a national and international level (Carr 1996/1997). As Paul Wilkinson (1996: 6) points out: 'armed forces can contribute the firepower, force projection capability and expertise, such as hostage rescue commandos, sophisticated bomb disposal teams, and specialist marksmen, which the civilian police is unable to provide'. On the offensive side, the military can be used to target terrorist groups or the state involved in sponsoring or harbouring them. Direct military action can be used to find and destroy the infrastructure of terrorist groups, reduce their capabilities, expose their vulnerability and undermine their status and deter further acts of terrorism (Shultz and Vogt 2003).

However, the use of military means against terrorists can also be heavily criticized. For one, some have questioned the use of employing the military as an additional force to enhance internal security. In contrast to the police, the military lack legitimacy and accountability in the eyes of the general public and are unfamiliar with local conditions and communities (Wilkinson 2000). Soldiers are generally not trained for internal security duties where, in contrast to their normal working environment, war zones, it is difficult to identify a clear enemy. There is a constant risk of overreaction which can trigger further violence. In situations such as Northern Ireland or the Basque Country, where parts of the population are at least supportive and sympathies with the goals of terrorist groups, a heavy military presence can lead to the escalation of violence by polarizing the groups involved in the conflict.

Apart from the question of whether terrorists can really be deterred by the threat of military action, there are a number of other practical problems in using military strikes against terrorism. Critics of a military approach to terrorism have pointed out that terrorists do not use ordinary or conventional combat methods found in a 'normal' war and generally do not engage in extensive operations with thousands of combatants which could be prevented by the deployment of a large number of troops (Light 2002). Similarly, one has to note that terrorist groups do not generally present many or even any targets or high value infrastructure which a government could strike at. One could therefore argue that military retaliation against primitive training camps with million dollar cruise-missiles or laser-guided bombs often does little more than rearrange rocks in a barren landscape in the middle of nowhere.

Due to the unreliability of intelligence mentioned above, violent military responses always involve the possibility of so-called 'collateral damage', i.e. causing the tragic, unintended death of innocent civilians (Ross 2006: 204). This is not only problematic from a normative perspective but can quickly become a practical political issue in an anti-terror campaign as it can greatly damage one's image and gravely impede the struggle for the heart and minds of the general public around the world (Steven and Gunaratna 2004). Besides the problem of the legality of military strikes against terrorist in international law, this can mean not only the loss of the moral high ground and the support of international public opinion, but it can strain existing international and regional alliances and lead to the situation where other states may be less willing to cooperate against terrorism in the future (Wilkinson 2000). It can make the attacking state look no better or even worse than the terrorist group it is fighting against. So it can lead not only to the loss of legitimacy by the state involved in the strike, but can also increase the legitimacy of the terrorist group they are fighting by portraying terrorists as soldiers and violence as a solution to the conflict (Chalk 1996: 97).

As Table 16.1 indicates and in contrast to many of the other policies mentioned above, there is probably the least agreement among Europeans as to whether the military is an appropriate tool against terrorism (see Chapter 15, in this book). In this respect one can roughly divide Europe into four different groups: the first group of governments is or was highly supportive of the US-led military engagement of terrorism around the world. And there are a number of 'old' and 'new' European states which have had troops both in Afghanistan and Iraq. For example Italy, the Netherlands, Spain and Denmark as well as newer EU member states such as Poland, Rumania and Bulgaria all had fairly significant numbers of troops in both countries. Yet the most prominent example within this group is the United Kingdom which was the only country in this group to actively take part in early combat operations both in Afghanistan and in Iraq. And it is fair to say that the United Kingdom has been at the European forefront of the military fight against terrorism. It was the only country to deploy troops on the first day of military engagement in Afghanistan and initially the public support for

Table 16.1   *European military presence in the 'war on terror'*

	Number of troops in Afghanistan in 2010 (peak in brackets)		Peak number of troops in Iraq after the invasion	Deployed to and withdrawal from Iraq
United Kingdom	9500		8500	Invasion–July 09
Germany	4590	(4665)	–	–
France	3750		–	–
Italy	3400		3200	July 03–Nov. 06
Poland	2630		2500	Invasion–Oct. 08
Romania	1750		730	July 03–July 09
Spain	1550		1300	April 03–April 04
Denmark	730	(750)	545	April 03–Dec. 08
Belgium	575	(590)	–	–
Bulgaria	540		485	May 03–Dec. 08
Sweden	530		–	–
Czech Republic	500	(525)	300	Dec. 03–Dec. 08
Netherlands	380	(2200)	1345	July 03–March 05
Hungary	360		300	Aug. 03–March 08
Slovakia	300		110	Aug. 03–Dec. 07
Portugal	250	(265)	128	Nov. 03–Feb. 05
Lithuania	245		120	June 03–Aug. 07
Latvia	170	(175)	136	May 03–Nov. 08
Estonia	160		40	June 05–Jan. 09
Finland	80	(115)	–	–
Greece	75	(170)	–	–
Slovenia	70	(75)	–	–
Luxembourg	9	(10)	–	–
Ireland	6	(10)	–	–
Austria	3	(5)	–	–
Cyprus	–		–	–
Malta	–		–	–

Source: Nato (2010) and Brookings (2010)

the war on terror was high. The UK's involvement in the early air campaign involved the provisions of support aircraft and use of Tomahawk missiles launched from Royal Navy submarines. At the start of the campaign in Afghanistan the government deployed 1,700 combat troops and then played a vital role in Operation Enduring Freedom and the International Security Assistance Force (ISAF) (Dorman 2003). Troop numbers in Afghanistan have consistently risen to around 9,500 with a large bulk of them deployed in the volatile southern Helmand province. In addition, the United Kingdom was the only European country apart from Poland which was directly involved in the invasion of Iraq with around 45,000 troops. And overall the UK was the largest European contributor to post-war Iraq with a peak of around 8,500 soldiers. Interestingly, as Table 16.1 shows, Romania and Estonia were the only other European states which remained in Iraq until 2009, apart from the United Kingdom.

The second group of countries was very supportive of the military engagements in Afghanistan, but was opposed to the invasion of Iraq. This included countries such as Sweden, Belgium and France. Interestingly, despite the image of the pacifist soft power, Germany in particular has played a large role as Afghanistan has been central to Germany's military involvement against terrorism. It has taken an active role in the country and even directly participated in Operation Enduring Freedom (OEF) by offering the United States up to 3,900 troops in support (Hyde-Price 2003). However, the motion in favour of military action was passed in parliament with a majority of only ten votes. Even though the vote in parliament might suggest otherwise, there was in fact widespread support for German participation in a military response after 9/11 (Spencer 2010). The seemingly close vote was due to the fact that Chancellor Gerhard Schröder linked the proposal of military action to a question of confidence in his government. This meant that the opposition parties such as the Christian Democrats (CDU/CSU) and the Liberals (FDP) voted against the motion even though they supported the participation in military action (Maull 2001; Hyde-Price 2003). Similarly, however, one has to consider that the closed ranks of the SPD and the Green Party could also be partly attributed to the question of confidence rather than to the support of military action. Apart from engagement in Afghanistan, Germany is also involved in patrolling shipping routes around the Horn of Africa to prevent the movement of terrorists and the cutting of supply chains. In addition, Germany sent 1,200 German soldiers to Afghanistan as part of the International Security Assistance Force (ISAF). These were deployed in addition to the 3,900 troops committed to OEF (Oswald 2004). The mission aims at creating a safer and more stable environment for the reconstruction of Afghanistan. The mandate for the ISAF mission has to be reapproved every year by the German parliament. Since the first deployment, the number of German troops has risen to around 4,590, and Germany is now the third largest troop contributor, and is in charge of Regional Command North. However, importantly, the German mandate for ISAF does not allow the *Bundeswehr* to participate in combat operations in the south and east of the country (Miko and Froehlich 2004). Despite the increased involvement of German troops, public support for military involvement in Afghanistan has continued to dwindle and in 2010 around two-thirds of the population appear to be against increased involvement of German soldiers.

The third group of countries was moderately supportive of the military engagement of terrorism and has provided only a limited number of troops to both conflicts. This group includes mainly new EU member countries from Eastern Europe, such as the Baltic States, Hungary or Slovakia. In particular, Hungary's military response to terrorism and the participation in the 'war on terror' in Afghanistan has been fairly moderate in comparison to the efforts of the UK and Germany. Although Hungary has not contributed directly to Operation Enduring Freedom it has nevertheless participated in the ISAF mission in Afghanistan. At the end of 2010 Hungary had around 360 troops in Afghanistan and has in recent years taken a more prominent leadership role in the country (Marton and Wagner 2008). In 2003 Hungary also sent a 300-strong military transport battalion to Iraq to assist in the stabilization of the country. However, public opinion opposed the military participation in Iraq and the Hungarian political elite were strongly divided on the issue (Valki 2005). As a result the troops were withdrawn and sent home only two years later. Similar to Hungary and despite the unreserved vocal support for the US in the 'war on terror' (Samson 2005), Slovakia's military contribution to fighting terrorism has been fairly moderate. In Afghanistan, Slovakia joined the other coalition forces in Operation Enduring Freedom in 2002 and deployed around 40 military engineers to the vicinity of Baghram air base responsible for demining and rebuilding the airport. In 2004, the government committed a small number of troops to the ISAF operation, and in October 2007 it approved plans to further boost troop levels within ISAF to around 300 (Farkasová 2007). Slovakia has also sent 110 army engineers to Iraq as a stabilization force based in Al Hillah, between Baghdad and Basra, who were mainly tasked with demining and dismantling arms and munitions. However, similar to Spain, a change in government in June 2006 resulted in the withdrawal of all Slovak troops from Iraq in 2007 (*International Herald Tribune* 2007).

The fourth group of countries only provided very limited or no military support for the 'war on terror'. This group includes Luxemburg, Ireland and Austria but only Malta and Cyprus did not send any military personnel to Afghanistan or Iraq. It is interesting to note that all new EU member states from Eastern Europe participated in the military engagement of terrorism in some shape or form.

Conclusion

Identifying general trends in European counter-terrorism remains difficult. While the United Kingdom and a number of other European states such as Poland and Italy are closely allied to the United States with regard to its military engagements and the extent of counter-terrorism legislation, Germany, France and Belgium have been more critical of the US. The emphasis that the different countries have placed on counter-terrorism varies greatly. Generally the emphasis given to counter-terrorism and the resulting concern for civil liberties is much higher in the 'old' EU member states than in the 'new' ones. In Eastern Europe counter-terrorism is not often an issue on the domestic political agenda and due to the reduced importance there seems to be less concern for the erosion of civil liberties. However, despite this lack of public interest there is no real indication that civil liberties are being eroded more strongly than in Western Europe.

While all states have implemented new counter-terrorism measures, the measures of the 'old' EU members states have risen out of their historical experiences with terrorism in their own countries. In contrast, the new member states do not have much experience with domestic terrorism. They have therefore tended not to develop their own approach but have used instead foreign templates and have implemented these measures due to external pressure from European Union and NATO rather than their own concern with terrorism (Rihackova 2006). Similarly one could explain the military response and ultimately the half-hearted and small participation in the war in Iraq with these countries' very recent membership of NATO.

As a response to the opposition to the Iraq war US Secretary of Defence Donald Rumsfeld in 2003 famously said: 'Now, you're thinking of Europe as Germany and France. I don't. I think that's old Europe' (BBC 2003). So there are two major dividing lines in Europe concerning counter-terrorism, and both involve the 'old versus new' Europe distinction. The first divide between the old and the new member states concerns the threat perception and the perceived importance of balancing civil liberties with security. The second divide concerns the involvement in Iraq: while parts of Europe including the United Kingdom, Italy, Spain and many of the new EU members have supported the US, others such as Germany and France have not. So despite the gloss of unity, Europe appears to remain divided at least on some aspects of counter-terrorism.

Suggestions for Further Reading

Chapter 2

The literature on the financial crisis is vast. Taleb (2004), Bookstaber (2007) and Das (2006) provide prescient insider accounts of the financial innovations that caused the crisis. Speaking before the US Congress, both Bookstaber (2008) and former Federal Reserve Chairman Alan Greenspan (2008) provide frankly disturbing analyses of unfolding events. Finally, Cooper (2008), Wolf (2009) and Kling (2010) offer valuable suggestions as to what should be done to keep such events from recurring. Unfortunately, few governments are willing to follow their advice. This is hardly a new situation. Kindleberger (2000) shows how often we have gone through this and Kindleberger (1986) shows how much effort is required to pull us out again. The situation in Europe is particularly uninspiring. Not only is there little evidence of coherent leadership (Jones 2010) but what institutional changes are on offer are sure to be insufficient. Both the EU writ large and the eurozone within it are likely to suffer from instability as a result.

Chapter 3

For excellent overviews, covering mostly, but not exclusively, developments in the 'old' member states, see Cowles *et al.* (2001); Featherstone and Radaelli (2003); Graziano and Vink (2007); and Ladrech (2010). For the Europeanization of candidate countries, see e.g. Grabbe (2006); Jacoby (2004); Schimmelfennig and Sedelmeier (2005a); Schimmelfennig *et al.* (2006); and Vachudova (2005). For the EU's impact in its neighbourhood, see Weber *et al.* (2007); Lavenex and Schimmelfennig (2009); and Schimmelfennig (2009).

Chapter 4

For a thorough treatment of parliamentary and presidential government, see Lijphart (1992); a rigorous comparative analysis of political systems using principal–agent analysis is provided by Strøm and Müller (2003), who have also edited a broadly comparative study on coalition government (Müller and Strøm 2000). Lijphart (1999) gives an excellent account of how different institutional features combine to produce a more majoritarian or consensual mode of governing. Poguntke and Webb (2007) provide comparative evidence on the shift towards more centralization and personalization of executive power while

Peters *et al.* (2000) focus on the internal workings of government. Egeberg (2006) and Curtin and Egeberg (2008) present valuable discussions of the emerging order of executive politics in the EU multilevel system. Several contributions scrutinize the EU impact on domestic actors. O'Brennan and Raunio (2006a) as well as Benz and Auel (2005) provide useful overviews and discussions of how EU politics affects the role of national parliaments. Bulmer and Burch (2009) is a good example of the Europeanization of executives in long-standing EU member states. The authors analyse the Europeanization of the British core executive. Zubek (2009) gives a comparative account of the Europeanization of core executives in the new member states of the EU after the Eastern enlargement.

Chapter 5

With respect to the array of pathologies said to be afflicting political parties in Europe today, readers can refer to a wide range of sources. General treatments of this topic can be found in Dalton and Wattenberg (2000), Webb *et al.* (2002) and Webb and White (2007). Readers interested in the literature on popular disillusion with politics more generally should consult Pharr and Putnam (2000), Dalton (2004), Stoker (2006), Hay (2007) and Norris (2011). These volumes include significant amounts of material on representative politics. Jordan and Maloney (2007) offer a focus on the role of pressure groups in modern democracy. On the theme of the impact of the modern mass media on see Barnett (2002), Lloyd (2004) and Russell (2005). For recent work on populist politics in Europe, see especially Albertazzi and McDonnell (2007) or Mudde (2007). On the personalization of politics the main comparative works are Poguntke and Webb (2007) and Karvonen (2010), while an interesting take on the issue of more radical participation as a possible 'remedy' for the ailments of representative democracy is provided by Bengtsson and Mattila (2009).

Chapter 6

An authoritative general text on party politics in Europe specifically is Mair *et al.* (2004), while an excellent reference work for party politics in Europe and elsewhere in the democratic world is Katz and Crotty (2006). On electoral systems, Gallagher and Mitchell (2005) and Klingemann (2009) outline how electoral laws shape the nature of electoral competition. The most recent comprehensive works on the nature of European voting behaviour are Thomassen (2005) and Knutsen (2006). Assessments of party system dynamics in contemporary Europe include Webb *et al.* (2002), Webb and White (2007). The decline of party identification and citizen disaffection are analysed in Dalton (2004), while the emergence of new cleavages is discussed in Ignazi (2003), Szczerbiak and Taggart (2008) and Swenden and Maddens (2009).

Chapter 7

Essential readings include Dalton and Klingemann (2009), an edited volume providing a general overview of comparative political behaviour. Norris (2002) also provides a comparative review. Other work usually focuses upon on specific dimension of the subfield, including Franklin (2004) on voter turnout, Putnam (2000) and Hooghe and Stolle (2003) on social capital, Tarrow (1994) on social movements (a third edition of Tarrow's work was published in 2011), Dalton and Wattenberg (2001) on political parties, Dahlgren on the role of political communications, Burns *et al.* (2001) on gender inequalities in political participation, Goerres (2009) and Dalton (2008) on generational patterns, Zittel and Fuchs (2006) on the impact of institutional innovations.

Chapter 8

On the impact of globalization, European integration and decentralization on cities and regions see Brenner (2004) Carter and Pasquier (2010), Crouch *et al.* (2003), Keating (1998) and Sassen (1991). On the rescaling of governance and the development of urban and regional capacities see Cole (2006), Le Galès (2002), Keating (2008), Loughlin (2001) and Pasquier (2003).

Chapter 9

For recent empirical studies on trust and politics, see Gabriel and Walter-Rogg (2008), Zmerli *et al.* (2006), Teorell *et al.* (2006) and Rothstein (2004); an excellent discussion of definitional and theoretical issues is Warren (1999). On social capital theory, the starting point is Putnam *et al.* (1993) and Putnam (2000), but it is well worth revisiting the classic study by Almond and Verba (1963), and also contrasting Putnam's account with that of Coleman (1990). On links between corruption and trust, see Della Porta (2000) and Warren (2001), and Eurobarometer special reports 245, 'Opinions on Organised, Cross-Border Crime and Corruption' (European Commission 2006); 291, 'The Attitudes of Europeans towards Corruption' (European Commission 2008); and 325, 'Attitudes of Europeans towards Corruption. Full Report' (European Commission 2009).

Chapter 10

The key texts for the debates raised in this chapter are Hall and Soskice (2001), Hancké, Rhodes and Thatcher (2007), and Hall and Gingerich (2004). Hancké (2009) reviews the debate on varieties of capitalism, with critical papers on the central points made by the 'varieties of capitalism' literature. For more on the logic of the Single Market from the perspective of comparative capitalisms, see Thatcher (2007). On EMU the articles by Iversen and Soskice (1998), Hall and Franzese (1998), and Hancké and Rhodes (2005) offer useful ways into the debate. Eastward enlargement is somewhat understudied from this perspective, but Greskovits (2005) and Feldman (2007) demonstrate how a comparative political economy perspective helps understand developments in Central Europe.

Chapter 11

The literature on post-industrial welfare states is particularly prolific. A very recent and comprehensive introduction to the study of welfare states worldwide and of their evolution and characteristics is the *Oxford Handbook of the Welfare States* (2010). The pioneer contribution of Esping-Andersen on the *Three worlds of welfare capitalism* (1990) also represents an excellent introductory volume. As for recent policy reforms, Scharpf and Schmidt (2000) examine the impact of globalization and the open economy on welfare policies in a comparative perspective, Armingeon and Bonoli (2006) analyse the impact of new social risks on European welfare states and Palier (2010) provides an insightful overview of the transformations and changes of the Bismarckian systems of social protection. The EU social dimension is examined in depth by Zeitlin and Pochet (2005) and more recently by Wallace, Pollack and Young (2010). Finally, from a theoretical point of view, Pierson (2001) on the explanatory hypotheses of the 'era of permanent austerity' and the revision of neo-institutional welfare studies provided by Streeck and Thelen (2005) are still essential readings.

Chapter 12

The literature on religion and politics and church-state relations in modern Europe has grown markedly in recent years. Remond (1999) places European church–state–society issues in their historical context. Boyle and Sheen (1997) and Evans (2001) provide useful surveys of developments in the area of human rights. Robbers (2005) gives useful country by country surveys of church-state relations in the member states of the EU and Anderson (2003) supplements these with coverage of a number of Eastern European countries under conditions of transition to liberal democracy. Madeley and Enyedi (2003) included both thematic and country-study treatments from across the Continent and van Hecke and Gerard (2004) surveyed the varying fortunes of European Christian Democracy since the end of the cold war. Fox (2008) places European state–religious patterns in a global context while Leustean and Madeley (2009) covers legal as well as political aspects of religion and politics in the context of European integration.

Chapter 13

In the vast literature on European immigration policies, descriptive country- and (sub)policy-specific case studies still predominate, reflecting the incoherence, complexity, and fast-moving nature of policy even in any one country. The key text for theorizing immigration policy in cross-sectional and cross-national perspectives is, for some fifteen years now, Freeman (1995), which should be read together with the commentaries by Rogers Brubaker and Ted Perlmutter, and Freeman's rejoinder. Important empirical-cum-theoretical moves beyond Freeman's political economy model are Money (1999) and Joppke (1998). Good comprehensive overviews of the European scene are Messina (2007) and the respective country chapters in Cornelius et al. (2004). Indispensable for following up on current events and trends at member state and EU level is the Brussels-based monthly *Migration News Sheet*. The best website is that of the Migration Policy Institute in Washington, DC.

Chapter 14

Essential reading about EU energy policy includes policy documents such as the European Commission's energy strategy towards 2020 and its Communication about energy infrastructure priorities. In a broader context, it is worth consulting the International Energy Agency's World Energy Outlook 2010 (IEA 2010). For a more specific focus on the security of European energy supplies, see Checchi et al. (2008), Larsson (2007), Noël (2008), as well as the SECURE project's webpage (www.secure-ec.eu). On climate change, additional reading includes Egenhofer *et al.* (2010) and Stern (2006).

Chapter 15

For contemporary foreign policy-making, see Smith *et al.* (2007) and Hill (2003). For EU foreign policy, see Keukeleire and MacNaughton (2008), Smith (2008), and Smith and Hill (2011). Manners and Whitman (2000) contains chapters considering the extent to which EU member states' foreign policies have been 'adapted' in the area of foreign and security policy. The Internet is a useful source of freely available analysis of both European states' and EU foreign policies – see in particular the European Council on Foreign Relations (www.ecfr.eu), the European Union Institute for Security Studies (www.iss.europa.eu), the Centre for European Policy Studies (www.ceps.eu) and CFSP Forum (http://www.fornet.info/CFSPforum.html).

Chapter 16

For further information on counter-terrorism in European countries, see Reinares (2000), van Leeuwen (2003), Shearman and Sussex (2004), von

Hippel (2005) and Zimmermann and Wenger (2007). With regard to different legislative approaches against terrorism see Beckman (2007) and for the relationship to the United States see Lansford and Tashev (2005) and Rees (2006). For more insight into counter-terrorism in the EU see Brown (2010) and Eckers (2010) and for an overview of the conflict between counter-terrorism, civil liberties and human rights see Donohue (2008) and Whittaker (2009).

Bibliography

Adrian, C. and D.A. Apter (1995) *Political Protest and Social Change: Analyzing Politics*. New York: New York University Press.

Aglietta, M. (1977) *A Theory of Capitalist regulation: The US Experience*. London: New Left Books.

Aja, E. (2003) *El Estado Autonomico. Federalismo y Hechos Diferenciales*. Madrid: Alianza.

Akerlof, G.A. and R.J. Shiller (2009) *Animal Spirits: How Human Psychology Drives the Economy and Why It Matters for Global Capitalism*. Princeton, NJ: Princeton University Press.

Albertazzi, D. and D. McDonnell (2007) *Twenty-first Century Populism: The Spectre of Western European Democracy*. Basingstoke, UK: Palgrave Macmillan.

Allen, D. (1996) 'Conclusions: The European Rescue of National Foreign Policy?', in C. Hill *The Actors in Europe's Foreign Policy*. London: Routledge.

Allen, D. (1998) ' "Who Speaks for Europe?" The Search for an Effective and Coherent External Policy', in J. Peterson and H. Sjursen (eds), *A Common Foreign Policy for Europe?* London: Routledge.

Almond, G.A. and S. Verba (1963) *The Civic Culture: Political Attitudes in Five Nations*. Princeton, NJ: Princeton University Press.

Almond, G.A. and S. Verba (eds) (1980) *The Civic Culture Revisited*. Boston, MA: Little Brown.

Alti, T. and M. Jessoula (2010) 'Italy: An Uncompleted Departure from Bismarck', in B. Palier (ed.), *A Long Goodbye to Bismarck? The Politics of Welfare Reform in Continental Europe*. Amsterdam: Amsterdam University Press, pp. 157–82.

Alunni, A. (2009) 'The Financial Crisis in Italy and the Case of UniCredit Group', in L. Beke and E. Jones (eds), *European Responses to the Global Financial Crisis*. Bologna: Clueb, pp. 69–82.

Amable, B. (2003) *The Diversity of Modern Capitalism*. Oxford: Oxford University Press.

Amin, A. (1994) 'Post-Fordism: Models, Fantasies and Phantoms of Transition', in A. Amin (ed.) *Post-Fordism*. Oxford: Blackwell, pp. 1–39.

Amin, A. (2004) 'Regions Unbound: Towards a New Politics of Place', *Geografiska Annaler*. 86B/1, pp. 33–44.

Anderson, J. (2003) *Religious Liberty in Transitional Societies: The Politics of Religion*. Cambridge: Cambridge University Press.

Andonova, L.B. (2005) 'The Europeanization of Environmental Policy in Central and Eastern Europe', in Schimmelfennig and Sedelmeier (eds), *The Europeanization of Central and Eastern Europe*, pp. 135–55.

Armingeon, K. and G. Bonoli (eds) (2006) *The Politics of Post-Industrial Welfare States: Adapting Post-War Social Policies to New Social Risks.* London: Routledge.

Aspalter, C., K. Jinsoo and P. Sojeung (2009) 'Analysing the Welfare State in Poland, the Czech Republic, Hungary and Slovenia: An Ideal-Typical Perspective', *Social Policy and Administration*, 43(2), pp. 170–85.

Audi, R. (1989) 'The Separation of Church and State and the Obligations of Citizenship', *Philosophy and Public Affairs*, 18(3), pp. 259–296.

Auel, K, and A. Benz (2005) 'The Politics of Adaptation: The Europeanisation of National Parliamentary Systems', *The Journal of Legislative Studies*, 11(3), pp. 372–93.

Austin, R. and M. Tjernström (2003) *Funding of Political Parties and Election Campaigns.* Stockholm: International IDEA.

Bader, V (2007) *Secularism or Democracy? Associational Governance of Religious Diversity.* Amsterdam: Amsterdam University Press.

Bagnasco, A., P. Le Galès (eds) (2000) *Cities in Contemporary Europe.* Cambridge: Cambridge University Press.

Bagnasco, A., and C. Trigilia (1993). *La construction sociale du marché: Le défi de la troisième Italie.* Cachan: Editions de l'Ens.

Balme, R. (ed.) (1996) *Les Politiques du Néo-Régionalisme.* Paris: Economica.

Balme, R. and L. Bonnet (1994) 'From Regional to Sectoral Policies: the Contractual Relations Between the State and the Regions in France', *Regional Politics and Policy*, 4(3), pp. 51–71.

Bamford, B.W.C. (2004) 'The United Kingdom's "War Against Terrorism"', *Terrorism and Political Violence*, 16(4), pp. 737–56.

Banchoff, T. (ed.) (2007) *Democracy and the New Religious Pluralism.* New York: Oxford University Press.

Bárándy, P. (2003) 'The response of the justice system – civil and criminal – to terrorism', Sofia: Council of Europe, 25th Conference of European Ministers of Justice, Speech held by the Hungarian Minister if Justice, 9–10 October.

Barbe, E., O. Costa, A. Herranz, E. Johansson-Nogues, M. Natorski and M.A. Sabiote (2009) 'Drawing the Neighbours Closer ... To What? Explaining Emerging Patterns of Policy Convergence between the EU and Its Neighbours', *Cooperation and Conflict*, 44(4) pp. 378–99.

Barbou des Places, S. and H. Oger (2005) 'Making the European Migration Regime: Decoding Member States' Legal Practices', *European Journal of Migration and Law*, 6, pp. 353–75.

Barnes, S. and M. Kaase (1979) *Political Action: Mass Participation in Five Western Democracies.* Beverley Hills, CA: Sage.

Barnett, S. (2002) 'Will a Crisis in Journalism Provoke a Crisis in Democracy?', *Political Quarterly* 73(4), pp. 400–8.

Barrett, D. (ed.) (1982) *World Christian Encyclopaedia: A Comparative Study of Churches and Religions in the Modern World AD 1900–2000.* New York: Oxford University Press.

Barrett, D. et al. (eds) (2001) *World Christian Encyclopaedia: A Comparative Study of Churches and Religions in the Modern World*, 2nd edn. New York: Oxford University Press.

Barro, R.J. and R. McCleary (2005) 'Which Countries Have State Religions?' *Quarterly Journal of Economics*, 4, pp. 1331–370.

Barry, B. (2002) *Culture and Equality: An Egalitarian Critique of Multiculturalism*. Cambridge: Polity Press.

Bartolini, S. and P. Mair (1990) *Identity, Competition and Electoral Availability*. Cambridge: Cambridge University Press.

Bauer, M.W., C. Knill, and D. Pitschel (2007) 'Differential Europeanization in Eastern Europe: The Impact of Diverse EU Regulatory Governance Patterns', *Journal of European Integration*, 29(4) pp. 405–23.

BBC (2003) 'Outrage at "old Europe" remarks', *BBC News*, 23 January, available at: http://news.bbc.co.uk/2/hi/europe/2687403.stm (accessed: 17/09/10).

Beckford, J.A. (1985) *Cult Controversies: The Societal Response to the New Religious Movements*. London: Tavistock.

Beckford, J.A. (2003). *Social Theory & Religion*. Cambridge: Cambridge University Press.

Beckman, J. (2007) *Comparative Legal Approaches to Homeland Security and Anti-Terrorism*. Aldershot: Ashgate.

Behrens, A (2010) 'The Role of Renewables in the Interaction between Climate Change Policy and Energy Security in Europe', *Renewable Energy Law and Policy Review*, 1(1), pp. 5–15.

Behrens, A, J. Núñez Ferrer, C. Egenhofer (2008) 'Financial Impacts of Climate Change: Implications for the EU Budget', *CEPS Working Document*. no. 300, August.

Bengtsson, A. and M. Mattila (2009) 'Direct Democracy and Its Critics: Support for Direct Democracy and Stealth Democracy in Finland', *West European Politics*, 32, pp. 1031–48.

Bennett, S.E. (1986) *Apathy in America 1960–1984: Causes and Consequences of Citizen Political Indifference*. Dobbs Ferry, NY: Transnational.

Bensahel, N. (2006) 'A Coalition of Coalitions: International Cooperation Against Terrorism', *Studies in Conflict and Terrorism*, 29(1), pp. 35–49.

Benz, A. and K. Auel (2005) 'The Europeanization of Parliamentary Democracy', a special issue of *Journal of Legislative Studies*, 11(3–4).

Benz, A., S. Lütz, U. Schimank and G. Simonis (2007) 'Einleitung', in A. Benz, S. Lütz, U. Schimank and G. Simonis (eds), *Handbuch Governance*. Wiesbaden: VS-Verlag, pp. 9–25.

Berger, P., G. Davie and E. Fokas (2008) *Religious America, Secular Europe? A Theme and Variations*. Aldershot: Ashgate.

Berger, S. and M. Piore (1981) *Dualism and discontinuity in industrial society*. New York/Cambridge: Cambridge University Press.

Berkowitz, B. (2002) 'Intelligence and the War on Terrorism', *Orbis*, 46(2), pp. 289–300.

Bhagwati, J. (2004) *In Defense of Globalization*. Oxford: Oxford University Press.

Bigo, D. (2002) *To Reassure, and Protect, After September 11*. New York: Social Science Research Council. Available at: www.ssrc.org/sept11/essays/bigo.htm (accessed: 17/09/10).

Blais, A. (2000) *To Vote or Not to Vote? The Merits and Limits of Rational Choice Theory*. Pittsburgh: University of Pittsburgh Press.

Blais, A. and A. Dobrzynska (1998) 'Turnout in Electoral Democracies', *European Journal of Political Research*, 33(2), pp. 239–61.

Blauberger, M. (2009) 'Compliance with Rules of Negative Integration: European State Aid Control in the New Member States', *Journal of European Public Policy*, 16(7) pp. 1030–46.

Blyth, M. and R. Katz (2005) 'From Catch-All Politics to Cartelization: The Political Economy of the Cartel Party', *West European Politics*, 28(1), pp. 33–60.

Bomberg, E., and J. Peterson (1998) 'European Union Decision-Making: the Role of Sub-national Authorities', *Political Studies*, 46(2), pp. 219–35.

Bonjour, S. (2009) 'Reducing diversity: the framing of civic integration abroad policies in France and the Netherlands'. Unpublished manuscript (on file with editors).

Books, J.W. and C.L. Prysby (1988) 'Studying contextual Effects on Political Behavior: A research Inventory and Agenda', *American Politics Quarterly* 16, pp. 211–38.

Books, J.W. and C.L. Prysby (1994) *Political behaviour and the local context*. New York: Praeger.

Bookstaber, R. (2007) *A Demon of Our Own Design: Markets, Hedge Funds, and the Perils of Financial Innovation*. Hoboken, NJ: J. Wiley and Sons.

Bookstaber, R. (2008) 'Testimony of Richard Bookstaber: Submitted to the Senate of the United States, Senate Banking, Housing and Urban Affairs Subcommittee on Securities, Insurance and Investment for the Hearing: "Risk Management and Its Implications for Systemic Risk", 19 June'. Mimeo.

Börzel, T.A. (2001) 'Non-Compliance in the European Union: Pathology or Statistical Artefact?' *Journal of European Public Policy*, 8(5) pp. 803–24.

Börzel, T.A. (2002) *States and Regions in the European Union. Institutional Adaptation in Germany and Spain*. Cambridge: Cambridge University Press.

Bourne, A.K. (2003) 'The Impact of European Integration on Regional Power', *Journal of Common Market Studies*, 41(4), pp. 597–620.

Bowler, S. and D. Farrell (1992) *Electoral Strategies and Political Marketing*. Basingstoke, UK: Macmillan.

Boyer, R. (1986) *La Théorie de la Régulation: Une Analyse Critique*. Paris: Editions La Découverte.

BP (2010), *BP Statistical Review of World Energy*, June.

Brender, A. and F. Pisani (2009) *Globalized Finance and Its Collapse*. Belgium: Dexia Asset Management.

Brenner, N. (2004) 'Urban Governance and the Production of New State Spaces in Western Europe, 1960–2000', *Review of International Political Economy*, 11(3), pp. 447–88.

Brookings (2010) *Iraq Index. Tracking Reconstruction and Security in Post-Saddam Iraq*, available at: www.brookings.edu/iraqindex (accessed: 17/09/10).

Broughton, D. and H.M. ten Napel (2000) *Religion and Mass Electoral Behaviour in Europe*. London: Routledge.

Brown, D. (2010) *The European Union, Counter Terrorism and Police Co-operation, 1992–2007: Unsteady Foundations?* Manchester: Manchester University Press.

Bukowski J., P. Simona and M. Smyrl (eds) (2003) *Between Global Economy and Local Society: Political Actors and Territorial Governance*. Lanham: MD Rowman & Littlefield.

Bulmer, S. and M. Burch (2009) *The Europeanisation of Whitehall: UK Central Government and the European Union*. Manchester: Manchester University Press.

Burleigh, M. (2005) *Sacred Causes. Religion and Politics in Europe from the Enlightenment to the Great War*. London: Harper.

Burleigh, M. (2006) *Earthly Powers: Religion and Politics from the European Dictators to Al Qaeda*. London: Harper.

Burns, N., K. Lehman Schlozman and S. Verba (2001) *The Private Roots of Public Action*. Cambridge, MA: Harvard University Press.

Byrnes, T. and P.J, Katzenstein (eds) (2006) *Religion in an Expanding Europe*. Cambridge: Cambridge University Press.

Calavita, K. (2005) *Immigrants at the Margins: Law, Race, and Exclusion in Southern Europe*. New York: Cambridge University Press.

Caramani, D. (2004). *The Nationalization of Politics: The Formation of National Electorates and Party Systems in Western Europe*. Cambridge: Cambridge University Press.

Calmfors, L. and J. Driffill (1988) 'Centralization of Wage Bargaining', *Economic Policy*, 6, pp. 13–61.

CARIM (2005) *Mediterranean Migration 2005 Report*. P. Fargues (ed.) Florence: European University Institute.

Carr, C. (1996/1997) 'Terrorism and Warfare. The Lesson of Military History', *World Policy Journal*, 13(4), pp. 1–12.

Carter, C. and R. Pasquier (2010a) 'Studying Regions as spaces for 'politics: rethinking territory and strategic action', *Regional and Federal Studies*, 20(3), pp. 281–94.

Carter, C. and R. Pasquier (2010b), 'Europeanization of Regions as Spaces for Politics: A New Research Agenda', *Regional and Federal Studies*, 20(3), pp. 295–314.

Casanova, J (1994) *Public Religions in the Modern World*. Chicago: University of Chicago Press.

Castiglione, D., J.W. van Deth and G. Wolleb (2009) *The Handbook of Social Capital*. Oxford: Oxford University Press.

Castles, F.G. (2004) *The Future of the Welfare State: Crisis Myths and Crisis Realities*. Oxford: Oxford University Press.

Castles, F.G. (2006) 'The Welfare State and Democracy: On the Development of Social Security in Southern Europe, 1960–1990', in R. Gunther, P.N. Diamandouros and D.A. Sptiropoulos (eds), *Democracy and the State in the New Southern Europe*. Oxford: Oxford University Press, pp. 42–86.

Castles, F.G., S. Leibfried, J. Lewis, H. Obinger and C. Pierson (eds) (2010) *The Oxford Handbook of the Welfare State*. Oxford: Oxford University Press.

Catterberg, G. and A. Moreno (2006) 'The Individual Bases of Political Trust: Trends in New and Established Democracies', *International Journal of Public Opinion Research*, 18(1), pp. 31–48.

Caul, M.L. and M.M. Gray (2000) 'From Platform Declarations to Policy Outcomes: Changing Party Profiles and Partisan Influence over Policy', in R.S. Dalton and M.P. Wattenberg (eds), *Parties Without Partisans: Political Change in Advanced Industrial Democracies* Oxford: Oxford University Press, pp. 208–37.

Cerami, A. (2010) 'The Politics of Social Security Reform in the Czech Republic, Hungary, Poland and Slovakia', in B. Palier (ed.) *A Long Goodbye to Bismarck? The Politics of Welfare Reform in Continental Europe*, Amsterdam: Amsterdam University Press, pp. 233–253.

Chalk, P. (1996) *West European Terrorism and Counter-Terrorism – The Evolving Dynamic*. Basingstoke, UK: Macmillan Press.

Chalk, P. and W. Rosenau (2004) *Confronting the 'Enemy Within'. Security Intelligence, the Police, and Counterterrorism in Four Democracies*. Santa Monica: RAND.

Checchi, A., A. Behrens and C. Egenhofer (2009) 'Long-Term Energy Security Risks for Europe: A Sector-Specific Approach', *CEPS Working Document*. no. 309, January.

Citrin, J. and J. Sides (2007) 'European Opinion about Immigration', *British Journal of Political Science*, 37(3), pp. 477–504.

Clarke, H., D. Sanders, M.C. Stewart, and P. Whiteley (2004) *Political Choice in Britain*. Oxford: Oxford University Press.

Clasen, J. (2005) *Reforming European Welfare States: Germany and the United Kingdom Compared*. Oxford: Oxford University Press.

Coen, D. and M. Thatcher (2005) 'The New Governance of Markets and Non-Majoritarian Regimes', *Governance: An International Journal of Policy, Administration and Institutions*, 18(3), pp. 329–46.

Cohen, A. and A. Vauchez (eds) (2007) *La Constitution Européenne: Elites, Mobilisations, Votes*. Brussels: Presses de l'Université de Bruxelles, pp. 113–27.

Cole Durham, W. (1996) 'Perspectives in Religious Liberty: A Comparative Framework', in J.D. van der Vyver and J. Witte (eds), *Religious Human Rights in Global Perspective*.

Cole, A. (2006) *Beyond Devolution and Decentralisation. Building Regional Capacity in Wales and Brittany*. Manchester: Manchester University Press.

Coleman, J.S. (1990) *Foundations of Social Theory*. Cambridge, MA: Harvard University Press.

Collett, E. (2008) 'The proposed European Blue Card system: arming for the global war for talent?', Retrieved from the website of the *Migration Policy Institute*, Washington, DC.

Conway, M.M. (2000) *Political Participation in the United States*, 3rd edn. Washington, DC: CQ Press.

Cook, L.J. (2010) 'Eastern Europe and Russia', in F.G. Castles, S. Leibfried, J. Lewis, H. Obinger and C. Pierson (eds), *The Oxford Handbook of the Welfare State*. Oxford: Oxford University Press, pp. 671–86.

Cooper, G. (2008). *The Origin of Financial Crises: Central Banks, Credit Bubbles and the Efficient Market Fallacy*. Petersfield, Hampshire, UK: Harriman House Ltd.

Cooper, R.N. (1968) *The Economics of Interdependence: Economic Policy in the Atlantic Community*. New York: McGraw-Hill for the Council on Foreign Relations.

Cornelius, W., T. Tsuda, P. Martin, and J. Hollifield (eds) (2004) *Controlling Immigration: A Global Perspective*, 2nd edn. Stanford: Stanford University Press.

Costa Lobo, M. (2007) 'The Presidentialization of Portuguese Democracy?', in Poguntke and Webb (eds), *The Presidentialization of Politics. A Comparative Study of Modern Democracies*, pp. 269–88.

Cottey, A. (2009) 'The Kosovo War in Perspective', *International Affairs*, 85(3), pp. 593–608.

Council of the European Union (2008) *European Pact on Immigration and Asylum*. Brussels: DG H 1B, 13440/08.

Cowles, M.G., J.A. Caporaso and T. Risse (eds) (2001) *Transforming Europe: Europeanization and Domestic Change*. Ithaca, NY: Cornell University Press.

Crouch, C. (2005) *Capitalist Diversity and Change: Recombinant Governance and Institutional Entrepreneurs*. Oxford: Oxford University Press.

Crouch, C., P. Le Galès, C. Trigilia, and H. Voelzkow (eds) (2003) *Local Production Systems in Europe. Rise or Demise?* Oxford: Oxford University Press.

Crown Copyright (2009) *The UK Low Carbon Transition Plan, National Strategy for Climate and Energy*. HM Government, 15 July.

Culpepper, P. (2002) 'Powering, Puzzling and "Pacting": The Informational Logic of Negotiated Reforms', *Journal of European Public Policy*, 9(5), pp. 774–90.

Curtin, D. and M. Egeberg (eds) (2008) 'Towards a New Executive Order in Europe?', special issue of *West European Politics*, 31(4), pp. 639–61.

Daguerre, A. (2006) 'Childcare Policies in Diverse European Welfare States: Switzerland, Sweden, France and Britain', in K. Armingeon and G. Bonoli (eds), *The Politics of Post-Industrial Welfare States: Adapting Post-War Social Policies to New Social Risks*. London: Routledge, pp. 211–26.

Dahl, R.A. (1971) *Polyarchy: Participation and Opposition*. Yale University Press, CT: New Haven.

Dahlgren, P. (2009) *Media and Political Engagement: Citizens, Communication and Democracy*. Cambridge: Cambridge University Press.

Dalton, R.J. (1999) 'Political Support in Advanced Industrial Democracies', in Norris (ed.), *Critical Citizens: Global Support for Democratic Government*, pp. 55–77.

Dalton, R.J. (2000). 'Value Change and Democracy', in S. Pharr and R.D. Putnam (eds), *Disaffected Democracies: What's Troubling the Trilateral Countries?* Princeton, NJ: Princeton University Press, pp. 252–69.

Dalton, R.J. (2004) *Democratic Challenges, Democratic Choices: The Erosion of Political Support in Advanced Industrial Democracies.* Oxford: Oxford University Press.

Dalton, R.J. (2008) *The Good Citizen: How a Younger Generation is Reshaping American Politics.* Washington, DC: CQ Press.

Dalton, R.J. and H.-D. Klingemann (eds) (2009) *The Oxford Handbook of Political Behavior.* New York: Oxford University Press.

Dalton, R.J. and M. Wattenberg (2002) *Parties without Partisans: Political Change in Advanced Industrial Democracies.* Oxford: Oxford University Press.

Damgaard, B. and J. Torfing (2010) 'Network Governance of Active Employment Policy: The Danish Experience', *Journal of European Social Policy*, 20(3), pp. 248–62.

Das, S. (2006) *Traders, Guns, and Money: Knowns and Unknowns in the Dazzling World of Derivatives.* London: FT Prentice Hall.

Davie, G. (2002) *Europe: The Exceptional Case.* London: Darton, Longman, Todd.

de Beer, P. and T. Schils (eds) (2009) *The Labour Market Triangle: Employment Protection, Unemployment Compensation and Activation in Europe.* Cheltenham: Edward Elgar.

de Giorgi, E. (2010) 'Gli equilibri della coalizione di governo', in M. Giuliani and E. Jones (eds), *Politica in Italia 2010.* Bologna: Il Mulino, pp. 137–57.

de Hart, B. (2006) 'Introduction: The Marriage of Convenience in European Immigration Law', *European Journal of Migration and Law*, 8, pp. 251–62.

de Schoutheete, P. (1980) *La Coopération Politique Européenne.* Brussels: Editions Labor.

de Vreese, C. (2005) 'The Spiral of Cynicism Reconsidered', *European Journal of Communication*, 20(3), pp. 283–301.

Delbeke, J (2006) (ed.) *The EU Greenhouse Gas Emissions Trading Scheme. EU Energy Law*, vol. IV. Leuven: Clays & Casteels.

Delhey, J. and K. Newton (2003) 'Who trusts? The Origins of Social Trust in Seven Societies', *European Societies*, 5(2), pp. 93–137.

Delhey, J. and K. Newton (2005) 'Predicting Cross-National Levels of Social Trust: Global Pattern or Nordic Exceptionalism?', *European Sociological Review*, 21(4), pp. 311–27.

Della Porta, D. (2000) 'Social Capital, Beliefs in Government, and Political Corruption', in S.J. Pharr and R.D. Putnam (eds), *Disaffected Democracies: What's Troubling the Trilateral Countries?* Princeton, NJ: Princeton University Press.

Detterbeck, K. (2005) 'Cartel Parties in Western Europe?', *Party Politics*, 11(2), pp. 173–91.

Dimitrov, V., K.H. Goetz and H. Wollmann (2006) *Governing after Communism. Institutions and Policymaking.* Lanham, MD: Rowman & Littlefield.

Dimitrova, A. and B. Steunenberg (2000) 'The Search for Convergence of National Policies in the European Union: An Impossible Quest?', *European Union Politics*, 1(2) pp. 201–26.

Dimitrova, A. and D. Toshkov (2009) 'Post-Accession Compliance between Administrative Co-ordination and Political Bargaining', *European Integration online Papers*, 13(2).

Dingeldey, I. (2007) 'Between Workfare and Enablement. The Different Paths to Transformation of the Welfare State: A Comparative Analysis of Activating Labour Market Policies', *European Journal of Political Research*, 46, pp. 823–51.

Dodd, V. and C. Bailey (2006) 'Terror law an affront to justice – judge', *The Guardian*, 13 April. Available at: www.guardian.co.uk/politics/2006/apr/13/humanrights.terrorism (accessed 17.09.10).

Dolowitz, D. and D. Marsh (2000) 'Who Learns What from Whom: a Review of the Policy Transfer Literature', *Political Studies*, 44(2), pp. 343–57.

Donohue, L. (2008) *The Cost of Counterterrorism: Power, Politics, and Liberty*. Cambridge: Cambridge University Press.

Döring, H. (1995) (ed.) *Parliaments and Majority Rule in Western Europe*. Frankfurt/New York: Nomos.

Döring, H. and C. Hönnige (2008) 'Parlament, Regierung, Staatsoberhaupt', in O.W. Gabriel and S. Kropp (eds), *Die EU-Staaten im Vergleich. Strukturen, Prozesse, Politikinhalte*, 3rd edn. Wiesbaden: VS-Verlag, pp. 451–81.

Dorman, A. (2003) 'Loyal Ally. The United Kingdom', in M. Buckley and R. Fawn (eds), *Global Responses to Terrorism. 9/11, Afghanistan and Beyond*. London: Routledge, pp. 66–78.

Downs, A. (1957) *An Economic Theory of Democracy*. New York: Harper & Row.

Duverger, M. (1980) 'A New Political System Model: Semi-Presidential Government', *European Journal of Political Research*, 8, pp. 165–87.

Dyson, K. (ed.) (2006) *Enlarging the Euro Area: External Empowerment and Domestic Transformation in East Central Europe*. Oxford: Oxford University Press.

Dyson, K. (ed.) (2008) *The Euro at 10: Europeanization, Power, and Convergence*. Oxford: Oxford University Press.

Eberlein, B. and E. Grande (2005) 'Beyond Delegation: Transnational Regulatory Regimes and the EU Regulatory State', *Journal of European Public Policy*, 12(1), pp. 89–112.

Eckers, C. (2010) *EU Counter-Terrorist Policies and Fundamental Rights: The Case of Individual Sanctions*. Oxford: Oxford University Press.

Eckstein, H. (1961) *A Theory of Stable Democracy*. Princeton, NJ: Princeton University Press.

Egeberg, M. (2008) 'European Government(s): Executive Politics in Transition?', *West European Politics*, 31, pp. 1–2, 235–57.

Egeberg, M. (ed.) (2006) *Multilevel Union Administration – The Transformation of Executive Politics in Europe*. Basingstoke, UK: Palgrave Macmillan.

Egenhofer, C. (2003) 'The Compatibility of the Kyoto Mechanisms with Traditional Environmental Instruments', in C. Carraro and C. Egenhofer (eds), *Firms, Governments and Climate Policy: Incentive-Based Policies for Long-Term Climate Change*. Cheltenham: Edward Elgar, pp. 17–57.

Egenhofer, C. (2007) 'The Making of the EU Emissions Trading Scheme: Status, Prospects and Implications for Business', *European Management Journal*, 25(6), pp. 453–63.

Egenhofer, C. (2009) 'The New EU Emissions Trading Scheme: A Blueprint for the Global Carbon Market?', in J. Harris and N. Goodwin (eds), *21st Century Macroeconomics: Responding to the Climate Challenge*. Cheltenham UK and Northampton MA: Edward Elgar Publishing, pp. 246–63.

Egenhofer, C. *et al.* (2004) 'Market-Based Options for Security of Energy Supply', *Fondazione Eni Enrico Mattei Working Paper* 117.04.

Egenhofer, C., A. Behrens and A. Georgiev (2010), 'EU Strategies for Climate Change Policy beyond 2012', in H.G. Brauch, U. Oswald Spring, P. Kameri-Mbote, C. Mesjasz, J. Grin, B. Chourou, P. Dunay and J. Birkmann (eds.), *Coping with Global Environmental Change, Disasters and Security: Threats, Challenges, Vulnerabilities and Risks, Hexagon Series on Human and Environmental Security and Peace*, vol. 3. Berlin: Springer, pp. 1319–32.

Eisenstadt, S. (2008) 'The Transformation of the Religious Dimension and the Crystallisation of New Civilisational Visions and Relations', in G. Motzkin and Y. Fischer (eds), *Religion and Democracy in Contemporary Europe*.

Elff, M. (2007) 'Social Structure and Electoral Behavior in Comparative Perspective: The Decline of Social Cleavages in Western Europe Revisited', *Perspectives on Politics*, 5(2), pp. 277–94.

Elgie, R. (1999) 'France', in R. Elgie (ed.) *Semi-Presidentialism in Europe*. Oxford: Oxford University Press, pp. 67–85.

Elgie, R. (2009) 'Duverger, Semi-presidentialism and the Supposed French Archetype', *West European Politics*, 32(2), pp. 248–67.

Elias, A. (2008) 'Introduction: Whatever Happened to the Europe of the Regions? Revisiting the Regional Dimension of European Politics', *Regional and Federal Studies*, 18(5), pp. 483–92.

Ellerman, D., F. Convery and C. de Perthuis (2010) *Pricing Carbon*. Cambridge, Cambridge University Press.

Enyedi, Z. (2008) 'The Social and Attitudinal Basis of Political Parties: Cleavage Politics Revisited', *European Review*, 16, pp. 287–304.

Enyedi, Z., and G. Tóka (2007). 'The Only Game in Town: Party Politics in Hungary', in Webb and White (eds), *Party Politics in New Democracies*, pp. 147–78.

Epstein, R.A. (2008) *In Pursuit of Liberalism: International Institutions in Postcommunist Europe*. Baltimore, MD: Johns Hopkins University Press.

Epstein, R.A. and U. Sedelmeier (2008) 'Beyond Conditionality: International Institutions in Postcommunist Europe after Enlargement', *Journal of European Public Policy*, 15(6) pp. 795–805.

Esping-Andersen, G. (1990) *The Three Worlds of Welfare Capitalism*. Cambridge: Polity Press.

Esping-Andersen, G. (2009) *The Incomplete Revolution: Adapting to Women's New Roles*. Cambridge: Polity.

Esping-Andersen, G. and M. Regini (eds), *Why Deregulate Labour Markets?* Oxford: Oxford University Press.

Esping-Andersen, G. *et al.* (2002) *Why We Need a New Welfare State.* Oxford: Oxford University Press.

Eurobarometer (2008) *The 2009 European Elections.* Special Eurobarometer. F/w March–May 2008. Brussels: European Commission. http://ec.europa.eu/public_opinion/archives/ebs/ebs_299_en.pdf

European Commission (1995) 'An Energy Policy for the European Union', Communication from the Commission to the European Council and the European Parliament. COM(95) 682.

European Commission (2000) 'Towards a European Strategy for the Securing of Energy Supply', Communication from the Commission to the European Council and the European Parliament. COM(2000) 769.

European Commission (2005a) *Green Paper on an EU Approach to Managing Economic Migration.* Brussels: COM (2004) 811 final.

European Commission (2005b) *Policy Plan on Legal Migration.* Brussels: COM (2005) 669 final.

European Commission (2007) *Proposal for a Council Directive on the Conditions of Entry and Residence of Third-Country Nationals for the Purposes of Highly Qualified Employment.* Brussels: COM (2007) 637 final.

European Commission (2007a) 'An Energy Policy for Europe', Communication from the Commission to the European Council and the European Parliament. COM (2007) 1 final, 10 January.

European Commission (2007b) 'Limiting Global Climate Change to 2°C – The Way Ahead for 2020 and Beyond', Communication from the Commission to the European Council and the European Parliament. COM(2007) 2 final, 10 January.

European Commission (2008a) 'Impact Assessment – Accompanying Document for amending Directive 2003/87/EC so as to improve and extend the EU greenhouse gas emission allowance trading system', *Commission Staff Working Document.* SEC (2008) 52, 21 January.

European Commission (2008b) 'Impact Assessment – Accompanying document for package of implementation measures for the EU's objective on climate change and renewable energy for 20', *Commission Staff Working Document.*

European Commission (2008c) 'Eurobarometer 70 – Public Opinion in the European Union', *Standard Eurobarometer 70.* December.

European Commission (2009) *Eurobarometer 72.2: Attitudes of Europeans towards corruption.* Available at http://ec.europa.eu/public_opinion/archives/eb_special_en.htm (accessed 25 January 2010).

European Commission (2010) 'EU Energy and Transport in Figures', *Statistical Pocketbook 2010.*

Eurostat (2009–10) *Population and Social Conditions,* Statistics in Focus.

Evans G. and S. Whitefield (2000) 'Explaining the Formation of Electoral Cleavages in Post-Communist Democracies', in H. Klingemann, E. Mochmann, K. Newton (eds), *Elections in Central and Eastern Europe: The First Wave.* Berlin: Sigma, pp. 36–68.

Evans, C. (2001) *Freedom of Religion under the European Convention of Human Rights.* Oxford: Oxford University Press.

Evans, G. (2006) 'The Social Bases of Political Divisions in Post-Communist Eastern Europe', *Annual Review of Sociology*, 32, pp. 245–70.

Falkner, G. and O. Treib (2008) 'Three Worlds of Compliance or Four? The EU-15 Compared to New Member States', *Journal of Common Market Studies*, 46(2) pp. 293–313.

Fallaci, O. (2002) *The Rage and the Pride*. New York: Rizzoli.

Faria, Joao R. (2006) 'Terrorist Innovation and Anti-Terrorist Policies', *Terrorism and Political Violence*, 18(1): 47–56.

Farkasová, M. (2007) 'More Slovak Troops Heading to Kosovo and Afghanistan', *Slovak Armed Forces*, 2, p. 13, available at: www.mod.gov.sk/267/slovakia-in-nato-/-slovak-armed-forces.php?mnu=201&PHPSESSID=7ed8eb33e0ed7b189d922cb4fce354c5 (accessed 17.09.10).

Farrell, B. (1971) *Chairman or Chief? The Role of the Taoiseach in Irish Government*. Dublin: Gill & Macmillan.

Farrell, D. and P. Webb (2000) 'Parties as Campaign Organizations', in R. Dalton and M.P. Wattenberg (eds), *Parties Without Partisans: Political Change in Advanced Industrial Democracies*. Oxford: Oxford University Press, pp. 102–28.

Featherstone, K., and C. Radaelli (eds) (2003) *The Politics of Europeanization*. Oxford, Oxford University Press.

Federal Constitutional Court (2009) 'Press Release No. 72/2009 of 30 June 2009. Judgment of 30 June 2009 – 2VvE 2/08, 2 be 5/08, 2BvR 1010/08, 2 BvR 1259/08 and 21 BvR 182/09,' www.bverfg.de/en/press/bvg09–072en.html (accessed: 10/08/09).

Feldman, M. (2007) 'The Origins of Varieties of Capitalism: Lessons from Post-socialist Transition in Estonia and Slovenia', in Hancké *et al.*, *Beyond Varieties of Capitalism: Conflict, Contradictions and Complementarities in the European Economy*, pp. 122–45.

Ferrari, S. (1999) 'The New Wine and the Old Cask: Tolerance, Religion, and the Law in Contemporary Europe', in A. Sajo and S. Avineri (eds), *The Law of Religious Identity: Models for Post-Communism*, pp. 1–15.

Ferrari, S. (2003) 'Church and State in Post-communist Europe', in S. Ferrari, W. Cole Durham and E. Sewell (eds), *Law and Religion in Post-Communist Europe*, pp. 411–30.

Ferrari, S. (2008) 'State Regulation of Religion in The European Democracies: The Decline of the Old Pattern', in G. Motzkin and Y. Fischer (eds), *Religion and Democracy in Contemporary Europe*.

Ferrari, S., W. Cole Durham and E. Sewell (eds) (2003) *Law and Religion in Post-Communist Europe*. Leuven Uitgeverij: Peeters.

Ferrera, M. (1996) 'The Southern Model of Welfare in Social Europe', *Journal of European Social Policy*, 6(1), pp. 17–37.

Ferrera, M. and E. Gualmini (2004) *Rescued by Europe? Social and Labour Market Reforms in Italy from Maastricht to Berlusconi*. Amsterdam: Amsterdam University Press.

Ferrera, M., A. Hemerijck and M. Rhodes (2000) *The Future of Social Europe: Recasting Work and Welfare in the New Economy*. Lisbon: CELTA/Ministério do Trabalho e da Solidariedade.

Fetzer, J.S. and J.C. Soper (2005) *Muslims and the State in Britain, France and Germany.* Cambridge: Cambridge University Press.

Fiers, S. and A. Krouwel (2007) 'The Low Countries: From 'Prime Minister' to President-Minister', in Poguntke and Webb (eds), *The Presidentialization of Politics: A Comparative Study Modern Democracies,* pp. 128–58.

Fleurke, F., R. Willemse (2006) 'The European Union and the Autonomy of Sub-National Authorities: Towards an Analysis of Constraints and Opportunities in Sub-national Decision-making', *Regional and Federal Studies,*16(1), pp. 83–98.

Foley, M. (2000) *The British Presidency: Tony Blair and the Politics of Public Leadership.* Manchester: Manchester University Press.

Forlong, R. (1999) 'Slovak Secrete Service accused of kidnap', *BBC News,*01.02.1999, available at: http://news.bbc.co.uk/2/hi/europe/270052. stm (accessed: 17/09/10).

Fox, J. (2008) *A World Survey of Religion and the State.* Cambridge: Cambridge University Press.

Fox, J. and F. Godement (2009) *A Power-Audit of EU–China Relations.* London: European Council on Foreign Relations.

Franklin, M.N. (2004) *Voter Turnout and the Dynamics of Electoral Competition in Established Democracies Since 1945.* Cambridge: Cambridge University Press.

Franklin, M.N., T. Mackie and H. Valen (1992) *Electoral Change: Responses to Evolving Attitudinal and Social Structures in Western Countries.* Cambridge: Cambridge University Press.

Franz, M. (2006) 'Familienzusammenführung in der Einwanderungspolitik der Europäischen Union', *IMIS-Beiträge* (Osnabrück), pp. 45–68.

Freeman, G. (1995) 'Modes of Immigration Politics in Liberal Democratic States', *International Migration Review,* 29(4), pp. 881–902.

Freud, D. (2007) 'Reducing Dependency, Increasing Opportunity: Options for the Future of Welfare to Work', *Department for Work and Pensions.* London: Her Majesty's Stationery Office.

Freyburg, T., S. Lavenex, F. Schimmelfennig, T. Skripka and A. Wetzel (2009) 'EU Promotion of Democratic Governance in the Neighbourhood', *Journal of European Public Policy,* 16(6) pp. 916–34.

Frieden, J.A. and R. Rogowski (1996) 'The Impact of the International Economy on National Policies: An Analytical Overview', in R.O. Keohane and H.V. Milner (eds), *Internationalization and Domestic Politics.* Cambridge: Cambridge University Press, pp. 25–47.

Gabriel, O.W. and M. Walter-Rogg (2008) 'Social capital and political trust', in H. Meulemann (ed.) *Social Capital in Europe: Similarity of Countries and Diversity of People? Multi-level Analyses of the European Social Survey 2002.* Boston, MA: Brill.

Gallagher, M. (1991) 'Proportionality, Disproportionality and Electoral Systems', *Electoral Studies.* 10(1), pp. 33–51.

Gallagher, M. and P. Mitchell (eds) (2005) *The Politics of Electoral Systems.* Oxford: Oxford University Press.

Gallie D. (ed.) (2004) *Resisting Marginalization: Unemployment Experience and Social Policy in the European Union*. Oxford: Oxford University Press.

Gamble, A. (2009) *The Spectre at the Feast: Capitalist Crisis and the Politics of Recession*. Basingstoke, UK: Palgrave.

Gastil, J. and P. Levine (eds) (2005) *The Deliberative Democracy Handbook: Strategies for Effective Civic Engagement in the Twenty-First Century*. New York: Jossey Bass.

Gearty, C. (1997) *The Future of Terrorism*. London: Phoenix.

Gijsberts, M., and P. Nieuwbeerta (2000). 'Class Cleavages in Party Preferences in the New Democracies in Eastern Europe: A Comparison with Western Democracies', *European Societies*, 2(4), pp. 397–430.

Goerres, A. (2009) *The Political Participation of Older People in Europe: The Greying of our Democracies*. Basingstoke, UK: Palgrave Macmillan.

Goetz, K.H. (2000) 'European Integration and National Executives: A Cause in Search of an Effect?', *West European Politics*, 23(4), pp. 211–31.

Goetz, K.H. (2002) 'Europeanisation in West and East: a challenge to institutional theory', paper presented at ECPR conference on EU Politics, Bordeaux; 26–8 September 2002.

Goetz, K.H. (2006) 'Power at the Centre: The Organization of Democratic Systems', in P.M. Heywood, E. Jones, M. Rhodes and U. Sedelmeier (eds), *Developments in European Politics*. Basingstoke, UK: Palgrave Macmillan, pp. 73–96.

Goldsmith, M. (1993) 'The Europeanization of local government', *Urban Studies*, 30(4/5), pp. 683–99.

Goodin, R. and A. Reeve (eds) (1989) *Liberal Neutrality*. London: Routledge.

Gourevitch, P. and M. Hawes, M. B. (2002) 'The Politics of Choice among National Production Systems', in R. Boyer (ed.), *L'Année de la regulation. No. 6*, Paris: Presses de Sciences Po, pp. 241–70.

Goyer, M. (2007). 'Capital Mobility, Varieties of Institutional Investors, and the Transforming Stability of Corporate Governance in France and Germany', in Hancke *et al.* (eds), *Beyond Varieties of Capitalism: Conflict, Contradictions, and Complementarities in the European Economy*, pp. 195–220.

Grabbe, H. (2001) 'How does Europeanization affect CEE governance? Conditionality, Diffusion and Diversity', *Journal of European Public Policy*, 8(6), pp. 1013–31.

Grabbe, H. (2005) 'Regulating the Flow of People across Europe', in Schimmelfennig and Sedelmeier (eds), *The Europeanization of Central and Eastern Europe*, pp. 71–134.

Grabbe, H. (2006) *The EU's Transformative Power: Europeanization through Conditionality in Central and Eastern Europe*. Basingstoke, UK: Palgrave.

Grabbe, H. and U. Sedelmeier (2009) 'The Future Shape of the European Union', in M. Egan, N. Nugent and W. Paterson (eds), *Research Agendas in EU Studies*. Basingstoke, UK: Palgrave, pp. 375–97.

Graham, B. (1993) *Representation and Party Politics: A Comparative Perspective*. Oxford: Blackwell.

Grande, E. (2000) 'Multi-Level Governance: Institutionelle Besonderheiten und Funktionsbedingungen des europäischen Mehrebenensystems', in E. Grande and M. Jachtenfuchs (eds), *Wie problemlösungsfähig ist die EU? Regieren im europäischen Mehrebenensystem*. Baden-Baden: Nomos, pp. 11–30.

Graziano, P., and M. Vink (eds) (2007) *Europeanization: New Research Agendas*. Basingstoke, UK: Palgrave.

Green-Pedersen, C. (2007) 'Denmark: A "World Bank" Pension System', in E.M. Immergut, K.M. Anderson and I. Schulze (eds), *The Handbook of West European Pension Politics*. Oxford: Oxford University Press, pp. 454–95.

Greenspan, A. (2008) 'Testimony of Dr Alan Greenspan, Committee of Government Oversight and Reform, October 23, 2008'. Mimeo.

Greider, W. (1998) *One World, Ready or Not: The Manic Logic of Global Capitalism*. New York: Simon & Schuster.

Greskovits, B. (2005) 'Leading Sectors and the Varieties of Capitalism in Eastern Europe', *Actes de Gerpis*, 39, pp. 13–128.

Groenendijk, K. (2006) 'Family Reunification as a Right under Community Law', *European Journal of Migration and Law*, 8, pp. 215–30.

Grönlund, K. and M. Setälä (2007) 'Political Trust, Satisfaction and Voter Turnout', *Comparative European Politics*, 5(4), pp. 400–22.

Gualmini, E. (1998) *La politica del lavoro*. Bologna, Il Mulino.

Gualmini, E., and V. Schmidt (2010). 'The role of state leadership and policy ideas in state-influenced economies: differential responses in Italy and France.' Manuscript. Department of Political Science, University of Bologna.

Gunther, R., P. Nikiforos Diamandouros and H. Puhle (eds) (1995) *The Politics of Democratic Consolidation: Southern Europe in Comparative Perspective*. Baltimore, MD: Johns Hopkins University Press.

Gutmann, A. and D. Thomson (2004) *Why Deliberative Democracy?* Princeton, NJ: Princeton University Press.

Habermas, J. (1991) *The Structural Transformation of the Public Sphere*. Cambridge, MA: MIT Press.

Hacker, B. (2009) 'Hybridization instead of Clustering: Transformation Processes of Welfare Policies in Central and Eastern Europe', *Social Policy & Administration*, 43(2), pp. 152–69.

Hall, P.A. (2002) 'Great Britain: The role of government and the distribution of social capital', in R.D. Putnam (ed.), *Democracies in Flux: The Evolution of Social Capital in Contemporary Society*. Oxford: Oxford University Press, pp. 21–58.

Hall, P.A. (2007) 'The Evolution of Varieties of Capitalism in Europe', in Hancké *et al.*, *Beyond Varieties of Capitalism: Conflict, Contradiction and Complementarities in the European Economy*, pp. 39–87

Hall, P.A. and D. Gingerich (2004) 'Varieties of Capitalism and Institutional Complementarities in the Macroeconomy: An Empirical Analysis', Cologne: Max-Planck-Institut für Gesellschaftsforschung, Discussion paper 04/5.

Hall, P.A. and D. Soskice (2001) 'An Introduction to Varieties of Capitalism', in P.A. Hall and D. Soskice (eds), *Varieties of Capitalism: The Institutional Foundations of Comparative Advantage*. Oxford: Oxford University Press, pp. 1–68.

Hall, P.A. and K. Thelen (2009) 'Institutional Change in Varieties of Capitalism', *Socio-Economic Review*, 7(1), pp. 7–34.

Hall, P.A. and R. Franzese Jr. (1998) 'Mixed Signals: Central Bank Independence, Coordinated Wage Bargaining, and European Monetary Union', *International Organization*, 52(3), pp. 505–35.

Hancké, B. (2009). *Debating Varieties of Capitalism: A Reader*. Oxford: Oxford University Press.

Hancké, B. and A. Herrmann (2007) 'Wage Bargaining and Comparative Advantage in EMU', in Hancké, *et al.* (eds), *Beyond Varieties of Capitalism: Conflict, Contradictions and Complementarities in the European Economy*, pp. 122–47.

Hancké, B. and L. Kurekova (2008) *Varieties of Capitalism and Economic Governance in Central Europe*. Final report for Project CIT1–CT-2004–506392 (NewGov STACEE), September 2008. www.eu-newgov.org/database/DELIV/D20D09_Final_Report_STACEE.pdf

Hancké, B. and M. Rhodes (2005) 'EMU and Labor Market Institutions in Europe: The Rise and Fall of National Social Pacts', in *Work and Occupations*, 32(2), May 2005, pp. 196–228.

Hancké, B., M. Rhodes, and M. Thatcher (eds) (2007). *Beyond Varieties of Capitalism: Conflict, Contradictions and Complementarities in the European Economy*. Oxford: Oxford University Press.

Hardie, I. and D. Howarth (2009) '*Die Krise* but not *La Crise*? The Financial Crisis and the Transformation of German and French Banking Systems', *JCMS*, 47(5) (November) pp. 1017–39.

Hassel, A. (2006) *Wage Setting, Social Pacts and the Euro: A New Role for the State*. Amsterdam: Amsterdam University Press.

Hassel, A. (2007) 'What Does Business Want? Labour Market Reforms in CMEs and Its Problems', in Hancké *et al.* (eds), *Beyond Varieties of Capitalism: Conflict, Contradictions and Complementarities in the European Economy*, pp. 253–77.

Hay, C. (2007) *Why We Hate Politics*. Cambridge: Polity.

Haynes, J. (ed.) (2009) *Religion and Politics in Europe, the Middle East and North Africa*. London: Routledge.

Heffernan, R. and P. Webb (2005) 'The British Prime Minister: Much More than "First Among Equals"', in Poguntke and Webb (eds), *The Presidentialization of Politics: A Comparative Study Modern Democracies*, pp. 26–62.

Heinisch, R. (2003) 'Success in Opposition – Failure in Government: Exploring the Performance of the Austrian Freedom Party and other European Right-wing Populist Parties in Public Office', *West European Politics*, 26, pp. 91–130.

Helleiner, E. (1994) *States and the Reemergence of Global Finance*. Ithaca, NY: Cornell University Press.

Hemerijck, A., M. Keune and M. Rhodes (2006) 'European Welfare States: Diversity, Challenges and Reforms', in Heywood *et al.* (eds), *Developments in European Politics*, pp. 259–79.

Héritier, A., D. Kerwer, C. Knill, D. Lehmkuhl, M. Teutsch and A.C. Douillet (2001) *Differential Europe: The European Union Impact on National Policymaking*. Lanham, MD: Rowman & Littlefield.

Heymann, P.B. (2001/2002) 'Dealing with Terrorism – An Overview', *International Security*, 26(3), pp. 24–38.

Heywood, P.M., E. Jones, M. Rhodes and U. Sedelmeier (eds) (2006) *Developments in European Politics*. Basingstoke: Palgrave.

Heywood, P.M., and I. Krastev (2006). 'Political Scandals and Corruption', in Heywood *et al. Developments in European Politics*, pp. 155–77.

Hibbing, J. and E. Theiss-Morse (2002) *Stealth Democracy: Americans' Beliefs About How Government Should Work*. Cambridge: Cambridge University Press.

Hicks, A. and L. Kenworthy (2003) 'Varieties of Welfare Capitalism', *Socio-Economic Review*, 1, 27–61.

Hill, C. (1993) 'The Capability–Expectations Gap, or Conceptualizing Europe's International Role', *Journal of Common Market Studies*, 31(3), pp. 305–28.

Hill, C. (1996) *The Actors in Europe's Foreign Policy*. London: Routledge.

Hill, C. (1998) 'Convergence, Divergence and Dialectics: National Foreign Policies and the CFSP', in J. Zielonka (ed.), *Paradoxes of European Foreign Policy*. The Hague: Kluwer Law International, pp. 35–52.

Hill, C. (2003) *The Changing Politics of Foreign Policy*. Basingstoke, UK: Palgrave Macmillan.

Hix, S. (2011) *The Political System of the European Union*, 3rd edn. Basingstoke, UK: Palgrave MacMillan.

Hobsbawm, E.J. (1994) *Age of Extremes: The Short Twentieth Century, 1914–1991*. London: Michael Joseph.

Hocking, B. (2004) 'Diplomacy', in W. Carlsnaes, H. Sjursen and B. White (eds), *Contemporary European Foreign Policy*. London: Sage, pp. 91–109.

Hoffman, B. and J. Morrison-Taw (2000) 'A Strategic Framework for Countering Terrorism', in F. Reinares (ed.) *European Democracies Against Terrorism: Governmental Policies and Intergovernmental Cooperation*. Aldershot: Ashgate, pp. 3–29.

Holslag, J. (2006) 'The European Union and China: the Great Disillusion', *European Foreign Affairs Review*, 11, pp. 555–80.

Home Office (2002) *Secure Borders, Safe Haven*. London: Government Printing Office.

Home Office (2005) *Controlling Our Borders: Making Migration Work for Britain*. London: Government Printing Office.

Home Office (2006) *A Points-Based System: Making Migration Work for Britain*. London: Government Printing Office.

Home Office (2008) *The Path to Citizenship: Next Steps in Reforming the Immigration System*. London: Government Printing Office.

Home Office (2009) *Earning the Right to Stay: A New Points Test for Citizenship*. London: Government Printing Office.

Hood, C. (1991) 'A Public Management for All Seasons?', *Public Administration*, 69(1), pp. 3–19.

Hooghe, L. (ed.) (1996) *Cohesion Policy and European Integration: Building Multi-level Governance*. Oxford: Oxford University Press.

Hooghe, L., and G. Marks (1996). 'Europe with the Regions? Regional Representation in the European Union', *Publius: The Journal of Federalism*, 26(1), pp. 73–91.

Hooghe, L. and G. Marks (2001) *Multi-level Governance and European Integration*. Boulder, CO: Rowman & Littlefield.

Hooghe, M. (2003) 'Voluntary Associations and Democratic Attitudes: Value and Conference as a Causal Mechanism', in M. Hooghe and D. Stolle (eds), *Generating Social Capital: Civil Society and Institutions in Comparative Perspective*. New York: Palgrave Macmillan, pp. 89–112.

Hooghe, M. and D. Stolle (eds) (2003) *Generating Social Capital: Civil Society and Institutions in Comparative Perspective*. New York: Palgrave Macmillan.

Hopkin, J. and C. Paolucci (1999) 'New Parties and the Business Firm Model of Party Organization: Cases from Spain and Italy', *European Journal of Political Research*, 35(3), pp. 307–39.

House of Commons (2008) *Treasury – Fifth Report*. London: House of Commons (24 January). www.publications.parliament.uk/pa/cm200708/cmselect/cmtreasy/56/5602.htm

Howard, M.M. and L. Gilbert (2008) 'A Cross-national Comparison of the Internal Effects of Participation in Voluntary Organizations', *Political Studies*, 56(1), pp. 12–32.

Huckfield, R. and J. Sprague (1995) *Citizens, Politics and Social Communication*. Cambridge: Cambridge University Press.

Hudson, R. (2007) 'Regions and Regional Uneven Development Forever? Some Reflective Comments upon Theory and Practice', *Regional Studies*, 41(9), pp. 1149–60.

Hughes, J., G. Sasse and C. Gordon (2004) *Europeanization and Regionalization in the EU' Enlargement to Central and Eastern Europe: The Myth of Conditionality*. Basingstoke, UK: Palgrave.

Huntington, S. (1996) *The Clash of Civilizations and the Remaking of World Order*. New York: Simon & Schuster.

Huo, J. (2009) *Third Way Reforms: Social Democracy after the Golden Age*. Cambridge: Cambridge University Press.

Hyde-Price, A. (2003) 'Redefining its Security Role. Germany', in M. Buckley and R. Fawn (eds), *Global Responses to Terrorism. 9/11, Afghanistan and Beyond*. London: Routledge, pp. 101–12.

IEA (2007) *World Energy Outlook 2007*. Paris: International Energy Agency.

IEA (2008) *World Energy Outlook 2008*. Paris: International Energy Agency.

IEA (2009) *World Energy Outlook 2009*. Paris: International Energy Agency.

IEA (2010) *World Energy Outlook 2010*. Paris: International Energy Agency.

Ignazi, P. (2003) *Extreme Right Parties in Western Europe*. Oxford: Oxford University Press.

Ilsoe, A. (2007) 'The Danish Flexicurity Model. A Lesson for the US?', *Working Paper*, SAIS, Johns Hopkins University, Washington, DC (http://transatlantic.sais-jhu.edu/bin/y/k/Ilsoe_The_Danish_Flexicurity_Model.pdf).

Imbeau, L.M., F. Petry and M. Lamari (2001) 'Left–Right Party Ideology and Government Policies: A Meta-Analysis', *European Journal of Political Research*, 40, pp. 1–29.

IMF (2010) *Global Financial Stability Report: Meeting New Challenges to Stability and Building a Safer System – Statistical Annex*. Washington, DC: International Monetary Fund (April).

Inglehart, R. (1988) 'The renaissance of political culture', *The American Political Science Review.* 82(4), pp. 1203–30.

Inglehart, R. (1997) *Modernization and Postmodernization.* Princeton, NJ: Princeton University Press.

Inglehart, R. (1999) 'Trust, Well-being and Democracy', in Warren (ed.), *Democracy and Trust,* pp. 88–120.

Inglehart, R. and C. Welzel (2005) *Modernization, Cultural Change, and Democracy.* New York: Cambridge University Press.

Inglehart, R. and P. Norris (2003) *Rising Tide.* Cambridge: Cambridge University Press.

Inglot, T. (2008) *Welfare States in East Central Europe 1919–2004.* Cambridge: Cambridge University Press.

International Herald Tribune (2007) 'Slovakia to withdraw its last 2 soldiers in Iraq', 4 October.

Jackman, R.W. and R.A. Miller (1995) 'Voter Turnout in the Industrial Democracies during the 1980s', *Comparative Political Studies,* 27, pp. 467–92.

Jacoby, W. (2004) *The Enlargement of the European Union and NATO. Ordering from the Menu in Central Europe.* Cambridge: Cambridge University Press.

Jansen, J., K. Gialoglou and C. Egenhofer (2005) 'Market Stimulation of Renewable Electricity in the EU: What Degree of Harmonisation of Support Mechanisms Is Required?', *CEPS Task Force Report.* Brussels: CEPS.

Jeffery, C. (2000) 'Sub-national Mobilization and European Integration: Does it make any Difference?', *Journal of Common Market Studies,* 38(1), pp. 1–23.

Jeffery, C. (2005) 'Regions and the European Union: Letting Them In and Leaving Them Alone', in S. Weatherill and U. Bernitz (eds), *The Role of the Regions and Sub-National Actors in Europe.* Oxford: Hart Publishing.

Jeffery, C. (ed.) (1997) *The Regional Dimension of the European Union. Toward a third level in Europe?* London: Franck Cass.

Jennings, M.K. and J. van Deth (1989) *Continuities in Political Action.* Berlin: deGruyter.

Johnson, J. (2006) 'Two-Track Diffusion and Central Bank Embeddedness: The Politics of Euro Adoption in Hungary and the Czech Republic', *Review of International Political Economy,* 13(3), pp. 361–86.

Johnston, A. and B. Hancké (2009) 'Wage Inflation and Labour Unions in EMU', in *Journal of European Public Policy,* Special Issue 'Ten Years of EMU', 16(4), pp. 601–22.

Johnston, R. and C. Pattie (2006) *Putting Voters in Their Place: Geography and Elections in Great Britain.* Oxford: Oxford University Press.

Jones, E. (2003) 'Liberalized Capital Markets, State Autonomy, and European Monetary Union', *European Journal of Political Research,* 42(2) (March), pp. 111–36.

Jones, E. (2009) 'The Euro and the Financial Crisis', *Survival,* 51(2) (April/May), pp. 41–54.

Jones, E. (2010) 'Merkel's Folly', *Survival,* 52(3) (June/July 2010), pp. 21–38.

Jones, P. (1989) 'The Ideal of the Neutral State', in Goodin and Reeve (eds), *Liberal Neutrality*.

Joppke, C. (1998) 'Why Liberal States Accept Unwanted Immigration', *World Politics*, 50(20), pp. 266–93.

Joppke, C. (1999) *Immigration and the Nation-States: The United States, Germany, and Great Britain*. Oxford: Oxford University Press.

Joppke, C. (2002) 'European Immigration Policies at the Crossroads', in P. Heywood, E. Jones and M. Rhodes (eds), *Developments in West European Politics 2*. London: Palgrave, pp. 259–76.

Joppke, C. (2008) 'Comparative Citizenship: A Restrictive Turn in Europe?', *Journal of Law and Ethics of Human Rights*, 2, pp. 128–68.

Jordan, A. and D. Liefferink (eds) (2006) *Environmental Policy in Europe: The Europeanization of National Environmental Policy*. London: Routledge.

Jordan, G. and A. Maloney (2007) *Democracy and Interest Groups*. Basingstoke, UK: Palgrave Macmillan.

Kaase, M. (1999) 'Interpersonal Trust, Political Trust and Non-Institutionalised Political Participation in Western Europe', *West European Politics*, 22(3), pp. 1–21.

Kaiser, W. (2007) *Christian Democracy and the Origins of the European Union*. Cambridge: Cambridge University Press.

Karvonen, L. (2010) *The Personalisation of Politics: A Study of Parliamentary Democracies*. Colchester: ECPR Press.

Kassim, H., B.G. Peters and V. Wright (eds) (2000) *The National Co-ordination of EU Policy: The Domestic Level*. Oxford: Oxford University Press.

Katz, R.S. and W. Crotty (eds) (2006) *Handbook of Party Politics*. London: Sage.

Katz, R.S. and P. Mair (1995) 'Changing Models of Party Organization and Party Democracy: The Emergence of the Cartel Party', *Party Politics*, 1, pp. 5–28.

Katzenstein, P.J. (1985) *Small States in World Markets: Industrial policy in Europe*. Ithaca, NY: Cornell University Press.

Katzenstein, P.J. (2004) 'Multiple Modernities as Limits to Secular Europeanization?', in Byrnes and Katzenstein (eds), *Religion in an Expanding Europe*, pp. 1–33.

Kautto, M. (2010) 'The Nordic Countries', in F.G. Castles, S. Leibfried, J. Lewis, H. Obinger and C. Pierson (eds), *The Oxford Handbook of the Welfare State*. Oxford: Oxford University Press, pp. 586–600.

Kazepov, Y. and D. Carbone (2007) *Che cos'è il welfare state?* Roma: Carocci Editore.

Keating M., J. Loughlin and K. Deschouwer (eds) (2003) *The New Regionalism in Europe: a Comparative Study of Eight Regions*. Cheltenham: Edward Elgar.

Keating, M. (1998) *The New Regionalism in Western Europe: Territorial Restructuring and Political Change*. London: Edward Elgar.

Keating, M. (2008) 'Thirty Years of Territorial Politics', *West European Politics*, 31(1–2), pp. 60–81.

Keating, M, and J. Hughes (eds) (2003) *The Regional Challenge in Central and Eastern Europe. Territorial Restructuring and European Integration*. Brussels: P.I.E.–Peter Lang.

Keating, M. and J. Loughlin (eds) (1996) *The Political Economy of Regionalism*. London: Franck Cass.

Kelley, J. (2006) 'New Wine in Old Wineskins: Promoting Political Reforms through the New European Neighbourhood Policy', *Journal of Common Market Studies*, 44(1) pp. 29–55.

Kelley, J.G. (2004) *Ethnic Politics in Europe. The Power of Norms and Incentives*. Princeton, NJ: Princeton University Press.

Kelso, A. (2009) 'Parliament on its knees: MPs' expenses and the crisis of transparency at Westminster', *Political Quarterly*, 80(3), pp. 329–38.

Kenny, M. (2009) 'Taking the Temperature of the British Political Elite 3: When Grubby Is the Order of The Day ...', *Parliamentary Affairs*, 62(3), pp. 503–13.

Keohane, R.O. and H.V. Milner (eds) (1996) *Internationalization and Domestic Politics*. Cambridge: Cambridge University Press.

Kepel, G. (1994) *The Revenge of God: The Resurgence of Islam, Christianity and Judaism in the Modern World*. Cambridge: Polity Press.

Kettner. C., A. Köppl, S. Schleicher and G. Thenius (2007) 'Stringency and Distribution in the EU Emissions Trading Scheme – the 2005 Evidence', *Fondazione Eni Enrico Mattei Note di Lavoro Series*. 22.

Keukeleire, S., and J. MacNaughton (2008) *The Foreign Policy of the European Union*. Basingstoke, UK: Palgrave.

Kindleberger, C.P. (1986) *The World in Depression, 1929–1939: Revised and Enlarged Edition*. Berkeley: University of California Press.

Kindleberger, C.P. (2000) *Manias, Panics, and Crashes: A History of Financial Crises*, 4th edn. New York: John Wiley & Sons.

Kirchheimer, O. (1966) 'The Transformation of West European Party Systems', in J. LaPalombara and M. Weiner (eds), *Political Parties and Political Development*. Princeton, NJ: Princeton University Press, pp. 177–200.

Kitschelt, H. (1997) *The Radical Right in Western Europe: A Comparative Analysis*. Ann Arbor, MI: Michigan University Press.

Klaassen, G. (1996) *Acid Rain and Environmental Degradation: The Economics of Emissions Trading*. Cheltenham, UK and Brookfield, US: Edward Elgar.

Klausen, J. (2005) *The Islamic Challenge: Politics and Religion in Western Europe*. Oxford: Oxford University Press.

Kling, A. (2010) *Unchecked and Unbalanced: How the Discrepancy between Knowledge and Power Caused the Financial Crisis and Threatens Democracy*. Lanham: Rowman & Littlefield.

Klingemann, H., R. Hofferbert and I. Budge (1994) *Parties, Policy and Democracy*. Boulder, CO: Westview Press.

Klingemann, H.D. (1999) 'Mapping Political Support in the 1990s: A Global Analysis', Norris (ed.), *Critical Citizens: Global Support for Democratic Government*, pp. 31–56.

Klingemann, H.-D. (ed.) (2009) *The Comparative Study of Electoral Systems*. Oxford: Oxford University Press.

Kluver, R., N. Jankowski, K. Foot and S. Schneider (2007) *The Internet and National Elections*. London: Routledge.

Knutsen, O. (2006) *Class Voting in Western Europe.* Lanham, MD: Lexington.

Koenig, M. (2007) 'Europeanising the Governance of Religious Diversity: An Institutionalist Account of Muslim Struggles for Public Recognition', *Journal of Ethnic and Migration Studies,* 33(6), pp. 911–32.

Korpi, W. (1983) *The Democratic Class Struggle.* London: Routledge & Kegan Paul.

Kostadinova, T. and T.J. Power (2007) 'Does Democratization Depress Participation? Voter turnout in the Latin American and Eastern European transitional democracies', *Political Research Quarterly,* 60(3), pp. 363–77.

Krishna, A. (2008) *Poverty, Participation and Democracy.* Cambridge: Cambridge University Press.

Krugman, P. (1991) 'Increasing Returns and Economic Geography', *Journal of Political Economy,* 99(3), pp. 483–99.

Kubicek, P. (2003) 'International Norms, the European Union, and Democratization: Tentative Theory and Evidence', in Kubicek (ed.), *The European Union and Democratization* (London: Routledge), pp. 1–29.

Kulich, M. and M. Rybár (2002) *Terrorism – Destabilizing Phenomenon of the Present Era and the War against it.* Bratislava: Ministry of Defense of the Slovak Republic Security and Defense Institute.

Laakso, M. and R. Taagepera (1979) 'Effective Number of Parties: A Measure with Application to West Europe', *Comparative Political Studies,* 12, pp. 3–27.

Ladrech, R. (2010) *Europeanization and National Politics.* Basingstoke, UK: Palgrave Macmillan.

Laffan, B., R. O'Donnell, and M. Smith (2000) *Europe's Experimental Union: Rethinking Integration.* London: Routledge.

Lansford, T. and B. Tashev (eds) (2005) *Old Europe, New Europe and the US. Renegotiating Transatlantic Security in the Post 9/11 Era.* Aldershot: Ashgate.

Larsson, R. (2007) *Tackling Dependency: The EU and its Energy Security Challenges.* Stockholm: Swedish Defence Research Agency.

Larsson, T. and J. Trondal (2005) 'After Hierarchy? Domestic Executive Governance and the Differentiated Impact of the European Commission and the Council of Ministers', *European Integration online Papers,* 9(14).

Lasswell, H. (1930) *Psychopathology and Politics.* Chicago: University of Chicago Press.

Lavenex, S. and F. Schimmelfennig (2009) 'EU Rules Beyond EU Borders: Theorizing External Governance in European Politics', *Journal of European Public Policy,* 16(6) pp. 791–812.

Lavenex, S., D. Lehmkuhl, and N. Wichmann (2009) 'Modes of External Governance: A Cross-National and Cross-Sectoral Comparison', *Journal of European Public Policy,* 16(6) pp. 813–33.

Le Galès, P. (2002) *European Cities, Social Conflicts and Governance.* Oxford: Oxford University Press.

Le Galès, P. and C. Lequesne (eds) (1998) *Regions in Europe.* London: Routledge.

Le Galès, P. and H. Voelkow (2003) 'Introduction: The Governance of Local Economies', in C. Crouch, P. Le Galès, C. Trigilia and H. Voelzkow (eds),

Local Production Systems in Europe. Rise or Demise? Oxford: Oxford University Press, pp. 1–24.

Lefevere, J. (2006) 'The EU ETS linking Directive explained', in Delbeke (ed.), *The EU Greenhouse Gas Emissions Trading Scheme. EU Energy Law*, vol. IV, pp. 117–51.

Leiber, S. (2007) 'Transposition of EU Social Policy in Poland: Are There Different 'Worlds of Compliance' in East and West?', *Journal of European Social Policy*, 17(4) pp. 349–60.

Leonard, M. and N. Popescu (2007) *A Power Audit of EU–Russia Relations*. London: European Council on Foreign Relations.

Letki, N. (2004) 'Socialization For Participation? Trust, Membership, and Democratization in East-Central Europe', in *Political Research Quarterly*, 57(4), pp. 665–79.

Letki, N. and G. Evans (2005) 'Endogenizing Social Trust: Democratisation in East-Central Europe', in *British Journal of Political Science*, 35(3), pp. 515–29.

LETS Update (2006) 'Decision Makers Summary. LETS/LIFE Emissions Trading Scheme', report produced for the LETS Update Partners. UK: AEA Technology Environment and Ecofys.

Leustean, L.N and J.T.S. Madeley (eds) (2009) *Religion, Politics and Law in the European Union*. London: Palgrave.

Leustean, L.N. (2007) 'The Place of God: Religious Terms in the Debate on the European Constitution', in A. Cohen and A. Vauchez (eds), *La Constitution Européenne: Elites, Mobilisations, Votes*.

Levitz, P. and G. Pop-Eleches (2010) 'Why No Backsliding? The EU's Impact on Democracy and Governance before and after Accession', *Comparative Political Studies*, 43(4), pp. 457–85.

Lewis, J. (1992) 'Gender and the Development of Welfare Regimes', *Journal of European Social Policy*, 2(3), pp. 159–73.

Light, M. (2002) 'The Response to 11.9 and the Lessons of History', *International Relations*, 16(2), pp. 275–80.

Lijphart, A. (1971) 'Class Voting and Religious Voting in the European Democracies: A Preliminary Report', *Acta Politica*, 6, pp. 158–71.

Lijphart, A. (1999) *Patterns of Democracy: Government Forms and Performance in Thirty-Six Countries*. New Haven: Yale University Press.

Lijphart, A. (ed.) (1992) *Parliamentary versus Presidential Government*. Oxford: Oxford University Press.

Lipset, S.M. and S. Rokkan (eds) (1967) *Party Systems and Voter Alignments*. New York: Free Press.

Loughlin, J. (1997) 'Representing Regions in Europe: the Committee of the Regions', in C. Jeffery (ed.), *The Regional Dimension of the European Union*. London: Frank Cass.

Loughlin, J. (2005) 'The Regional Question, Subsidiarity and the Future of Europe', in S. Weatherill and U. Bernitz (eds), *The Role of the Regions and Sub-National Actors in Europe*. Oxford: Hart Publishing.

Loughlin, J. (ed.) (2001) *Sub-national Democracy in the European Union: Challenges and Opportunities*. Oxford: Oxford University Press.

Luciani, G. (2004) 'Security of Supply for Natural Gas: What Is It and What Is It Not?', *INDES Working Paper*, no. 2, Brussels: CEPS.

Luedtke, A. (2008) 'Why a European Union Immigration Policy?', paper presented at the 49th Annual Convention of the American Political Science Association, San Francisco, California, 26–9 March.

Madeley, J.T.S (2003a) 'European Liberal Democracy and the Principle of State Religious Neutrality', in J.T.S. Madeley and Z. Enyedi (eds), *Church and State in Contemporary Europe: The Chimera of Neutrality*. London: Frank Cass, pp. 1–22.

Madeley, J.T.S (2003b) 'A Framework for the Comparative Analysis of Church–State Relations in Europe', in Madeley and Enyedi (eds), *Church and State in Contemporary Europe: The Chimera of Neutrality*, pp. 23–50.

Madeley, J.T.S. (2006a) 'Still the Century of Antidisestablishmentarianism?', *European Political Science*, 5(4), pp. 395–406.

Madeley, J.T.S. (2006b) 'Religion and the State', in Heywood, *et al.* (eds), *Developments in European Politics*, pp. 237–56.

Madeley, J.T.S. (2008) 'Religion and the State', in J. Haynes (ed.), *Routledge Handbook on Religion and Politics*. London: Routledge, pp. 174–191.

Madeley, J.T.S. (2009a) 'Unequally Yoked: the Antinomies of Church–State Separation in Europe and the USA', *European Political Science*, 8(3), pp. 273–288

Madeley, J.T.S. (2009b) 'E Unum Pluribus: The Role of Religion in the Project of European Integration', in J. Haynes (ed.), *Religion and politics in Europe, the Middle East and North Africa*. London: Routledge, pp. 114–36.

Madeley, J.T.S. and Z. Enyedi (eds), *Church and State in Contemporary Europe: The Chimera of Neutrality*. London: Frank Cass.

Maier, S. and F. Schimmelfennig (2007) 'Shared Values: Democracy and Human Rights', in K. Weber, M.E. Smith and M. Baun (eds), *Governing Europe's Neighbourhood: Partners or Periphery?* Manchester: Manchester University Press, pp. 39–57.

Mainwaring, S. and E. Zoco (2007) 'Electoral Volatility in Old and New Democracies: Political Sequences and the Stabilization of Interparty Competition', *Party Politics*, 13(2), pp. 155–78.

Mainwaring, S. and M. Torcal (2006) 'Party System Institutionalization and Party System Theory after the Third Wave of Democratization', in R.S. Katz and W. Crotty (eds), *Handbook of Party Politics*. London: Sage, pp. 204–27.

Mair, P. (1987) *The Changing Irish Party System*. New York: St Martin's Press.

Mair, P. (1996) 'Party Systems and Structures of Competition', in L. Leduc, R. Niemi and P. Norris (eds), *Comparing Democracies: Elections and Voting in Global Perspective*. London: Sage, pp. 83–106.

Mair, P. (2002) 'In the Aggregate: Mass Electoral Behaviour in Western Europe, 1950–2000', in H. Keman (ed.), *Comparative Democratic Politics*. London: Sage, pp. 122–42.

Mair, P. and I. van Biezen (2001) 'Party Membership in Twenty European Democracies, 1980–2000', *Party Politics*, 7(1), pp. 5–21.

Mair, P., W. Mueller and F. Plasser (eds) (2004) *Political Parties and Electoral Change*. London: Sage.

Majone, G. (1996) *Regulating Europe*. London: Routledge.

Manners, I. and R. Whitman (eds) (2000) *The Foreign Policies of European Union Member States*. Manchester: Manchester University Press.

Marien, S. (2008) 'Trends and gender differences in political participation and political trust. A comparative analysis', working paper for PartiRep research network based on European social survey, available at www.partirep.eu/upload/1200903315.pdf (accessed: 25/01/10).

Marks, G. (1996) 'An Actor-Centred Approach to Multilevel Governance', *Regional and Federal Studies*, 6(2), pp. 20–40.

Marsh, A. (1977) *Protest and Political Consciousness*. Beverly Hills, CA: Sage.

Martens, M. (2008) 'Runaway Bureaucracy? Exploring the Role of Nordic Regulatory Agencies in the European Union', *Scandinavian Political Studies*, 31(1), pp. 27–43.

Martin, D. (1978) *Toward a General Theory of Secularization*. London: Robertson.

Marton, P. and P. Wagner (2008) 'The Netherlands and Hungary's Contribution to Operations in Afghanistan', *HIIA Papers: Periodical of the Hungarian Institute of International Affairs*. Available at: www.kulugyiintezet.hu/keklevel/MKI_hirlevel_2008–01.pdf (accessed 17/09/10).

Massachusetts Institute of Technologies (MIT) (2003) *The Future of Nuclear Power. An Interdisciplinary MIT Study*. Boston, MA: Massachusetts Institute of Technologies.

Massicotte, L., A. Blais and A. Yoshinaka (2004) *Establishing the Rules of the Game: Election Laws in Democracies*. Toronto: University of Toronto Press.

Mattelaer, A. (2008) 'The Strategic Planning of EU Military Operations – The Case of EUFOR TCHAD/RCA', *IES Working Paper 5/2008*, Brussels: Institute for European Studies.

Mauer, Victor (2007) 'Germany's Counterterrorism Policy', in Doron Zimmermann and Andreas Wenger (eds), *How States Fight Terrorism. Policy Dynamics in the West*. London: Lynne Rienner, pp. 59–78.

Maull, H.W. (2001) 'The Guns of November? Germany and the Use of Force in the Aftermath of 9/11', *German Foreign Policy Dialogue*, 2(5), pp. 13–15.

Maurel, M.C. (2004) 'Différenciation et Reconfiguration des Territoires en Europe Centrale et Orientale', *Annales de Géographie*, 636, pp. 124–43.

Mazey, S, and J. Richardson (eds) (1993) *Lobbying in the European Community*. Oxford: Oxford University Press.

McAdam, D., J.D. McCarthy and M.N. Zald (eds) (1996) *Comparative Perspectives on Social Movements*. New York: Cambridge University Press.

McAllister, I. (1999) 'The Economic Performance Of Governments', in Norris (ed.), *Critical Citizens: Global Support for Democratic Government*, pp. 188–203.

McDonald, M.P. and S.L. Popkin (2001) 'The Myth of the Vanishing Voter', *American Political Science Review*, 95(4), pp. 963–74.

McGoldrick, D. (2006) *Human Rights and Religion: The Headscarf Debate in Europe*. Oxford: Hart.

McNamara, K.R. (1998) *The Currency of Ideas: Monetary Politics in the European Union*. Ithaca, NY: Cornell University Press.

Meadows, D. (2006) 'The Emissions Allowance Trading Directive 2003/87/EC Explained', in Delbeke (ed.), *The EU Greenhouse Gas Emissions Trading Scheme. EU Energy Law*. vol. IV, pp. 63–115.

Merriam, C. (1931) *The Making of Citizens*. Chicago: University of Chicago Press.

Messina, A. (2007) *The Logics and Politics of Post-WWII Migration to Western Europe*. New York: Cambridge University Press.

Miko, F.T. and C. Froehlich (2004) 'Germany's Role in Fighting Terrorism: Implications for US Policy', *CRS Report to Congress*. 27 December, RL32710.

Milbrath, L.W. and M.L. Goel (1977) *Political Participation: How and Why do People get Involved in Politics?*, 2nd edn. Chicago: Rand McNally.

Miles, T.J. (2004) 'Felon Disenfranchisement and Voter Turnout', *Journal of Legal Studies*, 33(1), pp. 85–129.

Minkenberg, M. (2001) 'The Radical Right in Public Office: Agenda-Setting and Policy Effects', *West European Politics*, 24, pp. 1–21.

Mishler, W. and R. Rose (2001) 'What Are the Origins of Political Trust? Testing Institutional and Cultural Theories in Post-Communist Societies', *Comparative Political Studies*, 34(1), pp. 30–62.

Molina, O. and M. Rhodes (2007) 'The Political Economy of Adjustment in Mixed Market Economies: A Study of Spain and Italy', in Hancké *et al.* (eds), *Beyond Varieties of Capitalism: Conflict, Contradiction and Complementarities in the European Economy*, pp. 223–52.

Money, J. (1999) *Fences and Neighbors*. Ithaca, NY: Cornell University Press.

Monsma, S. and C. Soper (eds) (1997) *The Challenge of Pluralism; Church and State in Five Democracies*. Oxford: Rowman & Littlefield.

Montero, J.R., A. Westholm and J.W. van Deth (2006) 'Conclusion: The Realisation of Democratic Citizenship in Europe', in van Deth *et al.* (eds), *Citizenship and Involvement in European Democracies: A Comparative Analysis*, pp. 415–38.

Moravcsik, A. (1994). 'Why the European Community Strengthens the State: Domestic Politics and International Cooperation', *Center for European Studies Working Paper Series # 52*. Cambridge, MA: Center for European Studies, Harvard University.

Morlino, L. (1996) 'Crisis of Parties and Change of Party System in Italy', *Party Politics*, 2(1), pp. 5–30.

Motzkin, G. and Y. Fischer (eds) (2008) *Religion and Democracy in Contemporary Europe*. London: Alliance Publishing.

Mudde, C. (2007) *Populist Radical Right Parties in Europe*. Cambridge: Cambridge University Press.

Muller, E.N., and M.A. Seligson (1994) 'Civic Culture and Democracy: The Question of Causal Relationships', in *American Political Science Review*, 88(3), pp. 635–52.

Müller, F. (2007) 'Energy Security – Demands Imposed on German and European Foreign Policy by a Changed Configuration in the World Energy Market', *SWP Research Paper*, no. 2, Berlin: SWP.

Müller, W. C. and K. Strøm (eds) (2000) *Coalition Governance in Western Europe*. Oxford, Oxford University Press

Nannestad, P. and C. Green-Pedersen (2008) 'Keeping the Bumblebee Flying: Economic Policy in the Welfare State of Denmark, 1973–99', in E. Albaek, L.C. Eliason, A.S. Norgaard and H.M. Schwartz (eds), *Crisis, Miracles, and Beyond: Negotiated Adaptation of the Danish Welfare State*. Aarhus: Aarhus University Press, pp. 33–74.

Natali, D. (2007) *Vincitori e Perdenti. Come cambiano le pensioni in Italia e in Europa*. Bologna: Il Mulino.

National Security Office (2003) 'Main Scope of Activity of the National Security Office: Terrorism', Budapest: National Security Office.

NATO (2010) 'International Security Assistance Force Key Facts and Figures', 6 August, available at: www.isaf.nato.int/troop-numbers-and-contributions/index.php (accessed: 17/09/10).

Négrier, E. and B. Jouve (1998) (eds), *Que gouverne les régions d'Europe?* Paris: L'Harmattan.

Neller, K. (2008) 'Explaining Social Trust: What Makes People Trust Their Fellow Citizens?', in H. Meulemann (ed.), *Social Capital in Europe: Similarity of Countries and Diversity of People? Multi-level Analyses of the European Social Survey 2002*. Boston, MA: Brill, pp. 103–34.

Newton, K. (1999) 'Social and Political Trust in Established Democracies', in Norris (ed.), *Critical Citizens: Global Support for Democratic Governance*, pp. 169–87.

Newton, K. (2001) 'Trust, Social Capital, Civil Society and Democracy', *International Political Science Review*, 22(2), pp. 201–14.

Niemi, R.G. and H.F. Weisberg (eds) (2001) *Controversies in Voting Behavior*. Washington, DC: CQ Press.

Nieuwbeerta, P. (1996) 'The Democratic Class Struggle in Postwar Societies: Class Voting in Twenty Countries,1945–1990', *Acta Sociologica*, 39(4), pp. 345–83.

Nieuwbeerta, P., N.D. de Graaf and W. Ultee (2000) 'The Effects of Class Mobility on Class Voting in Post-war Western Industrialized Countries', *European Sociological Review*, 16(4), pp. 327–48.

Noël, P. (2008) 'Beyond Dependence: How to Deal with Russian Gas', *Policy Brief No. 9* London: European Council on Foreign Relations (November).

Norris, P. (1999) (ed.) *Critical Citizens: Global Support for Democratic Governance*. Oxford: Oxford University Press.

Norris, P. (1999) 'Institutional explanations for political support', Norris (ed.) *Critical Citizens: Global Support for Democratic Governance*, pp. 217–35.

Norris, P. (2000) *A Virtuous Circle? Political Communications in Post-Industrial Democracies*. Cambridge: Cambridge University Press.

Norris, P. (2002) *Democratic Phoenix: Reinventing Political Activism*. New York: Cambridge University Press.

Norris, P. (2004) *Electoral Engineering: Voting Rules and Political Behavior*. New York: Cambridge University Press.

Norris, P. (2007) 'Political Activism: New Challenges, New Opportunities', in C. Boix and S. Stokes (eds), *The Oxford Handbook of Comparative Politics*. Oxford: Oxford University Press, pp. 628–49.

Norris, P. (2008) *Driving Democracy*. New York: Cambridge University Press.

Norris, P. (2009) 'The Globalization of Comparative Public Opinion Research', in N. Robinson and T. Landman (eds), *The Sage Handbook of Comparative Politics*. London: Sage, pp. 522–40.

Norris, P. (2011) *Democratic Deficits: Critical Citizens Revisited*. New York: Cambridge University Press.

Norris, P. and R. Inglehart (2004) *Sacred and Secular: Religion and Politics Worldwide*. Cambridge: Cambridge University Press.

Noutcheva, G. and M. Emerson (2007) 'Economic and Social Development', in K. Weber, M.E. Smith and M. Baun (eds), *Governing Europe's Neighbourhood: Partners or Periphery?* Manchester: Manchester University Press, pp. 76–96.

O'Brennan, J. and T. Raunio (2006a) 'Introduction: Deparliamentarization and European Integration', in J. O'Brennan and T. Raunio (eds), *National Parliaments within the Enlarged European Union. From 'Victims' of Integration to Competitive Actors?* New York: Routledge, pp. 1–26.

O'Brennan, J. and T. Raunio (2006b) 'Conclusion: national Parliaments Gradually Learning to Play the European Game', in J. O'Brennan and T. Raunio (eds), *National Parliaments within the Enlarged European Union. From 'Victims' of Integration to Competitive Actors?* New York: Routledge, pp. 287–306.

OECD (2007) *International Migration Outlook: Annual Report*. Paris.

OECD (2008) *International Migration Outlook: Annual Report*. Paris.

Offe, C. (1999) 'How Can We Trust Our Fellow Citizens?', Warren (ed.), *Democracy and Trust*.

Offe, C. and S. Fuchs (2002) 'A Decline of Social Capital? The German Case', in R.D. Putnam (ed.), *Democracies in Flux: The Evolution of Social Capital in Contemporary Society*. Oxford: Oxford University Press.

Olsen, J.P. (2007) *Europe In Search of Political Order. An Institutional Perspective on Unity/Diversity, Citizens/Their Helpers, Democratic Design/Historical Drift, and the Co-existence of Orders*. Oxford: Oxford University Press.

Olson, M. (1965) *The Logic of Collective Action: Public Goods and the Theory of Goods*. Cambridge, MA: Harvard University Press.

Orenstein, M.A. (2008) 'Postcommunist Welfare States', *Journal of Democracy*, 19(4), pp. 80–95.

Orloff, A. (1993) 'Gender and the Social Rights of Citizenship: The Comparative Analysis of Gender Relations and Welfare States', *American Sociological Review*, 58(3), pp 303–28.

Oswald, F. (2004) 'German Security After 9/11', in P. Shearman and M. Sussex (eds), *European Security after 9/11*. Aldershot: Ashgate, pp. 90–106.

Palier B. (2010c) (ed.), *A Long Goodbye to Bismarck? The Politics of Welfare Reform in Continental Europe*. Amsterdam: Amsterdam University Press.

Palier, B. (2010a) 'The Dualization of the French Welfare System', in B. Palier (ed.) *A Long Goodbye to Bismarck? The Politics of Welfare Reform in Continental Europe*. Amsterdam: Amsterdam University Press, pp. 73–100.

Palier, B. (2010b) 'The Long Conservative Corporatist Road to Welfare Reforms', in B. Palier (ed.), *A Long Goodbye to Bismarck? The Politics of Welfare Reform in Continental Europe*. Amsterdam: Amsterdam University Press, pp. 333–87.

Pallavi, A. (2009) 'Europe Plays "Blue Card" to Bridge Skill Gap', *Business Standard* (India), 31 July (www.business-standard.com/india).

Paloheimo, H. (2007) 'Finland: Let the Force Be with the Leader – But Who Is the Leader?', in Poguntke and Webb (eds), *The Presidentialization of Politics. A Comparative Study of Modern Democracies*, pp. 246–68.

Panebianco, A. (1988) *Political Parties: Organization and Power*. Cambridge: Cambridge University Press.

Pasquier, R. (2003) 'From Patterns of Collective Action to the Capacity for Governance in French Regions', in J. Bukowski, S. Piattoni and M. Smyrl (eds), *Between Global Economy and Local Society: Political Actors and Territorial Governance*. Boulder, CO: Rowman & Littlefield, pp. 67–90.

Pasquier, R. (2004) *La capacité politique des régions. Une comparaison France–Espagne*. Rennes: Presses Universitaires de Rennes.

Pasquier, R. (2005) ' "Cognitive Europeanization" and the Territorial Effects of Multi-Level Policy Transfer: Local Development in French and Spanish Regions', *Regional and Federal Studies*, 15(3), pp. 295–310.

Pasquier, R. and C. Perron (2008) 'Régionalisme et Régionalisation dans une Europe Elargie: Les Enjeux d'une Comparaison Est/Ouest', *Revue d'Etudes Comparatives Est/Ouest*, 39(3), pp. 5–18.

Pasquier, R. and G. Pinson (2004) 'Politique européenne de la ville et gouvernement local en Espagne et en Italie', *Politique européenne*, 12, pp. 42–65.

Pasquino, G. (1995) 'The Politics of Civic Tradition Eclipsed', in *APSA-CP*, 6(2), pp. 8–9.

Pedersen, M.N. (1979) 'The Dynamics of European Party Systems: Changing Patterns of Electoral Volatility', *European Journal of Political Research*, 7(1), pp. 1–26.

Peters, B.G., R. Rhodes and V. Wright (2000) 'Staffing the Summit – the Administration of the Core Executive: Convergent Trends and National Specificities', in B.G. Peters, R. Rhodes and V. Wright (eds), *Administering the Summit: Administration of the Core Executive in Developed Countries*. Basingstoke, UK: Macmillan, pp. 3–24.

Petridou, K. (2008) 'EU-27 Foreign Direct Investment in Brazil, Russia, India and China more than doubled in 2007', *Eurostat Statistics in Focus*, 64/2008, http://epp.eurostat.ec.europa.eu/cache/ITY_OFFPUB/KS-SF-08–064/EN/KS-SF-08–064–EN.PDF (accessed: 12/11/10).

Pharr, S.J. and R. Putnam (eds) (2000) *Disaffected Democracies: What's Troubling the Trilateral Countries?* Princeton, NJ: Princeton University Press.

Philibert, C. and J. Reinaud (2004) *Emissions Trading: Taking Stock and Looking Forward*. IEA/OECD, Paris, COM/ENV/EPOC/IEA/SLT(2004)3.

Philpott, D. (2004) 'Religious Freedom and the Undoing of the Westphalian State', *Michigan Journal of International Law*, 25, pp. 981–98.

Pierson, P. (ed.) (2001) *The New Politics of the Welfare State*. Oxford: Oxford University Press.

Pillar, P.R. (2001) *Terrorism and US Foreign Policy*. Washington, DC: Brookings Institution Press.

Pillar, P.R. (2004) 'Counterterrorism after Al Qaeda', *Washington Quarterly*, 27(3), pp. 101–13.

Pintor, R.L. and M. Gratschew (2004) *Voter Turnout Since 1945: A Global Report*. Stockholm, International IDEA. www.idea.int.

Piore, M. and C. Sabel (1984) *The Second Industrial Divide*. New York: Basic Books.

Poguntke, T. and P. Webb (eds) (2007) *The Presidentialization of Politics: A Comparative Study Modern Democracies*. Oxford: Oxford University Press.

Poguntke, T., N. Aylott, E. Carter, R. Ladrech, K.R. Luther (eds) (2007) *The Europeanization of National Political Parties: Power and Organizational Adaptation*. London/New York: Routledge.

Polish Embassy in Dublin (2009) *Poland's Energy Policy until 2030*, 21 May, available at http://dublin.trade.gov.pl/en/aktualnosci/article/a,3286,Polands_Energy_Policy_until_2030.html (accessed: 24/07/09).

Powell, G.B. (1980) 'Voting Turnout in Thirty Democracies: Partisan, legal and socioeconomic influences', in R. Rose (ed.) *Electoral Participation: A Comparative Analysis*. London: Sage.

Powell, G.B. (1982) *Contemporary Democracies: Participation, Stability and Violence*. Cambridge, MA: Harvard University Press.

Powell, G.B. (1986) 'American Voter Turnout in Comparative Perspective', *American Political Science Review*, 80(1), pp. 17–43.

Pridham, G. (2008) 'The EU's Political Conditionality and Post-Accession Tendencies: Comparisons from Slovakia and Latvia', *Journal of Common Market Studies*, 46(2) pp. 365–87.

Pridham, G. (2009) 'Securing the Only Game in Town: The EU's Political Conditionality and Democratic Consolidation in Post-Soviet Latvia', *Europe-Asia Studies*, 61(1) pp. 51–84.

Putnam, R.D. (1988). 'Diplomacy and Domestic Politics: The Logic of Two-Level Games', *International Organization*, 42(3), pp. 427–460.

Putnam, R.D. (1993) *Making Democracy Work*. Princeton, NJ: Princeton University Press.

Putnam, R.D. (1995) 'Bowling Alone: America's Declining Social Capital', in *Journal of Democracy*, 6(1), pp. 65–78.

Putnam, R.D. (1995) 'Tuning In, Tuning Out: The Strange Disappearance of Social Capital in America', *Political Science & Politics*, 28(4), pp. 664–83.

Putnam, R.D. (2000) *Bowling Alone: The Collapse and Revival of American Community*. New York: Simon & Schuster.

Putnam, R.D. (2001) 'Social Capital: Measurement and Consequences', *Canadian Journal of Political Research*, 2(1), 41–51.

Putnam, R.D. (ed.) (2002) *The Dynamics of Social Capital*. Oxford: Oxford University Press.

Putnam, R.D., R. Leonardi and R. Nanetti (1993) *Making Democracy Work: Civic Traditions in Modern Italy*. Princeton, NJ: Princeton University Press.

Quaglia, L. (2009) 'The "British Plan" as Pace-Setter: The Europeanization of Banking Rescue Plans in the EU?', *JCMS*, 47(5) (November), pp. 1063–83.

Quillen, C. (2002) 'A Historical Analysis of Mass Casualty Bombers', *Studies in Conflict and Terrorism*, 25(5), pp. 279–92.

Radaelli, C. (2003), 'The Europeanization of Public Policy', in Featherstone and Radaelli (eds), *The Politics of Europeanization*, pp. 27–56.

Raunio, T. (2009) 'National Parliaments and European Integration. What We Know and What We Should Know', *ARENA Working Paper* 02/2009.

Rees, W. (2006) *Transatlantic Counter-Terrorism Cooperation: The New Imperative*. London: Routledge.

Regeringskansliet (2009) *A sustainable energy and climate policy for the environment, competitiveness and long-term stability*. 5 February.

Reinares, F. (ed.) (2000) *European Democracies Against Terrorism: Governmental Policies and Intergovernmental Cooperation*. Aldershot: Ashgate.

Rémond, R. (1999) *Religion and Society in Modern Europe*. Oxford: Blackwell.

Renner, G. (2005) 'Das Zuwanderungsgesetz-Ende des deutschen Ausländerrechts?', *IMIS-Beiträge* (Osnabrück) pp. 9–24.

Rhodes, M. (2000) 'Restructuring the British Welfare State: Between Domestic Constraints and Global Imperatives', in F.W. Scharpf and V.A. Schmidt (eds), *Welfare and Work in the Open Economy: Volume 2 – Diverse Responses to Economic Challenges*. Oxford: Oxford University Press, pp. 19–68.

Rhodes, M. (ed.) (1997) *Southern European Welfare States: Between Crisis and Reform*. London: Frank Cass 1997.

Rhodes, R.A.W. (1995) 'From Prime Ministerial Power to Core Executive', in R.A.W. Rhodes and P. Dunleavy (eds), *Prime Minister, Cabinet and Core Executive*. London: Macmillan, pp. 11–37.

Rhodes, R.A.W. (2003) 'What is New about Governance and Why Does it Matter?', in J. Hayward and A. Menon (eds), *Governing Europe. Memorial Volume for Vincent Wright*. Oxford: Oxford University Press, pp. 61–73.

Richardson, J. (1995) 'The Market for Political Activism: Interest Groups as a Challenge to Political Parties', *West European Politics*, 18, pp. 116–39.

Richardson, J.T. (2004) *Regulating Religion: Case Studies from Around the Globe*. London: Kluwer Academic/Plenum.

Rihackova, V. (2006) 'Counterterrorism Policies in Central Europe', EUROPEUM Institute for European Policy, available at: www.europeum. org/doc/pdf/854.pdf (accessed: 17/09/2010).

Riley, A. (2006) 'The Coming of the Russian Gas Deficit: Consequences and solutions', *CEPS Policy Brief*, no. 116, Brussels: CEPS.

Robbers, R. (2005) (ed.) *State and Church in the European Union*. Baden-Baden: Nomos Verlag.

Rodrick, D. (2007) *One Economics, Many Recipes: Globalization, Institutions, and Economic Growth*. Princeton, NJ: Princeton University Press.

Rodríguez-Pose, A. (2001) *The Role of the ILO in Implementing Local Economic Development Strategies in a Globalized World*. London: Local Economic Development Programme.

Rodríguez-Pose, A. (2003) 'Local Production Systems and Economic Performance in France, Germany, Italy and the United Kingdom', in C. Crouch, P. Le Galès, C. Trigilia and H. Voelzkow (eds), *Local Production Systems in Europe. Rise or Demise?* Oxford: Oxford University Press, pp. 25–45.

Rokkan, S. (1970). *Citizens, Elections, Parties: Approaches to the Comparative Study of the Processes of Development.* Oslo: Universitetsforlaget.

Rokkan, S. and D. Urwin (eds) (1982) *The Politics of Territorial Identity. Studies in European Regionalism.* London: Sage.

Rokkan, S and D. Urwin (1983) *Economy, Territory, Identity. Politics of West European Peripheries.* London: Sage.

Röller, L, J. Delgado and H. Friederiszick (2007) *Energy: Choices for Europe.* Brussels: Bruegel Blueprint.

Romero, V.C. (2003) 'Decoupling "Terrorist" from "Immigrant": An Enhanced Role for the Federal Courts Post 9/11', *Journal of Gender, Race and Justice*, 7, pp. 101–11.

Rose, R. and C. Haerpfer (1998) *New Democracies Barometer V: A 12-Nation Study.* Glasgow: Centre for the Study of Public Policy, University of Strathclyde.

Rose R., and I. McAllister (1986). *Voters Begin to Choose: From Closed Class to Open Elections in Britain.* Newbury Park, CA: Sage.

Rosenstone, S. and M. Hansen (1993) *Mobilization, Participation, and American Democracy.* Washington, DC: CQ Press.

Ross, J.I. (2006) *Political Terrorism – An Interdisciplinary Approach.* New York: Peter Lang.

Rothstein, B. (2004) 'Social trust and honesty in government: a causal mechanism approach', in J. Kornai, B. Rothstein and S. Rose-Ackerman (eds), *Creating Social Trust in Post-Socialist Transition.* Basingstoke: Palgrave Macmillan.

Ruggie, J.G. (1982) 'International Regimes, Transactions, and Change: Embedded Liberalism in the Postwar Economic Order', *International Organization*, 36(2) (spring), pp. 379–415.

Saalfeld, T. (2005) 'Deliberate Delegation or Abdication? Government Backbenchers, Ministers and European Union Legislation', *Journal of Legislative Studies*, 11(3/4), pp. 343–71.

Samek Lodovici, M. and R. Clemenza (2008) 'The Italian Case: From Employment Regulation to Welfare reforms?', *Social Policy and Administration*, 42(2), pp. 160–76.

Samson, I. (2005) 'Slovakia', in T. Lansford and B. Tashev (eds), *Old Europe, New Europe and the US. Renegotiating Transatlantic Security in the Post 9/11 Era.* Aldershot: Ashgate, pp. 219–38.

Sandler, T. (2003) 'Collective Action and Transnational Terrorism', *World Economy*, 26(6), pp. 779–802.

Sartori, G. (1994) *Comparative Constitutional Engineering: An Inquiry into Structures, Incentives and Outcomes.* Basingstoke, UK: Macmillan.

Sasse, G. (2008a) 'The European Neighbourhood Policy: Conditionality Revisited for the EU's Eastern Neighbours', *Europe-Asia Studies*, 60(2) pp. 295–316.

Sasse, G. (2008b) 'The Politics of EU Conditionality: The Norm of Minority Protection During and Beyond EU Accession', *Journal of European Public Policy*, 15(6) pp. 842–60.

Sassen, S. (1991) *The Global City: New York, London, Tokyo*. Princeton, NJ: Princeton University Press.

Saxonberg, S. and T. Siròvatka (2009) 'Neo-liberalism by Decay? The Evolution of the Czech Welfare State', *Social Policy and Administration*, 43(2), pp. 186–203.

Schanda, B. (2005) 'Church and State in the New Member Countries of the European Union', *Ecclesiastical Law Journal*, 4, pp. 186–98.

Scharpf, F.W. and V.A. Schmidt (eds), *Welfare and Work in the Open Economy: Volume 2 – Diverse Responses to Economic Challenges*. Oxford: Oxford University Press.

Schattschneider, E.E. (1942) *Party Government*. New York: Rhinehart.

Schedler, A. (2006) *Electoral Authoritarianism: The Dynamics of Unfree Competition*. Boulder, CO: Lynne Rienner.

Schimmelfennig, F. (2008) 'EU Political Accession Conditionality after Enlargement: Consistency and Effectiveness', *Journal of European Public Policy*, 15(6), pp. 918–37.

Schimmelfennig, F. (2009) 'Europeanization Beyond Europe', *Living Reviews in European Governance*, 4(3). www.livingreviews.org/lreg-2009–3.

Schimmelfennig, F. and F. Trauner (2009) 'Introduction: Post-Accession Compliance in the EU's New Member States', *European Integration online Papers*, 13(2).

Schimmelfennig, F. and H. Scholtz (2008) 'EU Democracy Promotion in the European Neighbourhood: Political Conditionality, Economic Development and Transnational Exchange', *European Union Politics*, 9(2) pp. 187–215.

Schimmelfennig, F. and U. Sedelmeier (2004) 'Governance by Conditionality: EU Rule Transfer to the Candidate Countries of Central and Eastern Europe', *Journal of European Public Policy*, 11(4), pp. 661–79.

Schimmelfennig, F. and U. Sedelmeier (2005b) 'Introduction: Conceptualizing the Europeanization of Central and Eastern Europe', in Schimmelfennig and Sedelmeier (eds), *The Europeanization of Central and Eastern Europe*, pp. 1–28.

Schimmelfennig, F. and U. Sedelmeier (eds) (2005a) *The Europeanization of Central and Eastern Europe*. Ithaca: Cornell University Press.

Schimmelfennig, F., S. Engert and H. Knobel (2006) *International Socialization in Europe: European Organizations, Political Conditionality and Democratic Change*. Basingstoke: Palgrave.

Schmid-Drüner, M. (2006) 'Germany's New Immigration Law: A Paradigm Shift?', *European Journal of Migration and Law*, 8, pp. 191–214.

Schmitt, H. and S. Holmberg (1995) 'Political Parties in Decline?', in H.D. Klingemann and D. Fuchs (eds), *Citizens and the State*. Oxford: Oxford University Press, pp. 95–133.

Schmitt-Beck, R. (2008) 'Mass media and social capital in Europe: Evidence from Multilevel Analyses' in H. Meulemann (ed.), *Social Capital in Europe: Similarity of Countries and Diversity of People? Multi-level Analyses of the European Social Survey 2002*. Boston, MA: Brill, pp. 159–90.

Schwartz, H. (2001) 'The Danish "Miracle": Luck, Pluck, or Stuck?', *Comparative Political Studies*, 34(2), pp. 131–55.

Schwartz, H. (2007) 'Dependency or Institutions? Economic Geography, Causal Mechanisms, and Logic in the Understanding of Development', *Studies in Comparative International Development*, 42, pp. 115–35.

Schwellnus, G. (2005) 'The Adoption of Nondiscrimination and Minority Protection Rules in Romania, Hungary, and Poland', in Schimmelfennig and Sedelmeier (eds), *The Europeanization of Central and Eastern Europe*, pp. 51–70.

Schwellnus, G., L. Balazs, and L. Mikalayeva (2009) 'It Ain't over When It's Over: The Adoption and Sustainability of Minority Protection Rules in New EU Member States', *European Integration online Papers*, 13(2).

Scott, A.J. (1996) 'Regional Motors of the Global Economy', *Futures*, 28, pp. 391–411.

Scott, A.J., and M. Storper (eds) (1986). *Production, Work, Territory: The Geographical Anatomy of Industrial Capitalism*. London: Allen & Unwin.

Sedelmeier, U. (2007) 'The European Neighbourhood Policy: A Comment on Theory and Policy', in K. Weber, M.E. Smith and M. Baun (eds), *Governing Europe's Neighbourhood: Partners or Periphery?* Manchester: Manchester University Press, pp. 195–208.

Sedelmeier, U. (2008) 'After Conditionality: Post-Accession Compliance with EU Law in East Central Europe', *Journal of European Public Policy*, 15(6) pp. 806–25.

Sedelmeier, U. (2009a) 'Post-accession compliance in the enlarged EU: Why are the new member states so good?', paper presented at KFG conference, Berlin, 9–11 December.

Sedelmeier, U. (2009b) 'Post-Accession Compliance with EU Gender Equality Legislation in Post-Communist New Member States', *European Integration online Papers*, 13(2).

Sederberg, P.C. (2003) 'Global Terrorism: Problems of Challenge and Response', in C.W. Kegley (ed.) *New Global Terrorism: The Characteristics, Causes and Controls*. Upper Saddle River, NJ: Prentice Hall, pp. 267–84.

Senato della Repubblica Italiana (2007) *Uno sguardo sulle pensioni: politiche pubbliche nei paesi dell'OCSE*, Roma.

Serrano Pascual, A. and L. Magnusson (eds) (2007) *Reshaping Welfare States and Activation Regimes in Europe*. Brussels: Peter Lang Publishing.

Shachar, A. (2006) 'The Race for Talent: Highly Skilled Immigrants and Competitive Immigration Regimes', *New York University Law Review*, 81, pp. 148–206.

Sharpe, L.J. (1988) 'The Growth and Decentralization of the Modern Democratic State', *European Journal of Political Research*, 16, pp. 365–80.

Sharpe, L.J. (1993) *The Rise of Meso-Government in Europe*. London: Sage.

Shearman, P. and M. Sussex (eds) (2004) *European Security after 9/11*. Aldershot: Ashgate.

Shiller, R.J. (2008) *The Subprime Solution: How Today's Global Financial Crisis Happened, and What to Do about It*. Princeton, NJ: Princeton University Press.

Shonfield, A. (1965) *Modern Capitalism: the Changing Balance of Public and Private Power.* London, New York: Oxford University Press.

Shultz, R.H. and A. Vogt (2003) 'It's War! Fighting Post-11 September Global Terrorism through a Doctrine of Preemption', *Terrorism and Political Violence*, 15(1), pp. 1–30.

Sikk, A. (2005) 'How Unstable? Volatility and the Genuinely New Parties in Eastern Europe', *European Journal of Political Research*, 44, pp. 391–412.

Sissenich, B. (2005) 'The Transfer of EU Social Policy to Poland and Hungary', in Schimmelfennig and Sedelmeier (eds), *The Europeanization of Central and Eastern Europe*, pp. 156–77.

Skjærseth, J. and J. Wettestad (2008) *EU Emissions Trading.* Aldershot: Ashgate.

Slovak Ministry of Foreign Affairs (2001) 'Co-operation in the Area of Justice and Home Affairs', in *Negotiating Position of the Slovak Republic.* Bratislava: Government of the Slovak Republic, ch. 24.

Smith, A. (1996) *L'Europe politique au miroir du local. Les fonds structurels et les zones rurales en France, en Espagne et au Royaume-Uni.* Paris: L'Harmattan.

Smith, K.E. (2005) 'The Outsiders: The European Neighbourhood Policy', *International Affairs*, 81(4) pp. 757–73.

Smith, K.E. (2008) *European Union Foreign Policy in a Changing World.* Cambridge: Polity.

Smith, M., and C. Hill (2011) (eds.) *International Relations and the European Union*, 2nd edn. Oxford. Oxford University Press.

Smith, S., T. Dunne and A. Hadfield (eds) (2007) *Foreign Policy: Theories, Actors, Cases.* Oxford: Oxford University Press.

Smyrl, M. (1997) 'Does European Community Regional Policy Empower the Regions?', *Governance*, 10(3), pp. 287–309.

Soper, C. and J. Fetzer (2003) 'Explaining the Accommodation of Muslim Religious Practices in France, Britain, and Germany', *French Politics*, 10(1), pp. 39–59.

Soskice, D. (1999) 'Divergent Production Regimes: Coordinated and Uncoordinated Market Economies in the 1980s and 1990s', in H. Kitschelt, P. Lange, G. Marks and J. D. Stephens (eds), *Continuity and Change in Contemporary Capitalism.* Cambridge: Cambridge University Press, pp. 101–34.

Soskice, D. and T. Iversen (1998) 'Multiple Wage Bargaining Systems in the Single European Currency Area', *Oxford Review of Economic Policy*, 14(3), pp. 110–24.

Soskice, D. and T. Iversen (2000) 'The Non-Neutrality of Monetary Policy with Large Price or Wage Setters', *Quarterly Journal of Economics*, February 2000.

Spence, D. (1999) 'Foreign Ministries in National and European Context', in B. Hocking (ed.), *Foreign Ministries: Change and Adaptation.* Basingstoke: Macmillan.

Spencer, A. (2006) 'Counter-Terrorism in New Europe', *International Public Policy Review*, 2(2), pp. 92–112.

Spencer, A. (2010) *The Tabloid Terrorist. The Predicative Construction of New Terrorism in the Media.* Basingstoke: Palgrave.

Standard Eurobarometer (2007) no. 67, Spring 2007, available at: http://ec.europa.eu/public_opinion/archives/eb/eb67/eb67_en.pdf (accessed: 11/11/08).

Steiner, V. and K. Wrohlich (2005) 'Work Incentives and Labor Supply Effects of the "Mini-Jobs Reform" in Germany', *Empirica* 32, pp. 91–116.

Stepan, A. (2000) 'Religion, Democracy and the Twin Tolerations', *Journal of Democracy*, 11(4), pp. 37–57.

Stern, J. (2002) 'Security of Natural Gas Supplies', *Journal of Royal Institute of International Affairs*, London, July.

Stern, J. (2006) 'The New Security Environment for European Gas: Worsening Geopolitics and Increasing Global Competition', *Oxford Institute for Energy Studies*, NG 15, October.

Stern, N. (2006) *The Stern Review on the Economics of Climate Change.* Cambridge, Cambridge University Press.

Steunenberg, B. and D. Toshkov (2009) 'Comparing Transposition in the 27 Member States of the EU: The Impact of Discretion and Legal Fit', *Journal of European Public Policy*, 16(7), pp. 951–70.

Steven, G.C.S. and R. Gunaratna (2004) *Counterterrorism – A Reference Handbook.* Santa Barbara, CA: ABC-Clio.

Stiglitz, J. (1999) 'Whither reform? Ten years of the transition'. Keynote address, World Bank Annual Conference on Development Economics.

Stiglitz, J. (2002) *Globalization and Its Discontents.* New York: W.W. Norton & Company.

Stoker, G. (2006) *Why Politics Matters: Making Democracy Work.* Basingstoke, UK: Palgrave Macmillan.

Stolle, D., M. Hooghe and M. Micheletti (2005) 'Politics in the Supermarket: Political Consumerism as a Form of Political Participation', *International Political Science Review*, 26(3), pp. 245–69.

Stone, C. (1989) *Regime Politics: Governing Atlanta.* Lawrence, KS: University Press of Kansas.

Storper, M. (1995) 'The Resurgence of Regional Economies, Ten years Later: The Region as a Nexus of Untraded Interdependencies', *European Urban and Regional Studies*, 2(3), pp. 191–221.

Storper, M. (1997) *The Regional World.* New York: Guilford Press.

Streeck, W. (1992) *Social Institutions and Economic Performance.* Beverly Hills, CA: Sage

Streeck, W. (2009) *Re-forming German Capitalism.* Oxford: Oxford University Press.

Streeck, W. and K. Thelen (2005) 'Introduction: Institutional Change in Advanced Political Economies', in Streeck and Thelen (eds), *Beyond Continuity: Institutional Change in Advanced Political Economies*, pp. 1–39.

Streeck, W. and K. Thelen (eds) (2005) *Beyond Continuity. Institutional Change in Advanced Political Economies.* Oxford: Oxford University Press.

Strøm, K. (2000) 'Delegation and Accountability in Parliamentary Democracies', *European Journal of Political Research*, 37, pp. 261–89.

Strøm, K. and W. C. Müller (2003) *Delegation and Accountability in Parliamentary Democracies*. Oxford, Oxford University Press.

Swedish Energy Agency (2006) *The EU Emissions Trading Scheme after 2012*. A report from the Swedish Energy Agency and the Swedish Environmental Protection Agency.

Swenden, W. and B. Maddens (eds) (2009). *Territorial Party Politics in Western Europe*. Basingstoke: Palgrave Macmillan.

Szczerbiak, A. and P. Taggart (2008) *Opposing Europe? The Comparative Party Politics of Euroskepticism*. Oxford: Oxford University Press.

Szikinger, I. (2003) 'National Security in Hungary', in J.P. Brodeur, P. Gill and D. Töllborg (eds), *Democracy, Law and Security. Internal Security Services in Contemporary Europe*. Aldershot: Ashgate, pp. 81–109.

Taleb, N.N. (2004) *Fooled by Randomness: The Hidden Role of Chance in Life and Markets*. New York: Random House.

Tarrow, S. (1994) *Power in Movement*. Cambridge: Cambridge University Press.

Tarrow, S. (1996) 'Making Science Work across Space and Time: A Critical Reflection on Robert Putnam's *Making Democracy Work*', *American Political Science Review*, 90(2), pp. 389–97.

Tarrow, S., P. Katzenstein and L. Graziano (eds) (1978) *Territorial Politics in Industrial Nations*. New York, Praeger.

Taylor, C. (2007) *A Secular Age*. London, Cambridge, MA: Belknap Press.

Taylor, T. (2002) 'United Kingdom', in Y. Alexander (ed.) *Combating Terrorism: Strategies of Ten Countries*. Ann Arbor, MI: University of Michigan Press, pp. 187–224.

Taylor-Gooby, P. (ed.) (2004) *New Risks, New Welfare: The Transformation of the European Welfare State*. Oxford: Oxford University Press.

Teixeira, R.A. (1992) *The Disappearing American Voter*. Washington, DC: Brookings.

Teorell, J., M. Torcal and J.R. Montero (2006) 'Political participation: Mapping the terrain', in van Deth *et al.* (eds), *Citizenship and Involvement in European Democracies: A Comparative Analysis*, pp. 334–57.

Thatcher, M. (2005) 'The Third Force? Independent Regulatory Agencies and Elected Politicians in Europe', *Governance: An International Journal of Policy, Administration and Institutions*, 18(3), pp. 347–73.

Thatcher, M. (2007) 'Reforming National Regulatory Institutions: the EU and Cross-National Variety in European Networked Industries', in Hancké *et al.* (eds), *Beyond Varieties of Capitalism: Conflict, Contradictions and Complementarities in the European Economy*, pp. 147–72.

Thérien, J.P. and A. Noël (2000) 'Political Parties and Foreign Aid', *American Political Science Review*. 94, pp. 151–62.

Thomassen, J. (ed.) (2005) *The European Voter: A Comparative Study of Modern Democracies*. Oxford: Oxford University Press.

Tilly, C. (1978) *From Mobilization to Revolution*. Reading, MA: Addison-Wesley.

Tocqueville, A. de (2000) *Democracy in America*, trans. and eds, H.C. Mansfield and D. Winthrop. Chicago, University of Chicago Press.

Tomka, P. (2001) 'Slovakian statement to the United Nations: measures to eliminate international terrorism', New York: 56th Session of the General Assembly, October, Agenda item 166.

Trauner, F. (2009a) 'From Membership Conditionality to Policy Conditionality: EU External Governance in South Eastern Europe', *Journal of European Public Policy*, 16(5) pp. 774–90.

Trauner, F. (2009b) 'Post-Accession Compliance with EU Law in Bulgaria and Romania: A Comparative Perspective', *European Integration online Papers*, 13(2).

Trigilia, C. (1986) 'Small-Firm Development and Political Subcultures in Italy', *European Sociological Review*, 2(3), pp. 161–75.

US Department of State (2004) *Country Reports on Human Rights Practices – 2003*, Slovak Republic, available at: www.state.gov/g/drl/rls/hrrpt/2003/27863.htm (accessed: 17/09/10).

US Department of State (2007) *Country Reports on Terrorism – 2007*, available at: www.state.gov/s/ct/rls/crt/2007/index.htm (accessed: 17/09/10).

Uslaner, E. and G. Badescu (2004) 'Honesty, Trust, and Legal Norms in the Transition to Democracy: Why Bo Rothstein Is Better Able to Explain Sweden than Romania', in J. Kornai, B. Rothstein and S. Rose-Ackerman (eds), *Creating Social Trust in Post-socialist Transition*. Basingstoke, UK: Palgrave Macmillan.

Uslaner, E.M. (1998) 'Social Capital, Television, and the "Mean World": Trust, Optimism, and Civic Participation', *Political Psychology*, 19(3), pp. 441–68.

Uslaner, E.M. (1999) 'Democracy and social capital', in Warren (ed.), *Democracy and Trust*, pp. 121–50.

Uslaner, E.M. (2002) *The Moral Foundations of Trust*. Cambridge/New York: Cambridge University Press.

Vachudova, M.A. (2005) *Europe Undivided: Democracy, Leverage and Integration after Communism*. Oxford: Oxford University Press.

Vachudova, M.A. (2008) 'Tempered by the EU? Political Parties and Party Systems before and after Accession', *Journal of European Public Policy*, 15(6) pp. 861–79.

Vachudova, M.A. (2009) 'Corruption and Compliance in the EU's Post-Communist Members and Candidates', *Journal of Common Market Studies*, 47(1), pp. 43–62.

Valki, L. (2005) 'Hungary', in T. Lansford and B. Tashev (eds), *Old Europe, New Europe and the US. Renegotiating Transatlantic Security in the Post 9/11 Era*. Aldershot: Ashgate, pp. 239–257.

van Deth, J.W. (1995). 'A Macro-Setting for Micro-Politics', in J.W. van Deth and E. Scarborough (eds), *The Impact of Values*. Oxford: Oxford University Press, pp. 46–75.

van Deth, J.W. (1998) *Comparative Politics: The Problem of Equivalence*. London and New York: Routledge.

van Deth, J.W. (2008) 'Political Involvement and Social Capital', in H. Meulemann (ed.), *Social Capital in Europe: Similarity of Countries and Diversity of People? Multi-level Analyses of the European Social Survey 2002*. Boston, MA: Brill, pp. 191–218.

van Deth, J.W. (ed.) (1997) *Private Groups and Public Life: Social Participation, Voluntary Associations and Political Involvement in Representative Democracies*. London: Routledge.

van Deth, J.W. and W. Maloney (eds) (2010) *New Participatory Dimensions in Civil Society: Professionalization and Individualized Collective Action*. London: Routledge.

van Deth, J.W., J.R. Montero and A. Westholm (eds), *Citizenship and Involvement in European Democracies: A Comparative Analysis*. London: Routledge.

van Hecke, S. and E. Gerard (eds) (2004) *Christian Democratic Parties in Europe since the End of the Cold War*. Leuven: Leuven University Press.

van Kempen, H. (2007) 'Media–Party Parallelism and its Effects: A Cross-National Comparative Study', *Political Communication*, 24 (3), pp. 303–20.

van Kersbergen, K. (1995) *Social Capitalism: A Study of Christian Democracy and the Welfare State*. London: Routledge.

van Leeuwen, M. (ed.) (2003) *Confronting Terrorism: European Experiences, Threat Perceptions and Policies*. The Hague: Kluwer Law International.

Veltz, P. (1996) *Mondialisation, Villes et Territoires*. Paris: PUF.

Veltz, P. (2008), *Des Lieux et des Liens. Essai sur Les Politiques du Territoire à L'heure de la Mondialisation*. Paris: Edition de l'Aube.

Verba, S. and N.H. Nie (1972) *Participation in America: political democracy and social equality*. Chicago: University of Chicago Press.

Verba, S., K. Schlozman and H.E. Brady (1995) *Voice and Equality: Civic Voluntarism in American Politics*. Cambridge, MA: Harvard University Press.

Verba, S., N.H. Nie and J. Kim (1978) *Participation and Political Equality: A Seven-Nation Comparison*. Cambridge: Cambridge University Press.

Véron, J., S. Pennec and J. Légaré (eds) (2007) *Ages, Generations and the Social Contract*. Dordrecht: Springer.

Vis, B., K. Van Kersbergen, and T. Hylands (2010). 'Did the financial crisis open up opportunities for welfare state reform?', manuscript. Department of Political Science, VU University, Amsterdam.

Vis, P. (2006) 'Basic Design Options for Emissions Trading', in Delbeke (ed.), *The EU Greenhouse Gas Emissions Trading Scheme. EU Energy Law*, vol. IV, pp. 39–62.

von Hippel, K. (ed.) (2005) *Europe Confronts Terrorism*. Basingstoke, UK: Palgrave.

Walker, C. (2003) 'Policy Options and Priorities: British Perspectives', in M. van Leeuwen (ed.) *Confronting Terrorism: European Experiences, Threat Perceptions and Policies*. The Hague: Kluwer Law International, pp. 11–35.

Wardlaw, G. (1989) *Political Terrorism – Theory, Tactics, and Counter-measures*, second edition, Cambridge: Cambridge University Press.

Ware, A. (1987) *Citizens, Parties and the State*. Oxford: Polity Press.

Warren, M.E. (1999) 'Introduction', in M.E. Warren (ed.) *Democracy and Trust*. Cambridge: Cambridge University Press, pp. 1–21.

Warren, M.E. (2001) 'Social capital and corruption', paper delivered at EURESCO Conference on Social Capital, University of Exeter, 15–20 September.

Wattenberg, M. (2000) 'The Decline of Party Mobilization', in R.J. Dalton and M.P. Wattenberg (eds), *Parties without Partisans: Political Change in Advanced Industrial Democracies*. Oxford: Oxford University Press, pp. 64–76.

Weatherill, S. (2005) 'Finding a Role for the Regions in Checking the EU's Competence', in S. Weatherill and U. Bernitz (eds), *The Role of the Regions and Sub-National Actors in Europe*. Oxford: Hart Publishing.

Webb, P. (2002) 'Political Parties and Democratic Control in Advanced Industrial Societies', in Webb, *et al.* (eds), *Political Parties in Advanced Industrial Democracies*, pp. 438–60.

Webb, P. and S. White (2005) 'Political parties in new democracies: Trajectories of development and implications for democracy', in Webb, *et al.* (eds), *Political Parties in Advanced Industrial Democracies*, pp. 345–70.

Webb, P. and S. White (2007) *Party Politics in New Democracies*. Oxford: Oxford University Press.

Webb, P. and T. Poguntke (2007) 'The Presidentialization of Contemporary Democratic Politics: Evidence, Causes and consequences', in Poguntke and Webb (eds), *The Presidentialization of Democracy: A Study in Comparative Politics*, pp. 336–56.

Webb, P., D. Farrell and I. Holliday (2002) *Political Parties in Advanced Industrial Democracies*. Oxford: Oxford University Press.

Webb, P., T. Bale and P. Taggart (2010) 'Deliberative Versus Parliamentary Democracy in the UK: An Experimental Study', *SEI Working Paper* 118.

Webber, M. and M. Smith (2002) *Foreign Policy in a Transformed World*. Harlow: Prentice Hall.

Weber, K., M.E. Smith and M. Baun (eds) (2007) *Governing Europe's Neighbourhood: Partners or Periphery?* Manchester: Manchester University Press.

Weller, P. (2005) *Time for a Change: Reconfiguring Religion, State and Society*. London: T&T Clark.

Weigel, G. (2005). *The Cube and the Cathedral: Europe, America, and Politics without God*. New York: Basic Books.

Welzel, C. (2007) 'Are Levels of Democracy Affected by Mass Attitudes? Testing Attainment and Sustainment Effects on Democracy', *International Political Science Review*, 28(4), pp. 397–424.

Wessels, W., A. Maurer and J. Mittag (2003) *Fifteen into One? The European Union and its Member States*. Manchester: Manchester University Press.

White, B. (2001) *Understanding European Foreign Policy*. Basingstoke: Palgrave.

Whiteley, P. and P. Seyd (2002) *High-Intensity Participation: The Dynamics of Party Activism in Britain*. Ann Arbor, MI: University of Michigan Press.

Whitley, R. (1999) *Divergent Capitalisms: The Social Structuring and Change of Business Systems*. Oxford: Oxford University Press.

Whittaker, D. (2009) *Counter-Terrorism and Human Rights*. Harlow: Longman.

Wilkinson, P. (1996) 'The Role of the Military in Combating Terrorism in a Democratic Society', *Terrorism and Political Violence*, 8(3), pp. 1–11.

Wilkinson, P. (2000) *Terrorism versus Democracy: The Liberal State Response.* London: Frank Cass.

Wolf, M. (2009) *Fixing Global Finance.* New Haven, CT: Yale University Press.

Wolfinger, R. and S. Rosenstone (1980) *Who Votes?* New Haven, CT: Yale University Press.

Wong, R. (2005a) 'The Europeanization of Foreign Policy', in C. Hill and M. Smith (eds), *International Relations and the European Union.* Oxford: Oxford University Press, pp. 134–53.

Wong, R. (2005b) *The Europeanization of French Foreign Policy: France and the EU in East Asia.* Basingstoke, UK: Palgrave Macmillan.

Wood, S. (2001) 'Business, Government, and Patterns of Labour Market Policy in Britain and the Federal Republic of Germany', in P. Hall and D. Soskice (eds), *Varieties of Capitalism: The Institutional Foundations of Comparative Advantage.* Oxford: Oxford University Press, pp. 247–74.

Zapfel, P. and M. Vainio (2002) 'Pathways to European Greenhouse Gas Emissions: History and Misconception'. *The Fondazione Eni Enrico Mattei Nota di Lavora Series.* 85.2002.

Zimmermann, D. and A. Wenger (eds) (2007) *How States Fight Terrorism. Policy Dynamics in the West.* London: Lynne Rienner.

Zittel, T. and D. Fuchs (eds.) (2006) *Participatory Democracy and Political Participation: Can Participatory Engineering Bring Citizens Back In?* London: Routledge.

Zmerli, S. and K. Newton (2008) 'Social Trust and Attitudes toward Democracy', *Public Opinion Quarterly*, 72(4), pp. 706–24.

Zmerli, S., K. Newton and J.R. Montero (2006) 'Trust in people, confidence in political institutions, and satisfaction with democracy', in van Deth *et al.* (eds), *Citizenship and Involvement in European Democracies: A Comparative Analysis*, pp. 35–65.

Zsohar, I. (2004) *The Risk of Terrorism in Europe and Hungary.* Budapest: National Security Office.

Zubek, R. (2008) *Core Executive and Europeanization in Central Europe.* Basingstoke, UK: Palgrave Macmillan.

Zysman, J. (1983) *Governments, Markets and Growth: Financial Systems and the Politics of Industrial Change.* Ithaca, NY: Cornell University Press.

Index

When locators are in **bold** following an author's name, this indicates the chapter they have contributed to this volume.